IN HANUMAN'S HANDS

CHEENI RAO

IN HANUMAN'S HANDS

a memoir

HarperOne
An Imprint of HarperCollinsPublishers

HarperOne

HarperCollins books may be purchased for educational, business, or sales
promotional use. For information please write: Special Markets Department,
HarperCollins Publishers, 10 East 53rd Street, New York, NY 10022.

HarperCollins Web site: http://www.harpercollins.com

HarperCollins®, 📖®, and HarperOne™ are trademarks
of HarperCollins Publishers

FIRST EDITION

Library of Congress Cataloging-in-Publication Data

Rao, Cheeni.
In Hanuman's hands : a memoir / Cheeni Rao. — 1st ed.
p. cm.
ISBN 978–0-06–073662–0
1. Rao, Cheeni. 2. East Indian Americans—Biography. 3. Hindus—United
States—Biography. 4. Young men—United States—Biography. 5. Drug addicts—
United States—Biography. 6. Homeless persons—United States—Biography.
7. Drug addicts—Rehabilitation—United States—Case studies. 8. Redemption—
Case studies. 9. Hanuman (Hindu deity) I. Title.
E184.E2R375   2008
973'.04914—dc22   2008055421

09 10 11 12 13   RRD(H)   10 9 8 7 6 5 4 3 2 1

This is not a good, old-fashioned memoir. It isn't a factually accurate recounting of my life either, but it is a memoir nonetheless. The line between fiction and nonfiction is as thin as that between myth and history, caught in a perpetual tug-of-war between the myths we call memories and then proclaim as fact, and the truths that fade to whispered voices in our collective dreams.

I have pulled from my experiences and from the stories of my relatives. There is the ancestral temple itself, weathered by the years, and there are the written records of my family's service, carved into wood slats centuries ago in a language scholars have forgotten. It is our native language, now only remembered in speech, the characters of the text an unbreakable hieroglyphic code. Even the wood into which the symbols are carved mystifies scientists. The wood should have rotted into indecipherability by now, but due to a lacquer whose formula is lost in the tomb of our language, the secrets of my ancestors are incorruptible. Our language has become a secret to ourselves, and our history a mystery for us to re-create.

Those who do not have power over the story that dominates their lives, power to retell it, power to rethink it, deconstruct it, joke about it, and change it as times change, are truly powerless, because they cannot think new thoughts.

—**Salman Rushdie**

I asked God for strength that I might achieve. I was made weak that I might learn humbly to obey. I asked for health that I might do greater things. I was given infirmity that I might do better things. I asked for riches that I might be happy. I was given poverty that I might be wise. I asked for power that I might have the praise of men. I was given weakness that I might feel the need of God. I asked for all things that I might enjoy life. I was given life that I might enjoy all things. I got nothing that I asked for, but everything I hoped for. Almost despite myself, my unspoken prayers were answered. I am, among all men, most richly blessed.

—**Unknown**

For the Oasis

IN HANUMAN'S HANDS

Whenever virtue declines and unrighteousness rises, I manifest myself as an embodied being. To protect the saints and sages, to destroy the evildoers and to establish dharma, I am born from age to age.

—Bhagavad Gita 4.7–8

Long ago my ancestors lived in Kashmir, trapped in frozen valleys by the broad shoulders of the Himalayas. We weren't vegetarians yet—that would come hundreds of years later, after the Hindu faithful borrowed Buddha's nonviolent message. In Kashmir, we considered yak a delicate vegetable, and raised the sturdy beasts to help us plow the earth when it thawed. We slit their throats and offered up the meat in the *puja*, or sacrificial fire, to the Gods when winters lingered. We were priests in a hungry land, surrounded by sleeping demons disguised as mountains. We were needed and loved. We had no reason to leave.

During one of my drug overdoses, while a doctor pumped activated charcoal into my stomach through the tubes he'd coaxed down my throat, I saw one of those long-dead Kashmiri relatives. One moment I was looking into the eyes of a sweating Indian doctor, hearing him chant the mantra, "Don't die, you stupid bloody fool," and the next moment the sourness of my own vomit was replaced by the faint sweetness of the smoke of *ghee* and flowers and a revelation of frigid mountain air, the dull trickle of charcoal in my belly fading to absence. A man with hair on his body like thick black fur tended a puja fire. He crouched outside a temple that had been carved into the skin of the mountains, the puja smoke signaling to the sleepless eyes of the Gods above. The man burned bundles of wood, flowers, and cups of rice and ghee whenever he ended a mantra. His chanting trembled like snow before an avalanche, ringing like the crack of ice after each *sloka*. My relative looked up at the night sky, then over at me. He motioned me toward him, gently took my hands within his, then began binding them with an itchy twine. He kissed me on the forehead.

He pulled out a long, thin knife, tilted my head back. The blade was quick against my throat, a sliver of ice pressed deep into my skin, followed by my body's gasp at the heat of myself flooding away. He didn't need to push me into the fire—I knew what I was supposed to do. I lay down upon the bed of coals, the acrid smoke curling around me, the flames shriveling my skin. I was the sacrifice.

I looked into the night at the uncountable stars and watched as, one by one, they were shaken free. My relative would yell a mantra, pour ghee onto my burning body, and another star would fall. The Gods were plummeting toward us, flames streaming in their wake.

My family doesn't talk about why my relatives left Kashmir, but the night of my overdose, I learned a truth that makes sense. My ancestor, like many of the family line that lay between us, had wanted to be a god. He sacrificed a demon to show his power so that the Gods would lift him up and ask him to join them. He sacrificed his own distant grandson to show that he had no attachment to the human world.

But you can't change fate. We run this circle of time again and again, unchanged and unchanging. To ask to be a god is to make war against the fundamental nature of our universe, and so, as the Gods fell in a rage toward us, they cursed Kashmir to be forever at war, and they cursed us.

When I blinked my eyes, the cracked white ceiling paint of the critical care unit loomed over me. A hospital band wrapped my wrist and IV lines snaked from my veins, but my once-hairy hands had been singed clean. Thick burns crisscrossed my fingers.

Our family curse is a forgotten secret. The current generation of my family is sure our misfortunes are solely due to bad luck, inbreeding, and stupidity. My family won't believe because none of us are priests anymore—we have become devotees of logic, engineers and doctors sacrificing faith at the altar of science. When I first told my father about the curse, he scolded me for making up stories, and promised to disown me if I didn't enter into a drug rehab program. But in the time when my ancestors had sense to believe in the curse, we fled before it, doomed to wander the lands aimlessly in search of a God that would forgive us. For generations we searched.

In the past, when my ancestors tended the temples, the Gods spoke to them, reminded them of their sins, protected them, and guided them on a path that would lead to our family line's eventual salvation. My father had abandoned our ancestral temple and forgotten how to hear the Gods. But that night, as I lay in the hospital bed, my mind afloat on a chemical sea, drifting between the shores of my world and the transcendent, I realized that the drugs gave me the power to hear the divine in the way my ancestors had. It was the crack pipe that enabled me to see the reason for the curse, that I was part of the cause of it. The kiss of the needle revealed my dharma. I would need to find a God that would forgive me.

It took me years, but I finally found one in Chicago in an alley behind a *tacqueria*.

Seetharama Rao, my grandfather on my mother's side, could pour molding *bandtha* on a cold skillet, whisper a mantra, and produce *masala dosai*s as delicate as gold foil. The feverishly ill, their souls moments from Yama's noose, would storm outside to play passionate cricket at the fiery kiss of his green-chili-, onion-, garlic-, and cilantro-studded *oothapam*. Chefs and priests made pilgrimage to his restaurant in Madras, hoping to learn the secrets of the Gods and taste divinity.

"You should never hide what Gods teach you," he said to me once. "What they tell us, they need us to share."

Seetharama taught me many lessons during the summers my siblings and I visited him in India: how to spell my name in Kannada, that good Brahmins did not throw rocks at beggars from the terrace, that our family line was descended from divine blood and had a unique responsibility because of it. He held an orange peel near my face during a lesson and told me, "Look! Look!" and when I did, he squeezed the peel, stinging my eyes with the spray. Thus I learned not to look where people wanted me to.

When we sat together in the early mornings, his eyes closed in prayer, my gaze wandered, fixating on the flicking tongues of the clammy-skinned *pullis,* the little lizards scuttling up the walls in search of flies. The pullis were like jade figurines with large opal eyes—they reminded me of my female cousins in their green school jumpers, hair oiled into perfect pigtails, ponytails, French braids and twists, hop-scotching on the terrace oblivious to my stares. I tried capturing *pulli*s by grabbing their tails, but they always escaped, abandoning their tails in my fingers. I would climb the bars on the windows meant to keep thieves out, chasing a pulli, its captured tail safe behind one of my ears, hoping that perhaps it would be lured by the sight of the part of itself I'd claimed for myself. It never was.

Seetharama whispered to the plants he tended on our terrace. He secretly paid for others' education when he found out they were in need. He would take out his dentures and let me brush them. He never hit me. When we walked together, he would tell me why the monkeys never left Tirupathi, the secret ways to befriend a raging elephant.

He also taught me the Ramayana. In the comic books I'd read, the Ramayana revealed itself as an Indian *Iliad*. Ravana, an evil *Rakshasa* king, had stolen Sita, Rama's wife. Rama and Sita were incarnations of the powerful Gods Vishnu and Laxmi, born again on the earth to cleanse it of evil, but even with all their power, fate bound them to a path of suffering. After a long search for Sita, Rama eventually attacked Ravana's island with an army of monkeys led by the monkey God Hanuman, killed Ravana, and saved Sita. The version of the Ramayana Seetharama taught was nothing like what I'd read in comic books, but he explained that there are as many varieties of the Ramayana as there are people. He was telling me the version I needed to know.

"I will tell you the true story," he said. "Have I told you what happened to Rama and his brother Laksmana when they were in exile?"

"What is exile?"

"When you run from your father, you are in exile."

I nodded.

"Agni came to them. Who was Agni?"

"The sun!" I said.

"You are a smart boy. The sun was worried for Sita. He told Rama, 'Ravana will kidnap Sita, and that action will seal his fate and guarantee his death at your hands, but it is not proper that Sita, the incarnation of the goddess Laxmi, should be touched by Ravana. I shall keep Sita safe with me and give you a phantom Sita instead.'"

"There was only one Sita in the comics," I said.

"No—the sun gave Rama a *Mayasita*, a twin illusion of Sita, without his brother noticing. And then the sun took Sita with him to the heavens so that she would be safe."

"Did she cry?"

"Why should she cry? She went to the sun's palace in the sky."

"It would be scary. I would miss Rama. And isn't the sun too hot? Did he burn her?"

"Yes, but he gave her ice cream. He also had the coldest air-conditioning in the universe, so Sita was very happy."

"That is all she needed to be happy? Didn't she miss Rama?"

"Ice cream is all I need to be happy," Seetharama said. "Would you like some?"

I nodded eagerly, and Seetharama gave me a sly grin.

"Of course, if you have ice cream, then I should have ice cream too. I must make sure that what you are eating is the best possible dessert."

The doctor had told him that he was not to eat sweets anymore, but he ate them anyway. When he was young he had been too poor to have good food, so now that he was older, he made himself ice cream whenever he desired.

We shared his latest creation: mango and lime, a hint of cardamom, thickly creamy, soft as his belly, with an aching sweetness that stung my cheeks.

"This is special ice cream," Seetharama said. "It is like you, filled with God's blessings and power."

I laughed at him for being silly.

"I am not making stories," he said, smiling. "Hanuman whispered this recipe to me. He even showed me where I could find the best mangoes, the freshest limes. He said he stole the cardamom from the table of the prime minister."

"Hanuman is just a story," I said, laughing. "He isn't real."

Seetharama shook his head.

"Hanuman is a God," Seetharama said quietly. "Perhaps he didn't steal the cardamom, but he is here in this room right now, protecting me. He will protect you too if you ask."

I couldn't see any Gods in the room, nor any monkey Gods for that matter, so I laughed and ran out of the room whooping like the monkey God I thought he wanted me to be.

Seetharama didn't follow me. He stayed in the room and whispered prayers to the God I couldn't see.

I'd seen monkeys in the temples of Tirupathi and Mangalore during my childhood visits, and had gotten used to their typical behavior: masturbating, screaming unintelligibly, throwing shit at visitors. I'd had no idea they were important to my family until Seetharama told me of his bond with Hanuman. When I was nine, a week before he died, he told me of an ancient temple guarded by monkeys, nestled between the jungle and the sea, that he had found when he was a child. He had wandered endlessly, thirsty and tired, lost until he had forgotten how to hope. He turned to prayer and Hanuman appeared. Hanuman led him to the temple and blessed him, and from then on Seetharama's life had been marked by an inordinate amount of good fortune.

"You will need to find Hanuman too," he said, "or you will lose yourself in America."

"Do you have a map to his temple?"

Seetharama laughed.

"You cannot find him with a map," he said. "Live like him, and you will find him."

I found a shortcut to Hanuman by smoking rock. I thought all those Hindu priests with their mantras, pujas, *homas*, oil lamps, and incense were doing it the hard way. They chanted his name, they prayed to him, but they just didn't feel him the way a crackhead does. Meditation and ritual require learning, years of dedication before you have the skill necessary to even have a chance of luring a God into looking at your road. Succeed and you might only hook the sleepy-eyed and blissed-out incarnation of your God of choice, because that God is the one most attuned to your peaceful and happy meditation brain waves. At best, it might rouse itself from its nap and whisper fragments of new-age philosophy, or give a minor blessing to your loved ones. When I was at my lowest, though, alone in an alley, another man's blood on my jacket, craving the absolution of crack, Hanuman came to me. Not happy little Hanuman who might let you play jump rope with his tail. Mine had fists of ill will and steel wool for fur, and he came from the version of the Ramayana where Rama is a crackhead and Hanuman is his formerly rock-smoking sponsor.

In the crackhead Ramayana, the evil Rakshasa king Ravana, hopped up on angel dust, grabs Sita because he's horny and can't think straight, motivated by desire because desire is the only thing he can feel anymore. Rama and Laksmana want Sita back, but not having a clue where she's gone or who's taken her, end up bumming around India. Every once in a while they have a good adventure and help some folks out, but they spend most nights by campfires, puffing joints and huffing pipes, talking about all the shit they're going to do when they find Sita, or crying about how much they've screwed up their lives.

But then they hook up with hardcore ex-con tattooed Hanuman, and Hanuman saves them. He sponsors them in recovery, finds Sita after he gets tired of hearing Rama say he misses her so bad he'd rather smoke a rock than think about it, and rallies the monkeys to fight in the war with a big recovery-house potluck reunion. Hanuman and his monkey army create a bridge across the ocean, one boulder at a time, then cross into Ravana's kingdom of Sri Lanka. Hanuman gets as big as a mountain, as small as an ant, hides the sun in his armpit when that's what it takes, but, most impressively, he gets the guys to sober up for a bit, just enough to get their lives back in order.

The crackhead Ramayana is about more than good and evil, fate and duty, because all the heroes are monkeys and junkies. Picking sides in this version is like choosing which set of gangbangers you want to win your local turf war. Everyone's screwed up, and though some of them mean well, you don't want them hanging around your kids. Ravana's kid brother comes over with a peace offering just before the big battle, but Rama's so high he thinks he's an assassin and spears him. Ravana's so busy with his pipe that the battle starts without him. His kids have to go out and fight for him, making up a bullshit cover story about how he's readying himself for battle. During the last few days of the war, Ravana sends his son Indrajit into battle. Indrajit is a bathtub wizard, the kind that can make LSD from scratch, and when he gets involved, Rama's people overdose and go down like a waterfall of dominoes. Rama hunts for Indrajit, but when he finds him, Indrajit unleashes a magical weapon—the *Brahmastra*.

In every version of the Ramayana they say the Brahmastra was like a snake, that it had a terrible venom worse than the king cobra's. The truth is that the Brahmastra was rock. It was crack cocaine. It was super-fine white in a spoon. It was the junkie's dream.

Rama goes down. He's too high to fight. He's let himself fall deeply in love with the kiss of the needle and the crackle of the pipe. He'd gotten himself straight, but now he's relapsed again. And it says in every version of the Ramayana that they sent Hanuman to find the cure.

Hanuman knows where to find the cure. It's called the *Sanjeevani* root. It's on the Hill of Herbs, between the Rishabha and Kailasa mountains in the Himalayas. But when he goes for the Sanjeevani root, instead of wasting time looking for it, he rips the entire hill out of the ground and tries to carry it back to Sri Lanka.

He's got it with him still.

I was born flushed and shaking, screaming at the morning, in a hospital in the heart of Chicago. My mother, Pushpanjali, says I was the easiest pregnancy—no mean kicks in the gut while she was savoring her daily cottage cheese, no manipulative attempt to twist my umbilical cord around my neck and force her to the hospital early. She gained weight with steady ease, reading books on how to have a painless childbirth while walking my two brothers and sister to school, reading *Pride and Prejudice* while wielding a cantankerous hand-me-down vacuum cleaner in our confined apartment. My father, Sreepada, was trapped in hospital halls, trying to prove that he deserved to practice medicine in America. My father's mother, Varadha, nearly blind, her mind full of memories of threshing rice in the shadow of the Western Ghats as the monsoon clouds curled over the mountain, spent her time hunched on our threadbare sofa, wondering why she had to live in a land full of concrete walls.

I was an omen of change. My mother and father hadn't been trying for another child, but despite all the laws of probability and chemistry, the pill stopped working for a moment, and my horoscope became an inevitability. My mother says that she felt no pain when she delivered me, as if the Gods told her I was ready for the earth, and convinced her body that there was no need to cling any further. My family thought it was a divine blessing, noting the auspicious paw print of monkey hair on my back, but when I came into the world, my body knew better. My own blood tried to kill me.

Platelets. They are a billion Vishnus in our blood, rushing to any cut, throwing their many arms into the breach and holding tight, walling off the enemies of the world from the magic of our hearts, keeping the world free of the needless spilling of our blood. But in my body, the Vishnus did not want to fight for me. They lounged in the twists of my veins, nonviolently resisting their duties. Blood seeped from tiny fissures within me with the Gods' blessings.

In mythic times, that would have been enough. I would have lain shuddering in my mother's arms, wide-eyed and gasping at the horror of the world until Yama's noose encircled my neck. But in America, the doctors at the hospital were not so willing to trust in the purpose of fate. They rushed me into an intensive care unit and began pumping me full of blood. Not the blood of my own family, but the blood of strangers, of people of Chicago. High school kids, college dreamers, drug addicts, prostitutes, priests. The doctors pumped me full of American blood, and injected steroids to reduce the inflammation.

My father was a man of logic and science, but in that moment he closed his eyes and prayed.

Before my family line on my father's side could dream its way into America, we were priests in the Marigudi temple of Kapu, bonded by land and lineage to serve Kali. We had served this Goddess of vengeance from the time Kerala had risen from the sea. Back before time was recorded with numbers, when all that was known was sung in song, we came to the land because a God finally asked us to.

The legends say that God came to earth as a Brahmin, in order to cleanse the earth of the evil of kings and rulers. God in this form was known as Parasurama, Rama of the Ax, the warrior-priest. Parasurama drenched the land with the blood of the wicked and freed the people from the chains of kings, but when he was done, he needed a place free of the blood he had spilled in order to meditate and do penance for the violence he had brought into the world, and to praise the end of the evil that he had removed. So he stood at the top of the highest peak in the Western Ghats and threw his ax into the Arabian Sea, and the sea receded from the point where his ax had landed, creating a new land. He called for other Brahmins to join him, and my father's side followed, hoping this new God would forgive us. To us he gave a special honor. We would be the caretakers of Kapu, the area nearest where the ax had landed. We would preserve the memory of God's vengeance.

We were given other gifts as well. We lived on *devashya*, land whose title was held in Kali's name, and were granted three acres of fertile land to farm as our own. Our house was made of hardened clay, and the roof was composed of *hunchu*, laboriously crafted ceramic tile that was as precious as gold. And we were respected, or at least feared, by the devotees who would trek through the bloodred clay of the surrounding hills and bring offerings of goats, sheep, or chickens for mother Kali. They would chop the heads off the beasts outside the temple, and we would carry the offering to the Goddess. We told the outside world of the blessings or curses that had been bestowed by Kali. We were allowed to be the arms of the Goddess on earth.

The catch was that we were never supposed to leave. Kali would protect us from the family curse as long as we served her. Each generation had to produce a son, and that son had to stay to continue the tradition. A family without a male child was incomplete, and so no matter how many daughters were produced, each generation would offer lavish sacrifices to Kali until blessed with a son. Daughters never stayed. They would get married, cross the river, and settle in with their husbands in a different land, only coming back if they were pregnant and needed a place to rest. Vedantic continuation of our religious duties required a son, and the family salvation, or *moksha*, depended upon a male to perform the death rites, or *shrardha*, for the previous generations until we could find an end to the curse, so the males were tied to the land. For a soul to find peace, its name had to be recalled at the shrardha for three generations. A man who left would not only be cursing the generations that begat him, but those that followed in his footsteps as well. For servants of a lesser God this might not have been as potent a curse. What trouble could come from displeasing the Goddess of grasses? But no one would ever cross a Goddess known for her swords and her wrath. Only a fool would reject her protection. The world was too small to hide from Kali.

There are people who whisper that my father was too proud, that he shouldn't have stood up to the Gods. For millennia we had trusted that the events of our lives were part of a divine script, and so we cowered before tragedy, taking it as divine punishment, or happily threw the Gods' favorite foods into the puja fire in thanks when blessings touched upon us. But when my father was eleven and those he loved lay around him dying, their gasped prayers to the Gods unanswered, he had a revelation. God was not watching from the shadows, doling out reward or punishment to steer us along his path. God did not exist. People were born into the world with whatever talents genetics provided them, and the rest of their lives was determined by what they did with those talents. Those who worked hardest attained success and power and made the lives of everyone around them better. If his family was looking for a God to rescue them from the stifling poverty of temple life, he would have to be that god. He would have to be perfect.

So he was. He worked hard in the fields and helped out in the temple, but spent every waking moment studying. He could only get the money to go to high school if he won the scholarships reserved for the top five finalists on the entrance exam, so he studied hard enough to ensure he was the highest scorer. He needed scholarships in order to attend college, so he made sure he placed in the top ten in his state on every qualifying exam. After he had blazed his way through medical school, he found out that the Americans were offering a test in India for the first time—the top scorers would be permitted to practice medicine in America. So he sat down to take the test, alongside his own instructors from his medical school, and beat them all.

My father was perfect because he wouldn't allow himself to be anything less. People that driven blaze their way through the world; they expect to arrive in America and achieve success. My father did. Through his efforts, he was able to save himself and his brothers and sisters. They all escaped the temple and the rice fields and have comfortable lives in different corners of the world. When the family clan gathers for weddings, they all pay their respects to my father—hundreds of cousins and second cousins and wives and children clamoring for him to notice them, love them, and advise them. They give him this respect because he did something only a god could do: he rescued our family line and forever changed the lives of generations.

You would expect my father to show some sign of what he'd done— a glimmer of happiness, perhaps, or an aura of achievement that lent confidence to his words. If nothing else, you would expect him to stand tall, with pride, and to look you in the eye. But my father is not the same eleven-year-old boy who left on his adventure with an unshakable belief that curses do not exist, that fortune is what we make of it. Today he is a balding man with a tired sag to his shoulders. His skin is worn and loose, his eyes haunted. He now wakes up before sunrise to read the Ramayana or Swami Chinmayananda's analyses of Hindu philosophy, thumbing through pages he has read too many times, searching for answers that could bring him peace. He gave all that he had to save his family, and now it seems as if he has little energy left in reserve for himself. I asked him when I first went into treatment if he had any regrets, and he whispered, "I should never have left India." It was more than the predictable utterance of a nostalgic expatriate. It was the lament of a man broken by the weight of a thousand-year curse, forsaken by his ancestral Goddess, and betrayed by his youngest son.

You are fools to think that by noting what aspect of *dharma*, of *kama*, or of *artha* is most important you could ever choose which path you take, how you will live, or what you will be remembered by. In the end, my brothers and sisters, our fate, our *karma* will decide for us. And we, as befits all good people, will follow our path in wonder at its mystery.

—Yudisthera, the Mahabharata

The Oasis stood between the charred remains of a two flat and a boarded-up three flat. It had clean glass windows, and a roof so new I could smell the tar from inside the taxi. There was a man sitting on the front porch, a coffee can between his legs. He looked thick, muscleman biceps and chest softening into a big gut that poured over the waistband of his jeans. He had long, clean blond hair streaked with gray, a trimmed beard and mustache, and a white T-shirt. A long cigar smoldered in his hand.

I double-checked the address. I pulled my garbage bag of clothes out of the trunk of the taxi, gave the cabbie the last of my money, then made my way up to the man on the porch. He had at least three thousand dollars' worth of tattoos on his arms: two big blue men shooting flaming arrows, a naked Barbie chained to a tree, a monkey sitting on a train.

"This the Oasis?" I asked him. "What you smoking?"

"You're late," he said.

"Taxi came as fast as it could, but you know how traffic is on LSD. All those kids trying to hit the beach."

"I been waiting an hour. It's already noon."

"Started late."

"Then you shoulda called. You ain't startin' off on the right foot."

He got up, hitched his pants a bit higher, then pinched the cherry off the tip of his cigar. He stuck his hand out at me.

"My name's Tats. I'm the house manager. If you ever got a problem with me, with the rules, or with the house, then you can leave."

I shook his hand.

"Good. Welcome. Now come inside. I got some coffee for you. None of that decaf treatment-house shit. Real coffee. Probably burnt now, though."

I grabbed my bag and followed him in.

"I hate burnt coffee," he said. "There'll be consequences for that. Don't piss me off anymore today."

Tats removed his hiking boots and put them on a rubber mat beside the door, next to a pair of mud-stained cowboy boots with cracked leather. He picked up some clean tennis shoes that were also on the mat, and said, "House shoes."

Tats seated himself on the first step of a spiraling staircase and stared at me while tying the laces on his tennis shoes. The oak flooring glistened, each knot and swirl differentiated by years of stain and sealant, a topography of swirling mountains surrounded by vast plains and aching chasms. I touched the floor. It was like running my hands over the glass casing of a museum display. I took in the lacquered baseboards, the walls around me like movie screens: white, perfect, untouchable. Above were a distant ceiling, a hint of the second floor (a wooden banister, gleaming spindles), and, suspended by a shimmering chain—a mystery of glass bulbs, crystal teardrops, gold filigree, the crystal whispering of lavender, crimson, bright sunlight—a chandelier.

"That floor's over a hundred years old," Tats said. "We dry mop it each day with furniture polish. Get your shoes off before you ruin it."

"What's wrong with my shoes?"

My Nikes had a few holes, but I'd cleaned them in treatment with soap and water.

"You're gonna keep them on the mat, like everyone else. And your socks," he said. "I don't want fungus getting on everyone."

"My shoes are fine," I said. I felt a familiar sourness creep along my tongue, my hands becoming fists.

"They smell like shit. You been standing in the gutter all day long? And you want to bring that in my house?"

A thought flickered in my mind. I could walk up to him, shoe in hand, and slam a Nike in his mouth. I could grab his throat with two hands, and squeeze until my hands ached.

I concentrated on setting my shoe back down. I looked at him and he stared back. I picked up my shoes, took them to the mat, peeled my damp socks off and balled them in my shoes. I walked back to Tats, my feet clammy, sullying the beautiful wood, and said, "Don't ever think I did that because you said to."

"Don't be so goddamn sensitive. Alls I said is that your shoes stink. I was giving you a pull-up. Telling you what needed fixing."

"I know what needs fixing."

"This is my house," Tats said. "Used to be my grandparents', then it was my folks', then my brothers', but now they're all dead. I'm in charge. You don't like it, you can go back out there to whatever Dumpster you call home and piss on yourself for all I fucking care."

I looked away. I'd get him for that.

He walked over to me. His voice began again, soft. "I know your road. Twelve fuckups jammed together in this place, and we all know your road. You want to talk about the best chance you'll ever get—it's here. Jimmy, over at the ADD center, pulled heavy strings to get you in here. He told me you needed a chance, that you still got a piece of good in you."

He was trying to con me. I could taste it like I could taste powdered sugar and baking soda in a cut bag of coke—too sweet, too soft, not enough bitter to be real.

I looked at him, rubbed my palms together, crossed my hands over my chest to make it look like a revelation had hit me deep in the gut, looked down, took a deep breath.

I said, "Just give me a chance," letting the words slide from the back of my throat, letting the word "chance" catch a little as I took a breath.

Tats smiled. He put his arm around my shoulder. He leaned in and whispered in my ear, "If you try to fuck me, or anyone in the house . . ." He let the words hang. His grip grew tight on my shoulder. He stared me straight in the eye and I felt my breath slow to the point of nothingness. There, in the darkness of his pupils, I saw a reflection of myself, small, distorted, imprisoned by his blue irises. His pupils dilated, and I grew, the curve of my neck elongating, my head spreading, misshapen.

The dark people, bare chested, hauled nets filled with the freshly dead from their rowboats, dragging them across the sand. They shouted, yelled at each other, and one of them paused in his dragging to squat in the sand, lift his *dhoti*, and piss in a long hissing stream.

Seetharama whispered in my ear in Brahmin Thulu, "Those are the *Mogera*s. Watch them." The fishermen continued yelling in their Shudra Thulu.

"Get outta my way! You gonna rip my net," an old man said, yanking at a younger man's net.

"Daughter-fucker, the sea's a farm, and all the good fish just vegetables for the grabbing!" the younger man said. "If you can't catch your own fish, go suck your granddaughter's milk!" He spat on the old man and shoved him aside.

"Evil curse you!" the old man yelled, looking up from the sand. He waved his cupped palm at the other man, like the hood of the cobra, evoking the hissing Pambu, king of the Nagas, and said, "*Thathasthu*," the words rolling off his tongue full of a powerful and ancient venom. We turned our backs and faced the setting sun.

Seetharama held me, his arm tight around my shoulder. We'd walked from the ancestral temple of my father's family, through the hills and mud-caked streets of Mangalore, west to the sea. The smoke from the puja, the endless ladles of rice poured into the sacrificial flame, topped with ghee, *gelabi*, *halwa*—the favorite sweets of the Gods—had burned my eyes. The hours spent sitting on the floor, the priests chanting the hundreds of names of God, praying for protection from Rakshasas, had exhausted me.

I'd asked Seetharama who the Rakshasas were, why we prayed so long for the Gods' protection from them. He had led me to the beach, a hundred meters from the sea.

"I have seen them. Can we go?"

"These are not the Rakshasas," he said. "These are people. They are our people."

I looked at the fishermen again. They were dirty. I could smell them. I wrinkled my nose.

"Some call them 'untouchables' because they were born into this caste. Yet they speak the same language as us, if a bit rougher. They are as poor as we were growing up. They have as much capacity for good or evil as any of us. Show them respect and compassion and they will be loyal friends. No matter where despair leads them, however, they will never be Rakshasas. Imagine a people coming from the sea. Dark, like these, with fangs, swords, yelling words you do not understand. They come with nets into our village, and they take the women, the men. They eat some. Others they drag in nets to the sea, laughing, killing. We cannot stop them. They knock our temples down. They are Rakshasas."

"I would kill them," I said.

"A Brahmin can't kill. Would you be like them? Eating meat, killing?"

"I would do what is needed to protect us," I said.

"But what if you cannot recognize them?"

"I would see them."

Seetharama laughed. "Only Rakshasas can kill. And Gods. Or a man given God's blessing. So we pray to Gods."

I sat down in the sand. "My father said that Gods never answer prayers."

Seetharama looked at me and said, "When the Rakshasas last came, one of my family line had the wisdom to pray to Hanuman. He did severe *tapas* in the forest—renouncing food, water, even air, and finally Hanuman came to him, dropping from the sky. When Hanuman landed, the trees for miles around fell to the ground as if axed. The air smelled of burning coconuts. Hanuman looked at our ancestor and opened his mouth, and inside his mouth our ancestor saw the stars—the Whale, the Net, the Water Bearer, the Furnace—and our world, spinning, slowly. Then Hanuman disappeared. When our ancestor came back to Mangalore, the Rakshasas were gone. And they have never returned."

My grandfather pulled a plastic prescription bottle filled with ashes from the puja from his shirt pocket. He took a pinch from the bottle, and drew a stripe from my forehead to the bridge of my nose. His touch was soft, the *prasadam* like talcum, the mark on my forehead his promise of divine protection.

The night was cool and heavy with the sea. I'd tuned out the men with their nets and loud voices. I looked out into the crash of the ocean, to the horizon, and up at the dome of the sky, so far away, a deep purple fading into black. And I looked at my grandfather. He was only a small man with a silk dhoti and a clean white shirt.

We would be protected so long as we followed our dharma, performing our righteous duty and upholding the truth, and our dharma lay in the simple and eternally binding Brahmin rules. Never marry an outsider. Never drink alcohol or smoke. Never harm another living thing. Pass on the knowledge of our people. By following these rules we could live in peace with our world, and promote peace. We would always be pure. We would be genetically unsullied. Our actions would reify dharma, and dharma would define us as the chosen people.

My father told me, "If you marry an American, we will have to perform the shrardha for you. Everyone will forget you. None of your cousins will ever talk to you, because you will be dead. The priests will curse your mother. And if your American wife gives you children, the Americans will beat them up at school. Your wife will make them eat meat and wear crosses. And then, of course, your American wife will divorce you and take them away. That is their way."

Our lives would never be tainted by the confusion and doubt that plagued the Western mind. We knew what we were supposed to do. We had been provided a rule book and a script for our lives. Only a fool would disregard a perfect system refined by centuries of pious living.

But I had American blood coursing through me. When I said mantras, my accent was too thick. The sacred smoke of the puja fire made me cough, made my eyes burn. I could not stand the heat of my parents' native land, and often fainted from dehydration. When I drank our blessed water, I got diarrhea and lay lifeless, and mosquitoes bit my arm incessantly until it seemed a braille manuscript detailing my weaknesses. If I tried to communicate with the divine through ritual, my mind buzzed with static, but when I was supposed to be focused on schoolwork or on what my parents were yelling at me, a divine whisper agitated me. I could not fully sense the words, or tell which God they came from—if it was Kali coaxing me into self-destruction or Hanuman tricking me into making a fool of myself—so my explanations to my parents for why I'd set the bushes in front of the school on fire, or slugged the principal in the gut, never satisfied. My parents should have set me afloat in a basket in a river, an outsider who could not be trusted, an enemy who would inevitably bring ruin to them. They treated me like a son instead.

If asked why they did, they would say they raised me as their own because that is what parents do. The truth, however, is that they raised me as their son because they had been commanded to do so.

On a chilly March day in Chicago, with dark clouds curdling above a playground filled with parents and children decked out in fashionable plaid bell-bottoms, I toddled my way out into a busy street, compelled by a voice inside me to commit suicide while my mother was distracted. The Gods flung a blue car with sharp tail fins at me, and I stood in the middle of the pavement awaiting my fate.

My mother doesn't remember screaming or fainting, but she does remember that something flew from the sidewalk, faster than anything human, and grabbed hold of me. The car and the being and her child were inches apart, and then the being spun. She heard the screech of tires.

She remembers a crowd parting around her to allow a tall, dark hooded figure near. He set me in her arms, touched her cheek, and said, "Keep him safe, always." And then, just like that, he walked away and vanished into an alley.

She had wanted to thank him, but when his long-fingered hands had touched her face, the words seemed meaningless. She could see the fine hair coating the back of his hand, and in his eyes she saw the hint of distant worlds. Her ears rang with a slow pulsing beat, and she knew who had saved me. If she had her wits about her, she would have asked why.

My horoscope shows that I should have died at birth. It shows that I should have died that day when the Gods shot their blue-finned car at me. It shows eleven times when I was fated to die, and each time Hanuman stepped from the shadows and took me in his hands.

I smelled pork, burnt, overseasoned. I smelled coffee.

"You sure alls you did is touch him, Tats? You didn't punch him or nothin'?"

"Son of a bitch. I'm calling 911."

"Ravenswood's just down the street, Tats."

"You gonna carry him?"

Something was in my mouth. I could barely breathe, the stink of a lit cigar suffusing me. I felt myself rising. I felt a tightness on my ankles, under my arms, pulling me, my body sagging. I bucked, I kicked, I yelled.

"He's going into DTs! Why's he moaning?"

"Seizures. Keep your wallet stuffed in his mouth so he don't swallow his tongue."

I felt my feet hit the ground.

"Drop him, Tats!"

"He'll hit his head."

I felt something soft forced deeper in my mouth. I spat. I kicked. Something hit the back of my head. The ache in the back of my skull seemed a beacon, and I focused my mind on it.

"You dropped him too hard."

"How the hell was I supposed to know?"

"Is he breathing?"

The panic in the scent of their sweat was like smelling salts.

"Goddamn it, leave me alone!" I tried to yell.

"He's choking on yer wallet!"

"Naw, he's comin' out of it, Tats. We gotta slap him or he'll slip into a coma."

"That don't make sense."

"Medicine don't always make sense. Trust me. I saw it on TV."

A red glow exploded at the edge of my darkness accompanied by a thunderclap.

"Damn it, T.T.! That kung fu shit'll tear his head off."

"That's how they did it on the show, though."

The red glow flashed again, the pain a current. My eyes snapped open against my will.

Tats loomed above me.

"I'm fine," I said.

Tats waved two fingers over me.

"How many fingers I got?"

"A shitload. I'm fine." My throat burned. I felt queasy.

"Give him a pork chop, T.T.," Tats said.

"Goddamn it, I only got two cooking."

"And some coffee."

I heard the other man clomping off.

"I'm hungry," I said.

"When's the last time you ate?"

"Lunch, yesterday."

"Didn't they feed you at ADD?"

I groaned. I felt like a puddle of mud trapped in a bag of my own skin.

"My head's killing me."

"Can you sit up?"

My eyes felt dry. I blinked. Tats lifted me and sat me on a couch.

I sat for a few minutes, my head in my hands, trying to get my eyes to focus on the wood floor. The floor loomed near one instant, then faded away, grew hazy as if fog had rolled in, then became so distinct that I felt like I was flying across ravines and plateaus, small specks swooping far below me across a wooden world, vast brown rice fields on the plateaus with little brown cows grazing, and long lines of men walking single file across bridges spanning gaping chasms. I closed my eyes.

Tats left the room and came back with a cup of coffee. "I stirred in some milk and sugar," he said. "Let this settle in, and then I figure you can dig into some pork chops."

I leaned back and took a deep breath. I looked at Tats and wanted to explain that I wasn't on anything, that I was clean, thirty-six days, in fact, thirty-six shitty days, but time all the same. Maybe it was the food, something old, followed by hours of nothing, my stomach folding in on itself. Tats and I looked at each other.

We were seated on a burgundy couch. A fake potted cherry tree leaned in one corner of the room. Across from us hunkered a TV too big for me to steal by myself.

"This is a real nice place," I said, running my hand along the vinyl of the couch. There were no holes.

"I want guys to be proud of it," Tats said. "I figure the reason other places have so many guys breaking bad is because they're shitholes. Stoves that don't work. Busted-up TV for thirty guys. Sofas smelling of piss and sweat. There's no respect for the place, no discipline. But here, you can bring a lady friend by and tell her, yeah, this is where I live, and you can say it proud, because it's good and it looks nice."

"It's better than Bill's Family," I said. "When I was there, guys would be drunk half the time. They'd come home and piss in the sink."

"What's the motto there? 'Bullshit walks'?"

I shrugged. If we'd had a motto at Bill's Family, I'd never bothered to learn it.

"We got no motto here," Tats said. "We keep it simple, like in the Big Book of AA."

Tats laid out the rules. The rules were as simple as they had been in treatment. No drinking. No drugs. No stealing. No fighting. No destroying property. No sex on the property. No gambling. Work a decent job. Pay rent each week to Tats. Keep everything clean, Marine-style. If you messed up on any of the rules, then there were consequences. Tats determined what the consequences were. Keeping things clean meant no dust was allowed, no dishes left out, no ashtrays left out, the sink had to be spotless, and the entire house had to be cleaned, swept, and mopped every day by six o'clock. Cleaning shifts were called detail, and two people did detail every day of the week, except Sunday, when everyone did a thorough detail, which was followed by a Sunday meeting where people could bitch about any problems they had with anyone else. People with seniority got certain privileges, like being allowed overnights, which was the only way any of the guys could get laid. Everything had to be cleared with Tats.

The minimum consequence was extra detail, the maximum was getting kicked out, and, from the look on Tats' face when he said it, possibly getting the shit beat out of you in the process. There were a lot of consequences that fell in between. Tats ran a tight ship.

We sat in silence. I felt hungry, but I could at least feel the world around me.

"Could I see the rest of the place?" I asked.

"You feeling alright?"

I wasn't, but I nodded anyway.

Tats got up and motioned toward the TV. "You can watch TV in here." Tats moved toward the doorway. He motioned to his left. "Dining room." In it was a big unfinished cedar dining table and unfinished cedar chairs. There were green cloth place mats on it, giving space for eight people all around. "You eat in here, and you keep it clean."

"Don't keep it clean, and there's a consequence," I said.

Tats stared at me.

I said, "Just wanted to let you know that I'm listening."

"If you want the tour, shut up."

He went through another doorway into a hallway. There was a kitchen to our left. I could see a skinny guy working a stove in there. To our right the hallway went straight to the foyer and the front door, the stretch broken only by another doorway, through which I could see a hint of stairs leading down. He motioned to our right. "That's the way to the front door."

He pointed to the stairs. "That's the basement," he said. "We got a TV down there, and a washer and dryer, and a foosball table. You can go down there anytime, but after ten there's no foosball, except for on weekends. Consequence on that is detail for a week. You can watch TV anytime, just not too loud. The phone's down there too. It's a pay phone, and there's a ten minute limit sos that people don't get a busy signal every time they call in, so don't hog it too much. And I don't have change for it. Get change across the street at the Walgreens. Bother me about the phone and I'll give you a consequence on that too."

He led me into the kitchen. "This is the kitchen. And that's T.T. over there on the stove. He's the house foosball champ, so give him respect, even if he is an asshole."

I nodded toward T.T., and he nodded back. He was screwing up a pair of pork chops, dumping chili powder all over them, splattering grease everywhere. There were the stove; a big fridge in a corner; a microwave; a toaster with openings for four slices of bread; and two coffeepots, one plastic and rickety, the other with nozzles and metal pipes; and a full pot of coffee on a molded hotplate.

"This coffeepot is mine," Tats said, motioning to the coffee machine, "and you get a cup out of it today, but if I catch you messing with it any other day, I'll kick your ass."

"Don't even try to clean it," T.T. said.

"That's right," Tats said. "I clean it special."

He opened the fridge door and pointed to the lower right-hand corner of the bottom shelf. "That's your spot in the fridge."

"I don't have any food," I said.

"There's a Butera across the street," Tats said.

"I don't have any money."

T.T. turned from his pork chops, looked me over. "You Mexican?"

I stiffened. "What's it matter to you? You a fucking racist?"

He shrugged. "Maybe I am. What's your name?"

My mind clicked through possibilities. "Eduardo. Eddie for short," I lied.

"So you're Mexican," T.T. said.

Tats looked at me for a second, raised an eyebrow, then turned to his coffeepot.

When I first entered college, people kept asking what my real name was. I would write my real name in Kannada and say "Cheeni," even though I'd written "Srinivas." They'd ask if my name meant anything. I'd tell them that it was the name of a God.

My mother told me that the reason Indian parents named their kids after Gods was so that when parents were on their deathbed, they could call out to their children, and their last words would be the pained gasping of Gods' names. It would be a blessing on their death.

Having a name like that while committing crimes in America is just plain stupid. It would always mark me as Indian, that tall dark guy, over there in a corner, snorting coke. It's better to be called Mike or Bill, a name that brings to mind hundreds of different faces and forms—the fat Mike that works at Colonial's Pizza, the blond-haired Bill who plays drums on the Quads, black Mike who got thrown in front of the Metra.

So I became like Ravana, the Rakshasa who turned into a golden stag to hide from Rama's eyes and to lure Sita into his trap. I could stop shaving, call myself Muhammad and become Muslim, or wear a turban and become a Sikh. I could call myself Jorge and become Hispanic; I could shave my face and call myself Eduardo. With each name I could fade into the forest, leaving the policeman to ask me if I know Nasir, a man about my height, Muslim. He is a drug dealer and is wanted for questioning about a murder. *No hablo Inglés*, I could say, and walk toward the El.

"Would you tell me, please, which way I ought to go from here?"
"That depends a good deal on where you want to get to," said the Cat.
"I don't much care where—" said Alice.
"Then it doesn't matter which way you go," said the Cat.
"—so long as I get somewhere," Alice added as an explanation.

—Lewis Carroll, *Alice's Adventures in Wonderland*

In the brochure my college sent to emphasize the rustic New England charm of my freshman dorm, ancient trees shaded a manicured field, the earthy colors of the dorm's brickwork balancing the jubilant green of the land. Ivy scurried along the mortar lines, wreathing windows. The college listed the famous and powerful people who had slept in that dorm, as if the dorms contained a special energy that steered the thoughts of students and elevated them above common humans.

My dad and I agreed that I should visit the school to check it out. We didn't think we needed to visit any of the other colleges. My dad had driven by the local colleges and determined that they were safe and sturdy places to get an education. The big Ivy League schools didn't need a visit either—everyone wanted to get into those schools, so we should want to as well. But we'd never heard of my college. Nobody we knew ever talked about the school, and the only reason we'd applied was because it had a good liberal arts reputation and had been highly ranked in magazines. My dad was sure the college had fine professors, but he'd read that it was in a rural area, and he wanted to make sure I wouldn't be lynched when I asked for a vegetarian Whopper at the local Burger King.

"They are still racist in the small towns," he warned me. "In the good towns, they try to hide it. You may see many people staring at you meanly, looking like they want to thulp you. You call me if it looks like this."

My dad expected I'd investigate the college laboratories, the shops and restaurants of the town. I spent my entire time in search of a party. I'd lived with the Brahmin rules for my entire life, never allowed to date or go out and party. The other kids in high school got drunk, got laid, had adventures, and they seemed happy for the experience, not the shattered demons my parents said they were. None of their warnings about what was dangerous, what would lead to trouble, had anything to do with personal experience, and none of the consequences they warned me of ever seemed to happen to the high school kids I saw. Since it was my first unsupervised time away from home, and I didn't have to worry about how to hide it from my parents, I'd get a chance to do my own research and knock off a few items from my checklist of family taboos.

The school shuttled us around in groups during the day to visit the various departments, but I spent those times talking to the other prospective students, especially the girls. I knew my college didn't have anything scheduled for the nights, and I wanted to find people I could make plans with. As a result, I didn't learn anything about the college. The only memories I had of the place as I flew back to Chicago were of a cute, brown-haired prospective student who had been invited to play on the volleyball team; the paroxysm of coughing I had when I choked on a beer funnel; and the smell of the toilet I embraced for most of the last night.

The decision to lock myself into my college for at least the next four years of my life was, as a result, based on the hazy, drunken memory of the brown-haired volleyball player. The possibility of meeting her again inspired me to bullshit my father about the wonders of the college. I told him I had seen the school's conjurers of chemistry wielding test tubes like wands, evoking cures and Nobel prizes with the deft manipulation of their Bunsen burners. There were hundreds of Indians nestled in fabulous homes in the surrounding hills, just waiting to erect a glistening marble temple that they would use as the headquarters of the vegetarian revolution America desperately needed. As with any good lie, I mixed in elements of the truth. The college didn't allow fraternities and sororities, which meant I could rub shoulders with the wealthy children of the powerful without feeling the need to impress them with displays of stupefying drunkenness. Although the truth of it, as a sophomore put it to me when I was visiting the school, was that "there's nothing to do in this shit town, and no place to go, so all we're ever trying to do is get shit-faced and laid," the school brochures painted a reassuring picture. My father trusted me and, though I had enough scholarships to go to a state school for free, he agreed to put a second mortgage on the house so I could have a chance at being educated with the elite.

On the long drive from O'Hare, my dad chattered with pride. He told me again the magical story of how he'd escaped the rice fields of India and saved his family. My other brothers hadn't understood that work ethic or had his innate intelligence. They struggled through school, and he worried that America had made them lazy and dull. But in me, he had found his successor. I had competed in national and international competitions for math and science, leading my high school math team to the state finals and my school science bowl team to the national championships. I had straight As, was an accomplished athlete, and had rounded myself out with debate and writing awards.

His family hadn't been able to help him along his path, but by paying my way through an expensive private college, he could ensure I realized my full potential.

I loved it when my dad was happy. I didn't see the point in telling him the truth. The person he knew was just a part of who I really was. That was my Indian immigrant high-achiever mask, a useful disguise that put everyone at ease because that kind of person was wholesome and passionately dedicated to success. Now was not the time to tell him that I felt imprisoned by success, a trophy he displayed on the mantel. I couldn't explain the confusion within myself to him because I couldn't articulate it at the time. All I knew was that an excitement had been building within me from the day I'd first been accepted at my college because going to college would give me temporary freedom from the strict rules of my family. If my father had known where that path would ultimately lead me, he would have forced me on the next plane to India.

Freshman year roommate pairings are a random act of cruelty. At best, the college arbitrarily lumps students together. At worst, they waste time going over applications to determine which students would get along well. Of course, applications never tell the truth about a person. The people described within application essays and circumscribed by test scores are fictional creations intended to trick the admissions department into letting them in. In my essays I portrayed myself as an earnest, ethical young man eager to make a contribution to the world. I left out the little details that admissions departments never want to see: the two suicide attempts in high school, my nighttime addiction to breaking and entering houses, the fact that I'd burned my neighbor's house down in a fit of rage but had never been caught by the cops. My teachers and guidance counselors did their best to cover up my rough spots in their recommendations as well. Nobody mentioned the schoolyard fights, the suspensions, or my arrogance and belligerence. According to my application, I was a good kid, as smart as they come, and well suited for college.

The college had me rooming with three other guys my freshman year. We were packed into two tiny closets with beds, and used our Spartan common room when we needed to study. Despite what I'd written on my applications, my biggest desire upon reaching campus was to find people I could party with. High school was where bookworms like me cultivated our intellectual sides. College was where we learned how to have fun. Why else would anyone place thousands of students together without parental supervision and surround them with bars and liquor stores?

My roommates, though, were of a different mind. Before I could say my name to the slender African American in starched button-downs and pressed slacks allocated to share one of the closet bedrooms with me, he told me he liked to study late into the night in bed and would be leaving the lights on. He told me he was an economics major three different ways before he finally introduced himself as "Kenny from Jersey." He reminded me of my oldest brother, Kartikkeya, who advised me that life was a video game where you only got points for accumulating gold, and that anything that wasn't about getting gold was a waste of time. Once Kenny realized we wouldn't be in the same classes, he had nothing more to say to me.

In the other closet bedroom were Salvatore and Jonas. Salvatore introduced himself with a vigorous handshake and a lilting hello that let you know, before he inevitably said it, that he was originally from Italy. Long hair cascaded down his back, but the crown of his head was completely bald.

"That some kind of Italian fashion?" I asked. "What's with the Friar Tuck?"

"Oh, this! This is holy," Salvatore explained. "How does one say? It is . . . electric that does this?"

"You stick a fork in an outlet when you were a kid?"

Salvatore crinkled his eyebrows in confusion.

"No. From the sky it comes. One day, I walk in the hills. Big clouds, small rain, I not concerned. The sky, you know how it is, when it growls with the rain and you do not worry because it is always make

33

its noise. And then, I remember light and a burning. The tourists, they help me. And then again, last year, it happens again! It is God, twice, giving me blessings."

His verbal fumbling grated on me the way my father's did when we went to the restaurant and I had to translate his request for a "boof-ate" to the server as, "Do you guys have a buffet here?"

"You're bald because you got hit by lightning?" I asked.

"I am not bald!" Salvatore said vehemently. "I am blessed. It was a sign that I should study physics." He paused and smiled. "But, yes, twice I am struck. Light-ing. This is the word?"

"Yeah. Tell folks you were hit twice by lighting, and they'll know exactly why you're fucked up."

And that's exactly what Salvatore told everyone for the entire first semester until Kenny pulled him aside to explain the difference between "lightning" and "lighting," and that, honestly, nobody really needed to hear him tell the story every single day.

The roommate I found most interesting, however, was the one among us that would have blended into any picture. Jonas looked like a typical football jock—big sturdy muscles filling out a six-and-a-half-foot frame, a ruggedly handsome face, and a tree-trunk neck. Perched on his nose was a set of wire-rimmed glasses so delicate it seemed as if he could snap them if he blinked too quickly. He kept running a hand through his hair to keep his shoulder-length curly black locks out of his eyes. After our initial greetings and get-to-know-each-other small talk, I'd asked Salvatore if he wanted to join me that night in a search for a party. He had hugged me in his excitement. Kenny had simply nodded and said, "I have nothing against a good par-tay." I'd turned to Jonas, hoping to have him join us. A big man watching your back is always a good thing, especially if you have a propensity for getting into fights.

"Rivers of beer, ladies of luxury. You've gotta come," I said.

"I don't want to," Jonas said, a slight smile on his lips.

"Are you afraid of the women?" Salvatore asked. "Do not worry! I will teach you the poetry of ladies!"

"I don't drink, and I don't date," Jonas said. "I'd rather stay here and read. I wanted to translate a book I've got."

Back in Chicago, if somebody said something like that, the guys would have called him a faggot. At my college people were throwing around the words "politically correct," which I didn't fully understand, but I could see the way their words tiptoed around the labels my crew back home slapped on anyone. The college kids wore new Patagonia and J. Crew clothes, so with my Kmart hand-me-downs and blue-light-special tongue, I knew I'd have to watch myself. The college was a new country, and I was still just another foreigner in a strange land. I didn't want to piss anyone off and risk getting my ass deported to a state school.

"What's so important that you've got to translate it tonight?" I asked.

"It's a book my parents gave me. The Reverend Moon thought I should study it." Jonas smiled.

"Oh God," Kenny said, flipping his paper aside. "Don't tell me we're rooming with a fucking Moonie."

"Don't call me that," Jonas said. His jaw clenched, his meaty hands curled into fists, even the air took on a chill as if it were afraid of him. "I'm a member of the Unification Church. Don't judge what you don't understand."

"I know exactly what you are," Kenny said, rising from his chair. "You guys are a cult. Mass weddings, brainwashed idiots wandering around selling flowers, and lording over it all is some freak who thinks he's the Second Coming of Christ."

In less than a breath Jonas bulled into Kenny. His thick mitts gripping Kenny's shirt near the collar, Jonas raised him in the air and pinned him against a wall. Kenny's feet kicked helplessly.

"And I know what you are," Jonas said, thumping Kenny's scrawny body against the wall. "A dressed-up fool trying to buy and lie his way into God's kingdom."

"Put him down, Jonas!" I yelled, grabbing hold of one of his arms. I was like a flea clinging to an elephant.

"Who's the idiot now?" Jonas growled.

"We are all *idiotas*," Salvatore squeaked from a corner. "*Dovremmo essere amici*. We should be friends, no? We live together this year."

Kenny's hands twitched at his sides, the veins on his neck like branches growing from Jonas's throttling hands. His eyes were wet with terror.

"You're killing him," I pleaded.

Jonas banged Kenny against the wall. Kenny feebly kicked his legs.

"A man of God would not do this," Salvatore said. "God does not love killing."

Jonas's hands snapped back and Kenny slumped to the floor. Jonas took a few steps back, his eyes bewildered, his hands rubbing his forearms. Kenny wheezed on the ground.

"I promised," Jonas said, his voice suddenly soft and full of a sadness that seemed bigger than any I had ever known. He stared at Kenny and shook his head. "I'm sorry," he said, and he rushed out the door.

Salvatore and I ran to Kenny, helping him sit up. Kenny arched his head up, gasping for air. I patted Kenny on the hand while Salvatore cooed something in Italian.

After a couple of minutes, Kenny nodded at us.

"I'm okay," he said, still breathing heavily. "Thanks for getting that fucker off of me."

"We should get you to the infirmary," I said.

"No," Kenny said, shaking his head, "the infirmary can wait. I'm going to the dean. I'm getting that psycho expelled."

"Just cool off for a bit," I said. "I'll bring Jonas back here and we'll see if we can't settle this shit on our own. If you still want him gone after that, then fine. There are a lot of angles going on here, though, that you're not seeing. Play this wrong, and we'll all get burned."

"What the hell are you talking about?" Kenny called out as I rushed out the door. "He assaulted me!"

With brothers six and nine years older than me, I'd always been an easy target for teasing. If I put a thumbprint on the Mylar bag protecting one of my brothers' comics, or took the last of something tasty in the fridge that they'd had their eyes on, I got a knee in the back, a punch in the arm, or a shove down the stairs. The walls of our house were festooned with blood marks and the telltale dents and holes of our wars for household supremacy. In time, since my father couldn't stomach the idea of paying anyone to paint the house but didn't have the time to do it himself, those marks overwhelmed the underlying paint, so anyone who walked into our house could see that this was a place at war with itself, a breeding ground for madmen.

The more time I spent in a corner of a room reading books, the less I had to face my misery and anger, so I read everything we had in the house. Since I had a near-photographic memory, all that reading only created trouble at school.

For a long time, I took the beatings of my brothers and classmates with a classic Hindu passivity. It was my fate and there was nothing to be done about it. I could cry or not cry. It made no difference. One day, after I had come home weeping because the kids on the school bus had depantsed me and called me a sand-nigger, my sister, Kamalavati, pulled me aside.

"Quit crying and feeling sorry for yourself," Kamalavati commanded me. "Your brothers won't respect you, and the kids at school will only pick on you more since you don't do anything about it. You have to fight back every chance you get. Make them afraid of you."

Kamalavati was ten years older than me and like a second mother. All the times my mother had been lost in her own grief, my sister had been around, advising me.

"Can you teach me how to fight?" I asked her.

She laughed.

"What don't you already know? Haven't you been beaten up enough to know how a punch works?"

"Yeah, but I don't really know how to throw a punch. What if I miss?"

"Then kick them in the nuts," she said, a gleam in her eyes. "Poke them in the eyes. Pull their hair. Bite them and spit their own blood back in their face. You do that and no one will ever mess with you again."

"But that's not fighting fair."

"Fair? There's no such thing. Besides, you're a boy. Our parents will say that anything you do is okay," she said. "Be thankful you weren't born a girl. At least you get a chance to determine what your life is like."

I was too caught up in my own thoughts to notice her sadness, the way she clutched herself tight as she spoke. I ran off to contemplate how I was going to use her new style of fighting.

That night, when one of my brothers gave me a charley horse because I'd taken the last can of Coke, I slugged him back in the stomach. I got more bruises than usual in the ensuing rumble, but I felt better afterward because I'd gotten in a few good shots. And though my body hurt, I didn't cry. Crying was a sign of weakness, and I swore to myself that no one would ever see me cry again. The next day at school, when another bully shoved me down, I got back up and punched him square in the face, and he ran off crying with a broken nose. When I fought, I felt no pain, no sadness. When I was done, I only felt the euphoric rush of adrenaline. Though the school tried to control me with detentions and suspensions, and my parents pleaded with me to be a good boy, I was addicted.

A few weeks later, while I was sitting in my fourth grade classroom, reading a book while the teacher taught the other kids the day's lesson, I heard a knock on the door. Peering in through a pane of glass in the window was the principal, and behind him, I could see Kamalavati.

I was led out into the hall. Kamalavati clutched at me, sobbing, before I could say a word. My father leaned against the wall, a scowl on his face.

"I'm sorry," I said. I grabbed his arm. "I promise I won't fight."

"Nothing is wrong," my father said.

"I have to go," Kamalavati sobbed. "They're sending me to India."

"It's not her fault!" I said.

"Keep your voices down," the principal whispered, leaning back on his heels and looking sidelong down the hallway.

"Leave him be," my father said to Kamalavati. "It is getting late."

"You'll be back soon, right?" I asked.

She shook her head and clutched me tighter.

"But why?"

She turned and looked at my father, but he shook his head.

"She will write you letters," my father said. "For now, she will only be saying good-bye."

My sister kissed me fiercely, and then was led away by my father. I sat back down in my class, dazed.

When the bus took me home after school, I ran to her room hoping to catch her. Her clothes were gone. Only her books, and the cloying flowery smell of her perfume, remained.

Many years later I learned that she had been exiled because a boy from her college had called her at home hoping to go out on a date with her. She hadn't really known him, but my parents had been listening in on the phone and assumed the boy wouldn't have asked her out unless something serious was going on. The family couldn't risk any shame, so she was sent to Bangalore where she could be under the tight watch of family until she had her arranged marriage.

My parents and our relatives in India expected that we would continue the treasured family tradition of inbreeding. Nobody in our extended family had done anything other than get an arranged marriage, so, like our family's centuries-old traditions of vegetarianism, abstinence from drugs and alcohol, and service to the temple, we were expected to unquestioningly follow the tradition. My family married my sister off as early as possible—they trusted our relatives in India to select a suitable boy whose adherence to custom could rein in her recklessness. For us boys, things would work out differently. Both my brothers thumbed through pictures and résumés of prospective brides before arranging a sightseeing tour of the top picks. The pool was limited, restricted by caste and family lineage, but they each had their pick of the most beautiful Thulu-speaking Brahmin girls, and found well-educated former beauty queens among our third and fourth cousins whom they ended up marrying.

My parents felt that arranged marriages were the best way, and they pointed to themselves as examples. They were sure dating-fueled marriages inevitably blew up in divorce. They talked about the beauty of our religion and the importance of our rituals, but never explained what any of it was or meant. We were taught mantras, but not their meanings, so religion became a daily chore of spouting gibberish. We were taught that our religion accepted all people and believed in the innate goodness and equality of all beings, but then told over dinner about the dangerous blacks in America, the devious whites with their lawyers, and reminded that if we ever married any of those people our family would have nothing to do with us and we would be forbidden from entering the ancestral places in India. If I argued, they labeled me "hormone-fevered." They were older and wiser and could see the world clearly. I couldn't understand, they explained, because I was too young.

My brothers and my sister were six to ten years older than me and so at least had each other. They could secretly talk among themselves and counsel each other on how to handle my parents' rules. By the time I seriously started questioning my parents' ways, however, my brothers and sister were gone. My brothers were off in college and not interested in the whining of their annoying kid brother, and my sister was by that time consumed by her marriage. Though coaches at school had begun channeling my rage and confusion into sports, the schism between my Indian and American selves was tearing me apart. I soon realized that the only way to handle the situation was to lie my ass off. I could tell everyone at school that things were great, and secretly sneak off on dates and to parties so that I felt a part of America, and could pretend to be a good, studious Indian boy while at home with my parents. One of my favorite things to do was tell my parents about stuff I had been doing, but to talk about it as if it was a story I had heard about some other kid. Together we would bemoan the madness that had twisted that poor, deluded young man into getting drunk at an away football game and smashing car headlights in the parking lot. I could feel the guilt and the pride all at once, the intoxication that comes from leading a double life. I learned that people believe you when you tell them what they want to believe. In that way, my parents raised me to be the best of liars.

I wandered through the library in search of Jonas. A few students roamed amidst the towering bookshelves, and a tired couple slept intertwined on two plush sofas pulled together, but the library was otherwise empty. The whisper of a snore echoed along the linoleum, and for a moment I thought the library itself was dozing. It turned out to only be a librarian napping with her head on her desk, her mess of blond permed curls fanning over her arms.

On the second floor I found rows of cubicles stacked two high, with a tiny opening in the side for entrance. Embedded rungs in the sides of the lower cubicles allowed a person to climb to the higher ones where at least they had open air over their heads, but I couldn't imagine ever stuffing myself into one of those little coffins with their hard wooden seats. In the back of one of the rows, squeezed into a cubicle, I found Jonas thumbing through a book.

"You can't run from me, Jonas," I said. "It's a small town."

Jonas set down his book. "I know you want me to apologize."

I climbed up into the cubicle in front of him, and standing on the seat, leaned on the barrier between us.

"He's the one who should apologize. He started it. You just finished it."

Jonas cracked a smile but it quickly faded.

"They're going to expel me. Before I even sit down in my first class."

"How you so sure?"

"It's in the student handbook."

"I've done worse. It's no big deal as long as you can fake a sincere apology."

Jonas stared at me.

"What did you do that's worse than trying to choke someone to death?"

"A fire. Everyone survived. My point is, all you did was stand up for yourself. At least now he knows not to fuck with you, and if you apologize, I'm sure he'll let it go."

He traced the edge of his book with his finger. "My whole life people called me names because of what my family believes in. And every time I end up getting into trouble because I lash out. I know I have to apologize, but I can't."

"Because of the promise?"

Jonas glared at me.

"Who told you about that?"

"It's what you said when you ran."

Jonas leaned back and sighed.

"I promised myself I wouldn't get into fights anymore. I've got enough trouble as it is."

I laughed.

"That's a dumb promise to make when you're a foreigner."

"I was born here . . ."

"I mean foreign as in different from everyone else," I said, waving him off. "Me and you, we're freaks to these people. When I was a kid, I told people about arranged marriages, and they acted like I was a Satan worshipper."

Jonas's eyes lit up.

"You're supposed to have an arranged marriage too?" He stood up quickly and nearly busted the table in front of him in his excitement. "What are the odds on the two of us being roomed together?"

I shrugged.

"The admissions department got our files, simple as that."

He paused and looked me over. "You don't drink or smoke either, do you?"

"I'm not supposed to."

Jonas's grin lit up his face. He thumped his book, tucked it under his arm, and climbed out of his cubicle.

"What's the hurry?" I said, hopping down after him.

"The sooner I talk to Kenny, the sooner you and I can sit down and talk about arranged marriage. You tell me about yours, and I'll tell you about mine."

He was like a giddy kid ready for show-and-tell.

"One thing you should know," I said. "All those rules of my religion about not drinking, arranged marriage, being vegetarian . . . those are my parents' kind of things. I'm not planning on following them. Except the vegetarian thing. Meat's always looked kinda nasty to me."

Jonas slung one of his massive arms around my shoulders.

"That's why we should talk. I think I can help you rediscover your faith."

4

Krishna said, "Do your duty, Arjuna, as your nature dictates.
All work fetters, as all fire gives smoke. Only selfless duty saves.
Fix your mind on me. Surrender all deeds to me. All problems
will be solved by my grace. Pride will lead only to your moral ruin.
If, filled with pride, you say, 'I will not fight,' it is all in vain. You
are foolish. Fight you will; your nature will make you fight. Your
karma will make you fight. You will fight in spite of yourself."

—Bhishma, the Mahabharata, Book Six

The villagers, and even people within his own family,
told my father, Sreepada, that the biggest dream he
had the right to have was to be a priest in our ancestral Kali temple like
his father before him. If he couldn't remember the mantras, at least he
could work as a dish boy in a hotel in Mangalore. But he remembered
how his father, Narasinga, would walk barefoot from the temple and
swim through the swollen river between the temple and his school,
clothes in a sodden bundle on his head, just to meet him when school
let out for the day. He remembered the smile on Narasinga's face
when he handed him his graded schoolwork, his father holding the

papers close to his heart as if they were a sign from the Gods of blessings to come. The rice fields were failing. The temple gave the family only one rupee a week. But in his son there was a power that he knew could change the future. And so, though duty bound him to teach his son the mantras of the temple, my grandfather whispered to Sreepada that his schooling was more important. He taught him that the perfect marks on his schoolwork were a more powerful prasadam from the Gods than the holiest protections of the temple.

One night, before exams for entrance into junior high, Sreepada needed to find a place to study. There was no electricity in the house, and the moon was obscured by the first wisps of clouds that would become the monsoon blanket of the night, so he had to go into the crowded Kali temple where the torches would bring the words in his book flickering to sight. He went inside the temple and sat with his back against the cool stone. The stone felt soft to his back, as if the touch and scrape of thousands of praying hands through the centuries had evoked compassion from the rock. The night air pressed hot against his face, heavy with the sour scent of desperation. The villagers filled the temple, awaiting word from Kali concerning their fields. Some had already packed for Mangalore, as if they knew the land was dying. In the city, at least, they could work in a restaurant and find food.

The villagers pushed in, but around Sreepada they left a circle of space, for he was a Brahmin, the son of the priest, and they did not want to invite a curse from Kali for having strayed too near one of her chosen servants. Sreepada read, the words of his books swimming in the light, intoxicating him with dreams of distant lands where men flew in the sky and built concrete towers that kissed the clouds. In other lands, it seemed, the people did not need Gods. What they wanted, they created. What they feared, they could destroy.

Narasinga led a bare-chested man into the temple, and the crowd parted as he passed, for the man was the *pathri*, the one selected to channel the voice of Kali. The man was covered in sweat, his voice a cantillating song in a language none of them could understand. He stopped before the idol of Kali and his singing became louder, his arms and legs jerking to an internal music. He grabbed hold of a few long saffron-colored vines of golden *pingara* flowers, pressed them up to his nose, and inhaled wide-eyed. He began to whip his body with the pingara, pollen flying up in a thick yellow cloud, tiny seeds sticking to the sweat on his body. His skin turned yellow from the pollen, his eyes open but seeing beyond the crowd gathered around him.

"Who will ask the first question?" Narasinga asked the crowd.

The crowd hung back, the men looking at their feet. From outside, where the untouchables stood, a woman called out.

"My son won't work the fields. He only plays cricket all day. What does mother Kali say I should do?"

Narasinga pulled the golden pathri close to him and whispered in his ear. The man broke free, his song like the birds' when the rice lay freshly harvested and waiting for their greedy mouths. Suddenly, he stopped, and nodded slowly. My grandfather rushed over to him and the man whispered in my grandfather's ear before spinning off to dance and sing again.

"He plays because he hates the fields," Narasinga said. "You have not punished him appropriately, for he must learn to fear you more than he fears work. Stop feeding him. Hunger brings wisdom."

Sreepada smiled to himself as he studied from his books. The people of the village believed that they were witnessing Kali speaking, but it had to be a trick. All one needed to speak for the Gods was common sense and a platform.

"I have a question," a man said, pushing himself close to my grandfather. "My elder brother and I lived together peacefully in the same house with our parents, even after we were married. Though it was crowded, we enjoyed each other's company and had no complaint, and our fields were always well tended. Now that our father has died, however, our family fights. We fight in the fields, and our wives yell at each other. There is no peace anymore. What can we do?"

The man gave Narasinga a cup of milk and motioned toward the pathri. The pathri was hopping from foot to foot before the Kali idol, shaking his head, his belly undulating as he gasped for air. The crowd gave him a wide berth, although from time to time a man would dart forward from the crowd to touch the pathri before rushing back to the comfort of the throng. Narasinga pushed forward, the cup of milk in his hand, and waved it in front of the pathri's eyes. Narasinga leaned in and whispered in his ear. The pathri snatched the milk and staggered toward the Kali idol. He poured the milk slowly over Kali, its whiteness dripping down the black stone of her face, mixing with the dried blood on her fangs.

Sreepada bent his head over his books to keep from smiling. He traced the words on the pages with his finger in order to lock them in his mind. Most of the people in the village knew of the problems in the man's family. The rumor was that the trouble came from the wives. The wife of the elder son had come from a family with fruit fields, and she had thought that when the patriarch had died, her husband would inherit the fields of his father. With all the land to their name, her husband would seem more respectable to her family. The patriarch had left one day for Tirupathi and had never returned, fortunately able to spend his last days praying in the holy shrine before dying at the idol's feet. When the patriarch had left, however, the fields needed harvesting, and so the sons had worked hard together. When their father didn't return, they decided to share the house and fields. The elder son's wife took her frustrations out on the younger son's wife, bossing her around as if she were a servant, and she had responded by whispering gossip to her husband. Each wife had turned the ear of their husband and sown the seeds of dissension. The sons were noble men like their father, and inclined to share peacefully, but their wives were a different matter.

Sreepada thought that if the man had offered a chicken as sacrifice, along with a few rupees, my grandfather would have told them the truth. The solution was simple: the wives hated each other, so the only choice would be for the brothers to find separate houses. But offering a cup of milk meant the man likely didn't want to know the truth. A cup of milk would likely only get him a standard response: be patient, or, if Narasinga was in a businesslike mood, that the family should light an elaborate puja to the Gods and make donations to the temple.

The pathri had been whirling before Kali, the pingara flowers lashing his flesh like whips. Suddenly he stopped, the crescendo of his song cut off as if he had been punched in the stomach. He crumpled to the ground, shrieking and covering his ears. Narasinga rushed forward and leaned beside him. The pathri sobbed against his shoulder, his undecipherable ranting coming now in gasps.

Narasinga recoiled. He staggered back toward the man, closing his eyes for an instant, rubbing his ears. My grandfather stood before the man and uttered a mantra my father had never heard before. Sreepada struggled to follow the Sanskrit words he spoke, but they were beyond him. Narasinga's deep baritone resounded through the hushed temple, and even the pathri, suddenly clear-eyed, seemed afraid. Some of the villagers glanced questioningly toward Sreepada—they did not know Sanskrit. It was the secret language of priests, and of the people in the room, only Kali, Narasinga, the pathri, and perhaps Sreepada had any chance of understanding. It was the mantra of warding, the mantra that kept Kali from bursting forth into our world.

Narasinga touched the man's hands.

"Your father is buried in the northeast corner of your fields. You must raise his body and cremate him properly."

The man blinked back tears.

"He is in Tirupathi. My brother and his wife saw him leave on the bus."

"They lied."

The man ran off into the night and raced toward his home, the temple crowd rushing after him. A few of the villagers lingered within the temple, afraid to venture into the night. One cautiously approached my grandfather and asked if his question could be answered that night—he wondered about the coming rains, the future of the crops, the life that lay ahead for him and his family. My grandfather called the pathri over. The pathri sipped from a cup of water, and paused to dab at his eyes with the edge of a towel.

"You will have to wait until next week," the pathri said, shaking his head.

"Just this one question," the man pleaded. "Surely Kali will speak on this matter. I have brought a goat."

"I cannot speak with Kali anymore tonight," the pathri said. "Come again next week."

The man wandered off, and slowly the remaining villagers left with him. My grandfather joined Sreepada and sat against the wall of the temple, and soon the pathri joined them. Sreepada stared at the floor.

"Read," my grandfather commanded, opening my father's book and placing it before him.

"But I am afraid."

"You are not the one who should be afraid," the pathri said.

Sreepada was not allowed to go to the cremation, so he helped his mother in the fields, toiling with those of his three brothers and four sisters who were old enough to be useful. The youngest ones played tag alongside the rice fields, chasing each other back and forth, the toddlers making bewildered half turns as the action passed them by. From time to time a villager paused to gossip with his mother.

They had found the body late in the night, but when confronted, the elder son had said that he knew nothing of the death, and his wife had stood by his side. They claimed to have seen their patriarch leave on the bus. How the body ended up in the fields was unknown to them.

"Why would I kill my own father?" the elder son had asked. "If I killed him for the land, wouldn't I have also killed my brother so I wouldn't have to share it?"

"They are Rakshasas" was the village gossip. "Rakshasas came and killed the oldest son and wife and then pretended to be them. And now we are all cursed because of them. They are the reason for the drought."

The villagers had surged forward to kill them, but my grandfather held them off with words.

"If they are Rakshasas, none of us could kill them. If they are people twisted by evil, spilling their blood on our land will not lift the curse. We can judge their actions, but the remedy must come from Kali."

The body of the murdered father was cremated that day, and my grandfather spent the night in the temple with Kali.

The next morning, no trace could be found of the eldest son and his wife. Some claimed to have seen them running off into the night.

"They did not flee," Narasinga corrected them. "Kali has cursed them and will never allow them peace. They are dead to the world till the ending of time. Their crimes called her forth into this world. They were fools, forgetting that once welcomed, Kali can never be removed unless she is appeased. She took their souls to feast upon, and I can only hope they have sated her."

The rain began to fall that night and continued for several days. My grandfather walked Sreepada to the school for his exams because he was worried that Sreepada might stumble in fording the swollen river. Narasinga lifted Sreepada upon his shoulders and crossed it. Nobody in the family had ever even tried to take the junior high examinations. Schooling had never seemed that important when the rice fields were plentiful, or when the kings of old had provided for the priests. And even after the kings fell before the British, and the fields slowly lost their strength, school still seemed a useless luxury. None could afford proper schooling when every scrap of money needed to be put toward buying food, and scholarships were so rare that one might as well have asked Kali if she would be willing to raise a mortal into the kingdom of the Gods. In the old system, Brahmins had been given every opportunity to succeed. They had been expected to be cared for and allowed to study their mantras in peace. In the new India, nobody wanted any special allowances for the Brahmins anymore. If the state offered only one hundred scholarships, the vast majority would be reserved for the "backward" classes. The few that were available to Brahmins often went to the rich Brahmins in the cities who had the ability to afford private tutoring and bribes.

My grandfather knew what no one else in the village could even dream. He walked Sreepada to school, and on the day of the exams, as the rains poured down, he stood outside the school and stared through the window at his eldest son, his blessing from God. Sreepada sat in the front row, near the instructor, and as each test was passed out, his pencil danced across the pages with such fervor that it seemed the lead could spark the paper to burning. Sreepada pressed so hard on the paper that sometimes the pencil snapped with a crack that startled him. He pulled out his razor and furiously sharpened a new tip. The other children labored along, sweat dripping onto their sheets, each question contorting their bodies like a poke to their ribs. But with each exam, Sreepada seemed to gain in energy. He would finish quickly, pause to lick his pencil, and then look outside the window and smile at his father.

At the end of the day they walked back to the village, hand in hand.

"You did well," my grandfather said.

"I was perfect with the math," Sreepada said, ticking exams off his fingers, "and science was quite easy. They may disagree in principle with some of my social topics' responses, but my arguments were well reasoned. The time was more than enough, so I checked all my answers."

"Intelligence is a blessing. In this new world, an intelligent man can go far. When the government comes and bothers the temple with legal forms, you will be our village politician and you will weave such words that they will never take from us again. And people will come from far away to visit our temple, because they will know your wisdom. You will learn all the sacred texts, and when there is a question, the people will come to you for answers. It will be like the past, like it is for our family at the Eshwara temple. There, did you know, they still carry the name Shastri that was given to them by the King of Mysore. Shastri: the great learned people. You will be the Shastri of Kali."

They walked in silence for a while, Sreepada stamping his feet in the puddles on the path.

"I will not be a priest," Sreepada whispered.

The rain poured down and Narasinga pushed his dripping hair from his eyes.

"What else but a priest could you be?"

My father shrugged and kept walking. My grandfather sped up to keep pace.

"This is what was chosen for us by God," my grandfather said.

"I could be a president. Or an architect. Maybe I will be a judge," Sreepada said, eyes gleaming. "And there would be justice and we wouldn't have to wait for God."

"Don't be silly. That is not what God wants for us. It is not appropriate for our caste. We are bound to Kali."

They walked on, hurrying their steps before the onslaught. Overhead, thunder shook the sky.

"One of my younger brothers could be the priest. How do you know that isn't what God wants? Why does it have to be the oldest son?"

"It doesn't," Narasinga said, "but it is better that way. Otherwise, what if the next eldest doesn't want to be a priest either? You can't pass the responsibility to your brothers. It was not meant for them. One could say that he doesn't want to be a priest, and then the next, and then finally the youngest may not have the wits to be a priest. The temple would fall, and the village would lose its faith, and there would be no protection for anyone in this world from Kali's vengeance."

"God would send a priest."

"What if God didn't because the one that was meant to continue the tradition decided that his desires were more important than his dharma? God would curse such a man, and the town he was meant to protect. Perhaps God would feel that the time had come for *Kaliyuga* and the ending of existence."

They came to the river and my grandfather lifted Sreepada to his shoulders. The river was thick with rain but slow, a fat serpent winding its way through the trees. It was as high as his chest, but if he walked slowly, he could carry Sreepada across.

Narasinga focused on his path through the water, but Sreepada thought of the path of his life. The water lapped at his ankles like the traditions that threatened to bind him to the village. People could try to swim through, fall, and drown, never to be heard from again, or reach the other bank too spent to go much farther beyond. Or they could be carried across, and reach the other bank with all their energy, and leave the river behind like memory. Most people had no choice. They had to swim in the river. But God had given him intelligence, and it would be his intelligence that would carry him across.

"I know how to tell what the Gods' will is," Sreepada said.

Narasinga lurched in the river, then righted himself, but not before he took a deep swallow of the water. "Be careful what you say," he spluttered.

"Our fate is determined by God," Sreepada said. "We have choices, but they are limited by our duties, and they are affected by the strengths and weaknesses that have followed us from our past lives. I do not know my fate, but I know that God has given me intelligence. I took the exams, and I am sure I did very well."

"This does not mean you aren't fated to be a priest."

"But it does not mean that I am fated to be one either."

My grandfather reached the other bank of the river. My father clambered to land and reached back to help my grandfather onto the riverbank. My grandfather lay on the ground, his breath coming in ragged gasps.

"The odds are against me getting a scholarship," Sreepada said.

My grandfather rolled over to spit out some water.

"If I don't get the scholarship, I cannot go to school. If I cannot go to school, then I will have to study the mantras of the temple. I will accept that as my fate if that is what God decides."

"And if you get the scholarship?"

"Then you must accept that it is my fate to continue my schooling, wherever that takes me."

Kali struck Narasinga, riding the monsoon clouds like chariots, swallowing the ocean in gulps, and raining the water down upon the land until every valley lay submerged, the rice fields overwhelmed. She sent water into my grandfather's lungs until he had to lay propped up in order to breathe. Sreepada went to the temple and prayed, but Kali would not answer him. He ran to the village doctor, and the doctor named the curse of Kali "influenza," but would not come to help unless they could pay him. My father ran back to the temple and begged all those who came to pray to lend him a few rupees so that he could pay the doctor, but he was only a beggar in the house of Kali. Kali would save his father or she wouldn't, people said. What use would it be to give him money when he would probably only use it to buy candy?

Sreepada went back into the temple and prayed before Kali. She did not answer him or send any messengers to give him a sign. She was nothing more than a stone idol garbed in the finest silks the village could provide, wearing a necklace attached to an ancient gold coin. He looked around, but nobody else was in the temple, so he stripped Kali of her silks and ripped the necklace from her neck. He ran to the doctor and bartered Kali's belongings for his father's life.

Sreepada rushed back to the house with the doctor only to find his father, his grandfather, Bhagavatha, and his grandmother, all wheezing and gasping in their beds. His aunt was trying to help, but there was little she could do. The doctor asked Sreepada to bring him a cup of water. He took the cup to each of the sick family members, made them take a brief sip, then drew water from the cup with a syringe and injected it to their arms.

"That isn't medicine," my father hissed.

The doctor stared at him. "You aren't a doctor, so you wouldn't know. But this will help. I am helping to hydrate them. If you want stronger medicine, bring more money."

Over the next few days, Sreepada tended to his family. His grand-mother was the first to go, her breathing shuddering to a stop in the middle of the night. A few hours later, Narasinga pulled him near, kissed him, then closed his eyes. Bhagavatha lasted longest. The fire of fever raged across him, but he chanted until hoarse, sputtering and coughing, his phlegm thick with blood. From time to time he would strike his own chest with one of his meaty hands, as if trying to thump the illness out of himself, leaving welts on his chest.

After a week, Bhagavatha finally seemed to tire. His words faint, he spent most of the day in a stupor, his eyes unfocused. Sreepada cried beside him, his aunt holding him, herself wracked with sobs.

Suddenly Bhagavatha raised his hand and motioned Sreepada close.

"Leave the tears for others. You are the man of this family now. Bring us honor. Be a model of dharma. Use your blessings for good."

He gripped Sreepada's head in his hands and pulled him close. He tilted his head forward and blew gently on his scalp at the point where the bones of the skull meet.

"I pass my wisdom and my blessings to you," Bhagavatha said.

Sreepada gripped his hand and cried.

"Oh no, child," Bhagavatha said. "This is not the end. It is only a temporary parting."

He closed his eyes. All his responsibilities, all his duties, now passed to my eleven-year-old father.

From that point, my father was fueled by the vengeance of Kali. The doctor who wouldn't help his family—he would show him. Those people in the village who could have spared a bit of money to heal his family—he would show them. He sealed himself from all emotion except anger, and threw his heart into studying. He would never enter the priesthood. He would never help Kali. What had she done for him except bring misery to his family and leave their prayers unanswered? What had the Gods ever done? No, he would not be like the rest, hoping for a divine blessing to rescue him. He would rescue himself. He would save them all.

Tats poured me another cup of his coffee, and gave me a splash of his milk. I stirred in two sugars and joined him in the dining room. He brought an ashtray with him.

"You smoke?" he asked, pulling a pack of Winstons from his hip pocket.

"I quit in treatment," I said.

"Go ahead and smoke," he said, giving me a cigarette. "Trying to quit everything at the same time is damn tough."

I borrowed his lighter. I took to smoking like I'd never left off.

He watched me smoke for a bit, then said, "I've never seen the reason in quitting. In a house full of guys, everybody smoking, the nonsmokers are the ones that get it raw. It's like they're smoking without getting any of the good out of it."

"How long you been here?"

He said, "I am the Oasis, and the Oasis is older than you."

"And before that?"

"I talk about my road with my sponsor, not with you. I tell you my story, it'll just get me drunk."

He lit up a cigarette, set it in the ashtray, and took a sip from his coffee. "Drink your coffee," he said.

I took a sip, then another. I let it soak in.

After I had another cup of coffee and five more of his cigarettes, Tats put two identical sheets in front of me. They listed the rules and had spaces for two signatures at the bottom. I signed in the appropriate places and he shook my hand.

"I'll get the security deposit to you as soon as I can," I said.

"How much money you got on you?"

"Nothing."

He drummed his fingers on the table and looked me in the eye. "What kinda work you do?"

"I'll do anything."

He shook his head. "I know that. What's your trade?"

"I don't have one."

"Then what can you do? I'm talking honest work."

"I could teach maybe. I got some college."

"You're shitting me."

"Serious. I went to college. Two years," I lied.

He blinked, took a sip from his coffee. "Keep it simple for me, Eddie. I'm trying to figure out how we're gonna get you some money."

"Teachers make good money," I said. "Twenty thousand or so."

Tats rubbed his hands together, pressed them to his face.

"I'm serious," I said.

"You don't even have a lead on a job. You'll be lucky if you make six bucks an hour."

I took a deep breath and stared into my cup of coffee.

Tats said, "Just think straight. Nobody cares if you were the goddamn president of the country or Jimi Hendrix with his magic guitar. Who the hell's gonna hire you?"

I looked up at him and tried to will the muscles in the back of my neck to unknot. He didn't understand. I was young, twenty-two, and smart. That counted for something in the real world.

"Nobody hires drunks," he said, "except for other drunks. And we know better than to pay more than five bucks an hour." Tats shook his head and chuckled a bit. "If you want real work, I can set you up. No charity, though."

I took a sip from my coffee and looked up at Tats.

"Do you want the work or not? They pay in cash."

I nodded. I knew something I could do with cash.

"Good. That's what I want to see. I line something up for you, you gonna bust your balls and make me look good?"

I nodded.

"I'll try," I said.

I would honestly try to get high. When I was in college I got high, and later, when I was sleeping under the jungle gym at Clemente High School, I got high. I'd drifted thousands of miles in a perpetual search, walking alone except for the whispering voices in my head. Anyone else who touched my life either died or disappeared, and yet I kept searching. I didn't have to do anything anymore.

When I first hit the streets, I tried keeping up appearances for awhile. One night I decided to shave. I thought that if I looked good then maybe I could get a girlfriend for the night, no one beautiful, but at least no one whom I'd have to pay with cash or rocks. I went into the Broadway shelter, stayed the night, borrowed some shaving gear from the front desk. There wasn't any shaving cream, not even any soap to lather up with, so I used plain water. The blade on the shaver was so dull it yanked at my beard. I looked at the blade—it was covered in blood. I wiped the blood off using the sleeve of my T-shirt, but some of it persisted. When I looked closer I realized that specks of other people's blood were dried on the blade: dark brown, black, flaking away.

I never trusted anything in the shelters. I'd have to wait a couple hours just to get a mattress that smelled like rotting piss. If I fell asleep, I'd wake up without shoes. The first time I went into a shelter I'd had a garbage bag full of memories I'd stolen from home. I'd used it as a pillow on one of those mattresses. When I woke up, it was gone. Pictures of my mother, an address book, phone numbers, my high school diploma.

It was better on the streets. At least I had some dignity. The cops never let me stay in any one place long, just "move along, move along," all night long so it got hard to sleep at all—constantly moving, no one to talk to, just silence and stares, and people kicking my ass because it was something to do. I needed someone to talk to. Being alone drives people crazy. I'd try to keep moving all night long, stopping in twenty-four-hour places at night to warm up for as long as they'd let me stay.

Getting through the night was the trick. I had all kinds of different cons to keep alive. Sometimes I'd last an entire night on the El or shuttling back and forth on a bus. Or I'd check apartment buildings, trying to find one where the front door could be jimmied open, or one where the front door didn't completely close, and I'd last another night. For the most part, though, living meant trying to find a way to stay alive on the outside. I knew one woman everybody called Bloody Mary, who walked the streets muttering to herself. She wasn't crazy at all, but most folks took pity on her because her con was that good— crazy enough for sympathy, quiet enough that you could let her into your Dunkin' Donuts and know that she wouldn't start screaming or start hassling you for free food. She had a quiet dignity about her. She also would just let her period run, dribbling down her legs and through her pants. That kept her from getting raped.

I always kept a good long piece of pipe on me. One night I caught a whiff of smoke coming from an alley behind a tacqueria. I looked in. I saw a kid about my age, maybe eighteen or nineteen, about my size, but dressed clean, all alone deep in the shadows. I crept up on him in the darkness, and when I got close I saw him flicking a lighter over a pipe.

From walking the streets all night long, my face had gone numb, my ears burned. When the wind blew, it would bring tears to my eyes. My hands and feet, legs and arms, were no longer my own, but could move, searching for a warm spot, a place to rest, while my mind wind-milled with self-pity. Walking all night makes a man crazy, makes him replay memories.

I looked at that boy on the street. My height, my hair. Would he turn around to show me my face? I could ask him, "What right do you have?" And he'd reply, "It's my life." Wasn't that my pat answer to everything back then? All my teachers, my parents talking about what potential I had. They had dreams.

I crossed the alley. Gripping the pipe with two hands like a baseball bat, I planted my lead foot, turned my hips, rotated my upper body, and swung with all one hundred and fifty pounds of what was left of my drug-ravaged body. I got myself clean in the base of the skull. I gave a short grunt, as if I had driven the soul clean out of myself.

The body pitched forward, forehead smacking the alley wall, body crumpling, right arm splayed out, twitching. I hit it a couple more times to keep it quiet.

I got thirty-four dollars, a red lighter, a new black leather wallet, pictures of a girlfriend or sister (good smile, green eyes, long brown hair), a high school ID and driver's license, new shoes (Reeboks a size too small), a clean white T-shirt, a black sweatshirt, and a nice big gray Starter jacket that made me look like the Michelin Man.

According to the ID, my new name was Jorge Chavez. I lifted the skinny body, soft and warm, flopping everywhere, but I finally leaned it against a wall. I didn't want to look. But yes, there I was. Undeniably. It was me, older. My hands froze.

My face was bruised, bloody, like somebody had used it as a battering ram. Despite the mess, I could see my thick lips, an almost square jaw, same sharp cheekbones, and coarse, thick black hair. My skin, where it wasn't bleeding or puffed out and purple from bruising, was oily, thick, slightly wrinkled. I was still breathing, somehow.

The moon shone bright deep in the alley, and the street looked far away, veiled by a mist that must have drifted in from the lake.

"You made another mistake," a voice said in my right ear.

I turned, but there was nothing there, only the gleam of the light on the brick walls of the alley, the sheen of the mist.

"You aren't dead yet, but you will be if you keep listening to Kali," the voice said. It was a deep voice, with a hint of an Indian accent.

My mind filled with memories. I saw a point in the mist thicken, become a ball, a torso, and finally, a body. The body walked near me. It had two feet, bare, covered in hair. Two hands that reached to touch my face. The backs of the hands were covered in dark brown hair, rough like wool. I could see a hairy chest, thick and muscled, at my eye level. I looked up and nearly a foot above me was a face, covered in hair, with thick gray lips, a wide flaring nose, protruding eyebrows. The eyes were gray. There was a thick ring of gold set atop the head and gold studs along his right ear. I felt something brush along my feet and looked down to see a tail curling around my leg.

"You need to focus, Rama," the voice said. "The war is only beginning."

I felt a brush of softness caress my check. His tail flitted before my eyes. It was Hanuman.

He crouched before me, bringing his face to my level. The monkey God looked me in the eye and winked. "Yes, Rama. I have to save your ass again, don't I?"

A person will worship something, have no doubt about that. We may think our tribute is paid in secret in the dark recesses of our hearts, but it will out. That which dominates our imaginations and our thoughts will determine our lives, and our character. Therefore, it behooves us to be careful what we worship, for what we are worshipping we are becoming.

—Ralph Waldo Emerson

Back at the dorm, the reconciliation between Jonas and Kenny went as smoothly as could be expected. Jonas walked over to Kenny and extended his hand for a handshake, and Kenny warily eyed his arm like it was a sword poised to plunge. Jonas gruffly said he was sorry for choking Kenny, and that as long as Kenny didn't insult his church, they would have no problems. Kenny angrily said that he was going to have Jonas expelled because he was dangerous, and I yelled at Kenny and called him a fucking fuck and told him that if he reported Jonas, that I'd report him for starting the fight. Kenny looked to Salvatore for support, I glared at Salvatore, and Salvatore threw up his arms in defeat. Kenny stomped off into his room, Salvatore sat down on the couch and tried to read a book, and Jonas leaned against the wall with a smile flickering across his face.

Outside, the lanterns above the field in front of the dorm blazed to life. The sound of someone singing "When the Levee Breaks" in an off-key falsetto grew louder, and then came a rat-a-tat of knocks on our door.

A stumpy, double-chinned guy with mottled, cocoa skin I'd seen on the front steps of our dorm opened our door.

"Hey, hey, sexy," he said. "I heard you want a party. We're meeting up in my room, first floor, in about an hour." He scanned the room. "You can come too, big man. You too, baldy."

"Salvatore," Salvatore said.

"*Salud* to you too."

"Where's this party at, anyway?" I asked.

He pointed in one direction, then another, then threw up his hands.

"It's at my brother's house. He's a senior and he's got a place off campus. I don't know exactly where it is right now, but I can call him."

"What's your name?" I asked.

He gave me a mock salute and stood stiffly at attention.

"I am Lucas, sir. I do not know what I'm fucking majoring in, but I'm from Connecticut."

His shoulders slumped and he shook his head.

"It's the exact same question from everyone every time. We should get buttons printed that list this stuff so we can talk about more important shit."

"I'm from Chicago," I said. "I'm supposed to want to be a doctor."

Lucas smiled. "I know that feeling," he said. Then, tapping his watch and giving me a knowing nod, he turned and hurried off down the stairs.

"You're going to a party?" Jonas asked.

"You can come too."

"Can I?" Salvatore asked.

"I thought we were going to talk. About religion."

"We can talk at the party. Or on the way. I've never been to a college party, not one where I didn't have to worry about sneaking home to my parents."

"Can I come?" Salvatore asked.

"Go by yourself then," Jonas said.

"Look, Jonas," I said, "nobody's going to force you to drink, and I doubt anyone, even if they're completely wasted, is going to try to jump your bones. You can think of it as research into all the reasons why you shouldn't do the shit I'm about to."

"Can I come?" Salvatore asked.

After dinner, Kenny was still sulking, so Jonas, Salvatore, and I went to Lucas's room. There we found a crowd of eager faces, and when Lucas yanked out his violin and strutted out the door, the crowd followed him. We wandered down tree-lined streets, Lucas stopping every hundred feet or so to bow at his violin and warble a few off-key lines from rock ballads. After wandering up and down the same blocks for so long that I thought our Pied Piper had gotten us lost, I finally heard the deep reassuring bass thump of a house party down the block. As we drew near, I could see the porch filled to capacity with plastic cup-swilling students.

"Freshmen!" they yelled out. "Hide the beer!"

"How can they tell?" Salvatore asked.

A tall black man stepped off the porch and strode toward us.

"Lucas," he said, "I told you to bring a few friends, not your entire dorm."

Lucas nodded. "I told a few friends, and they talked. Can't stop that, Micah. They're all cool, though."

"The keg won't last."

"Get another."

"We're not in New York."

"Just ask them for money."

Micah shook his head and brushed past Lucas. He stood in front of us and waved us quiet with his arms.

"If Lucas brought you, then you can come. Ten dollars for beer, though, and you get served after upperclassmen."

The crowd groaned.

"You don't like it, then you can walk. But that's the way it has to be. We've only got one keg. They've got some old-time liquor laws in this town, and I can't change that."

I heard a chorus of "Screw this!" and "Rip-off" as a chunk of our horde splintered off to find their way back to the dorms, but I saw just as many begin digging into their wallets and purses. Quite a few handed Micah their crumpled bills and pushed their way into the house.

"That seems a bit expensive for beer," Jonas said.

"You're not kidding," I told him, nodding at Micah. "But that man's a genius. He's going to make a killing."

"I don't have ten dollars," Salvatore said.

I walked over to Micah.

"We don't have cash, but we don't want beer. Because of my religion, I don't drink. Same goes for Jonas. And Salvatore's Italian. He's only into wine. Mind letting us in?"

"I could do that," Micah said.

"So what all's going on in there?" I asked, peering around his wiry frame.

"Drinking. Some folks are dancing on the back lawn. There's a poker game upstairs."

I had exactly $100. It was my dad's parting gift when he'd finished helping me move into the dorm.

I pulled Jonas and Salvatore along with me toward the party.

"I don't know how to play poker," Salvatore said.

"Don't worry. You're not playing."

"I don't want to watch you gamble your money away," Jonas warned.

"You just make sure nobody tries to grab the money off me after I win it," I said.

We used to play card games all the time in the back of the math team bus. My experiments in poker amidst a group of math junkies who could count cards taught me one thing: understanding the small edges in probability helped, but not as much as the ability to read players' strengths or weaknesses from the way they breathed, the way they moved their eyes. I'd been born with a quick calculator in my brain, and I loved lying as much as I loved spotting the bullshitters. I figured that walking into a cash game amidst a bunch of drunk college kids would be a way to make some easy money.

The house was packed, the smoky air inside stiflingly muggy. It was cooler outside, but in the house the collective lust of the ogling drunks lent a sweaty heat. Some in torn T-shirts and cutoff shorts, others studiously casual in crisp shirts and thin khakis or skirts, like clumped with like and smirked at the unfamiliar passersby. A few girls with melting mascara, sweat streaks cracking their pancaked faces, fanned each other with studied grace in a corner by the front door. I glanced at them surreptitiously, wondering if they were different from the pretty girls I'd lingered by in high school. There had been a few friendly ones in high school, but they'd never allowed us to be more intimate than hallway gossipers. I'd come to believe that the reasons were many, and all hinged on the same thing: I was too smart, too brown, and too ugly to be cool enough for intimacy. College was supposed to be different, though, and since no one knew me, there was always the chance that I could be funny enough on first impression that they deigned to get to know me better. I didn't expect anything deeper than that—experience had conditioned me to believe that only an Indian woman would view me as anything other than a dog—but I desperately hoped that in college I might be able to talk to the pretty girls about things that mattered without them cringing as if I'd just tried to sniff their crotch. I'd lived for so long inside myself, building a wall of small talk and inanities to keep people from peering too closely at me, that I craved real and honest interaction. Most people lived behind the same walls, and it seemed such a tragedy that we all protected our loneliness, even when encountering people we could safely reveal ourselves to. Whether or not I or anyone else could actually be real and honest was still to be seen, but if Jonas was any indication, college was the place to find people who were willing to try. If I was lucky, I could find a woman who was tired of being bullshitted to.

As Jonas, Salvatore, and I wandered through the house, I gave the people who looked at me a confident nod and my best practiced smile, a good old Chicago "Hey there, guy," and a thump on the back as if I belonged and knew I belonged. A few of them gave me the look you give a familiar friendly face—that acknowledging nod, the hint of a smile. That was a good foundation for a friendship, because that meant that if I ran into them a few days later and started talking to them, a part of their mind would maybe recall my face, and they'd feel compelled to chatter back without any of the cold curtness we use to let strangers know we don't trust them.

Wisps of smoke curled out from under the door of a second-floor room, and Jonas began coughing before we even entered the fog bank that lay inside. The room was larger than I expected, as if the door opened into another dimension. In the center was a long dining table draped with green felt, with eight players pelting chips into the middle to punctuate their steady stream of trash talk. Only men sat at the table, but along the walls of the room, lounging on beanbags or straddling metal folding chairs, a mixed crowd chattered inanities with the easy nonchalance of those who think they're truly cool. On the sofa, a couple necked to the hoots of the drunks teetering nearby, groping each other methodically, as if they were the paid entertainment, a moving sculpture intended to inspire the horny. A few of the women in the room were clearly girlfriends of the players at the table, stumbling over with plastic cup in hand to heckle or cheer their boy depending on the fall of the cards. I watched a few hands, eyeing the way the players handled their chips. The only player I recognized was Micah. It looked as if each of the players had several hundred in front of them, and he had at least five hundred stacked neatly in plain view.

Salvatore pulled a scowling Jonas along with him toward a pretty, curly-haired girl puking into a wastebasket in the corner. Jonas leaned against the wall, scanning the room like a preacher in a whorehouse. Salvatore knelt beside the girl and rubbed her back.

I pulled up a chair at the poker table and slipped my cash from my wallet.

"Hey, fresh meat, I don't know you," said a player with a scraggly beard and a mountain of cash in front of him. He had on a crisp red flannel shirt, top two buttons open to reveal a snake tooth and coral necklace tangled in the burgeoning brush of his chest hair.

There were two ways I could play it. Most people would act soft and compliant, wanting the strangers to feel safe around them. That kind of style wouldn't fly with these guys, though. If they thought I was nice, they wouldn't respect me. I figured I needed to be Chicago around them—tough, blue-collar straight talk, and ready to throw down.

"What's your problem? Micah said there was a game."

"Yeah? Well, how do you know Micah?"

"Like it matters. You think I'm some undercover cop come here to ride your ass? Micah's bro's my hookup."

"Micah doesn't have a brother. He's a fucking eunuch."

"I've got a brother," Micah said. "A freshman."

"You're still a fucking eunuch."

"Do you even know what that means, Alex?" Micah asked.

"You," Alex said, jabbing his beer cup in my direction. "Just put your money on the table and shut up. I don't know you, so I don't like you, and so you can't talk unless you're playing."

"My money's already on the table," I said.

"Then keep quiet while you lose it. I'm not here to listen to fresh-man bullshit."

We quickly got to the business of cards, each player choosing a poker variant to play when it was his turn to deal. Most of the other players looked a lot like Alex to my eyes—drunk, pissed off, but in new, clean clothes. They favored baseball caps as their fashion accessory, kept their shoes clean, and ironed their khakis, but not always their blue jeans. At the end of the table, one of them, a clean-cut baby face in a collared cobalt shirt, kept adding to a massive pile of money in front of him as the night progressed. As Alex sniped at the baby face, I learned that Alex had lost a big pot to him, that the boy was a sophomore, and that his name was Hamilton.

I would later learn that all the players, and the majority of the people in the room, had known each other from childhood. They came from some of the richest families in America, and their families were part of the money aristocracy obliged by their station to present an image of dignity and class. I'd heard that some pretty well-connected people were on campus—guys like Walker Stapleton, who was somehow related to President Bush, and Hussain Aga Khan, whose family was one of the wealthiest in the world and could trace their lineage to Ali, cousin of the prophet Muhammad. I'd likely never get a chance to hang out with guys like that, but the kids in the room were future lords and ladies, too, and I wanted to be part of their circle. The kids in the room would inevitably take positions of leadership in the political and economic fiefdoms of our quasi-democracy, aided, of course, by the considerable influence of their collective families. Like their mothers and fathers before them, it was expected that they'd blow off a little steam during their college days, and so their gestures of rebellion— the unkempt hair, the discreetly placed scandalous tattoo, the education sacrificed in favor of a few years of competitive hedonism—were understood as a forgivable rite of passage, so long as they didn't go so far as to irrevocably damage the family name. They were willing to try anything, safe in the belief that their families would smooth things out if they went too far, rationalizing it all as a necessary adventure that would enable them to truly understand the mind-set and problems of the people they would eventually rule.

Hamilton was a tight but aggressive player who made astute plays, and though we weren't working together, we got good cards for the first hour and carved the table up between us as if we were a team of seasoned card sharks. I was grateful for every dollar I swept into my pile, and always felt a little sick when I lost a pot. My parents argued about nickels, groaning when they had to spend more than ten bucks on a pair of jeans, and so they'd drilled into me their immigrant respect for the dollar. I didn't have my dad's nearly pathological fear of being reduced to poverty, but I wasn't going to ignore a penny I found on the road either. The guys at the poker table, though, were a different breed. When Alex blew through his money, he dug into a pocket and flipped five crisp hundreds on the table with a laugh.

I saw another player fly through hundreds of dollars, and when he ran out, he got up with a smile.

"That's it till tomorrow," he said, "unless one of you can spot me."

A couple players threw him some bills. They didn't write IOUs, and with all the beer they were drinking, I was sure they wouldn't remember it in the morning. I was playing with money, but if they lost, if they won, if they set fire to the table, what did it matter?

Still, it was one thing to lose to each other, and entirely another to lose to an outsider like me. When I dragged in a pot after a particularly outrageous bluff attempt by Alex, he grabbed the deck of cards and flung them across the room.

"I know exactly what's going on," he said pointing at me and then Hamilton. "You two walk in here, acting all innocent, but I know cheaters when I see them."

"Save the bullshit for your girlfriend," I snapped. "I don't need to cheat to beat a dumbass like you."

The rest of the table roared, but Alex wasn't laughing with them.

"You two are working together."

Hamilton shook his head.

"I've never met him before in my life," he said.

I got up from the table and started organizing my money into a neat bundle.

"Sit down and play, Exeter boy."

"I'm not from Exeter," I said.

"That's where Hamilton went, and I know that's where you went too. That's where you worked out this scam."

"I'm from Chicago and that's where I went to school. Public school, not some private party my rich daddy bought me into," I said, leaning over the table. "You ever want some lessons on how to play"—I snapped a twenty off the wad and tossed it at him—"consider the first lesson free. Twenty bucks for the next one, and you can find me in Lucas's dorm."

The table burst out laughing, and Alex, after a moment's hesitation, gave me a crooked grin.

"That's good," he said, but I could tell from his eyes that he saw nothing good about it.

"It's just luck," Hamilton said, tapping the table with his fingers. "Sit down and play. We're all cool here."

"Fucking beginner's luck," Micah said, laughing. "Somebody get him a beer."

"Spliff 'em both up," another player said, pulling something from his pocket.

"Oh, come on," Alex said. "We are *not* sharing that."

"What is that?" It looked like a tampon, and though I was interested in having some sexual adventures while at my college, none of my fantasies involved tampons and a group of greasy men.

Alex put the thing to his lips, pulled out a lighter, and lit it up. He pulled long and hard, then passed it to his left.

"Heaven," he said in a strange choked voice. A tendril of smoke rolled out with his words. He leaned back and closed his eyes, and smoke billowed from his nostrils.

I knew what it was now, and I didn't want anything to do with it. Drugs were for losers, the group we called "Skids" in high school in part because they seemed to spend most of their time screeching about in the school parking lot in their rusted jalopies, and in part because there was nothing breaking their descent into complete uselessness.

"I don't need that shit," I said.

Hamilton put the joint to his lips and pulled hard, the cherry turning a bright red. For a moment the flame reflected off his pupils, a fire flickering in his cold brown eyes.

"You will," he said, a bank of smoke rushing from his lips.

I smelled the smoke as it curled by. It reminded me of the cheap incense devotees left as an offering at our ancestral temple, of the house I set fire to and watched burn to the ground. I should have run from that table and sworn never to hang out with those guys again. But just like on the night my neighbor's house burned, I didn't move. I watched, and secretly, I felt glad.

"College is about experiencing things, right?" I said. "Well, I promised myself that I'd try. When you're driving down the highway of life in a Mercedes, only an idiot doesn't check out what all the buttons do."

"You're not a fucking Mercedes," Micah said.

"You're a monkey. And this here," Hamilton said, holding the joint up high, "is the super-kind Humboldt skunk banana. You were made for each other."

He was right.

6

The tectonic layers of our lives rest so tightly one on top
of the other that we always come up against earlier events
in later ones, not as matter that has been fully formed and
pushed aside, but absolutely present and alive.

—**Bernard Schlink**

Monkey" was what they called me in school ever since
junior high, and I'd long stopped thinking of it as
a racial slur. In junior high I'd popped in on a friend during an after-
school basketball practice, just wanting to sit in the bleachers and
watch the guys play and to bullshit with them after. They were short a
couple players due to a nasty virus making its way through the school,
though, and the coach had hollered at me to come out and play with
them so that he could at least get a decent full-court scrimmage going. I told him I didn't know much about basketball other than what
I'd learned watching Bulls games with my dad, but he told me not to
worry—he just wanted to have me fill out the second team for a bit
and he wasn't expecting me to do anything spectacular. I'd already
shot up to six feet tall by seventh grade, and so the coach thought I

was big enough to at least give the starting center something to think about. I didn't know how to dribble or how to shoot anything other than a point-blank shot since my dad discouraged wasting time on anything other than schoolwork, but I figured that I could scrap my way through the scrimmage.

A few times people passed me the ball, and I made a royal mess of things, bouncing the ball off my leg or throwing passes that smacked my teammates in the back. The coach pulled me aside and told me that all he wanted was for me to try to keep the center from scoring, and for me to try to act like a gorilla under the boards, going after every rebound.

The next time the center had the ball, I bellied up against him. When he tried a sky hook, I spiked the ball out of bounds. When a ball clanged off the rim, I hopped high and snapped it down with both hands. Then one time I muscled my way inside when a player on my team took a shot. The ball rolled off the rim and I ripped it down. I thought I was supposed to shoot, but I didn't want to piss anybody off, so I waved the ball around, looking for someone to pass it to.

"Just dunk it," one of the players said with a laugh.

I didn't know he was joking, so I tried, flatfooted from under the rim. The ball boinged high off the back iron and bounced near the three-point line, and my hands, unsure of what else to do, clung to the rim. I hung there, startled, before letting myself drop to the ground.

The coach blew his whistle and charged over. The kids stared at me as if I'd pissed in the middle of the court.

"Boy," he said, "did you just try to dunk?"

I shrugged my shoulders.

"They told me to," I said.

The coach sunk to his haunches and let out a long whistle.

"Sorry," I said.

"None of these kids can dunk," he said, looking at me with a gleam in his eyes. "On a good day, they might be able to grab the bottom of the net."

I nodded, not believing him. I'd seen people dunking all the time on TV and figured it was something most people could do.

"You got legs," the coach said, "and they sure look pretty to me. Your daddy play ball?"

I laughed. "My dad doesn't believe in games."

"Then I just don't understand where you got that from," he said.

"Well, my mom says my family is descended from some monkey God."

The coach let out a low whistle.

"Monkey legs, huh?" he said. "Well, monkey, how'd you like to be on the team?"

No longer was I just a brain or a sand-nigger to be mocked. I'd entered into the glorified realm of athletics, that magical place where the ability to control the movement of a leather sphere was prized above all else. Nobody valued good grades—that was something all students could get if they really wanted to. Our family's legends, that we could trace our family line back a millennium, were equally unimportant— most of the kids at my school were multi-Anglo mutts, their family tree an irrelevant mystery, the world outside America filled with a confusing jumble of people who didn't speak English, and whom they would never want to visit because of it. I had monkey legs, though, and that was a special gift you could only be born with. It was as if I had special powers beyond the reach of mortals, and so their awe made me begin to believe the snippets of family history I'd heard, to search out the full story, and to accept that I had the monkey God Hanuman's blood coursing through my veins.

Growing up, I had a hazy sense of our family history. I knew Sreepada came to America in the early sixties, and that my two brothers, my sister, and my mother followed him a few years later. I knew we had family in India, and that each time we visited we spent what I thought was too much time visiting temples, but I never understood the connection between us and temples. I even got into a fight with one of my cousins when we were kids because I said a Brahmin had killed Gandhi, and when my cousin told me I was a Brahmin too, I slugged him in the gut. I knew we were Hindu, but I didn't think we were Brahmin because my dad never talked about the caste except to describe the fat and corrupt Brahmin priests as lazy people who used religion as a con to trick money out of people. When he'd snap open the *India Today* and mutter and shake his head, the offending group was always "North Indians" or "Pakistanis" or "Brahmins." I came to view the groups as a trinity of evil that threatened the world.

Our mythology and our history didn't matter to my father, so he didn't elaborate on them. They were bullet-point details I cut and pasted into my incomplete understanding of who we were. But every growing child craves the magic of stories, and so my father replaced the stories of religion with the stories of his life. The cocky boy in his high school class who thought he didn't need to study. The time he worked for the summer on a banana plantation and fell off a tree. The image of his blind grandmother mashing jackfruit into a tasty fruit leather, oblivious to the horde of ants that had found her jackfruit and which were now the secret ingredient in her food. When the thought struck him, he would finish each story by stating its moral: studying is important, be careful in trees, not knowing what's in your food can be a good thing. His favorite moral was that all play and no work makes Jack a dull boy. He would tell me this if he saw me frolicking outside for too long, telling me, quite seriously, that I should ask my teachers for more work.

My father worked from sunrise to sunset at a variety of hospitals, nearly always seven days a week. His beeper would go off even when he was at the dinner table, and my mother would hand him the phone (in his left hand, so he could keep eating). While listening, he ate, his right hand scooping steaming rice and *saar* into his mouth, pausing only to recite the appropriate mantra of prescriptions required for the patient. Sometimes when the beeper went off he'd rush out in his tan trench coat, armed against the elements with an enormous black umbrella. Night and day had no real meaning for him, it seemed. There was only work and home, and work was where he lived.

By junior high, I was old enough to be allowed to run along with him while he tended to patients. He could take a yowling beast from a crib, whisper a few words to a nurse, and in hours his magic would reveal an amiably drooling baby. The ability to do that commanded respect. Nurses gathered around him when he paused in his rounds, and other doctors nodded deferentially as he passed. Patients watched him with reverence. He was the local medical superstar, the man who knew the answer. But to my young eyes, the awe and reverence that greeted my father meant only one thing—he was someone special, like a God of myth. And standing there, watching the world pay homage to my father, I wanted to believe that genius was genetic, that divine power infused my family's blood.

Outsiders to my father's village feared my great-grandfather, Kupana Bhagavatha Rao, not just because he was a priest of Kali. He weighed well over two hundred pounds, but the weight sat well on his massive, broad-shouldered frame. Even as his paunch grew larger with age, the muscles of his chest and arms, hardened from years of farming and the secret mantras of Kali, made him seem more a boxer than a man of God. His forehead bare, the long hair on the back of his head hanging like thick rope between the blades of his back, he was easy to spot from a distance, and the villagers would often come running to him, both to be near the giant of Kapu and feel safe in the power that radiated from him, and to voice their troubles in hopes that he could find a solution that mortals could not. Once a local strongman had tried to steal land from some of the villagers by sending a band of toughs to scare the people into surrendering their fields. The villagers called upon Kupana Bhagavatha, and he went to the forest hideout of the strongman, and there, unarmed, surrounded by men unafraid of God, he reasoned with them in Kali's tongue. The next day, Kupana Bhagavatha performed a sacrifice at the Kali temple, and as a final offering, he began to string a necklace. He reached into a small bag attached to his waist and pulled out shards of teeth that he gently tied onto the necklace. He pulled out a knife, dug carefully into the space between the knuckles of his ring finger and middle finger, and pulled out a bloody incisor that he tied onto the necklace with the final knot. He put the necklace around Kali's neck, the blood and the bone a warning without words.

Sreepada only knew Bhagavatha as the old man who wandered the temple grounds and sometimes assisted his father with the temple pujas. But when the villagers spotted Sreepada walking down the street, they would often pull him aside and thank him for something his grandfather had done long ago. They would begin talking about the many great things Bhagavatha had done, sometimes squeezing my father's arm to see if he too had the same strength. They were always disappointed in my father. Bhagavatha had traveled from town to town in his teens, challenging the strongest in each village to a bare-knuckle boxing competition, until all of Kerala talked of the giant of Kapu, an invincible man, a man who was purported to be made of living stone, a man who could shatter mountains with one punch. My father was good at reading and good at math and could sometimes hold a hand-stand for as long as a minute. He could never compare.

They called him Bhagavatha, not because his godlike strength deserved a heroic name, but because he was known as a master of the Bhagavad Gita, the seven hundred verses better known to him than the names of his own children. On summer nights he would travel to the surrounding villages with a troupe of *kathakali* actors he had trained and perform an abridged version of the epic that lasted until dawn. If a drummer fell ill, he would fill in, maintaining a thundering beat on the *maddalam*. If an actor was indisposed, he would delicately paint his face into a mask with the *chutty* of lime, rice paste, indigo, and sulphur, then command the stage, his massive frame spinning through the dance, his hands showing their delicate mastery of the *mudras*, or hand signals and positions. He would sing the epic in his bass rumble as the actors danced before villagers, taking pauses only as other actors filled in with song, or banged drums during climactic battles. Although he loved the tales, he did not do the performance for free, and he would ask for payment from each village. If the village offered enough, he would even perform the Ramayana, his voice shaking the earth when Ravana, the Rakshasa king, wrestled with Hanuman.

Bhagavatha was accustomed to praise, but he didn't believe in any of it. He was a priest, nothing more. Yes, he'd been fighting most of his life, and with Kali's grace had somehow emerged unscathed, but he had always acted only to protect his own people, and he had acted without pride—it was his dharma. He was the preserver of vengeance, and when people were wronged, he had to stand for them, regardless of the risk to himself.

And so, naturally, villagers competed with each other in their stories about him, wrapping their facts in luscious layers of exaggeration. In one myth Bhagavatha had been performing a puja within a temple when Rakshasas suddenly attacked. With one hand he tended the sacrificial fire, while with the other he warded the Rakshasas off. The Rakshasas grew frustrated and tried to bring the temple crashing down, but Bhagavatha stood, and with a roar, braced the crumbling ceiling with his hands. Some say he only held the ceiling for an instant, enabling a dawdling child to escape, but others say he held the temple up for hours, intoning mantras so powerful that they vaporized the Rakshasas as they lunged at him. Even the British were scared of the myth of the warrior-priest of Kali, a giant with two long scimitars who could decimate an entire regiment of fully armed soldiers. Bhagavatha would smile at the stories, at the constant embellishment that turned his every act into a sign of the divine. My father said that Bhagavatha was celebrated because he was the only hero the people had, and it was because of him that the villagers still honored our family, but in my heart I believed Bhagavatha was celebrated because he was like me, divinely blessed, the blood of Gods coursing through his veins, destined to make a difference in the world.

One of my therapists in the thirty-day lockdown facility where I finally sobered up told me at the end of my stay that she understood the reasons behind my Hanuman and Kali fixation growing up. The kids at school treated me like crap, calling me names, the girls cringing like I was a leper if I showed any interest in them. But at the same time I was kicking ass in class, hearing folks in the stands cheering for monkey boy. The whole world was telling me I was different, and given the stories of my family history, it was only natural that I'd turn to the myth to reconcile the contradictions.

"I never wanted to believe people wanted to treat me different because of my race and skin color," she said, "but I accepted it. For you, it's easier to believe the lie. You want to think you have a special purpose. That makes the suffering something like what heroes go through, instead of just being the crap associated with being a person of color."

I laughed and gave her the smile I reserved for friends. She was one of the few people in the lockdown who weren't afraid to be honest about themselves. She'd even confided early in my stay that she used to hide under the stairs from her mean drunk dad, and I could tell from the way she told it that it wasn't just some detail she'd picked up off a television show to make the lockdown addicts trust her as somebody who knew her shit.

"You go ahead and write that down in my file," I told her. "That's a nice explanation that'll go over good with your bosses."

"What do you think of it?"

"You want the honest truth?"

"I always do."

"It's not a lie. Hanuman himself told me so."

She shook her head and got up from her desk to come give me a hug.

"You go ahead and believe that until you don't need to anymore, okay? Take care of yourself. You've got a good heart."

"That's because it's Hanuman's heart," I told her, "and one day, I'm going to prove it to you. I'm not like the other junkies you see, making big promises, getting locked up again a few weeks later. I'll be straight because that's what Hanuman wants. He'll kick my ass if I fuck up again."

Giving me a farewell peck on the cheek, she said, "I will too."

. . .

The days when I'd regret prostituting my soul in service to almighty crack cocaine were still a long way away, however, when I woke up in my bed in the dorm the day after that first party at Micah's place. I was tucked under my sheets, fully clothed. Jonas, seated in a wooden chair beside my bed, had an ice pack pressed to his cheek. I slowly sat up, tugging the sheets off me. Grass stains and vomit streaked my jeans, but at least I didn't have a hangover. I dug in my pockets, but they were empty.

"Where's my money?" I asked. "Did those bastards steal some from me?"

Jonas shook his head.

"You had nothing left when they kicked you out."

"They didn't kick me out."

"You kept smoking that stuff, and one of them kept letting you sip from some bottle he had. After you threw up on the table, they told me to take you home."

"Did they seem pissed?"

"They didn't seem surprised."

I grabbed Jonas by the hand.

"Seriously. Were they kind of laughing about it, or was it like one of those Jane Austen books where they say everything's fine, but they're so cold about it you know they hate you?"

I didn't want to think of them making fun of me when I was gone, acting like cool aristocrats who've just rid themselves of the peasant vermin. The thought of people laughing at me made my muscles spasm, made me want to stomp over and force them to respect me.

Jonas shook his head.

"Neither, really. You were out of it. So were they. You passed out at the table, and nobody noticed. One of the girls said I should take you home."

"You think they liked me?"

"Why do you care whether or not they liked you? I didn't like them."

I shrugged and ran my hands over my jeans.

"I guess I've got green jeans now."

"You wanted to walk on your own. I tried carrying you, but you insisted."

He set the ice pack down and rubbed his jaw.

"Who did that to you? You weren't causing any trouble last night."

"As I said, you insisted on walking. You've got a sharp right hook."

"Sorry," I said. "I have a bad habit of punching people, even friends."

Jonas shook his head.

"I don't understand any of this at all. Those people at the party, I didn't expect anything more out of them. Drinking, drugs, sex—they think that's the American way. But you were born in a different country, raised a different way. You know better."

"I was born in Chicago," I said, "but raised like we lived in India. That makes all the difference. Chalk it up to rebelliousness."

"What do you have to rebel against? Nobody here is telling you what to do."

"You are."

Jonas sighed.

"Look, Jonas," I said. "It was just a one-time thing. It's not like I'm going to get wasted every night. I went a little overboard, but it's no big deal. Today's a new day. I feel fine."

"Good. I hope so. I thought you were going to die last night."

I laughed.

"You really haven't been around a party before, have you?"

"Of course not." He shifted uncomfortably in the chair.

"You sit in that chair all night long?"

"Sometimes drunk people drown in their vomit."

I patted him on the leg and laughed.

"Good for you, Jonas. I'll let my mom know you're looking out for me. What did Kenny think of you being in the room all night long?"

"I don't know," Jonas said with a smile. "I didn't think to ask, and he didn't seem to have anything to say about it."

"Didn't I promise you I'd take care of that situation for you?"

"Did you?"

"Stick with me, Jonas. I'll always have your back."

It was a promise I intended to keep. Jonas was sincere and honest, incapable of lying. I needed that kind of ballast in my life. With all the bullshit I served folks in an effort to give them an image of myself that I thought they would like, it was easy to lose sight of who the real me was. Pulling off a good con is a lot like method acting. You study your subject, learn what he loves, what he hates, what makes him want to roll out of bed in the morning. And then, when you have enough to fill out the character, you become the character, and you stay in character until the performance is over. The better I was at it, the more addictive it became. It made me feel happy and in control when I was the tough guy with the golden heart. People respect what they fear, and I'd taught the poker guys that I was worth being afraid of. After all, I came from a line of warrior-priests, I told them, and so fighting came naturally. Violence was genetic. It wasn't out of control or anything, just a part of what made me who I was. It was better to have me around because a guy like me would do anything for his friends. That was the kind of loyalty their families had for each other, and what I would need to prove in order to be welcomed in their circle.

"I set fire to a guy's house once," I said during a bong session.

"You're shitting me," Alex said, tucking his necklace back in after leaning over the bong.

"That's what people like to think," I said.

Hamilton gave me a knowing smile.

"I've got a story like that one too. But if you say the details, everybody just laughs."

"What's your story?" I asked.

Hamilton giggled like a little kid. "I was at a friend's house, and we tried to smoke some cigars we found in his dad's office. Man, we gagged on those stogies so bad we just threw them down and ran to the bathroom to try to wash the taste out, and then we were hanging out in the kitchen slugging tall frosties of milk because we'd heard somewhere that that's what you do. Stogies lit some papers, which got the desk going, and then the whole office was torching. They had to live in their summer house for about half a year and our folks were pissed, but you know how it is—nobody hurt so it's not a big deal."

Alex, who'd been listening intently, nodded.

"That was Chip's place, right? You know they had some shit go down with their company, stockholders getting pissy and all that. I think they forced his dad out, and that family's been running that business since before there was oil."

Micah shook his head in disgust. He'd had it freshly shaved, and it gleamed dully in the smoky light. "That's so shitty. Chip's a good guy—now what's he going to do?"

"That's the way things go," Hamilton said. "People rob you because it's easier to steal what you've got than build it on their own."

"I set fire to my parents' carpet when I was fucking around inside with a model rocket engine," I said.

"See? It just doesn't sound the same when you tell the details. Now you just sound like a dumbass," Hamilton said.

"But I said I set fire to a guy's house once. I wasn't talking about torching my folks' carpet. I burned a house down and never got caught."

"Bullshit!" Alex said.

"He was an asshole," I said. "His girlfriend dumped him and started going out with one of my buddies. He got his crew together and one day they piled on my guy when he was walking home. Broke his leg, cut up his face real bad. The guy fucking pissed on him while my buddy was down. Sick shit like that."

"You're kidding," Hamilton said.

"So I go by the guy's house, Sunday morning while they're in church. Kick in the back door, take a can of gas from their garage, and start their house cooking."

The uneasy silence lingered until Hamilton leaned back in his chair and laughed.

"You spin some good bullshit. Look at everybody, pissing their pants, thinking they're with a psycho." He laughed again and glanced over at the bong. "Hey!" he said, a grin lighting up his face. "Anybody planning on loading that up?"

Alex patted himself until he found a thin bag of weed in a pocket.

"That's all that's left?" Micah asked. "We just got a fat lid off Matty two days ago."

"Just buy some more," I said.

"That's easy for a psycho mooch to say, but I ran into Matty at lunch," Alex said. "He's out, but his brother might mail him a care package."

"How long's that going to take?" Hamilton asked.

"Depends on how fast we get him the money. Figure a few days after that for his brother to get some shit, then a few more until the post office delivers it to Matty. A week, I figure."

"You guys need to get your shit together," Hamilton said. "We're going to be jonesing for a week because you dumbfucks don't know how to plan."

I expected the guys to get pissed off and cut him down. Hamilton was a sophomore, after all. But nobody said anything, some even looking down as if ashamed.

"Why do you guys need it mailed to you?" I asked. "You have to know someone local who's got some, right?"

Micah spat. "Screw the townies. Even if we found someone who had something, it'd probably be crap, and they'd be working for the cops. You can't trust the people around here."

Alex nodded. "Matty's the only way."

"I'll chip in," I said. "What's it cost? Fifty bucks?"

"Fifty?" Scruffy said. Micah ruefully shook his head. "We need a lid of kind, not a quarter of schwag."

"What's the damage, then?"

"Four hundred dollars."

"You're getting ripped off," I said.

"It's a great price, dumbass. As if you could find better."

"I heard that some guys got a pound in Boston once for a grand," one of the guys at the table piped in. He was a clean-cut sophomore with nappy hair that everyone called Scruffy.

"Yeah," Alex said, "and I heard of a guy who bought a winning lottery ticket with a dollar. Who gives a fuck? It didn't happen for me, it's not happening for me, so it doesn't matter."

"But if we went to Boston . . ."

"Like you know anybody in Boston."

"My grandma's got a place—"

"I know your drunk bitch of a grandma's got a place."

As the guys argued back and forth, my mind did the math. If it cost a thousand dollars for a pound of weed, and they were willing to pay four hundred an ounce, a person could make $5400 a pound off the poker guys. They smoked a lot, and they knew others who smoked too, so I figured a person could move at least a pound a month without attracting too much attention.

I could already envision how it would work out. I would talk to Matty and he would let me in on some secrets of the business. It wouldn't be too hard—how hard could dealing drugs be if idiots on the street were making a living doing it? The best part about it was that there was zero risk. There was no way I could lose money on the deal, and the police wouldn't care. The cops would want to go after people dealing the hard drugs, not a small group of pot smokers at an elite college. And even if they did find me out, I'd seen enough movies to know that they would probably offer me a deal so they could go after the bigger fish who had dealt to me. Best of all, hooking the poker guys up with a steady stream of pot would forever put me in their good graces. As they inevitably rose to positions of power as they grew older, they would remember me and I would rise with them.

7

Both the forces of good and evil will keep the universe alive for us, until we awake from our dreams and give up this building of mud pies.

—Swami Vivekananda

T.T. kept yammering away at me. I appreciated the pork chop—he had given me one of his after Tats had finished with me, and probably only because Tats had ordered him to—but I liked silence when eating.

"I didn't know you people ate pork."

"I'll eat anything."

It had become my motto as soon as I hit the streets. It was difficult to find a vegetarian Dumpster.

"You can never tell. Had a guy come through here. A carpenter. Tall guy by the name of Mike. Blond. Lasted a couple months. You know him?"

I shook my head.

"I was sitting down on the couch with him, watching *Cops*—damn good show—and I was eating M&M's. Peanut. I offered him some, you know, because that's being polite, and you know what he says to me?"

T.T. paused. He looked at me as if expecting me to answer. I continued to chew.

"He says that he's Muslim. Can you believe that?"

I swallowed.

I waited.

T.T. blinked at me, pulled a pack of Marlboro Reds from his pocket, and lit one up.

This house was filled with idiots.

"After we're done here, we can go down and play foosball until the other guys get here. Or we can go up to your room and get things straightened out. Want a cigarette?"

"I'm not done eating."

T.T. tapped his cigarette in the ashtray.

"You're not a fag or anything, are you?"

I looked him over. He was balding, junkie thin, and was wearing a frayed green flannel shirt.

"No. Are you?"

T.T. laughed, ashed again.

"Hell, no! But you gotta make sure. We had a guy come through here once. A guy like you. I think he was Navajo or something though. Caused all kinds of trouble. He was a fag. I kid you not. He had that look, you know what I'm saying?"

I put my fork down.

"I like it quiet when I'm eating," I said.

He waited in silence, smoking, looking at me, smiling. I finished eating.

"Why don't you show me my room," I finally said.

My room was on the third floor. According to T.T., it had originally been an attic. It had six beds in it and six dressers, and a high vaulted ceiling that peaked in the middle of the room. As the new guy I got the bed across from the stairwell, which curled down to the second floor and the better rooms that held the five guys with seniority. The room had a warm, musty odor, because, according to T.T., guys would come back from work and stretch out on their beds, damp socks, tired shirts, and all.

I started moving my things from the garbage bag into my dresser while T.T. milled around the room. He poked at the other beds. He stared out the window. He rearranged the pictures on other people's dressers.

"Don't you have a job you need to get to?" I asked.

"I don't start till five. Second shift. Punch press operator. I make dies. Coil feed, line feed, straight feed—you name it, I punch it. I run a fifty-ton Minster. You ever work with one of those?"

I kept folding.

"You want to play foosball? After you're done? We've got a couple hours till I need to leave."

"I'd like some quiet time alone."

"Yeah, me too. I got a nice room. Better than this. Me and Bob and Mike share a room downstairs. Tats gets the best, but he's house manager. You know he has a cactus farm in his room? In a little fish tank. A rainbow of cactuses. Not all of 'em hurt neither. He gets pissed if you mess with them, though."

"So you don't sleep in this room?"

"Hell, no! This is the hell room. Why would anyone want to sleep here with five other guys, snoring, stinking, yelling? We had a guy sneak in a bottle of vodka and hide it in his dresser, and he kept getting up in the middle of the night to take sips. One time he got so drunk he fell asleep in another guy's bed, and the other guy was so tired he didn't notice, till all of a sudden the drunk guy just up and pissed all over him—and I'm telling you—that was a fight."

I closed my drawers and lay down in my bed. T.T. took the hint and went downstairs.

I needed a shower. It felt like I'd been needing a shower for a long time. On the streets it's easy to get high, easy to find a place to sleep, but water isn't something you ever have enough of. Just a cup of water was sometimes a victory. Trying to find a working water fountain, where the water didn't taste like pennies, or wasn't filled with vomit, was like Rama trying to find Sita. "Where is she?" Rama would ask, and sages would point to the north or to the east, or say "Lanka" and not know where that was, leaving him to shoot up with Hanuman and bitch about how clueless those sages were.

"In India at least I could just drink from a river or something," I told Hanuman.

I was trying to stay warm in the underground El stop at Ashland and Milwaukee. Hanuman was standing on the tracks.

"All the rivers are poisoned. All the runoff from the fertilizers has polluted them," he said.

He squatted on the third rail of the El and sniffed it. "There is a deadly current running through this steel," he said.

I nodded.

"The trains come quickly here?" he asked.

"Every five minutes or so."

"You should take one."

"Where?"

He jumped from the middle of the tracks to the platform. He stood before me and brushed my hair with his tail. "Home, perhaps."

I shook my head.

"They don't want me back."

He curled his tail around my neck.

"So you've resolved to die out here."

I took a deep breath. My body ached. My mouth felt like it was filled with sand.

"There isn't anything else to do," I said.

Hanuman crouched before me.

"Do you remember when you were in the forest, after Sita had been taken away?"

"I'm not that Rama."

"Of course you are."

I shrugged, rolled my eyes.

"You asked everyone where she was, and nobody knew. You didn't know how to save her. And then you asked me. I didn't know either, but I began searching for her."

And he found her. I could remember Seetharama saying that, the smile spreading across his face. Hanuman had found Sita on an island across the sea.

"Yes. I found her. I can bring you anything. I can help you to find what you have lost."

And Hanuman opened his mouth, wide, until it seemed the El station had disappeared. I found myself surrounded by blackness and ribbons and swirls of stars. Purple and green gasses twirling in distant places, and in the center, there I was, alone.

Jonas and I often sat down for breakfast in the dining halls and talked about our dreams. It was a simple pleasure that I relished, and it reminded me of the early morning talks I used to have with my dad, the way he eagerly chattered on about how we would work together as pediatricians someday, me bullshitting him to keep him happy. My dad and Jonas were early risers for similar reasons—they woke up with purpose, ready to take on the next challenge in their quest for fulfillment. And they both gave me an early morning calm, a pleasant respite from the insomnia and nightmares that consumed my nights.

I never told Jonas the truth about what I wanted, just as I never was honest with my dad. It wasn't because I didn't want to be honest with them—they were both good men whom I knew I was safe with, whom I knew only wanted the best for me—but because I didn't know enough about myself to pinpoint what it was that I wanted, and because I was afraid of what they would think of me if I even hinted at the violent impulses that compelled me. If I could have told them the truth, I would have said that I wanted peace with myself. I knew that within me was a good person, an honest person just wanting to be, but he was a coward, too weak to stand up.

A counselor in treatment later told me that the weakness within me was a by-product of my strengths. The reason I excelled in classes was because I remembered with nearly word-for-word accuracy anything I heard, as if my mind etched those sounds onto a compact disc. The only problem was that my mind randomly blasted everything back at me at maximum volume, focusing more on criticism than praise, a jukebox with malicious intent.

I'd been searching for a long time for a way to quiet that internal voice. As a kid I found that the confident narrative of a good book could take hold of the microphone for as long as the pages lasted. When my dad got us a computer, I found that video games had a similar effect, the flashing blips and mini-quests startling the voice into catatonia. Then, toward the end of my high school years, I took to breaking into houses and stealing small things.

One night, I woke up at two in the morning, full of restless energy. I threw on black sweats and a pair of gym shoes, cranked open my bedroom window, and jumped out. I wandered a few blocks south in our neighborhood enjoying the autumn night air, cool and damp after days of rain. Suddenly I felt a pull toward a house to my right, two slick Mercedes parked neatly in the driveway, and I tromped across the grass of their front lawn. In my mind I could hear the sound of some distant foreigner's voice, accented, unintelligible, distorted by cheap speakers. If I turned from the house, the voice flared up, screeching so insistently that the only way to bear it was to strike myself in the head so hard that the ringing in my ears balanced out the voice. But if I moved without thought, giving the voice no resistance, all was calmness and bliss. So the voice and I moved toward the back of the house, peering in the window wells until we found the ground-level window that served as the basement's fire escape. We gently pushed the window in, lowering it to the floor, and though all was pure darkness in the basement, I found that if I closed my eyes the voice led us skillfully past the stored boxes of the owners' memories. As we walked up the stairs of the house, I noticed that my hand had found a hammer. We saw a large TV, ensconced between bookshelves of hefty tomes, and a long indigo leather sofa that gleamed with newness. Slowly we made our way up a spiraling staircase, past a chandelier glittering like the stars, to the double doors of a bedroom. A thin blond woman spooned against a hefty bald man on a kingly bed, the covers pulled tight to their chins.

"Open the curtains so the moon can know what we do," the voice said, and so I slid the curtains aside. "Their family line traded your ancestors' blood for gold," the voice said. "Look at them, peaceful, without guilt. Let us teach them the meaning of vengeance."

We raised the hammer high, but my arms froze, and I stood, a statue in the moonlight.

"Strike," the voice hissed, but my arm would not move.

The woman's eyes fluttered open, and she stared at me. She rubbed her eyes. She screamed.

I flung the hammer through the window and jumped out after it, hitting the soft grass hard, the pain bringing clarity. In the bedroom, lights flicked on. I ran, the voice a whisper now.

"You are a coward," it said. "You are not worthy of me."

Pot and alcohol helped, turning the voice into a more manageable whisper. And I found that what Seetharama had taught me worked quite well when the voice had been reduced to a whisper: if I hummed "om" at those moments, the self-hatred vanished completely. It made me want to stay high and drunk every hour of the day.

For my first semester, at least, anesthetizing the voice didn't cause too many academic problems. I'd taken ten advanced placement tests in high school as a way to get a year's worth of college credit while also boosting my class rank, but my college was one of the few that didn't give much credit to AP scores. If it started giving credit for the tests, a sizeable chunk of the school population would be able to graduate early, having polished off many of the academic requirements with the AP tests. Since the institution was in the business of making money, it wasn't in its best interest to let kids graduate early. So, rather than waste my time going to classes that I'd already taken, I spent most of my time getting high and playing poker. I would walk in on the days of tests for my premed classes, scribble my answers down as fast as possible, then race out to find something better to do with my time. I was also taking a poetry-writing class, but I'd been writing for a long time before I came to the college as a way of dealing with my internal chaos, and so though the poems I created were sorry jumbles of cliché, they at least showed an understanding of basic poetic forms. The instructor was perpetually grumpy, either pissed that getting tenure didn't excuse him from having to teach poetry to a bunch of hacks, or that people only recognized him as the weirdo who had somehow gotten a poem with the last lines "Put down your flamethrower, honey/you know I always loved you" into the Norton anthology. Since a couple of the students felt it was a class requirement that they talk more than the professor, even if it was only a monologue about the secret meaning of the poem they had scribbled before class, I soon stopped going to that class too.

Growing up, my parents ensured that I spent the majority of my time learning. When classes were too easy, they signed me up for more outside school. Although they thought sports were a waste of time, they kept me busy and looked good on college applications. My dad told me that if I didn't work hard, I would become boring and lazy and my mother said that boring and lazy people were ripe pickings for Rakshasas, the shape-shifting demons of our mythology. They told me that whatever grade I got was acceptable as long as I'd given the class my full effort. Of course, if I got an A-, they would pull me aside to ask if I had really tried my hardest. My mother warned me that I would have to work very hard to overcome my own barriers, that she'd noticed that I gave people "bad vibes," that there was something about me that would make people easily dislike me. My constant fighting, my occasional back talk—these were signs that the Rakshasas already had a firm grip on me. The only way to save me lay in convincing me that I wasn't doing enough with my life, because fear, pressure, and guilt were good things that kept people from the traps of idleness.

I sat down for dinner in the cafeteria with Salvatore and Jonas. Though I thought they were too constrained by their ideas of right and wrong for me to ever have any real fun with them, they had become an oasis from the chaos of my own hedonism. I could sit with them after a debauched night that made my skull feel like a tweeter thudding a bass line, my lungs and throat seared from a night inhaling the hot tars of weed and cigarettes, and their carefree voices would soothe me into a momentary peace. They reminded me of the math team guys I used to hang out with—good, decent people ostracized by the cool because they hadn't mastered the subtleties of social interaction. The difference between us was that they talked about themselves honestly and openly and seemed genuinely interested in the people around them, and they weren't going to change anything just to get others to like them. As a result, I viewed them with a bit of jealousy—I wished I could live with such simplicity and honesty, but I didn't know how to stop lying.

"Hamilton wanted both of you to come," I told them. "He's going, and he went out of his way to invite us. He wouldn't have done that if this was going to be an ordinary party."

"I've had more fun being heckled by Baptists," Jonas groaned.

"There is a good party I was invited to," Salvatore said. "It is with my friends from the play."

He'd auditioned for a part in a student-written work in order to meet the kind of students he'd never see in his science classes, but had assumed he'd at best get a small role. It had been a sort of social experiment for him, but we'd had to spend a night comforting him after the director sabotaged his plans by casting him as a monk with a big speaking part.

"Every time we go to a party the two of you get drunk and hit on girls," Jonas said. "Inevitably you tell them about my religion because you think it's something they would find interesting. I spend the rest of my night debating religion with atheists or fevered Catholics, the two of you pass out while the girls you were seducing wander away, and I end up dragging you back to the dorm."

"But you have fun doing it," I said.

"This Hamilton party," Salvatore said with a shake of his head, "I will not go to it."

"We could do both parties. Check out Hamilton's and then head to yours. He invited us, after all."

"He invited you," Jonas said. "He doesn't care if we come, and I'm sure he doesn't really care if you go either."

"It's not like that between me and him."

"He's not your friend," Jonas said.

"He is nobody's friend," Salvatore said.

I laughed. "He's got a ton of friends," I said. "He's maybe a little cold when you first get to know him, but you guys would like him if you gave him the chance."

Jonas shook his head in disbelief.

"Haven't you seen the way he talks to people, the way he looks at them? There's good in him somewhere—there always is with everyone—but as my dad taught me, you don't preach to a man when he insists on dancing with the devil. It's like your card games. You said a good player disguises his hand, tricks the other guy into thinking he has something he doesn't. He's been playing poker with you every moment you've known him."

"We go to his party first," Salvatore said. "Then we spend the rest of the night with my theater group. There is one girl—her hair the color of *grapa*. I will be falling in love with her."

"He's not playing me," I said to Jonas. "I'm playing him."

"You're as much in love with him as Salvatore is with his *grapa* girl. And both of you are too young to know what to do with feelings that strong."

"Fuck off. I'm not in love with him."

"You want to be him. You want the world he was born with. It's almost the same thing."

"I understand love," Salvatore said. "It is man's nature to understand love."

Jonas placed his palms facedown on the table as if he was steadying the world. "Eve trusted the snake as well, didn't she?" he said.

"She wasn't Indian," I said with a grin. "My people—we're born snake charmers."

"Her name is Eva," Salvatore said.

"I'm not talking about your *grapa* girl!" Jonas said.

"Yes, you are," I hissed. "You're like my mom, saying we're all fucked unless we do things your way. You've barely met Hamilton, and you've got him pegged as a sinner. You've never even seen grapa girl, and you're calling her a snake."

"It was a metaphor, about the apple—"

"I know what a fucking metaphor is, Jonas. And even silly pagans like me know that whole Bible story. I'm not some confused kid waiting for a preacher to save my soul."

"If Eva is an apple, then she is a good apple. And if she is a snake, I would not mind her beautiful sting."

"I'm talking about temptation, knowledge. You're opening yourself up to something you're not ready for."

"Nobody's ever ready, Jonas," I said, picking up my cafeteria tray. "I'm not ending up like my mom, perpetually afraid, hiding in her bedroom. I'm not going to preach about life based on what I've read in books either. You want to do that—go ahead. I'm a gambler, Jonas. I'll take my chances."

After dinner, Jonas made his nightly pilgrimage to the library while Salvatore and I prettied ourselves up for the party. Salvatore gelled his hair into a comb-over helmet and doused himself in bull-piss that he claimed was cologne. He threw on a baggy floral silk shirt full of lime greens and paradise pinks, and left the top three buttons undone, his chest hair tufting out like withered bulrushes. He squeezed himself into a tight pair of black jeans that forced his developing belly to crest over his waistband, then stuffed his hands into his pants to adjust his crushed genitals. I tried to convince him that he'd be better off if he shaved himself completely bald and paired a plain T-shirt with some comfy slacks, but he claimed that while snake charming might come naturally to Indians, Italians were the kings of fashion.

I wasn't as concerned with my appearance. I shaved since I knew girls liked the look of my jawline and appreciated being able to see my dimples. As long as I didn't smell, it wouldn't matter what I was wearing. The few times I'd gotten lucky so far during my time at college had all followed a similar pattern—the girl got very drunk, I small talked her, she'd find out I was Indian, and I'd spin a few stories about my family history. We'd hook up, and then, if I ever saw her again, she'd look away embarrassed. Sometimes I wondered if there was something I said or did that kept them from being interested in developing a relationship that lasted longer than a night, but the concern didn't last too long. I figured the girls were acting just like the guys I knew who kept track on a mental scorecard of all the people they'd fucked—I filled their Indian quota. The way people at the college chose who they fucked was like the way they selected classes—new ones every semester, never the same one twice, and always whatever worked easiest with their schedule. Nobody was planning on majoring in me, but I was a decent elective to pass the time with.

Salvatore and I caught up to Hamilton in his dorm room. I'd been invited to his room before, so I knew what to expect. Since Hamilton knew we were coming, the place would be clean—he felt it was important to have his place look good for guests, and he had the in-town maid service on speed dial. One time I'd wandered over unannounced after breakfast only to have a surly Hamilton tell me to fuck off. He'd opened the door a crack and I'd spotted beer bottles full of cigarette butts strewn on a table, one of them on its side, dripping. Vomit streaked with red splattered the wall, a few full pieces of paper towel sticking to it from an abandoned attempt to blot the vomit off. I'd asked him if he was alright, if he needed any help, and he slammed the door in my face. He apologized later, saying he'd been hungover, that he didn't like people dropping in on his private space anyway unless they'd been invited. I could only come over if he asked me to—that, he said, was an important rule that he asked everybody to respect.

When Salvatore and I showed up, the room smelled like French vanilla. Indirect lighting from gleaming brass lamp stands washed the room in a comforting glow. Along one wall was a full-service bar that looked like it had been carved from a single massive oak. There was no way it had been carried up four flights of stairs to his room— some artisan had built the thing for him right there. Above it, fluorescent beer signs glowed cheerfully, free of the caked-on soot and grime and residual despair they would have accumulated in a dive, so now they seemed like a playful suggestion for beverage choices rather than a ghosted neon whisper naming the lords of alcoholic tyranny. Black-and-white cityscapes in gold-edged frames lent a crispness to the freshly painted cobalt walls. In other dorm rooms I'd often see a poster of Bob Marley puffing a blunt, or Jim Morrison in faux crucifixion, all part of a tacked-on wall collage of anything free and colorful that could cover the dingy walls. That was the way I decorated, the principle behind how I dressed—whatever covered the crap was good enough. Hamilton, though, was a man of taste. Simply by being in his presence I had the chance to learn how to fake the dignity he was born with.

"You can't come like that," Hamilton said to Salvatore when he removed his coat. Hamilton stared at Salvatore's shirt, then shook his head fiercely. "Halloween's done and gone. This isn't even bad enough to be funny."

"It has color," Salvatore said, a little-boy frown petulantly taking control of his face. "It has history. A little old-fashioned, yes, but it was my grandfather's."

"They should have buried it with him. You'll never get laid in that— the chicks'll run screaming." He turned to me. "You've got to get it together. Didn't I tell you how important this was?"

Salvatore gave me a knowing look.

"I have a different party I need to go to. With friends," Salvatore said. "I am here to be polite, to say thank you for your invitation, but I did not want anyone to have to explain for me."

"Don't start crying on me. I'm doing you a favor. Good friends tell you the truth, and I'm saying now that you look like a clown. Back me up on this," he said, looking to me.

I shrugged.

"It's Salvatore's style. If he's cool with it, then why should I give a fuck?"

"Fine. Whatever." Hamilton scowled. "I hate that I always have to be the one to take care of this kind of shit."

"I am not asking you to do anything," Salvatore said coldly. He looked to me for support, but I didn't say anything. He'd handled it well enough and didn't need me, I figured.

We stood looking at each other, the familiar thrashing of Nine Inch Nails leaking into our silence from a room down the hall.

Salvatore grabbed a pen off the table and pulled my hand toward him. He scribbled "Freak Ballroom" on my hand and leaned in to whisper, "My friends are here. Come for our party." He gave Hamilton a brisk wave and walked out the door.

"He's a fucking tragedy," Hamilton said, slumping into his sofa. "I wanted to do him a favor, something good for him. It's like my dad says—you can't save anyone from themselves."

"He's cool with himself. You don't have to worry about him," I said.

"I'm always going to worry. I hate seeing people screwing it up, looking and acting like dorks and then wondering why they're so fucking miserable. I mean, it's so obvious, and the way to fix it all—I mean it's almost like there are all these simple little rules and strategies that everybody knows, but the losers just decide that they'd rather be losers. It makes no sense."

Hamilton dug his hands into the cushions of his couch and pulled out a small satchel.

"Might as well get going," he said, unzipping the satchel.

"You still haven't told me what this party's about, who's going to be there, why it's such a big fucking deal."

"It's a favor," he said, pulling a tiny mirror from the satchel, dumping the snowy contents of a vial on the glass.

"That what I think it is?"

"Yeah. You expecting a line?"

"I don't do that shit."

"Good." Hamilton pulled his college ID from a pocket and began chopping the powder. I felt a rush in me, a sense of danger, and I kept glancing over my shoulder wondering if the police were going to barge their way in. I'd thought that cocaine was pure, fine, white like powdered sugar, but the stuff Hamilton was cutting up seemed a mix of dull white sand and discolored clumps like what happens when you put a wet coffee spoon in the sugar bowl. By the time he was done preparing the coke it glinted in the light like a fresh field of snow, a sprinkling of tan the only hint that it hadn't always been that way.

Hamilton caught me staring at the powder and smiled.

"Yeah, she's beautiful, isn't she? She's mine tonight, though." He cocked his head. "You sure you don't want a line? I could spare you a small one."

I shook my head, but the excitement was there, the possibility.

"Some other time," I said.

Hamilton nodded and leaned his head over the mirror, snorting like a Hollywood pro. He rubbed his finger over the glass when he was done and looked over at me.

"Come here," he said, and I did. He motioned me down to his level, and I knelt before him. "Open your mouth," he said.

I felt his thick finger in my mouth, tracing my gums. A chill chased his finger, a sudden tingling numbness like when my foot fell asleep. And then it came—a hint of a glow, a spark of warmth alighting on me, comforting like a roaring blaze to someone freshly escaped from winter's wrath.

He leaned in and whispered in my ear, "Now you know what love is."

Our breath steamed into the night as we walked toward the Freak quad where Hamilton's party was supposed to rage. Though all the college buildings and dorms were within a few blocks of each other, the college had been divided by the students into cool and not so cool sections. There was "Alcatraz," a hideous concrete bunker honeycombed with dorm rooms that would have made a prison cell seem extravagant. Alcatraz housed most of the sophomores and had a reputation for drunken free-for-alls and middle-of-the-night fire alarms—most of the kids who chose to lock themselves into that dorm should have been handed AA pamphlets when they walked in so they'd be better prepared for their destiny. The other dorm complexes had similar reputations—there was the Russia House that held the more studious seniors and had a reputation for long periods of quiet punctuated by classy, yet raucous, binges where students in blazers and ties chugged White Russians; the strip of dorms along the highway, called Black-Out Row, which had been turned into a secret fraternity and sorority stretch by the rugby and football players who'd taken over. The Freak quad was actually one of the neater places on campus, but since a majority of the school's artists, writers, and eccentrics called it home, the rest of the school felt compelled to disparage it. The bisexual, gay, and lesbian union claimed it as its turf, and though its members threw the most creative parties and tended to be an open and friendly bunch, some things were simply never going to be accepted. As the fall semester drew to a close and the first hints of a bitter New England winter turned the strolls into a test of the insulating properties of jackets, most students avoided the inconvenient walk to the Freak quad. They'd make an exception when a drag ball was supposed to go down—the Alcatraz kids dutifully got hammered and heckled the cross-dressers—or when the Freak quad cafeteria offered its weekly spicy buffalo wing special.

Hamilton, bubbling with coke-induced euphoria, babbled as we walked, calling me his best friend one moment, cursing out his adulterous father the next, his hands slashing the air in grand gestures that he must have assumed only drove his point home stronger. Every few seconds he would stop and pirouette, staring up into the sky, and marvel at the profusion of stars that the lack of light pollution made visible. I couldn't help feeling even colder looking at the uncountable stars, visualizing the great distances between them and us, imagining the mysterious worlds that spun far beyond the reach of anything but dreams. Like so many others, I looked up and marveled at my complete insignificance.

"I could snort the sky!" Hamilton yelled. "Just what if, seriously, think about it—what if every star was just a big ball of coke? It blows my mind!"

I nodded. That, indeed, would be a surprising and amazing thing. "This party—" I said. "Are the guys going to be there?"

"In the Freak quad? You kidding me?"

"They got something else going on?"

"I didn't tell them about this. They wouldn't understand."

"What's to understand? There's a party—like they'd ever pass up on an excuse to get fucked up."

Hamilton stopped me, his hand gripping my forearm tightly.

"We don't talk about this with them, okay? This has to be secret."

I brushed his hand off and kept walking.

"It's not like their feelings are going to be hurt because you didn't invite them."

"That's the point. I can't invite them. I'm not even sure we can go in. A guy I know from high school—he was a year ahead of me—he told me about these parties because he owed me a favor. And then a couple weeks ago he told me they were planning on doing a party today. The parties these guys do—they call their spot the Den of Iniquity—anything goes. I mean anything."

"I'm sticking to weed. You can keep that coke shit to yourself."

Hamilton laughed.

"This isn't about getting high, at least not that way. These parties—they're different every time, twisted, cool shit you'll never get anywhere else. One time, my friend said, they had this girl, and she agreed to be blindfolded. They kept her in another room. Then a dozen guys volunteered, and they were blindfolded. They brought them in one by one to the girl, and she judged their size, and it was like a real contest—whoever she picked after testing them out, whoever she said was the winner, that was the person she fucked. She didn't know who it was, and the guy didn't know who she was."

"I don't want to fuck some prostitute. What's so cool about that?"

Hamilton shook his head.

"You don't get it, do you? This isn't some random whore with a bunch of losers. This is a girl you know. Somebody from the school. Each party, a bunch of folks get called together. There are regulars—kind of like club members—and then the folks they invite. They invite people they're interested in. Imagine that—what if you're a member, you invite who you're interested in—but they never know who invited them, they just get the invite. Whatever goes on, you don't know who it's with, or maybe you do, but it's all kept secret and nobody ever talks. You can do anything you've ever dreamed of and nobody will ever say anything."

"One girl for, what, thirty guys? I don't know, man. Jerking off in the shower has more dignity."

Hamilton rolled his eyes.

"It's not like that," he said. "You make it sound like something twisted and sick. These parties—there's always more than one girl. They keep things balanced so it doesn't get weird, unless you want it to get weird. And they're all normal folks like me and you—they're invited for a reason. You do what you want and nobody judges it. Nobody talks about it."

"I don't know, Hamilton," I said. "Maybe I'll just watch."

Hamilton shrugged. "If that's all you want, I figure they'll have no problems with it. That is, if you even get in."

"But you're in for sure?"

"No, but they'll let me in anyway."

The night was silent as we neared the Freak quad—the wind only occasionally fidgeting with tree branches, the ill-prepared crickets keeping their lamentations to themselves. Even nature had been sworn to secrecy. Images of students entangled in the dramas of their lives played out in the lighted windows of the surrounding dorms—the forlornly studious enshrining themselves within a tomb of books stacked on their desk, short-lived couples throttling their romance with the noose of remembered wrongs.

"Salvatore's party is here too," I told Hamilton.

"Him and his little friends are probably in some tiny single, sipping wine, listening to jazz. We should drop by later and let him know what his ugly shirt cost him."

"I don't think he'd care. Anyway, they're in the ballroom."

Hamilton stopped and yanked on the back of my coat to stop me as well.

"Salvatore's in the ballroom?"

"That's where he'd said he'd be."

Hamilton shook his head in disbelief.

"That fucker. He's got an invite too, and he didn't even mention it."

"Maybe it's not the same party," I said. "He didn't say anything like what you were talking about. He said it was just a party with his new acting friends."

"He knows," Hamilton said. "He was keeping quiet about it because nobody's supposed to talk. Why didn't he let us know where he was heading?"

"He told me."

Hamilton shoved through the doors and tromped down the steps to the ballroom, slinging his coat against the wall halfway down. I swam through the tipsy crowd clogging the steps, apologizing with a shrug and a halfhearted smile to the ones toppled in Hamilton's wake. I lost him at the door, parted by a foursome of women in white evening gowns and glow-in-the-dark lipstick, so I leaned against a wall and tried to pick him out from the crowd, my hands, in search of an anchor amidst the swirling mob, gripping woodwork smoothed into soft antiquity by decades of wallflowers. A fusion of jazz and techno murmured under the cackles of drunken laughter, the smiling faces around me menacing in the candlelight. A few students chattered in the casual comfort of a blue-jeaned clump, but the majority waltzed stiffly in the classic lace and cuff-link uniforms of debutante paradise. A slender girl with a sparkling tiara crowning cascading curls of mahogany hair sidled up to me. She leaned in as if to whisper in my ear, then bit my earlobe.

"Don't be shy," she ordered, "I know who you are."

"Who are you?" I asked, mesmerized by the nearly translucent whiteness of her skin, the startling bluegrass of her eyes, as if from a Kentucky field freshly misted with dew.

"I'm a nun," she giggled, "so quit looking at me like that. My priest sent me in search of his champion."

She pulled me toward the center of the ballroom. Salvatore's shirt had been converted into a bandana, and he stood with a drunken scowl on his face, silently listening as Hamilton lit into him while jabbing his chest. Nearby, a lithe blond man in a three-piece suit stared intently at the two, his eyelash extensions fluttering with anxiety. A saxophone hung around his neck, and he fingered the keys with the distracted fervor of a nail biter butchering his cuticles during an exam.

I clapped Hamilton on the shoulder and stepped between him and Salvatore.

"Whatever he did, this isn't the way to handle it," I said to Hamilton.

"I did nothing!" Salvatore slurred.

"That's my point," Hamilton said, stepping back, arms crossed tight. "You knew this was going on, and you kept it secret."

"He told you he was going to a party," I said.

"Right. He told us all the fucking details. Made us walk over like a couple losers when he could have brought us with him, introduced us. It was the same fucking party, and he knew it. He's embarrassed by us, but too fucking chicken to say it. Piece of shit."

"Pieces of shits and chickens, this is what you call me? This is how you treat me?" Salvatore took a menacing step forward, his belly bumping Hamilton backward, his suddenly loud voice roaring through Italian curses, wielding language like a mace.

Instantly two surly giants tromped over, their meaty paws parting Salvatore from Hamilton. They looked to the saxophone man for guidance. His eyelashes fluttered for a second, then he nodded toward Hamilton.

"He needs to leave. Be gentle," he said. The giants each took a firm grip on one of Hamilton's arms.

"You don't tell me what the fuck to do!" Hamilton yelled, squirming uselessly.

"He's a little coked up," I said, trying to pry one of the giants off Hamilton. "Just give him a second to cool off and he'll be okay."

Hamilton glared at me, and interjected, "I'm not on anything."

The sax-man looked at me quizzically.

"He can't handle his coke, and we're supposed to babysit for him?"

"Salvatore and him just had a little disagreement. It's nothing they can't work out."

"Is this what you think, Salvatore?" the sax-man asked.

Salvatore shrugged.

"My Indian friend is good-hearted," Salvatore said, "but this one"—he looked Hamilton up and down—"is like the garbage. Nice clothes, nice perfumes, but he is still the stinking garbage."

"Oh, I'm the fucking garbage, is that what you think you fucking greasy-assed—"

The sax-man nodded to the giants. They lifted Hamilton in the air. He squirmed in their mitts, and continued to yell as they carried him out. The moment he was out the door, the ballroom erupted in applause.

The sax-man smirked at me.

"Thank you for the entertainment. Salvatore promised you would be an interesting one to meet. Go mingle, and come with Salvatore for the after party."

He winked at me, put the saxophone to his lips, and began to play.

I lurked amidst the flickering reds of the candles ringing the room. Beyond the candles lay the pale blue moonlit lords and ladies. I would disappear if I walked into that world, my dark skin swallowing light, my body an unwelcome shadow. I sipped drinks and watched silently, wondering if this was how the Rakshasas had felt when they first glimpsed the heavenly court of Indra and his seductive Apsaras. I could imagine them peeking from perches in the trees, their throats thick with longing, their breathing a forgotten habit suddenly remembered in startled gasps and sighs. They could hide their dark skin and their coarse midnight hair with their powers of illusion, and attempt to con their way into paradise, but they would know the lie, they could never believe they truly belonged. If they stole their desires with scimitars, heaven would become a mockery, tainted by the curse of their touch. Faced with the choice between eternal longing or a delectable moment in paradise, they did what anyone would. They unsheathed their swords and murdered the Gods. They did not mourn when the holy trinity of Vishnu, Shiva, and Brahma struck them down and returned them to perpetual longing, or when the trinity guaranteed the resurrected Indra his throne until the death of death itself. They had tasted the forbidden and ruled the heavens, if only for a moment.

Salvatore stumbled around the ballroom with a drink in each hand, toasting anyone he bumped into. Everyone smiled when they saw him, leaning in to banter and nod at his witticisms, even though his hair was wild and wet with sweat, even though his shirt was forgotten somewhere in the shadows. He reminded me of the big-bellied priests gorging on mountains of rice that I saw at every important family ritual. I'd always averted my eyes when I saw one of those lumbering beasts. Lazy and unkempt, they waddled off when I asked them to explain the meaning of the mantras they chanted, and yet everyone else knelt in their presence when they pompously recycled gossip and proclaimed judgment. Salvatore, like the priests, was an embarrassment that the world inexplicably adored.

I moped in a corner as the voice in my mind ridiculed me for feeling sorry for myself. Why was I surprised, it asked. The ballroom was filled with the wealthy and beautiful, with people who knew they were better than me. I didn't belong in the school—for all my academic achievements, the school had probably only let me in to increase diversity, and I was sure everyone in the ballroom could sense it. It was like in junior high when I'd gone on a field trip with the school chorus. I'd had to sit next to a kid who hadn't taken a bath in weeks, and I could barely keep myself from gagging from the smell. The kids sitting in the row behind didn't know who was the source of the smell, but they assumed it had to be me since I was the only colored kid nearby. So they kicked at my chair and spritzed me with perfume and whispered insults in my ear. When I got mad and threw chairs and started pummeling the boy who'd been sitting behind me, I was thrown out. Later, one of the teachers called me in for a gentle discussion of personal hygiene. I told her the truth about what happened, and she smiled and didn't believe me. I could have showered just before I met her, and she would have sensed a foul odor all the same. What I was couldn't be washed away. The people in the ballroom instinctively knew it, the voice told me. It was why they kept away.

Alone, in the darkness, I sipped drinks and murmured to myself as the party staggered to its end. At first people peeled off in pairs, a knowing smile, a soft touch on the forearm all that was needed to catalyze a drunken hookup. Some of the couples surely cared deeply for each other, and spoke and kissed with the sincerity I longed for, but it felt better to believe that I was witnessing a tawdry series of drunken unions, a reflexive grab for a familiar fuck-buddy. If it was nothing more than an intoxicated impulse, then my solitude was due only to chance—the time would surely come when I could play the game with them. I couldn't tolerate the alternative explanation, that my race made intimacy impossible, that my race made me as alluring as a neutered boar. I didn't even bother thinking that my solitude might all be chalked up to my personality. At least if I felt like a martyr, I could wallow in anger. Rage, at least, had always been a faithful lover.

I was slumped in a corner, testing the sharpness of my switchblade by jabbing it into my palm, when light flooded the ballroom. The nun who had directed me to Salvatore when I first came into the party stood by the light switches near the door, her tiara dangling limply in one hand, her other hand shielding her eyes from the transformative glare. Crumpled plastic cups and cigarette butts floated in brownish pools. The walls rose into tobacco-stained dimness, the paint jaundiced yellow by the years.

"I've been looking for you," she said, tiptoeing through the mess to reach me. She leaned over me, her hair cascading into my face, soft and sweet and warm like the first hint of summer.

"What did you do to your hand?" she asked.

I wiped the blood off with my shirt. "Only me and the garbage left in this shithole."

She rolled her eyes.

"Then come to the after party. Nobody told you to sit here."

"Why the fuck do you care?"

"I don't," she said, shaking out her hair with a snap of her head and walking toward the door, "but I promised Salvatore I'd look for you."

I pulled myself to my feet.

"So you're Salvatore's girl?"

She stopped at the door and stared at me.

"I'm not for sale," she said coldly.

"I didn't mean anything. You're a pretty girl. I was just checking."

"Right. And because you're drunk, you think you're irresistibly cute."

"Am I?"

"We're on the second floor, room 208," she said as she walked out the door.

"I was just fucking around," I yelled after her, but she was already gone.

A chorus of friendly hellos greeted me when I knocked on the door. At least a dozen people filled the small room, some standing and talking, but most sprawled on the mattress on the floor under the only window in the room. I recognized Salvatore passed out on the bed, the nun patting his forehead; the sax-man smoking a joint with a couple kids from my poetry class; Lucas, the chubby, mixed-race guy from my dorm, drawing something on the wall with lipstick; but the rest were a threatening mystery. I could see them surreptitiously glancing at me, judging me. I snapped my knife open and closed with my bloody hand to give them something to think about.

The sax-man grabbed me around the shoulder, thrusting the joint in front of my face.

"That's a neat trick," he said, looking at my knife, "but you're not very good at it, and I don't allow knives in my room." He leaned in and whispered in my ear. "Whatever's pissing you off, talk about it. You're with friends now."

I gave him a sidelong glance, then double-puffed the joint. Immediately the sharp fever of my anger faded into a cottony glow, soft and sweet and safe like the ritual of warm creamy coffee shared with my dad after a Sunday afternoon nap.

"Weed always makes me feel better," I said with a wistful smile.

"Then I better make sure I send some back with you when you take off."

"You've got some to spare?"

"I've got a lot of things I could spare," he said with a wink. "All you need to do is ask."

I took a spot on the bed and quickly sank into conversation, lulled into comforting peace by the sweet buzz of weed and mellow thrum of the jazz playing in the background. The sax-man's name was Sebastian, and he was a junior theater major. A handful of the people in the room were acting in the play he'd written, and those who weren't either knew him through music circles or from plays he'd done the previous years. The nun, who'd been running her hand through the unconscious Salvatore's hair, revealed that her name was Eva and that she was a freshman too. She asked to see my knife, and soon it was being passed around the room like a second joint. I'd slipped into Chicago mode, and either because of my accent, my no-bullshit monosyllabic patter, or the cruel lines of my knife, the people in Sebastian's room treated me with the quiet respect reserved for gangsters. Respect, even if it was born of fear, was better than contempt, and far better than the invisibility of unimportance, so I played along. The knife, I explained, was a lucky charm that had pulled me through scrapes with the gangbangers that ran my high school. I had a gun, I said when asked, but I'd given it to a buddy in Chicago who'd taken care of a situation for me. I'd almost gotten locked up in juvey, but the judge had given me a second chance when he found out I'd been accepted at the college. School far from home was supposed to be my chance to get straight.

If they doubted my bullshit, they kept it to themselves. My stories were like a good poker bluff—there was no reason for them to call me on them. Even if they thought I was full of shit, I had come into the room with a knife and a bloody hand—nobody ever fucks with an armed and bleeding guy. And if I was telling the truth, and they got caught up in trying to say I was bullshit, there was no knowing how a thug like me might react. To put them at ease, I told them that I wasn't into that tough guy stuff anymore. It was a part of life in my hood, but I was in college because I was trying to get past all that.

"That's good," Eva said, adjusting her tiara on her head. She reached over and patted the hand I'd sliced up. "Leave that life behind, because it only hurts you."

"I just try to do the right thing these days," I said with my practiced wistfulness.

"You should write about it in your poems," one of the kids from my poetry class said. "That's what writing is about. Catharsis."

"You're a writer?" Eva asked, her eyes locking with mine. "So am I. You should join us on Mondays—there's a writing club where we read each other's work."

I shrugged.

"I like to write, but I can't write about that stuff. It's too personal."

"So what do you write about?"

"Being Indian. Or being crazy. I've got this one story about these two kids that live in this neighborhood where everybody's replaced their lawn with Astroturf and lives in these houses that look exactly like Warhol's variations on Campbell's soup cans. They murder this developer when he comes in trying to build a cookie-cutter two flat."

"You should read it at the writing club. I'm sick of hearing breakup stories and coming-of-age-while-hunting-with-dad stories."

"How come you haven't put up any of that wild stuff in class?" the kid from my poetry class asked.

"How the hell am I supposed to fit that into class assignments? He wants us doing new bullshit each week. Write a poem about a piece of art. Write a poem about nature. He rips the shit we do every week anyway, so what's the point in putting up something you care about?"

The poetry kid nodded.

"So is it worth it?" Eva asked. "I want to be a writer and I'm still trying to figure out which classes to take."

"What are you in now?"

She ran her hands slowly through Salvatore's thin hair.

"I couldn't get into any of the writing classes. I knew I needed some good samples of my writing if I was going to get into any of the classes, and I'd been working on that my senior year at high school." She shook her head. "I can't tell what's good and what's not anymore."

"We should sit down sometime," I said. "I'll help you."

The raging sex party that Hamilton anticipated never materialized. Maybe he'd heard about a different group of students, or maybe the entire thing was bullshit. As I sat there in Sebastian's room, sipping cheap wine and smoking joints, I didn't mind. The people around me were relaxed and down to earth, only verging into pretentiousness when they talked about their artistic efforts and how their work would revolutionize the world. I'd always been sympathetic to that kind of talk—all the people I knew back home were full of themselves too.

When the graduating high school seniors in the Indian community had gathered on a stage at the Chinmaya mission, all the parents sat with pride in the audience as their children got up one by one to tell the crowd what school they were going to, what they were majoring in. Kid after kid got up and named some state school, that they were going to be premed, or some engineering variant. Each time, the audience erupted in applause. The biggest applause was reserved for the kid going to Northern Illinois U who was planning on doing premed and electrical engineering. When I got up and told the crowd what my dreams were and where I was going to pursue them, I was greeted with silence. They couldn't look at me. They were ashamed, and in that moment, I learned to hate my own people. The college had a South Asian club, and I'd hung out there to meet the other Indian kids at the school. I thought they would be different, but they were like every other Indian I'd met. If you weren't planning on being a doctor or engineer, they looked on you with pity. It was more than the assumption I'd come across before, that I wasn't interested in medicine or engineering because I wasn't intelligent enough to handle the coursework. They looked at me the way people in my community stared at the white wife my dad's doctor friend had once brought to a family function: she was untrustable, unknowable, a dangerous outsider who would criticize our ways because she could never understand them. It was better not to talk to her. It was better to stare at her until she ran crying from the room.

That night in Sebastian's room I began to feel like I had finally found where I belonged. Since I had been lying from the moment I walked through the door, nobody there knew anything real or true about me other than that I liked to write weird stuff, but I could tell that I was with a group of people who didn't measure the quality of people by where they had come from or what they bragged they would do with their lives. Sebastian talked about being poor and gay. Eva talked about being rich and Jewish. Lucas talked about being overweight, gay, Mormon, and mixed-race. They didn't use those labels when talking about themselves, they just told their stories, and the people who listened didn't laugh at them. Sebastian talked about how his parents had ripped on him, his dad especially—this asshole former football jock—how they hadn't given a damn about whether or not he went to school. He talked about the time one of the kids at school tried to force Sebastian to give him a blow job and how Sebastian had nearly bit the kid's dick off, but couldn't run fast enough to escape. His dad hadn't even visited him in the hospital. He'd escaped Nebraska because of himself, because of his intelligence and his acting skills, and he was never going back. Eva talked about her dad, the big attorney for a pharmaceutical company, how he'd dragged her by her hair and thrown her on the curb when he thought he saw her kissing some black boy. Every night, and she didn't know why, she dreamed of watching him drown. Lucas talked about Micah and his "asshole" friends and how coming out had turned his family, his brother, and everyone his brother knew, against him. They looked at him with fear, even though he'd never done a damn thing to anyone. They wouldn't talk to him. His family didn't hug him anymore.

We traded stories and secrets like brothers and sisters around a campfire, huddling closer together to protect ourselves from the chill of our own words.

"I burned a house down," I admitted, "and I'm not sure why."

Nobody said anything. They looked at me and nodded. It was as if they knew I would tell them the truth if they waited, but they wouldn't think less of me if I didn't. We passed a bottle of wine around, a joint, and then another. Sebastian snorted a few lines of something brown with one of the poetry kids. In that moment I loved them all because they were healthy, and normal, and real. We were nice people in a shitty world, but if we stuck together we didn't need to ever feel scared or alone again.

"We're all good people here," Sebastian said quietly. "Even if the rest of the world doesn't think so."

As daylight crept into the room to the sound of the radiator's wake-up hiss and clank, my friends stumbled off into the world. Eva and Salvatore left first, cooing softly to each other, followed in ones and twos by the others. When Lucas finally left, muttering about having to turn in a paper he hadn't yet written, only Sebastian, myself, and a tall, gangly guy named Eduardo were left.

"I should get going," I said. "It'd probably be good to show up for my chem class since I heard the prof say he'd be going over what's supposed to be on the final."

Sebastian shrugged.

"You don't have to go. We're going to rip a few bong hits, maybe play some music, then head out for a walk along the river."

"There's this crazy old guy we found living in a tent out there," Eduardo said. "He's awesome with a guitar, said he used to play with Hendrix."

"No classes today? And aren't you guys tired?"

"Fuck the school," Eduardo said.

"If you did a line, you wouldn't be tired," Sebastian said.

I pulled myself to my feet, leaning on a wall for support.

"Not today," I said. "I'm done for a while."

Sebastian nodded then leaned into Eduardo and whispered in his ear.

"You wanted weed?" Eduardo asked me. "A dime bag?"

"An ounce, probably. Maybe more."

He leaned in to Sebastian and the two whispered fiercely to each other. Finally he turned toward me and stared into my eyes as if he was searching for something.

"You're not a pothead, and I've never met you before. Why so much? Trying to save money?"

"It's for these guys I know. I'm trying to make money."

"You a cop?" Eduardo asked.

Sebastian rolled his eyes. "I keep telling you that doesn't prove anything."

"Well, are you?" Eduardo asked.

"Yeah, sure," I said, "I've got my SWAT team waiting outside the door." I snatched my coat. "I'm beat," I said. "I've got to get to bed."

"I had to ask," Eduardo said. "I don't know who the fuck you are."

"And you could be an undercover cop trying to trap me," I said.

"This is ridiculous," Sebastian said.

"No it's not. My dad was helping one of the campus cops remodel his house and the guy told him the college wanted him to try to clear out drugs. He was talking about maybe calling on cops from some of the nearby towns for undercover."

"The school doesn't want that," Sebastian said with a dismissive wave. "It's all talk and you know it. They're not going to mess with their reputation by letting a big drug bust go down on campus."

"But if one does, I'm the one who takes the hit," Eduardo said. "You guys are in school. They'll protect you. But me, I'm just some townie kid."

I blinked blearily and leaned against the door. I knew so many people who'd be interested in buying weed, and if I was the guy who could provide it to them, I'd be in everywhere. It was such a simple thing. With one easy move, I could instantly become the cool guy people wanted to know, and I'd make a shitload of money in the process.

"I can unload an ounce a week, at least. If it's good," I said. I pulled my knife from my pocket, snapped it open, and drove the point into the door. "And where I come from, people know better than to talk. If I go down, I go down alone."

"You said you wanted someone who could help you out on campus when I'm gone," Sebastian said.

Eduardo nodded.

"I need to talk to my guy, make sure it's good with him."

"Teddy's not going to like him," Sebastian said.

Eduardo smiled. "He'll like an ounce a week."

"How good is it?"

"You like what you smoked last night?"

"You can get that again? That's better then what they've been smoking."

"Depends. Anything from hydroponic purple crystal skunk and northern lights with a Dutch twist to ditch weed. How much your guys willing to pay?"

"They want the best and they've got money. They're paying $400 for an ounce now."

Eduardo and Sebastian stared at each other.

"They like other things too?" Eduardo asked. "I can keep you stocked with whatever you need."

"I'm pretty sure I can move anything. I'll make sure you never have to worry about anything except collecting your money from me."

Eduardo came over and grabbed me by the hand, pulling me into a quick hug. He stepped back and nodded.

"Get your money together and call Sebastian when you're ready."

I could barely keep the smile off my face.

"This is absolutely perfect," I said. "And to think, Hamilton tells me you guys run some orgy. That's the only reason he came. But this is better."

"The Den of Iniquity?" Sebastian asked with a smile.

Eduardo grinned at him.

"Strange what people think goes on," Sebastian said.

"We're just drug dealers today," Eduardo said with a nod.

I looked toward both of them, waiting for an explanation. They grinned at me, children with a luscious secret.

And as for those
Who ungratefully repudiate Our signs
And accuse them of falsity,
They are the company of the fire;
They are the ones who stay in it.

—The Qu'ran

I was shaken awake. A guy with blue eyes, crooked teeth, and a chubby face smiled at me. The man had brown, clean-cut hair that he parted down the middle. He was wearing a blue pin-striped shirt with a solid black tie that hung loose from his collar.

"Eddie, get up. It's time for a meeting," he said.

"Who the hell are you?"

"You could stand to learn a few manners. Try to be civil."

I rubbed my eyes. He kept smiling. He would have been handsome if he was a touch thinner.

I stuck out my hand.

"My name is Eddie."

"And mine is Mike, but you should call me Walden, as that is what everyone else calls me. I am also the weekend RP. Do you know what that means?"

"No."

"It means I am the responsible person on the weekends. I am the one who takes over when Tats takes a night off on the weekends."

I nodded.

"Will you be coming to the meeting dressed like this?"

I was wearing jeans and a T-shirt, but both were pretty clean.

"What's wrong with my clothes?"

"Don't yell. I just wanted to make sure you were ready."

He grabbed hold of my hand and pulled me out of bed. He was strong.

"We're going to go to the Twelve-Step House. We will be walking. It's warm outside, so you won't need a jacket."

I followed him out of the house and we walked west on Wilson Avenue.

"Why you called Walden?" I asked.

Walden stopped and put his hand on my shoulder.

"Tats told me that you have an education. Were you lying?"

I shook my head.

"Well, then. My belief is that if you were fortunate enough to learn how to speak properly then it is your moral duty to speak properly. You are no longer living on the streets, Eddie. If we are going to have any success making a normal person out of you, then you are going to have to change a few things. I would suggest beginning with your speech habits."

We continued walking in silence.

"Coming up on your right is the Native American Museum. There is a large American Indian population in this area, drawn, perhaps, by the beautiful shade that these oaks provide," Walden said, motioning to the trees lining the road. They were majestic, as thick as four people standing together, and taller than the telephone poles.

"There is another senior resident here whom we call Zhivago. His name is actually Mike. In order to avoid confusion, we have taken different names. I work at Waldenbooks, thus, my name."

We passed the trees. Cars rolled along. A young mother with a stroller came down the sidewalk from the opposite direction. Walden swayed to the side to let her pass.

"Have you ever been in AA before?" he asked after she'd gone by.

"Not really. I went to meetings for a bit in Bill's Family, but I never really listened. I always just thought AA was bullshit," I said.

"I'm not sure it works either. The only way I will know is if I die sober."

As we walked, Walden gave me advice for the meeting. In AA, the old-timers held sway. A guy like Tats might talk, but he'd keep it simple, talking about what he was doing to keep things coming along, speaking about gratitude, things like that. If I spoke, the old-timers would yell, "Take the cotton out your ears and put it in your mouth!" or "Shut up and sit down!" or "All I'm gonna learn from you is how to get drunk!" The old-timers knew what it took. Walden said that if I stayed near the old-timers and listened, I would stay sober and have a chance.

Roaming the nights with Hanuman gave me a better chance of surviving the darkness. He was someone to talk to, someone who listened. He kept pestering me to go home, but he had his uses. If we found a warm grate, or a good shelter from the wind, he would stay awake while I slept. He would also remind me when it was time to go to the Dumpster behind the McDonald's on Western. At that McDonald's they would get rid of leftover food at nine o'clock at night, and if I was there on time the guy who came out with the garbage bags would sometimes give me the food. If he was in a bad mood he would just throw it over my head into the Dumpsters and make me scrounge.

Hanuman also reminded me when welfare and government checks came in. We would look for people who had cashed their checks, I'd mug them while Hanuman kept an eye out for the police, and then we'd hit the spot and pick up dime bags.

Hanuman never said a word about any of it. I kept expecting a lecture. One time I even asked him, "Doesn't any of this bother you?"

He shrugged. "Yes."

But that's all he said. Each day he would just watch me and wait, helping me in little ways.

"If you want help, ask," Hanuman kept saying.

And when everything ran out, and the shakes were coming, I'd start crying. I would curl up in a ball and cover my face with my hands. I wanted to be lying in a bed, my mother coming in with a tray and a big cup of rose milk, two *idlees* with mint chutney, and a crispy masala dosai. I wanted to feel her hand pressed to my forehead, checking my temperature. I wanted her to hold me. But most of all, I just wanted a rock.

"If that's what you want, then go under the bridges on North Avenue," Hanuman said.

"I'm not a fag."

"But you said you want to get high. And you said that you could make money under the bridges."

"I'm not doing that."

"Then forget the drugs. Or live for them. There will always be people who want someone brown, someone young, someone who knows the mantras whom they can practice the Kama Sutra with. They want to play tourist. They'll take you places. If they start liking you, then they will become regulars, and they would talk with you more. Maybe they could get you a place, a nice apartment. You want that, right?"

I went under the bridges. Hanuman shrunk himself down to the size of an ant and crawled inside my ear. A man in a black Nissan Sentra pulled up. He rolled down the passenger window.

"Are you looking to party?" I asked with my Indian accent.

"Get in, girl," he said.

"Forty bucks," I said.

"For what?"

"Anything."

He gave me two crisp twenties.

"This is your first time," he said.

When we got to his apartment he had me sit on his bed. He removed his shirt.

"Give me a back rub," he said.

His back was hairy and felt like dough under my hands.

"Have you ever heard of bondage? Do you like S and M?"

"You can still leave," Hanuman whispered in my ear.

The man got up from the bed, went to a closet. He returned with a black suitcase and opened it. I could see a leather suit and leather strips with buckles and a red ball attached to more leather.

"If you put some of this on, I'll give you fifty more dollars. I'll take pictures."

He helped me into a leather vest, then cinched it tight. He tied my arms to the sides of the vest with leather belts that came off of it. He tied my ankles together. He put the red ball in my mouth and tied it tight to my head with more leather straps.

I couldn't breathe. He began playing with himself.

"I can't help you," Hanuman said. He crawled out of my ear and made himself invisible. He watched.

"I'm going to shave your head," the man said.

I wanted to tell him to let me go, but the sounds that came from my mouth were muffled. The man grabbed my hair.

"I'm going to keep you under my bed," he said, "when I'm done with you. You'd like that, wouldn't you?"

I was crying. I tried to move my hands, anything.

After he finished, he let me go. He told me, "Never let anyone tie you up. There are a lot of perverts in the world." He gave me fifty more dollars.

I spent it all on dime bags. And when I looked at Hanuman, he did not look away. I wanted him to run, but he stood and watched me fill my pipe.

That first hit from the pipe, I watched Hanuman's eyes. They were the night sky, cloudless, full of light that only became stronger the longer I stared. I could feel a gentle tug, and in his eyes I saw stars inch closer together, tendrils of flame yanking them together. I could feel the wind swirl up around me, and then the familiar smell of burning flesh. A magenta sky glowered over me as I walked behind Hanuman. He was swinging a tree trunk, sending Rakshasas hurtling toward the sea. We were cut off, only the two of us, fighting a last battle in the sand. I held my bow in the air, and blew on my conch. I pelted the advancing Rakshasas with arrows, and still they came, staggering, falling, their blood pooling around my ankles. I had no fear. My arms would never tire. My arrows would never run out. I was Rama.

I smoked non-stop, inhaling all ninety dollars. Still, when it was gone, I needed more. My jaws ached. My skin felt like rubber. I was sweating in November.

As I walked down the street with Hanuman, looking for another trick, another hit, my knees buckled. As I lay there crying on the sidewalk, I remembered what my mother told me after I got kicked out of college, after I'd dropped out of treatment and begun wandering the streets.

She stood there behind the door of our house, crying. She wouldn't let me in. She told me, "I can do nothing for you. You are now in Hanuman's hands."

I knew there wasn't any Hanuman. There was no Sanjeevani root. There was nothing.

I felt the soft touch of his tail on my forehead.

"You're wrong," I heard him say.

Most of the students disappeared around Thanksgiving, but since I didn't have the cash for a plane ticket, or any real reason to head home—the American tradition of gorging on turkey and stuffing and cranberry whatnots as a way of showing gratitude, regardless of how the past year had treated them, being considered a blasphemous waste by my militant vegetarian family—I readied myself for solitude. The poker boys rushed home to family, and even Salvatore had plans—Eva had invited him to her family's summer home in the Berkshires, where the two were apparently going to attempt a Thanksgiving ritual on their own. Even Eduardo vanished, roaring off to Boston to pick up a "gift." Jonas suggested that I join him and his family since they lived only an hour away, but I figured that could only turn into a bad time once his parents realized I was the kind of pagan they'd dedicated their lives to saving. Although the thought of being by myself with no ready access to drugs of any kind made me feel unusually depressed, I bucked myself up by thinking of the advantages: without drugs I'd be able to cram a semester's worth of work in my head just in time to crush my finals. As well, since no one was around, I could break into people's rooms and take what I needed to bankroll my dealing.

The thought of ransacking the dorms filled me with a rush of excitement, as if a pretty woman I'd long admired had suddenly sat down beside me, smiled at me, and bit my ear. The day before Thanksgiving, though, I found Jonas still in the dorm.

"Aren't you going home?" I asked.

"I'm not leaving you alone."

"I don't need you to stay."

He smiled and shook his head.

"Too bad."

Thanksgiving morning I blearily wandered into our common room in my boxers, my hair poofed into a frizzy anvil by the press of pillows, to find our sofa filled with strangers. Jonas, standing in the middle of the room, had been loudly reading from his Korean book, but stopped to stare at me with a bemused half smile. Mr. Smith, a bald-headed boulder of a man with a bushy white mustache, stared at me vacantly from one side of the sofa, his eyes not quite focused on me as if he were coldly calculating the volume of my soul. In the middle, beaming and cherry cheeked, was Mrs. Smith, her sturdy glasses, the lenses thicker than any bone in her body, magnifying her irises into pale ivy flowers at home in the wheat of her hair.

"Close your eyes," the Smiths commanded the blushing girl they had squished into the other end of the sofa, but her hands already covered her eyes. She giggled.

"He doesn't look like the facebook picture you showed me, Jonas," she said. "He looks more vulnerable. Naked, somehow." She giggled again.

I ran back into my bedroom and threw on Kenny's bathrobe before coming back out.

"You might as well put on some real clothes," Mr. Smith said. "We were going to grab some breakfast, then take a walk."

"It's too chilly for a walk," Mrs. Smith said.

"Nonsense. We need to see the college's famous fall foliage." He enunciated as if the alliteration of the words was proof of the beauty of the land.

"Isn't it winter already?" Jonas's sister asked.

"The trees don't think so, Sarah," Jonas said.

Mr. Smith stared coldly at me, waiting.

"You think you're a tree or something? Get some clothes on," he ordered.

As usually happens when people bark orders at me, I secretly dream of ways to hurt them while I go about doing what they asked. I belted myself into my scruffiest pair of jeans and squeezed myself into a clean T-shirt and Cosby sweater that Kenny had left behind, as if that would show Jonas's dad that he shouldn't order me around. The gesture was as effective as it typically was with my dad—he grunted his approval and charged out the door, impatient for us to follow.

We traipsed around campus the rest of the morning, Mr. Smith stomping off toward whatever caught his eye—a tree with fiery leaves, a mossy church, a gargantuan station wagon embroidered in rust with a $1000 selling price soaped on the windows. We'd stop in front of each, and as Mrs. Smith fiddled with her disposable camera, Mr. Smith would extol the virtues of the object before us, Jonas nodding in agreement. The color of the leaves was a manifestation of God's passion but only a pale hint of what Moses saw, the colors washed out because mankind's spiritual fidelity had been diluted by those fanatically faithful to the blasphemy of science. The church, in the simplicity of its decay, was testament to the Lord's enduring power—men crafted bricks and walls into a symbol of their vanity, but God's soft touch of moss would inevitably transform that arrogance into humble dust. The station wagon was large and sturdy, an appropriately modest vehicle for transporting members of his congregation on their missionary work in the surrounding areas. He banged on the door of the station wagon owner's house, and, with us lurking restlessly in the background, hammered out a two-hundred-dollar concession from the owner and scheduled a meeting the following week when Jonas would drop by to discuss how the Unification Church could help the station wagon owner with his spiritual ailments.

Every place we stopped, Mrs. Smith would direct us into the same photographable clump—Mr. Smith in the center, Jonas to his left, me to his right, Sarah in the middle. My family did the same ridiculous thing on their trips, posing in every picture they took, the landmark out of focus and obscured behind them—a subtle and subversive proclamation that my family, with their clothes wrinkled by travel, their boredom poorly masked by the we're-taking-a-picture-now smile, was far more important than the eye candy that had inspired removing the lens cover. Mr. Smith and Jonas stuck to a tight-lipped frown, their hands clasped in front of them, as if it was a sin to be photographed, or, perhaps, that it was sinful to show any sign of happiness when in the company of an unapologetic pagan. Sarah, though, kept turning back to me with a giddy grin, reassuring me that she was my ally. The hint of red in her blond hair, her faint smell of lavender, the delicate swell of her adolescent breasts—she did not belong with these people. I imagined a time when we could hide ourselves in a secret garden and taste the salt of each other's sweat, our hands and hearts free to wander, my words freeing her from the chains of her father's faith.

Watching her, I felt like Ravana trembling in the forest when he first saw Sita. He had a harem filled with the daughters and queens of his conquests, and had grown so powerful that even the sun knelt in his presence, and yet when he saw Sita the meaninglessness of his life was revealed to him. He was a dark-skinned Rakshasa, doomed to grovel before the holy trinity, a member of a tainted and corrupted species held in contempt by all. The greater powers of the universe allowed his people a tiny allowance of happiness in their mortal lives—he had grabbed more because of his masterful manipulation of the *Vedas*, extracting boons of great power through his attention to the fine print. He could never hope to achieve the grace and peace of the divine, or their everlasting glory—they had made it clear that he would always be a villain, that they would find a way to destroy him. And so when he saw Sita in all her divine radiance, something snapped inside of him. He knew she was the bait in a trap. His advisors had told him that her beauty was a divine ruse, that she was a Goddess sent to earth, that it had been foretold that she would be the cause of his destruction. Maybe it was the delicacy of her beauty, the scent of absolute, absolving purity, the tang of ocean blossoms after years in the charnel house of war. Or perhaps it was simply that she was forbidden. In that moment with Sarah, I was Ravana without regret.

I gently teased Sarah as we walked in the wake of the Smiths. She was free from whatever spell Mr. Smith had cast on his son and wife to turn them into endlessly agreeing automatons. When Mr. Smith decreed the leaf blight ravaging a tree an accurate analogy of the effect of homosexuality on America, Sarah looked to me conspiratorially and rolled her eyes. When he looked at me and said that we all had to be wary of the influence of non-Christian elements, she gave him the evil eye. Later, while we lingered outside the local coffee shop waiting for Mr. Smith to return with what he'd selected for our lunch, she stepped away from her brother and mother and leaned in to me to whisper.

"He's an asshole, and I'm sorry you have to put up with it," she said.

"You're the one who lives with it," I said. "My parents are like that, but college ended that bullshit."

She shook her head sadly.

"I'm fifteen. I have at least two more years to wait," she said. "If I can even escape then."

"If you wanted to," I said, the rush of blood swelling inside me, "I could help you. They don't own you."

"But they do," she said quietly, "just like your family owns you. Jonas told me everything. They have our lives planned for us. Nothing we do, no matter how bad, could ever break their grip."

I laughed.

"That's awfully ominous. It's never that bad, trust me. Give yourself a few years and you'll see they've only got as much hold on us as we let them have."

She gave me a rueful smile.

"People keep thinking I'm too young to know," she said, "but I feel like there are parts of me that have been dying for forever. You ever get that feeling, that you know more than you should, that you're an actor trapped into following an ancient tragedy, that you were already dead before the play began?"

"If you really wanted, you could fuck shit up so bad that the director boots you out of the play."

"Maybe you're right," she said, grabbing my hand tightly.

"What's with all the whispering?" Jonas called out. The rest of the Smiths stood with cups of coffee staring at us.

I let Sarah's hand slip from mine.

"I was talking to her about you," I said.

"Saying good things, I trust," Mr. Smith said.

"He's not the worst demon I know," I said.

That afternoon in our dorm room, the Smiths set out a Thanksgiving spread of bread, deli slices, and potato salad, with a half gallon of chocolate ice cream for dessert. Mrs. Smith was genuinely startled when I told her I wouldn't be having any meat on my sandwich.

"I told you he was vegetarian," Jonas said.

"I thought that was a joke," Mr. Smith said. "Put some turkey on his," he ordered Mrs. Smith. "That's not really like meat anyway— think of it as a new kind of cheese. That way you'll be partaking in the American tradition."

Mrs. Smith hesitated over the meat, looking in confusion from me to Mr. Smith.

"He was kidding, Mom," Sarah said, and as if on cue Mr. Smith broke out in a toothy grin.

"He still doesn't have anything to eat," Mrs. Smith said, her fingers fluttering over our Thanksgiving feast in agitation.

"Bread, mayo, cheese, and lettuce," I said, trying to reassure her with a smile.

"But that's not enough!"

"It's too late to worry about that now," Mr. Smith said. "We make do with what we have and give thanks for it."

"Now that sounds more like Thanksgiving," I said, and I meant it. I felt like I was having my first authentic Thanksgiving ever. Hadn't the Pilgrims been like me, unwelcome foreigners in an unfriendly place, chasing after the idea of freedom, with little idea of what it would cost or really mean? And now, here I was, sitting down at the table with the native savages, picking through their half-assed cuisine, but grateful for the shit because I was hungry.

I inhaled a few sandwiches, then kicked back to watch Jonas eat. Sarah and Mr. and Mrs. Smith leaned back in their seats with a slight grin after they'd wrapped up their meals and watched too. Jonas stacked ham and cheese on turkey and mayo, then tried to wrap the bread with roast beef. If I hadn't seen him in the cafeterias, I would have thought it was all part of some deep-seated eating disorder, perhaps brought on by the presence of his parents. He ate with ravenous hunger, like a god just awoken after centuries of sleeping, and when he was done, he leaned back and smiled—pure, innocent, content. There was no victorious belching, no frat-boy thumping of the chest as if he should be recognized as some great champion because he'd shown his gluttonous power. His face had the quiet contentment of a man who has fulfilled his last need.

"You want some chocolate ice cream?" Mrs. Smith asked.

I glanced toward Sarah and found her staring back at me.

"Yes, please," Sarah said.

I pushed myself away from the table and shook my head.

"I shouldn't," I said, and I left in search of a bathroom to clear my head of Sarah's smile.

I took my time in the bathroom, fine-tuning my hair, practicing my smile. I sorted through my mental list of amiable small talk and rehearsed the tone of my voice, delivering my lines with hands crossed over my chest, or hands in my pockets, or one hand in my pocket, the other making sharp, efficient slashing gestures, all in hopes of finding the right way to disguise my longing. Looking at myself in the mirror, I hated my weakness. It made absolutely no sense to be attracted to Sarah. Sure, there were the coincidental similarities between our families, the same feelings of being trapped by their expectations, but Sarah was barely fifteen, and she was Jonas's sister. In ten years she might have found her own way free of those expectations and escaped her family—at that time it wouldn't be such a big deal. But right now, she was little more than beautiful trouble.

I splashed cold water in my face. An image of Sarah in a sheer slip, waiting for me on a plush divan under the massive arms of a banyan tree, flitted through my mind. I was a golden stag, pacing around the tree, snorting and stomping my hooves, tracing a ring in the dirt around her with the sharp tips of my antlers. Why was it that when I thought of her, I thought of wanting and taking, of the heat of my blood and the flush on her cheeks when I entered her? Who she was, what she dreamed, I knew my body didn't care even though I surely did. My mind could look at my lust and recognize the ludicrousness of it all—what was sex but a ridiculously romanticized physical function, a mindlessly mechanical insertion of tab A into slot B inspired by the arbitrary appeal of the curves and lumps of our flesh. Still, it wasn't my mind that moved me through my day. My mind was nothing but an annoying advisor, a dangling bell from the stag's neck that did little more than signal to the world that the stag was on the move again. It was my body's unfathomable, ungovernable desire that truly ruled me.

For everyone's sake, I secretly hoped that the Smiths would disappear before I made my way back down, that I'd misinterpreted the signs I'd seen in Sarah and that she would return home having quickly forgotten me. As much as I believed I had a sixth sense when it came to reading people in card games, experience had shown that women consistently befuddled me. I could only understand two kinds of relationships with women: the asexual familial I had with my mom and sister, and the hypersexual romantic I'd seen in movies. If a woman wasn't related to me, and showed any kind of warmth, I immediately assumed we were on the verge of a torrid romance. In my teens I'd even gotten confused a few times with my female cousins, rationalizing that since my parents were second cousins, and some of my uncles and aunts had married their first cousins, anything that developed between us was culturally blessed. Given all the evidence, I couldn't rule out the possibility that the attraction to Sarah was nothing more than another one of my fantasies, that her words and gestures were actually a secret signal that I was freaking her out.

When I returned to our common room, Jonas was polishing off the ice cream, nodding his head as his dad read a passage from his Bible, his mother glowing at the sight of her son shoveling in the rich cream. Sarah glanced at me with a shy grin, but when I looked her in the eyes, she quickly turned her head toward the Bible in her father's hands. Her father read on, but I was sure that, like me, Sarah wasn't hearing a word. When he was done, Mr. Smith snapped the Bible shut and looked right at me.

"That's a wisdom that even a non-Christian would agree with."

"It sounds like something I heard in the Ramayana," I said.

"It wouldn't surprise me," Mr. Smith said. "There's clear evidence that Christ brought his message to India, and it would make sense that your religion incorporated his teachings."

"The Ramayana predates Christ," I said.

Mr. Smith waved his hand dismissively.

"I'm sure there's a fake fossil somewhere to prove it too," he said. "But reasonable men, the preachers of your faith—I'm sure they are aware of what they owe to Christ, although I can understand their need to keep such knowledge suppressed."

Sarah covered her face with her hands and Jonas leaned back in his chair with a heavy sigh. Mrs. Smith nodded and smiled at me.

"You should talk more with Jonas and Sarah if you still have doubts," Mr. Smith said. "Since it's Thanksgiving, and she has no school, Sarah should stay with Jonas and show his friend some scripture."

"Really? I could stay?" Sarah asked.

"But you didn't bring a change of clothes," Mrs. Smith said.

"No way am I babysitting you," Jonas said. "I've got work to do, and this campus is not the place for kids."

"I've got nothing going on," I said. "I wouldn't mind looking out for her."

Mrs. Smith eyed me.

"It would be inappropriate to impose," she said, darting a look at Sarah.

"Nonsense," Mr. Smith said. "This will work out perfectly. Jonas's friend is ready to learn from the Bible, and Sarah is prepared to teach. You and I have to bring the new car home—we might as well do that today. Jonas can put her on a bus Sunday afternoon."

"She can be really annoying," Jonas warned me.

"I'm sure we'll be fine together," I said.

"You need a toothbrush, a change of clothes. You're completely unprepared," Mrs. Smith said.

"We can rustle something up," I said.

"I'll be fine," Sarah said. "I'm not a little kid anymore."

Mr. Smith clapped his hands. "It's all settled."

I could tell that Jonas and Mrs. Smith disagreed, but Mr. Smith was already readying his things to leave.

"Be good," Mrs. Smith warned Sarah.

Sarah nodded solemnly, her eyes flitting back to me.

We saw Mr. and Mrs. Smith off, Mr. Smith getting behind the wheel of the massive station wagon, Mrs. Smith following behind in their subcompact. Jonas waved until they made the turn out of the dorm complex, then turned to us and said, "I need to study, so keep it quiet tonight."

"You should hit the library if you want quiet," I said. "Nobody'll bug you there."

"It's closed," he said. "Didn't you see the sign they had at the front door? They won't be open till Monday."

I shrugged. I couldn't remember the last time I'd been in the library. I never really read the signs people put up around campus anyway, unless they were advertising for a party.

"I could still get you in if you really want," I said. "I've got a skeleton key."

"Really?" Sarah asked. "I thought those things didn't really exist."

Jonas laughed.

"He's talking about his hands," he said. "He's good at picking locks."

The kids in the dorm sometimes dropped by our room when they locked themselves out. Jonas had started up a sign-up sheet. I charged five bucks a pop, ten bucks for a late-night call, and sometimes got tips. I was a hell of a lot faster than the janitors with their dangling rings of keys.

"If you need the room," I said, "I could give Sarah a tour of campus, show her some good stuff."

"Watch what you show her," he said. "And no drugs, no drinking."

"As if I'd even do any of that," Sarah said.

"What the hell else is there to do in this shit town?" I said with a grin.

"I'm serious," he said, gripping my forearm tightly, looking me in the eye. "My mom would kill me for doing this. Sarah doesn't need any more crap in her life."

"Jonas!" Sarah said. "You need to forget about that. I know how to take care of myself."

"That's why bad things happen."

The two stared at each other, their bodies frozen, caught somewhere between the desire to flee and the need to pull tight, by some truth they saw freshly revealed in each other's eyes.

"I'll be fine with him," Sarah finally said, looking away.

Sarah was curiously quiet as I led her block to block, pointing out the points of interest, telling her their stories and historical significance.

"That's a church where they executed a British regiment," I said, "and over there, that huge oak, that was planted by the college founder."

"That's a birch, I think," she said.

I shrugged. Details. I couldn't be bothered with learning tree names—what value could that ever have? I didn't really know much about the town or its landmarks either, but I figured I knew more than her, and even if I was mainly spouting bullshit, she would never know.

We walked on and I pointed out the house that Lincoln had claimed was the finest in the land, the hill where Herbert Hoover lost his virginity.

"Every president who's been assassinated visited the college no more than a week before he died," I said.

"That's so spooky," she said, tugging at her coat, eyeing the buildings with renewed suspicion.

"Some say the college is cursed because the founder had a half-Native-American bastard son that he ignored. The kid died of tuberculosis, and now his ghost haunts the trees, fucking people over whenever he gets the chance just like the way his dad fucked him over."

"Jonas never mentioned it."

"Jonas's got book smarts," I said, "but nobody ever wrote about this."

"How did you find out about it?"

"I talk to people," I said, "and they tell me things because they trust me. People want to reveal their secrets—that's just human nature."

"Do you have any big secrets you haven't told anyone about?"

I shrugged.

"Nothing anybody needs to know."

"I've got two secrets," she said. "My family already knows one of them—they can't stop lecturing me about it. But the other one, that's just for me."

"Tell me," I said.

"You have to tell me yours first," she said.

Loose leaves fluttered by in the chill November breeze, pawing at me. The trees, their dark limbs sharp against the cloudless sky, bent in to listen.

"Not here. I'd just lie to you out here."

"You're kidding," she said, laughing unsurely.

I grabbed hold of her hand and pulled her toward the dorms.

Sarah bounced up and down on the sofa, running her hands ecstatically over the cushions.

"It's like fluffing up the rabbits at a petting zoo, but they've all been painted blue!"

"You want a drink?" I asked from the bar. The mini-fridge was stocked with a bottle of rum, a bottle of vodka—generic hangover specials—and enough Cokes to keep it palatable.

She stopped bouncing.

"Jonas will smell it on me."

"Not vodka."

"He'll be able to tell. I'm clumsy when I'm drunk."

"I'll tell him you caught the flu."

She shook her head.

"He's not an idiot, you know."

"I didn't say he was. People believe what they want to believe."

She looked around the room, then settled back into the cushions.

"Whose room is this anyway?"

"A guy your brother hates."

"We'll get in trouble."

"Nobody will know we're even here. The kid's so rich, he won't miss anything we take."

"I'm not a thief."

"If Hamilton was here, he'd be begging you to take a drink. Then he'd lay out some lines and plead with you to snort them with him. He'd probably be more offended if we stayed in his room and didn't touch anything than if we downed every bottle he has. He likes being a good host."

"He does cocaine?"

I nodded.

"Do you?"

"Fuck, no," I laughed.

"I've always wanted to try it. Just once, you know? Find a way to try it where I knew I'd never be able to get a hold of it again, just in case. What's it like?"

"It wouldn't be addictive if it wasn't a good experience," I said. "Hamilton once put some on my gums. You know what it felt like?"

I set a vodka and Coke in front of her.

"Like sex?"

"That's not what I was going to say."

"That's what every guy says. Any great experience—acing a test, running the mile really fast, a big bowl of pasta—they say it's like sex." She took a big slug from her drink. I tipped my cup to her and did the same.

"I didn't know your brother got laid."

"Okay, every guy except my brother. For him, every great experience is like seeing God or being in heaven, or any of that religious propaganda of my dad."

"I was wondering if you bought into any of that shit."

"Jonas's the only one who feels he has to. Me and my mom fake it."

"She's not faking it."

"She's got everyone fooled," she laughed. She pulled me over to sit beside her on the couch then punched my leg with playful ferocity. "So where's the fucking cocaine you promised me?"

I threw up my hands. "I don't know where he keeps it, if he even has any in here."

She poured the rest of her drink down her throat.

"There's only one way to find out."

. . .

Hamilton's dorm room had the same layout as the one I shared with my roommates, but by a suspicious bureaucratic snafu, he'd been roomed with three students who never actually showed up at the college. He'd arrived on campus to find that the spare bedroom didn't have any beds in it, and converted it into a walk-in closet replete with the finest chests and dressers that the college surplus had to spare. He hadn't wasted the extra space. The spare bedroom was lined wall to wall in silk ties and tailored suits, the finest dress shirts covering every color of the spectrum (except pink), and a suitable accompaniment of slacks. Shoes for every occasion—polished Italian leathers, cool-boy Air Jordans, even fucking-around-with-the-lawnmower sneakers—marched from one baseboard to the next. Heavy wooden chests squatted in the empty spaces, stuffed to overflowing with glittering CD jewel box cases, extra poker chips and cards, a menagerie of bric-a-brac crapperie. In one chest I found a stack of other students' tests and papers coated with the exultant praise of professors, the bundles arranged for each class he planned to take. We upended the chests one by one, sifting through the debris for a bag filled with white.

By the time we found Hamilton's spare stash of cocaine, the baggie sandwiched between the pages of Adam Smith's *Wealth of Nations*, we'd each downed a couple more drinks. I chopped up some lines the way I'd seen Hamilton do it, and I set them out between us on Hamilton's bed, using the Smith book as our snorting tray.

We mutually agreed that we should each try a tiny line first to see how we handled it. I snorted first since I was supposed to be the one with the most experience, but Sarah quickly followed after, snagging the rolled-up dollar bill from my hand when my head kicked back to revel in the rush. An Indian summer took root inside me, banishing the insistent chill that always seemed to wrap itself around my bones, and for a moment I remembered a play-off soccer game, my miraculous thirty-yard score as time ticked down, the kids, the parents, who had looked on me for so long with what I assumed was a secret loathing and contempt suddenly crushing me in jubilation, smiling at me, wanting to be the me of that moment. That one moment was one of the few where I didn't have time to remember the reasons I loathed myself, but I'd never been able to revisit the feeling—my mind recalling the soccer game as an inconsequential haze that was soon forgotten by everyone. The snort of cocaine was like a live wire pressed into the heart of the memory, resurrecting it with a crackling jolt. I did not want to let it die again.

Sarah sneezed, her eyes flicking up for a bit, giggling as she flopped back into Hamilton's flannel sheets. She reached for my hand, pulling my arm like rope until I lay beside her, our flushed cheeks warm against each other.

"Your skin feels like a moonless summer sky," she said, running her hands along my arm. She grazed the side of my neck with her nose. "You smell like a storm before it rains."

A sharp ache trembled within me, a horrifying emptiness washing over the tremulous warmth of the cocaine. I could feel myself tearing into pieces, mirror images of myself floating above me, one leering, one scowling.

I nuzzled up against Sarah, hugging her fiercely.

"There's so much beauty in the world, every day passing me by," I said. "So much I'll never have."

Her hand smoothed the hairs on my forearm.

"We should do another line," she said, licking her lips. She arched her back, drawing in a large breath of air. She turned and pressed her nose against mine. "One more so I'll never forget."

I could feel a chill coiling itself around me again, squeezing so hard that I wanted to stop breathing. I wanted to turn my body away, to wrap myself in a blanket and disappear, but my legs felt so good against hers, they snaked around her of their own accord. My chest heaved with sobs, my eyes betrayed me with tears.

"We should stop," I said, my fingers crawling under her blouse, cupping the side of her belly with a practiced gentleness. My body moved as it wanted, my conscience stuffed inside a bag and thrown into a closet of my mind. It wanted to speak, but I would not dare let it.

"You are my Sita," I whispered hoarsely, pulling her lips to mine, biting.

She flinched, pressing a hand to her lips. A jewel of blood glittered on her finger.

We lay together in the aftermath, Sarah draped over me, gripping my chest hair like a baby macaque clinging to its mother. When Sarah had pulled her blouse over her head, it was like being on my neighbor's lawn again, watching flames caress the cupboards in their kitchen. It was what Ravana felt in his hunting perch in the trees when he saw Sita bathing, when he realized that even the Gods were too far away to hear her scream.

"If I get pregnant, I'll run away," Sarah said. "I'll hide somewhere and wait for you."

Sarah got up from the bed and wrapped herself in the flannel sheets. She picked her cup up off the floor and walked out of the bedroom.

"You need a drink?" she called out from the other room.

I fished my boxers off the floor with my foot and pulled them on.

Sarah walked back in with the half-empty bottle of vodka and a Coke, sat down on the edge of the bed, and poured the Coke directly into the bottle. She sniffed it and passed it to me. I took a long pull and offered it back, but she shook her head and began putting her clothes back on.

"I'm not having an abortion again."

She buttoned up her blouse, turning away when she saw me staring. I threw a pillow at her back.

"Sit down and talk to me," I said. "You're acting like a kid."

She turned toward me, her eyes damp.

"Why talk? You already got what you wanted. Now you just want to make sure I don't cause you any trouble."

"If this was a fuck-you-and-forget-you deal, I wouldn't be trying to talk to you now."

She sat on the edge of the bed, almost hovering as if she would fly off at the slightest provocation. I eased over toward her and began rubbing her back. She leaned into my hands.

"Whatever happens, I'm with you," I said. I grabbed the bag of coke and coaxed a fat line out of the last pinch. "Do this. You'll feel better."

She snuffled the line down and gave me a watery smile. I began to massage her neck and shoulders.

"I'm sure our families will understand," she said with a tired laugh. "They'll say I'm too young to know anything, and that you're a pervert."

"My mom got married off when she was sixteen. My grandmothers were hitched before they hit their teens. We're just following a family custom."

"You pagans with your strange ways," she said, genuinely laughing. "My dad will gut you himself."

I wrapped my arms around her and hugged her tight.

She shook her head in disbelief. "I'm addicted to trouble," she said.

"Then we're perfect for each other."

Sarah hopped up the stairs to the coed shower to wash up, and I rattled around in Hamilton's room like a professional cleaner. By the time she came back down, squeezing her hair dry with her hands, Hamilton's place looked the same as when we'd entered it. He'd probably never miss the bottle of vodka and the bag of coke, and even if he did, he'd never know it was us unless he got the room dusted for fingerprints.

"It's pretty late," she said, seeing midnight clicking closer on the clock. "We need a story for Jonas. Let's say we went and saw a movie."

"Nothing's open in this hick town this late at night, except for the bars."

"He probably doesn't know that."

"We should say we watched a video—that's easier. Something classic."

"How about *An Affair to Remember*?"

I laughed. "My vote's for *Ten Commandments*."

"That's good," she said, nodding. "And afterward we had a good discussion about temptation."

"He's not going to quiz me or anything, is he?"

She shrugged.

"You know how to lie, don't you?"

"I've been practicing."

When we got back, Jonas barely looked up from his book. He had a big jar of chunky peanut butter open beside him on the couch, and didn't seem to notice the peanut butter smeared under his lips, on his fingers, on the edges of the pages.

"Heston's a great actor," he said when we finally told him about the movie we'd seen. "When I saw that movie, I was convinced he was Moses. Amazing that a Hollywood sodomite could pull that off."

"You're just saying what dad always says," Sarah said.

"My mom loves that movie too," I said, "but it's more because it reminds her of the nuns she had in Catholic school than because he's a Christian hottie. You ever see *Planet of the Apes*?"

Sarah nodded, but Jonas was already reading from his book again.

"It's about a world where us monkey boys have finally exterminated you Christian curs."

Sarah giggled. Jonas grunted the way my dad did when he wasn't listening to my mom—a clearing of the throat that meant that, yes, he'd heard her making noise, and he acknowledged her creation of noise, but he had more important things to do than waste time trying to understand her blathering.

"We were going to hang out and talk some more," I said. "We'll hang out in my bedroom and I'll close the door so we don't bother you."

Sarah pinched me, a warning in her eyes. Jonas looked up vacantly, but suddenly cocked his head when looking at Sarah.

"What happened to your hair?" he asked. "It looks wet."

I opened and shut my mouth, pinching myself to keep quiet. For some reason, I'd felt compelled to blurt the truth.

"I washed it," Sarah said.

I expected her to go on, but she knew her brother well. He grunted and looked back down at his book. I took Sarah by the hand and led her into my bedroom. We locked the door behind us.

We woke up the next morning to a banging at the door. At first I'd thought it was part of the ethnic drumbeat on the world music sampler CD that Sarah had put into Kenny's boom box to cover any incidental noises the bedsprings might make. She'd found it in Kenny's music rack and set the CD on repeat—Jonas had hollered initially that the music was too loud, but when she toned it down to an ambient murmur, he'd been appeased.

"Hold on a second," I'd yelled out, shaking Sarah awake and shoving her over toward Kenny's bed.

She'd just crawled under Kenny's covers, and I'd just finished kicking her discarded clothes underneath my bed when the door lock snapped with a crunch. Jonas filled the doorway, his face flushed, huffing like a bull.

"What the fuck," I said, rolling out of bed. "I was just about to open the door."

"You're naked," he said.

"That's just the way I like to sleep. Nothing happened."

Jonas looked long at the wisps of Sarah's hair peeking out from under Kenny's comforter. He turned to me, his face unreadable, and grabbed me by my hair and pulled me to my feet. I tried to smack his hands off me, but I was nothing more than a marionette in his grasp.

"Nothing fucking happened!" I yelled. "Jesus Fucking Christ! What kind of an asshole do you take me for?"

Jonas shoved me back down on the bed, my head smacking against the wall. He grabbed my jeans off the floor and flung them at me while I was rubbing my head, my hangover brought into sharp focus.

"Get dressed," he said. "You and I need to have a talk."

"I'm sleeping!" Sarah groaned, wrapping her head in Kenny's pillow. "Just let us sleep!"

Jonas clenched and unclenched his hands in time to the flaring of his nostrils, his lips a tight, bloodless line. He pointed at me, motioned out the door with his thumb, then rattled the door frame with a punch as he stormed out.

Sarah peeked out from under her pillow, her eyes wide. She shook her head and pressed a finger to her lips.

"Careful," she whispered as I jumped into my jeans and stretched into a T-shirt.

I tried to signal to her with my hands that if anything happened, she should call the police, but she only looked on my frantic gestures with confusion.

"Po-lice," I mouthed silently.

She nodded and went back to hiding under her sheets.

"Let's get coffee," Jonas had said when he shoved me out the dorm. As we walked, he kept shoving me ahead with his forearm. I felt like a goat who'd stumbled into the path of the cowcatcher on a train, an unwilling passenger doomed to die at the end of the line.

When we'd passed out of sight of the dorms, Jonas steered me into the wall of a building before turning me around to face him.

"What did you do with her?" he asked, gripping my face by the chin, forcing me to look him in the eyes.

My mom had always made me do that—look in her eyes when she thought I might try to lie. The key was to maintain eye contact and breathe easy, to plan out each sentence and the transition to the next before you opened your mouth.

"We talked. She slept in Kenny's bed. Nothing happened."

"Why was the door locked?"

"She was telling me secrets, things she didn't want you to hear. She didn't want you barging in."

"What secrets?" He shook my chin so hard that I accidentally bit my tongue.

I could feel the chill of the wind, the tickling warmth of the rising sun. Warm blood trickled from my nose and my face felt like I'd thrust it into a fire. I opened my mouth to speak, but the taste of my own blood curling around my tongue caused the words to freeze.

"You want to lie," he said, leaning in close, "but I know what you did."

He was bluffing. His eyes were too focused on me, his breath too still, as if he was waiting. He had suspicions, but he had suspicions about his suspicions. Suddenly confident, my mind returned to me.

"I can't tell you what she told me," I said softly. "I promised her I would keep her secrets safe. She needed someone to talk to who wouldn't judge her. That's all I did."

"You talked?" he said, his voice unsure.

"I listened," I said. "She's a confused kid. She needed me to listen. I told her to trust in her family, to open up to you guys. It's what worked for me when I was her age."

What had worked for me, actually, was jumping out my bedroom window late at night and running off to hang with my friends or bust into people's places.

Jonas stared at me some more, then suddenly nodded and covered his mouth with his hand.

"I'm sorry," he whispered.

"It's alright. I'd have done the same."

He shook his head. "You don't know what it's like to worry about her. Did she tell you about what happened this summer?"

I couldn't remember what she'd said, if she'd said anything at all. The memories of last night that came to mind had nothing to do with words.

"Not really. Maybe she was embarrassed," I guessed.

Jonas gripped me around the shoulder.

"She should have told you," he said. "Come on, let's get that coffee and I'll fill you in. She would want you to understand."

Jonas steered me back onto the path to the coffee shop.

"You have to trust me, Jonas. You can't fly off the handle like this."

"I know," he said, the familiar shame bowing his head.

We walked on, side by side, like brothers.

. . .

Jonas was so worried about people listening in to our conversation at the bagel shop where we got our coffee that he sat on the same side of the booth with me and whispered conspiratorially. With me dabbing my tongue with a blood-tinged tissue where I'd bitten it, a number of people paused on their walk past our booth to glance at me. A couple passersby seemed like they wanted to stop and give me advice on how to handle the bleeding or possibly coo in sympathy, but with Jonas thumping the table so hard when he got distraught that the glass window abutting our booth rattled from the force, they thought better of it, shying away from the hulking presence that had me pinned in a corner.

Sarah had been raped that summer, Jonas confided, and she was still in a state of denial about the whole thing. She'd always been a naïve, trusting girl, and when an old lacrosse buddy of his from high school, a sick loser living at home while he went to community college, took an interest in her, she hadn't known enough to stay away. The guy worked his seduction over the summer, tricking her by pretending to care about her, cajoling her into drinking beers with him, until he'd so confused her that she actually thought she loved him. One day Mr. Smith had come home to find Sarah naked in bed with the guy, so brainwashed by the guy's tricks that she actually yelled at her own father and tried to hit him when he called the police to report the rape. His family was still pushing for a court case so that the boy would be punished appropriately, but the prosecutor had a grudge against the Smiths, and kept saying that he wouldn't pursue the case. Though his dad had devoted himself to providing Sarah the counseling she needed, her healing was coming along slowly. She still lashed out at the family, claiming that they were ruining her life.

Jonas banged the table so hard I thought he would split it in half.

"She might never make a full recovery," he said.

"Sarah didn't really mention it. I don't think that's what's bothering her."

Jonas shook his head sadly.

"She can't see the sickness within her. She puts on a brave front, but we all know the damage that's been done. She's lost her purity, and because of that she's become more susceptible to the other weaknesses of the flesh. It's why she's so unhappy all the time. At least she can rest easy knowing that guy won't be touching her again."

"Sounds like your dad wouldn't let him within a hundred feet of the house."

Jonas nodded.

"That won't be a problem for a while. When I found out, I went over to the guy's house and explained that I never wanted to see him near my sister again."

"How'd he take it?"

"They ended up calling the police on me. That's the bit of legal trouble I still have to work through, but I'm sure God will watch over me for having done the right thing."

"How bad did you hurt him?" I asked, instinctively shrinking deeper into my corner of the booth.

"A part of me wanted to break his bones, to crush his jaw so they would have to wire it shut, but I didn't hurt him. Instead, I told him what I wanted to do, that I would do it without guilt if I ever saw him near my sister again, and that it would be nothing compared to what God would do to him when his day of reckoning came."

I envied Jonas's faith. Being an agent of God's wrath, or believing you were, made it easy to excuse anything. You could rape an adolescent and then parade through the streets of Jerusalem with her head on the end of a lance like the Crusaders did, or sleep easy under the comforting shade of a date tree while a man you'd gutted and tied to another tree screamed as the wild dogs tugged at his entrails. You never had to doubt yourself, never had to feel guilt. When Hanuman set fire to Ravana's kingdom, filling the air with the smell of roasting meat, he didn't have to bother himself worrying about the citizens cremated for the sins of their king. It ultimately didn't matter either that the whole Sita situation that had gotten Ravana into the mess in the first place was an elaborate trap the Gods had been planning for centuries. When you work for God, anything's cool as long as the job gets done.

Though my family no longer leaped onto forest paths and butchered British regiments with scimitars and spears, I knew that being an agent of divine vengeance was my birthright. It would have been convenient if I could have used that to rationalize my actions, to say that a burning house was just a bigger puja fire of devotion, that fucking my friend's sister was justified retribution for the rape of my ancestors by the British. I knew the little tricks of faith that allow a person to excuse anything, but no matter what I did, a hollowness pervaded me. It wasn't enough to believe that there was a demon within me that made me act, or that divine grace justified my every action. I felt like a child of both the Rakshasas and the Gods, the lonely son wielded like a mace by both sides in a nasty divorce. I loved them both, so I couldn't take sides. When Hanuman burned Ravana's kingdom to the ground, my own flesh cooked in the inescapable fire. When the Apsaras lay in the gardens of the Gods with their throats slit, I drowned in my own blood. I was both at once, cutting a swath of destruction through the good intentions of those that surrounded me, destroying the world in the name of the demon, obliged to destroy myself in the name of the Gods.

"Everything alright?" Sarah asked when Jonas and I came back, and we both nodded soberly. She rushed over when she saw me dab my tongue with a bloody tissue, but stopped short, her hands hovering uncertainly near my face.

"There was a misunderstanding," Jonas said. "I accidentally hurt him."

Sarah turned on him and punched him hard in the chest. The punch seemed to hurt her more than it hurt him, Sarah immediately clutching her hand while Jonas merely sighed, but Jonas's shoulders slumped, and he looked down at his shoes.

"One of these days you're going to kill someone. No one is ever going to trust you to lead the church! And for what? None of this is your business."

"He's being protective," I said. "Let it go."

"You're supposed to be his friend. Nobody wants to be your friend, Jonas. Because of this. Because you'd rather snap someone's neck than let them be who they are."

Jonas mournfully walked toward his room, muttering about needing to do penance. He closed the door behind him, but Sarah wasn't finished.

"You can't just walk away!" she yelled, banging on the door. "I'm not forgiving you."

"Let him be," I said. We'd get more benefit from his guilt if we stopped now and let it fester within him. "You and me, we should just get out of here, go do something fun."

Sarah's body shook, her face red and splotchy.

"You don't own me. And none of you can control me," she said. "We fucked because I wanted to."

Jonas's door banged open. He gripped the door frame, looming before us, his eyes focused on me.

"What did you just say?" he asked, breathing heavily.

I was out the door before she could repeat herself. I ran down the stairs, three at a time, Jonas thudding behind me. I raced out the front door of the dorm, then on down the road. I kept running until my lungs burned and seized up on themselves, until each breath was accompanied by a long wheezing cough. I ran because I knew Jonas wouldn't stop, and I kept going, four miles down the road, until I found the bus station and bus ready to leave for the closest town. I wasn't sure what would happen next, how things would shake out between me and Jonas and Sarah, but I was sure that whatever happened, it wouldn't be good.

9

Sometimes your medicine bottle has on it, "shake well before using." That is what God has to do with some of His people. He has to shake them well before they are ever usable.

—Vance Havner

One evening, when Bhagavatha was still young and un-married and could spend the entire summer trekking from town to town performing kathakali, a squat, spectacled man in a silk dhoti approached him after my great-grandfather had finished his dance.

"So you are the famous Kupana Bhagavatha," the man said. He adjusted his spotless white silk dhoti, looking up at Bhagavatha with a smirk. The man had a lazy eye, so as one eye focused on Bhagavatha, the other twitched as if in fear of his own voice. "You are the man they say no demon can kill."

"People make up stories. I'm just a simple servant of Kali," Bhagavatha said.

"Then why do the British run from you? Why else would all of Kerala call you Rama reborn?" The man leaned near and whispered,

"The people are forgetting the truth. Few now know the proper Rama-yana and Bhagavad Gita. Charlatans compose new verses and cloud the truth. I have studied, though, and I know you for who you are. It is foretold that as long as you live, as long as you have the strength to tell the stories, that the power of Rama will still safeguard the earth."

"I think the Gods would have mentioned that to me if that were the case."

The man shrugged. "See it as you will. What is most relevant is that you have the power to help us. The people of my village desperately need to see you and we are willing to pay appropriately."

"What do your people want? Do they want me to turn the moun-tains into fields? Raise their dead children to life? Have Kali extermi-nate the British?"

The man laughed. "It would be a blessing for us if you could do any of those things, but if not, then perhaps your troupe could perform the Ramayana for us tomorrow night as part of our Diwali celebra-tion. Think of what that would mean to my village—the descendant of Hanuman playing the role of Hanuman, destroying the Rakshasas of the story right in front of our eyes on the anniversary of Rama's tri-umphant return from battle. My village is only a day's walk from here, and I will pay in gold."

Most villages offered the performers a meal and small tokens of gratitude. On occasion the performers received a few small coins if the performance had gone especially well. One gold coin would feed his family for a year.

The man pulled a small bag from within his dhoti and poured ten gold coins in Bhagavatha's hand.

"We will pay an equal amount when the performance is finished."

Bhagavatha felt a flush of love for the man. With one performance, the kathakali troupe would earn more than they had in Bhagavatha's entire lifetime. He moved to grasp the man's hand in gratitude.

The man pulled back, a slight smile playing across his pinched lips.

"Gather your performers. I will show you the way to the village."

He stared at Bhagavatha with unblinking eyes. Bhagavatha could look into a man's eyes and see his secret hopes, but at that moment, staring into his new benefactor's glistening eyes, all he could see was himself, alone and naked in an ice-strewn field.

When Bhagavatha told the kathakali troupe of the promised bags of gold, the once-tired performers immediately packed their equipment. The maddalam player, a grizzled old man who still treated Bhagavatha like a precocious child, told everyone he would buy a set of protective metal rings that he could wear on his fingers to protect them while playing his drums, and iron-reinforced sticks for the *chenda* player. Some of the troupe talked of going to Mangalore and buying silks embroidered with gold that they could wear while watching the laborers they would hire to work their fields. One of them wanted to buy a rifle so he could hunt the British.

"I don't think we should go," Bhagavatha said. "It will take us too far from home."

The troupe looked at him incredulously.

"But we're already far from home," the maddalam player said.

"I tasted the gold," another performer said. "It is soft and sweet. It is real. And this man is offering more gold. I would walk anywhere with him."

"We are far from the temple, and it has been some days since I did puja to Kali," Bhagavatha said. "She may not want to protect us in this man's village. What if all of this is just a trick? Perhaps the man is a relative of some enemy of mine. They would kill us all and take our silks and instruments."

The troupe began laughing.

"Bhagavatha," the maddalam player said, "no one would be fool enough to attack us with you around. Enough joking. We should go find this man before he decides to give his gold to someone else."

"Gold," Bhagavatha said. "That at least should warn you of some danger. Who would pay gold? What if he is a friend of the British?"

"Maybe the Goddess Saraswati was pleased with our performance and has decided to bless us with wealth."

Bhagavatha looked at the hopeful faces around him. If he turned around and walked back to the Kali temple, the troupe would follow him. They might never forgive him, but he would have kept them safe. But what if they didn't follow him? The gold might lure them toward the man's village, and without Bhagavatha, what chance did they have if there really was a trap? If he didn't go with them, and word spread that Bhagavatha had been afraid, old enemies who had stayed away might lose their fear of him, and the villagers he had sworn to protect would suffer. His duty to protect his people meant that he would have to go to the man's village. That he seemed to have no choice in the matter re-assured him—he was clearly treading a path fate had chosen for him.

The troupe left that night. The man with the gold rode a white horse ahead of them, galloping ahead, waiting for them to draw near, then galloping off again. In the moonless night, the performers found it hard to see the path, so Bhagavatha lit a lantern and hung it from the handcart he was pulling, but its light flickered and did little to dispel the dark. Aside from telling the man that the troupe had agreed to travel to his village, Bhagavatha hadn't spoken with him since their meeting after the kathakali performance. When they paused in the middle of the night to rest, Bhagavatha expected the man to rest with them, perhaps even share a meal with them, but the man stayed on his horse the entire night, silently staring at them.

The next day was chill and gray, a thick fog rolling in over the land from the ocean. The troupe trudged on, heads bowed. The man rode ahead, gesturing impatiently for them to keep up.

"Tonight is Diwali. The festival of lights! The celebration of the victory of Rama and Hanuman over the Rakshasas," the man yelled, "and you are being paid well to perform on this holy night. Quick or we will be late!"

"If you wanted speed, you should have brought horses for every-one," Bhagavatha said. "At least hitch your horse to this cart if you are so impatient."

The man's lazy eye quivered and his fists tightened on the reins. His horse spun in a quick circle.

He looked down at Bhagavatha, a thin smile curling his lips.

"I don't have the proper harness. The great Bhagavatha will need to keep pulling his cart just a little longer."

The troupe tried to keep pace with the man on the horse. As they trudged on, the Kaiga forest loomed to their right, dense with vines and ordinary trees clumping around hoary teak and sandalwood giants as if they were the kingly trees' bodyguards. From the dark of the wood came the reassuring conversation of langurs screaming at civets who had come too close to their alphonso mangoes, of elephants warning the deer of creeping leopards. When the last of the forest slipped past, a gang of lion-tailed macaques gathered along the verge to stare at them, their thick manes ruffling in the humid breeze. The leader of the macaques held up his hand and screamed before swinging back into the heart of the forest along with the rest of his group. With the forest behind them, the land was now dotted with rice fields and well-groomed banana and coconut plantations. At one of the plantations, a sickly peacock chained to a coconut tree chirped mournfully to them, halfheartedly unfurling its fan. What fools would bring a curse to their family with such disrespect, the troupe wondered. Surely the Gods could see the injustice visited upon the bird through their ever-watchful eyes in the peacock's fan. It was an ill omen.

The cultivated land soon gave way to fields of tall grass interspersed with clumps of wild rice and black pepper. With each step, more of their world seemed to slip away, the grasses becoming thorny bushes, then tenacious scrabbling weeds, until finally all green seemed to have left the earth. They marched through a land full of boulders the size of houses that squatted on a red, parched land. The initial giddiness that had made some of the performers race ahead in babbling groups, or reach out at the plants along the road in search of the gentle tendrils of the white mallika or the delicate five-petaled golden champak to adorn their kathakali headgear, had faded into sullen silence. The

troupe now formed a weary clump around Bhagavatha, some clinging onto his handcart to ensure they didn't drift too far from his protection. A few stumbled in exhaustion, but packed as they were in a
tight group, they found themselves carried along by the hands of their
friends until their feet found the proper rhythm again.

The man led them up a steep hill, and at the top, he waited for
them. The troupe crested the hill and paused, staring into the darkness before them. They felt as if they had been walking for days, and
yet the dull gray of the sky remained as unchanged as when they had
woken up in the morning—a peculiar pea-green tint swirling amidst
the clouds as if they had passed not only into the twilight of day, but
the twilight between worlds.

Before them stretched a dark basin of land. A thick fog shrouded
the earth, interrupted only by the shadow of ramshackle huts roofed
in molding thatch. The man on the horse nodded at the sight.

"Welcome to my land," he said. "It may seem a dismal place, but I
promise you, when you wake tomorrow you will understand its beauty."

He dismounted from his horse and began to lead it down the twist-
ing path toward the village. The troupe lingered nervously at the crest
of the hill.

"Come, Bhagavatha," the man called out over his shoulder, "Diwali
is fast approaching, and your men will need time to prepare for the
performance."

Bhagavatha looked over his cowering troupe. The men, damp with
mist, shivered. Some looked back toward where they imagined their
village to be, but behind them it seemed as if the world were cloaked in
darkness. No birds or beasts rustled in the shadows behind. Ahead lay
only more darkness and chill. The man had disappeared into the fog.

"Stay close to me," Bhagavatha said, lifting his handcart into mo-
tion again.

"This land is cursed," the maddalam player hissed. "I am sure Yama
would find it enjoyable. I'm sure he will find enough corpses and spir-
its to harvest here, but I will walk no farther."

Bhagavatha set the handcart down and shook his head.

"Fate has touched us again. If this land is cursed, then you will not be able to simply walk back into our world. If it is not cursed, then we could leave—but we would have walked all this way and suffered hardship without collecting the gold that brought you here. We are fated to enter this valley."

One of the men threw himself on the ground, prostrating himself before Bhagavatha.

"We were fools. We should have listened. Let us leave this cursed place. Please, Bhagavatha."

Bhagavatha raised the man to his feet. The men were scared, but Bhagavatha knew he could not afford to let his own fear show. He whispered a mantra asking Kali for strength, but a chill of fear still lingered within him. He tried other mantras of power that he knew she loved, but felt nothing but the damp mist. Either they were too far from her, or she had abandoned them. Suddenly he smiled.

"It is Diwali," he said, a new confidence surging within him, "the time when Rama's influence is strongest in the mortal world. I just now recalled this mantra—it is a complex one, but it has tremendous protective powers on this day. Say it now with me, and say it any time fear strikes you tonight: *Agrathaha prastachasteva, praswastacha maha-balo, akarna purna thanwano, Rakshetham Rama Laksmano.*"

He repeated the mantra until the troupe found the proper intonation of the words. Still the men shook with fear, but Bhagavatha felt the thrum of holy energy building in his chest.

"This mantra will bring Rama and Laksmana to protect you from any Rakshasa demon that opposes you. They will come with bows drawn and protect you from all directions."

Bhagavatha picked up his cart.

"Bhagavatha," one of the men quietly said, "you said this mantra had power because Rama is strong today in the mortal world, but look at this land. Are you sure we are still in the mortal world?"

A tightness constricted Bhagavatha's chest.

"No demon has the power to transport Bhagavatha against his will into the demon world," the maddalam player said with a sudden confidence.

The others nodded at this, bowing their heads slightly to Bhagavatha in apology for having doubted him.

Bhagavatha pulled his cart down the hill and the others followed closely, some now poking fun at those who had moments before been so afraid. Bhagavatha, however, was silent. What the maddalam player had said was partially true. No demon could transport a God against its will. But the men had willingly entered into the land. And Bhagavatha was sure that though he was a terrifying warrior and priest, he was definitely not a God.

When Bhagavatha's cart finally reached the bottom of the hill, he paused along with the rest of the troupe. A few grasses sprouted from the earth, but their blades were a sickly white. The shattered remains of trees loomed in the fog like jagged teeth. Ahead, Bhagavatha saw a pale glimmer of flame. As he moved cautiously toward it, the men followed, their feet sinking deep into the fetid mud that coated the land.

They came upon a fire. The white horse that had led them there was tied to a fallen tree. The man stood nearby sharpening a long knife, bags of rice and bundles of wood surrounding him.

"You will perform over there," he said, motioning toward a barren but dry patch of earth a short distance away.

"You should send the children to us now," the maddalam player said, flexing his ancient calloused hands. "They always enjoy watching us practice with our drums, and we would enjoy painting some of them with the chutty."

"Children?" the man said, slicing open a bag of rice and setting it beside the fire. "There will be no children here tonight."

"Where are they?"

"Oh, we only have a few children. This is a small village. Some are sick, the rest are away."

"And what of the villagers that you said wanted to watch us perform?" Bhagavatha asked.

"They will come later," the man said, nodding at Bhagavatha. "They are all preparing for tonight."

"And you?"

"I have a sacrifice to perform," the man said, and with that he patted the horse on its head.

"Come," Bhagavatha said to the troupe. "Let us leave him."

The men quietly followed Bhagavatha to the spot the man had indicated would be their performance space, but as soon as they thought they were out of earshot of the man, they began to furiously whisper.

"What manner of Rakshasa puja is that?"

"It is a king's puja," Bhagavatha said quietly. "The king has a horse led through all the land. If any kingdom attempts to stop the horse, the king will wage war, but if none stop the horse, and he is able to bring it back to his kingdom for the sacrifice, then all the lands the horse has traveled become his, and all the people within it become his subjects."

"We can steal the horse—that would stop the sacrifice," one of the men said.

"None of you will do anything," Bhagavatha said, rubbing his thick hands together in agitation. "Prepare for the performance. I will worry about the horse."

While the men ground their makeup paste and set lanterns along the ground to light the performance area, Bhagavatha sat in the lotus position and tried to still his mind and ignore the fear that churned in his belly. The men still cast glances toward the horse, but Bhagavatha noticed that many of the men stared at him. Bhagavatha closed his eyes. They were all going to die because of him. They had come because they thought they were safe with him, and even now they still thought he was planning their escape. But there was no way to stop the sacrifice. The man would complete the ceremony and enslave their souls. And if they did somehow rescue the horse and stop the sacrifice? There was no hope there either. They were surely on Rakshasa land, an army of Rakshasas lurking somewhere in the mist. They were trapped on all sides.

But he could smell the tang of salt from the faint brush of a sea wind. He dug his hands into the earth and felt the chill, but when he lifted the caking dirt to his nose, it carried the musty spice of good hunchu clay. There was still life in this land, and if there was life, then that meant that Gods were still near.

Suddenly he stood up and motioned the men around him. They huddled close as he whispered his plan.

"When you run," he concluded, "don't wait for me."

The night came quickly, the last comforting hints of sunlight replaced by the pale light of the gibbous moon. With the moon came an unseasonal chill that made the men pause in their work. Some huddled together for warmth, warily looking toward the white horse in the distance.

"Start a fire, you fools," Bhagavatha growled.

"With what?" one of the men asked. There was nothing to burn in sight other than the damp and rotten trees lingering in the land.

Bhagavatha applied another stroke of green chutty to his face, then lined his eyes with kohl. When finished, he handed the chutty to another of the men, walked over to the handcart, and upended it. He grabbed hold of the handles and tore them off the cart, then stomped on the cart until it was left in shards.

"But how do we light it?"

Bhagavatha grabbed hold of a lantern and flung it onto the wood. Flames quickly curled over the shattered glass, dripping with the coconut oil onto the wood.

"You light it with fire!" Bhagavatha yelled. "You use common sense! Have you all lost your minds?"

The men scurried away and busied themselves with their makeup. The maddalam player set aside his drum and walked over to Bhagavatha.

"The men are scared," he whispered. "Scared men don't think clearly. Be kind to them."

"Then I need them to start acting like men instead of children. I can't watch over them—I need each to do his part without hesitation if we are to escape."

"They will. But for right now they need you to show them you aren't afraid. They have nothing else to cling to but you."

"Why me? Why not God? That is where I place my faith."

"But, Bhagavatha, you are a God," the maddalam player said. He leaned in and whispered, "I have known you long enough to know the truth, but these men need to believe in you. It is the only thing keeping them sane right now."

"They need to find their own strength," Bhagavatha hissed.

"Look at them. There is no strength left in any of them. They are looking to the giant of Kapu to rescue them, but they will be rescued because being with you makes a man feel stronger. They would not die for an ordinary man, but they will fight with everything they have for you if they think you are a God."

Bhagavatha nodded slowly.

"I don't know how to act like a God."

The maddalam player laughed. "You don't know how? But isn't that what you do in every kathakali performance?"

"That's different. This would be a lie."

The maddalam player gripped his forearm. "I know you are afraid. But you are the one who has allowed people to think of you as a God. I have seen how much you enjoy hearing the wild stories about yourself. You could have stopped them, or at least tried, but you didn't. And now you are afraid, because now you are in a place where only the Bhagavatha of the stories could succeed."

Bhagavatha sighed. "All I want right now is quite simple. I want a normal life. A wife. Some children. I don't want to be here. Why did we come at all?"

"Bhagavatha, I am an old man. I have seen much and I have had these things you want. You will have them too. Do you know how I know?"

Bhagavatha shook his head.

"Because in all my life, I have never seen a man like you. If ever there was a man that could be a God, it is you. How sure are you that you are not blessed with some secret power that could protect us? Haven't you wondered at how you escaped the British so many times? Bhagavatha, I know the stories about you are not completely true, but there is truth in them. Fate has brought us here. We would not have been brought only to be slaughtered. It is time for the true Bhagavatha to awaken. Lead us. If you are meant to be a hero tonight, God will guide your actions."

Before most performances, a crowd would have gathered around the troupe. Children, some painted in chutty, would be tugging at the performers, or trying to take the chenda player's drumsticks. The smell of food would be thick in the air, vendors trying to entice the audience with breaded and fried cucumber slices, or with the thick and sticky juice of overripe mangoes.

But that night was marked by silence. The troupe raised the *thiraseela* curtain, but still no one appeared. They extinguished all the lanterns except for the one in front of the performance area, and still, no audience. Only when the chenda and maddalam players began their drumming, first creating the sound of rustling leaves, then rising to the booming thunder of a storm, did bodies appear out of the mist. The figures stayed back from the lanterns, their hands behind their backs, their bodies rigid. Men and women with straggly long hair and pallid skin slowly surrounded the stage, bringing with them the fetid odor of days-old fish left in the sun. Their unblinking eyes stared only at Bhagavatha.

Although other kathakali troupes only had the energy to perform an episode of the Ramayana, Bhagavatha's troupe always promised to perform the entire Ramayana in a night, the climactic battle winding down just as the first rays of sun would peek over the horizon. So now they began slowly, even slower than usual, trying to conserve some energy for what they feared would follow the performance.

They started first with King Dasaratha, the kathakali performer holding the pose of sadness as the drums whispered like a distant waterfall. Dasaratha looked up, his hands communicating through mudras his plea to the Gods: please give me a son.

Then the performance shifted to Ravana, the Rakshasa king. Bhagavatha watched from the background as the performer pounded a dance of war. Ravana's face, a deep green with red flecks along the cheek, a long black streak like a knife down his nose, leered out at the audience. Bhagavatha expected the audience to react—they always did, but tonight they only stared, unmoving, as if they were waiting for something. Bhagavatha focused on one face, that of a slender man with thick brows. The man's eyes did not blink. His unflinching gaze remained on Bhagavatha. His arms hung loose by his sides, and his feet—Bhagavatha realized with a start that the man's bare feet seemed to hover above the ground, as if he were a marionette at rest. A Rakshasa never blinked—in this way they were never deceived by the illusions of the world the way mortals could be. And a Rakshasa's feet would never touch the ground—a Rakshasa would never touch the earth Goddess Bhoomi except with a sword.

Bhagavatha sidled over to the maddalam player. He flashed him the doublehanded mudra of *Katakam*: demons. The maddalam player nodded and picked up the pace.

Now the kathakali troupe raced through their performance, a palpable fear imbuing their every movement. They showed Ravana praying to the Gods and receiving the boon of invulnerability—and how in his arrogance he asked for protection against all things except humans. Ravana terrorized the three worlds, driving mortals, lesser gods, and even other demons to beseech the holy trinity of Brahma, Shiva, and Vishnu to save them, until Vishnu finally agreed to be reborn on earth as a man and to kill Ravana.

Bhagavatha burst onto the stage, his feet striking the ground hard in unison with the maddalam player's beat. He danced for the rebirth of Vishnu in the form of Rama, spinning only on the balls of his feet, his knees bent at first so deeply that his thighs bounced against his ankles. His hands, meanwhile, roared through the early years of Rama's life, the signs of his divinity, fingers forming mudras with the speed of hummingbird wings. As Rama grew in age, Bhagavatha incrementally rose higher from his crouch, the pace of his dance never slowing. Sweat shone on his skin, and in the flickering light of the lantern, he seemed like a man on fire. Minutes became an hour, and still he danced.

Finally he came to the time of Rama's banishment. The actors who played King Dasaratha and Queen Kaikeyi, the king's third wife, controlled the stage, their dance a tragedy. Kaikeyi, bewitched by the lies of her handmaiden, asked Dasaratha to grant her the boons he long ago promised her when she saved his life in battle. When she asked that Rama be banished and her own son put on the throne, Dasaratha fell to the ground. The drums rose to a crescendo.

Bhagavatha, meanwhile, had quietly slipped behind the curtain to join the other actors when King Dasaratha took the stage. He had grabbed hold of a stout staff from the stack of props and made his way to an apprentice actor. The young man, his eyes wide as if he would never sleep again, stood guard over the lanterns of the troupe near the edge of the cloth barrier that hid the troupe from the audience's view, his lips silently moving through some prayer.

"You won't be able to hear me," Bhagavatha said into his ear. "I forgot how loud this could be. Just count to one hundred and begin."

The apprentice, nodding his head, began to count on his fingers, his lips still in prayer. Bhagavatha ran toward the horse, swinging the staff back and forth in front of himself. He wasn't sure this would do anything if a demon did bar his way, but it seemed better than blindly walking forward.

He slowed down as he drew near. The man who had led them into the valley sat cross-legged before the fire, chanting mantras Bhagavatha had never heard before. He realized with a start that the man was chanting in Sanksrit, but in a strange accent, the mantras escaping his lips in guttural bursts. Words that he had thought sounded irrevocably holy now felt oily and unclean. The horse, nipping lazily at a hint of green struggling in the mud, was tethered nearby. In the distance he could hear the drums gathering for the crescendo when Dasaratha banished Rama.

He stepped closer to the fire, his staff raised. He could see the man, and the man could see him. Only the fire stood between them. The man's voice continued chanting, his arms and hands busy with the ritual, but his good eye took Bhagavatha in, his lazy eye quivering, the only part of him registering any emotion. With the sacrifice begun, the man was trapped—all would be ruined if he stopped now.

"I wish I could understand why you did this," Bhagavatha said. "The Rakshasas needed a man to do their dirty work. However it began, I will end it tonight. I release you." He raised the staff high in the air, ready to deal a mighty stroke.

Suddenly, from all around him, came a chittering noise, rising in intensity, as if a horde of cicadas had just awoken.

He brought the staff down with all his force. The man, at the last second, tried to roll aside, but the staff smacked him hard in the head, and he lay as if asleep. Bhagavatha ran to the horse.

The noise was now like the roar of a waterfall. In the distance he could see flames licking the sky—the thiraseela and all that could be burned was on fire. The apprentice had done his part.

He quickly slashed the rope and leaped upon the horse, but as he did so he noticed bodies running toward him: pale skinned, dank haired, unblinking eyes, wide-open mouths full of shattered teeth. The noise was coming from them. In the distance, he could faintly hear screams.

He wanted to race to his men, but the Rakshasas lay between them. Bhagavatha prayed. "*Agrathaha,*" he began, "*prastachasteva.*"

As the words of protection tumbled out of him, his voice grew stronger. The Rakshasas slowed their advance, their noise slowly dying to a hum. When he said "*Rakshetham Rama Laksmano,*" a bright blue haze began to billow around him, slowly forming into the shape of two ethereal figures in crowns. They were tall, slender but wiry strong, and carried jewel-encrusted bows in hand. Yet they were not altogether solid—Bhagavatha could see the advancing Rakshasas through them, the image rippling as if he were looking through water.

"We grant you protection, Hanuman Bhagavatha. Go, old friend."

Arrows began flying from their bows, clearing a path. The more Bhagavatha chanted the prayer, the more solid his protectors seemed to be, the faster their arrows flew, the quicker the Rakshasas fell. Bhagavatha slapped his horse and raced for the crest of the hill. He still heard screams behind him, but he dared not look behind. He could only hope that his men had remembered the prayer, and that they too saw Rama and Laksmana. He stood no chance against the Rakshasas, but the Gods would surely save his men.

The horse galloped quickly over the hill. Before him stretched a long plain. The horse rushed forward, faster now, but Bhagavatha finally pulled up on the reins. He had put some distance between himself and the valley, he hoped. He would wait now for his men to catch up. Exhausted, he fell off the horse, unconscious before he even hit the ground. The horse, untethered, did not stray.

Weeks later, when Bhagavatha finally found his way back to his village, only two men came with him. One was the apprentice whom Bhagavatha had entrusted with starting the fire during their escape. The apprentice admitted that he had been chanting the mantra in his head from the time Bhagavatha had taught it to them, and that when the time came, he found himself screaming it. The chenda player and the maddalam player had been nearby. They had grabbed several other members of the troupe and tried to herd them behind the apprentice. Nobody, it seemed, had remembered the prayer in the tension of the moment, and, sadly, many panicked and ran off by themselves. The maddalam player and some of the troupe tried to go back for some of the men. Only the chenda player stayed close to the apprentice.

Bhagavatha split the gold between them, taking four pieces for himself, and giving three each to the men. He immediately went to the temple and gave three of his pieces to Kali, and recommended to the others that they do the same, but neither listened. The chenda player fell mysteriously ill soon after, coughing up blood. "They are eating me from the inside," he whispered to Bhagavatha before he died. The apprentice remained in good health, but his mind was shattered. He walked during daylight like a haunted man, telling the story again and again to anyone who listened, searching for an answer that would bring him peace. Finally he found his answer in the friendship of a few men on the outskirts of the town who spent their days distilling *arack* with a makeshift still. He drank the rice liquor day and night, and though Bhagavatha tried to help him, the drink held a firm grip on the apprentice. He, at least, lasted nearly twenty years.

Bhagavatha seemed unaffected. His prodigious strength remained, and he used it now to help only the villagers—he never again performed kathakali outside the village. He wore the remaining gold coin on a necklace as a reminder of what had happened, and though he never spoke of the event in the years afterward, he would let the villagers touch the gold if they asked. From that day on, he helped his father in the temple, and soon took over the primary duties, working with an urgency that seemed fueled by guilt. They looked for a wife for him and found one in a nearby town. He readied himself for a more normal life, but without excitement.

Years after the incident, the apprentice revealed a detail about the story none had heard before. He had just finished telling some visitors to the village the story when a visitor piped in.

"Thank God for Bhagavatha," the visitor said. "Without him you all would have been lost. If he had not taught you that prayer . . ."

The apprentice spat at the man. His eyes looked up—a sudden clarity dispelling the drunken fog.

"We walked for weeks when we left that cursed place. Finally, we came upon the village where the man with the gold first met us. We asked a man there about the place we had just been. We pointed out where it was. He laughed and told us that nothing was there. Only the ocean. We told him it was a place of Rakshasas. He said that some old women claimed that the Chitradurga hill to the north was a place of Rakshasas, the home of the man-eating demon Hidimbasura. But that was north, and we had come from the northwest. The only reason we ever came to that accursed place was because of Bhagavatha. He was the one the evil man had looked for. Because of Bhagavatha, my friends died." He spat once more. "Never call him a hero in front of me again."

When the time came for Bhagavatha's wedding, everyone from the nearby villages attended, with the notable exception of the apprentice. Bhagavatha's wife was from the village across the river, and so their marriage was an excuse for the two villages to feast and celebrate together. The marriage lasted seven days, as was the custom at the time, and many other marriage alliances were cemented during the revelry of those days.

Bhagavatha's wife, however, soon fell blind. Bhagavatha tended to her, but the only way he could care for her was to have her at the temple with him. She would sit by the temple walls and listen to the voices, but her spirit seemed lost. It was as if her happiness had disappeared with her vision. When she finally became pregnant, Bhagavatha hoped that the child would give her comfort and companionship. But the first son, Narasinga, was sickly and weak. When his first daughter also was born with an illness that wouldn't leave, Bhagavatha beseeched Kali.

Bhagavatha's son and daughter spent many days lying sick in bed, and both grew to be thin and frail. Bhagavatha gave as much as he could to Kali, sleeping in the temple in order to tend to all her needs, performing pujas for his children on the side, but his children's health didn't improve. His son grew to be an able assistant at the temple, and his daughter was married easily enough due to Bhagavatha's reputation, so though Bhagavatha was concerned with naming and understanding whatever curse seemed to be upon them, he felt that they at least would have decent lives.

When his children were married, however, other facets of their curse began to manifest. His daughter had two children within the space of a few years. His daughter's husband was an educated man, and soon found work as a teacher in a nearby village. Each morning he would bicycle his way to work along the new highway the government had laid, and return before dark. One day, he didn't return. Bhagavatha and his daughter walked down the highway in search of him, but when they had gone only a few miles, they came upon a bus upon its side, a car smashed into a tree, and a mangled bicycle coated in blood. The car hadn't seen him, the witnesses said, and at the last second it had veered away. The bus, coming in the opposite direction, had turned to avoid the car. He hadn't suffered, one of the men whispered to Bhagavatha—the bus tire had rolled over his head. From that day, Bhagavatha's daughter and her two young children came to live with him.

Narasinga's only problem after marriage, aside from his worsening health, was that he couldn't produce a son. The family line needed a male heir, so they offered all the traditional sacrifices—bags of rice, heads of beloved farm animals, the pledge of their souls. Bhagavatha renounced food and water until Kali would give him a grandson, but Kali was obstinate, even as her most favored priest lay unconscious from dehydration. The family sold the few luxuries they had, but still, no son.

Bhagavatha, delirious from hunger, screamed at Kali.

"What more can I give you? I have given you all!"

He stumbled and fell to the ground, but as he did, the necklace snapped, and it, along with the gold coin it carried, bounced in the dirt. He grabbed hold of the necklace and raised it up.

"This?" he asked, incredulous. "But this is nothing! It is pain. It is a memory of foolishness. It is all that is left of my friends. It is not worthy of you."

The *deepa* flame before Kali flickered, and Bhagavatha understood. He placed the necklace upon Kali.

"I give you everything," he whispered. "Even my misery."

Months later, my father, Sreepada, was born. My father soon found himself surrounded by four sisters and two brothers, with a third on the way. With no land to call their own, except the devashya granted by the temple, they crowded together in the hunchu house, the children sleeping pressed together in a narrow hallway. One bedroom went to Narasinga and Varadha. Another was reserved for my grandfather's sister and her two daughters. The largest bedroom was reserved for Bhagavatha and his wife.

Sreepada quickly became Bhagavatha's favorite, for in him he saw Kali's forgiveness. Where his own son had been sickly, weak, and of normal intelligence, Sreepada was exceptional. Though he was astonishingly quick, able to climb trees as if he were born a monkey and bring fruit down to share with his siblings, most people were more impressed with his wit. At the age of six, he began engaging in political debate with the old men who drank coffee in the village square. By eight he had written a new variation of the Mahabharata for the kathakali. When Bhagavatha would tell him an obscure sloka or mantra, Sreepada instantly remembered it. The villagers took notice. Bhagavatha's strength was legend, but a new legend was growing. It was said that . Sreepada was like Bhagavatha—a blessed man, favored by Kali. Where Bhagavatha had strength of body, Sreepada had strength of mind.

After college Sreepada was accepted into a medical school in Madras, a huge city on the eastern side of India. The people there spoke Tamil, and though he had studied it some in school, he knew it would take a long time before speaking didn't immediately reveal him as a country bumpkin. Madras had started out as a British fort, but grew recklessly in the years after, a bustling maze of streets and concrete homes that stretched for miles. In his native village, my father could expect courtesy and a friendly hand, but Madras was a big, unfriendly city. Worst of all, his scholarships covered tuition and some of his housing expenses, but it wasn't enough. He mentioned the problem to his mother, and together they visited distant uncles and friendly priests in search of a benefactor. None wanted to help.

Just as they were about to lose hope, an ancient man who said he lived a few villages away visited them. They weren't completely sure how he was related to them—the web of intermarriage usually meant you could trace your way to the relative along both maternal and paternal lines. So, when they met him, my father called him grandfather, and Varadha bowed her head with respect. Varadha explained the problem and asked for his help. The old man smiled feebly but did not rise from his chair.

"Sreepada," the man said, his voice a guttural whisper. "You remind me of myself when I was younger."

"I hope that is a compliment."

"Sreepada has always been hardworking and good," Varadha said.

"But he wants to wander the world, does he not?" the man said, absentmindedly fussing at the gold earring in his right ear.

Varadha raised her eyes and looked directly at the man. "He would not leave if there was any other way."

The old man reached out for her hand and clasped it tenderly between his.

"But why does he need to leave? Don't you need him near? Some go to distant places, distant countries, just because they can. They go for their pride. I went to England once, because I could. There were things I thought I wanted there."

"What was it like, Grandfather?" Sreepada asked eagerly.

The old man shifted his dentures in his mouth, a pensive look on his face.

"You don't know who I am, do you?"

"I have so much family . . ." Sreepada began.

The old man waved him off. "No apologies. I was a good friend of your grandfather Bhagavatha. I saw you both often, long ago," he smiled kindly. "So tell me, Sreepada, what is your dream?"

"I want to be a doctor."

"So you want to be rich, respected."

My father shrugged. "That may happen, but that isn't why I want to be a doctor. Most of our people live in ignorance, at the mercy of those with power. The ones that get an education come back like kings, but they use their knowledge only to help themselves. The businessmen focus on how to make more money on the rice fields, but they don't make sure the workers get more food. The doctors trade lives for money as often as politicians."

"So you want to come back and help?" The old man smirked.

"My father, my grandfather, and my grandmother all died because a doctor wouldn't help. I can promise that money won't control whether or not I save a life."

The old man slapped his knee.

"A noble response, worthy of Bhagavatha himself. You know, when I went to England, I thought I would come back soon. Alone for the first time, though, I realized I could do anything as I pleased. Loved ones in India thought I would return, but how could I? There is so much more for a man with intelligence over there. But I had no family there. And now, when I finally return, it seems like I have no family here either. I have no home except my body, and even that is threatening to leave me soon."

"My brothers will visit you," Sreepada said. "There are so many of my cousins that would like to hear your stories too. We wonder what England is like. They show it in movies, and there are pictures in the books. It is so clean, so ordered!"

The old man smiled at my father.

"Very good. I see we have much we can trade. Your offer of family is accepted. Now I will tell you what you need to know to survive in Madras." He motioned toward a desk in the corner. "Find a pen. I will tell you the address of Seetharama."

"Is he a money lender there?" Varadha asked.

The old man laughed.

"Some might say that. But no, Seetharama is linked to your family. He is the son of Bhagavatha's wife's sister. He will help you without hesitation."

"He won't know who I am."

"Tell him you are Bhagavatha's grandson. Tell him of the promise his mother made to your grandmother. The sisters were born one year apart, and so they grew very close to each other. Some said that they were the same person. They shared everything. They even spoke in a secret language they had made up.

"When they reached adolescence, they realized they would get married soon. They would have to follow their husbands and for the first time live apart. So they promised to each other that they would be loyal to each other first, even above their husbands. If either one needed anything, she need only ask. Soon after your father was born and your grandmother went blind, they made another promise. The promise would extend to their children. The sisters are long dead now, and many of their children are scattered, but Seetharama was always his mother's favorite. His help is worth more than any money I could give you. Tell him that the friend he met long ago when he was lost as a child in the jungle has sent you to remind him that this is a promise he cannot break."

In Madras, Seetharama Rao had managed to create a comfortable life for himself. He had left his home at the age of eleven in order to find work to feed the family, and made his way to Madras, where he became a dish boy. He worked his way up the ranks, saved his money, then started a restaurant with a few of his friends, but his friends deceived him and stole the restaurant from him. Seetharama had always been a kind man, doing little things to help anyone, even untouchables. And so when the time came when he asked for help, he found many who would loan him money. He built one restaurant, then another, using recipes he had learned by sneaking in and watching the priests of Udupi when they cooked their sacred recipes in secret. All of Madras soon was eating in his restaurants.

By the time Sreepada showed up at Seetharama's home with an overflowing suitcase and the story the old man told him, Seetharama had already built a new four-story home to hold his family. With eight daughters, he needed the room.

It always struck me as strange that my mother said she'd had a "love marriage" to my father. In India that meant that a couple had avoided the arranged-marriage preferences of their parents and chosen their partners for themselves. The term implied a level of reckless passion, and most Indians looked at love marriages as business ventures doomed to failure. Passion faded, as everyone knew. A good marriage was an arranged marriage. The families of the prospective bride and groom would get together and determine if the couple had similar interests, and if the families respected each other, the match would be arranged. Of course the young couple would not know each other well, but supported by their respective families, they would be able to slowly grow together. In that way, they would develop a passion that would turn into undying love. At least, that was how it worked in theory. Since nobody ever divorced, and everyone always claimed that their arranged marriages had turned into happy, loving marriages, the only proof any of us had that we were being subjected to propaganda was the evidence we saw in the marriage of our parents.

I could understand why my mother considered her marriage a love marriage. She wasn't a stranger to my father when their marriage was arranged, and clearly both of them were drawn into the marriage by the pull of love. The only problem was that the love that brought them together was not for each other.

When Sreepada banged on Seetharama Rao's house in Madras, he never intended to find his future wife there. He was only hoping to find a friendly relative willing to honor an old promise and offer him a place to stay. It was the only realistic chance he had of being able to afford medical school—no free lodging or free food, and he'd quickly starve his way back to the Kali temple. Though Seetharama had a house full of daughters, he let my dad stay in a bedroom on the terrace of the house. He naturally was worried about how it would look to have an unmarried man near his daughters, but at least at night he could lock the door to the terrace and limit the potential for nighttime rendezvous with his daughters.

At six feet tall, and athletic from his years working the rice fields near the Kali temple, Sreepada seemed like a movie star to Seetharama's daughters. Most of the other men in the area were far shorter, pudgier, and darker. But my dad wasn't interested in flirting with the young girls. Seetharama realized that his daughters could prance nude before the young man, and just as the famous *rishi*s of old, deep in meditation and observance of the rituals of the Gods, had ignored the heavenly dancing Apsaras, the young man's eyes would stay glued to his books.

The girls tried their best to attract Sreepada's eye. As soon as they came home from school, they switched into their best clothing, re-plaiting their hair and washing their faces to remove any hint that they had just sweated through another sweltering Madras day in the convent school. The oldest daughter, Pushpanjali, soon gave up the effort. Slightly pudgy, with a lazy eye that made most visitors to her father's house think she was slow-witted, she had long before decided that she wasn't beautiful. For her sisters, wooing Sreepada was a com-petition, and Pushpanjali decided that the game wasn't worth playing. She wasn't going to waste her time competing in a beauty contest for the attentions of an aloof and distant man, no matter how handsome he was. Some days, when he came walking home, she would spit on him from the terrace, just to show him that she didn't care one little bit what he thought of her.

The only person Sreepada seemed to have any connection to was Seetharama. He was immensely grateful that Seetharama had let him stay in his house, and took to eating breakfast with him at Seetharama's nearest hotel. Over coffee and endless plates of idlees (which Seetharama never asked him to pay for), they talked politics, philoso-phy, and business. Seetharama was fascinated by the stories Sreepada told him of Bhagavatha and the Kali temple—he had heard rumors of Bhagavatha, but the stories paled beside the wide-eyed accounts of the young man who sat across from him. Yet what most interested him was my father's loss of faith. He pushed Sreepada on the issue, gently, but the young man was obstinately agnostic.

"So you stopped praying after your father died," Seetharama asked him one day, "just because it seemed to you God didn't answer your prayers."

"They let them all die. My father, Bhagavatha, my grandmother. If ever there was proof that there is no God, or that God doesn't care for our miseries, that was it."

Seetharama stirred his coffee and leaned close to Sreepada.

"God listened to your prayers. You have a blessed life."

Sreepada pushed himself away from the table and collected his books.

"Sit and talk," Seetharama said calmly. "Sit and think."

"I do think. That's the problem. Every day you badger me about God, but I know 'God' is just a word fools use to pretend that someone exists to correct the wrongs of the world. Now you want me to think my father's death was a blessing. In less than two weeks, my family lost everything, and we became beggars. There is no God!"

"Don't disrespect me with your anger."

"Not anger. Frustration. You do not know my past. Let us just agree that we see God in different ways. So far, in your life, you have been showered with blessings, so you think there is a God, and that he is kind and just. If you suffered as my family suffered, then you would feel as I do."

Seetharama's voice took a cold edge.

"I had to leave my family when I was little because they could not feed us. I came to this city alone, and I worked as a dish boy. Imagine being young, vulnerable, lonely, at the whim of those you work for. There is much I learned about the demons who pretend they are people and walk amongst us. So do not preach to me about suffering." With that he slammed the table, spilling his coffee.

Neither man moved to clean it up. The gentle murmur of others eating in the background was suddenly quiet. The men all around them stared at the two men, and even the busboy, rag ready in hand to clean the spilled coffee, hung back.

"What did they do to you?" Sreepada finally asked.

Seetharama shook his head and looked away.

"I survived because of some friends I worked with. I saved my money, started a small food stand, then used that money and built my first restaurant. And then one day those same friends kicked me out of my restaurant. They had bribed the right people, you see. There was no proof that I owned anything. I was married by then. And suddenly I had nothing."

Sreepada nodded, and without fully understanding why, reached out and took hold of Seetharama's shaking hands.

"I am sorry if I seemed rude," Seetharama whispered, "but I cannot accept that the evils in this world are due to God. I think our escape from the evils is the blessing of God. And, perhaps, the pain we feel is less than what it should have been. And sometimes the pain is a lesson that we must struggle to learn from. You know, I tried to kill myself on the Marinas Beach. I walked into the ocean, ready to end all my suffering. And God threw me back. As the waves roared around me, I heard him tell me that there was much for me to do. And because I believed in him, you are here now."

"I am honored that you trust me enough to tell me."

"I have learned by now to know whom I can trust. The moment you told me your story, I knew that you were like the man I used to be years ago, on the verge of walking into the sea."

"But I am little more than a stranger to you."

Seetharama shook his head and laughed.

"Our first child was a stillborn boy. Since then, only daughters. I asked the priests when a son would come, but they didn't know. And then I saw you."

"You realize that it was only a sequence of strange chance that brought us together."

"Chance. Yes. That is one of the many names of God." Seetharama patted his hand. "And so I will act as your father, even if you aren't sure you want to be my son."

The two were inseparable. For Seetharama, who had never had a formal education, Sreepada was an encyclopedia he could open at any time. Seetharama had never felt compelled to know anything other than how much his competitors charged for the same dishes, or how he could go about squeezing a little more profit from his hotels. All else had been God's business. There were, of course, items of science and history that he found curious, but he had little time to investigate on his own. He had taught himself how to read Tamil as a child, but his reading skills were limited, and the daily newspaper was challenge enough. He was embarrassed to admit to anyone that the famous owner of the Palimar hotels knew very little about how the world worked outside the realm of his business. Now, with Sreepada by his side, he found that he could ask the simple questions that embarrassed him, and learn the answers without judgment. They both pretended that Seetharama always knew the answer, that he was only asking the question to test the depths of Sreepada's education. And on those rare occasions when Sreepada didn't know the answer, such as how, exactly, an air conditioner worked, Seetharama delighted in chortling, "Aha. I have stumped you. See how much more you need to learn before you can be as wise as me?"

In his spare time, Sreepada looked over the hotel accounts and pointed out the various ways Seetharama's employees had been fleecing him. Seetharama had trusted his street sense to weed out the crooks who came to him looking for work, but Sreepada showed how the numbers in the daily account books proved that nearly everyone working at the hotels was a thief. Seetharama began to pull his employees aside. He fired many of the thieves on the spot, but whenever one explained that they had only stolen because they didn't have enough money to feed their family, he either increased the man's pay or promoted him on the spot.

"They'll only keep stealing from you," Sreepada said. "You can't run your business like a charity."

Seetharama shrugged.

"Business is not only about profit. Some will abuse the second chance I have given them. That is human nature. But many of these men have never been treated with dignity, except by me. They will want to prove that my trust is well placed. Watch. These men will be the most loyal. They will never steal again, and they will never allow others to steal."

Sreepada shook his head.

"I wish people were as good as you think they are."

"People always want to be good. Sometimes it is difficult for them, but if properly encouraged, even the lowliest bathroom sweeper will amaze you."

Seetharama's faith in others fascinated Sreepada. Other Brahmins, like the ones he had known in his village, were far less charitable. For them, the fact that they were Brahmin and of the highest caste meant that they were better than others they passed on the street, purer somehow. They expected to be treated with deference by the lower castes, even though the caste system had been abolished by the government. Even Seetharama's own wife, Laxmi, would yell at the untouchables who came to clean the house bathrooms if they strayed too close to one of her children. She persisted no matter how many times Seetharama pleaded with her to treat them with dignity, and Seetharama explained to Sreepada that, as for most Brahmins, change would be difficult for her. The attitude was based on a lifetime of habit. But Seetharama was different. The only time Sreepada ever saw Seetharama get angry was when he noticed a Brahmin treating a lower-caste person poorly. He would pull the untouchable aside and hug him, apologizing for what had happened. He often brought left-over food from the hotel with him when he walked home, and would distribute it to the beggars he passed along the way. If untouchables were new to the neighborhood, Seetharama's warmth would initially make them wary. They too, after all, had been conditioned to expect harsh treatment from the upper castes. But though Seetharama's example seemed to have little effect on the other Brahmins in the community, the beggars and lower-caste denizens of the neighborhood accepted him. Some even whispered that he was an emissary of God, and that eating the food from his hotels could cure any ailment.

As Seetharama's daughters grew older, his house became a frequent stop for emissaries from other Brahmin families intent on arranging a marriage. At first Seetharama met these people gladly. His eldest daughter, Pushpanjali, was almost sixteen, and it was important that she get married quickly. If he waited another year or two, people might begin to wonder at the delay. But when the emissaries came and set eyes on the cross-eyed Pushpanjali, they immediately began to ask if he was willing to have his second daughter married first.

"You understand, of course," one boldly said, "that even with your wealth and good name, the boy would be hesitant to marry Pushpanjali. But the second daughter—she has a healthy mind and the proper beauty."

Seetharama threw the man out.

One day, while his daughters chattered their way through dinner, Seetharama discussed the situation with Sreepada. Pushpanjali listened in, only pretending to nibble at her food.

"Perhaps I should send her to college," Seetharama said. "The Brahmins only see her lazy eye, but a degree would make them realize how smart she is."

Sreepada shook his head.

"College won't persuade them. Then they will think she is too educated to be a wife."

"They say she is too ugly and too stupid. They say this without looking at her closely, or even talking to her."

"There are men who will recognize her beauty," Sreepada said. "If she wears glasses, the lazy eye would be less noticeable. As well, the glasses will make them think she is intelligent, even if they don't bother to listen to her speak."

"She is a smart girl."

"I see her reading all the time. And she is beautiful in quiet ways that she does not see. She does not think she is beautiful—I never see her preening like your other daughters. But she is as good a wife as any man could ever hope for."

"You are the only one who seems to understand this."

"Then you need to find a man like me."

The men silently ate, pondering the situation, but for Pushpanjali, the sadness that had hung over her ever since the matchmakers had begun to visit the house vanished. She felt her cheeks flush and was scared to look up. It seemed clear to her that her father had slyly asked Sreepada if he would marry her. And it seemed equally clear that the handsome man who dominated her sisters' dreams was smitten with her. A nagging worry ate at her, however. Sreepada came from a poor family. She only hoped that he wasn't too embarrassed by his financial situation to ask for her hand in marriage.

A few weeks later, while she was sitting on the terrace reading a romance novel with her new glasses (she had recently taken to coyly batting her eyes at Sreepada whenever he passed her to go to his room on the terrace), her father approached her. From his broad smile, she knew what he was going to say. She set aside her book, ready to pretend surprise.

"Why are you so happy?" she asked.

"I have found a good match for you!"

"Is he tall and handsome?"

"But of course. And he is smart. A man of science. Brilliant and kind."

She giggled.

"Is he as strong as you? As generous?"

"Stronger. His arms are like Bheema's. He could split a demon in two."

"I accept. I knew he was interested. And—"she paused—"I am already in love with him."

"Of course you will accept. But love? You barely have spoken to him."

"Love can exist without words."

Seetharama clapped his hands.

"I was worried a little, I must admit. I thought you might think him too old, or perhaps you might not like that he doesn't have a thick head of hair."

Pushpanjali shook her head.

"Don't tease. Sreepada isn't so old."

"Sreepada?" Seetharama laughed. "Oh no. He is like your brother. No, today that Krishnamurthy man sent a proposal. Remember him— the chemical engineer?"

"That big fat man? He was so bald! And he was a widower!"

"His wife died through no fault of his. Come now. He is a good man. A good match. He comes from a respectable family. And he genuinely is interested in you. He said you were very witty, and he was not at all bothered by your eyes."

Pushpanjali grabbed her book and threw it at her father.

"How could you agree to that buffoon! It was supposed to be Sreepada! He is the one who loves me. You know we were meant for each other."

Seetharama rushed to his daughter and held her close, but her tears came fast and furious. She beat on his chest with her hands.

"Tell me you are joking. You are testing me," he said.

But his daughter could only wail like a widow at the pyre.

For weeks she wandered the house in a daze, frequently breaking out in uncontrolled sobbing. She could vaguely remember the Krishnamurthy man. He had seemed so pompous, constantly tweaking the broad red tie that pressed into the fat folds of his neck. How could he think she was witty? He had barely let her speak at all. It seemed like every other sentence he had felt compelled to remind everyone that he was a chemical engineer, that he had already bought his own house. Whenever he said "house" he had patted his belly as if the edifice had come fully formed from his gut.

Sreepada was completely oblivious. He had never paid much attention to the chattering of the girls in the house. One or the other was always swooning or wailing. He didn't understand the emotions of young women, and wasn't particularly interested in trying to learn. They were always trying to talk to him while he was studying, and so he had developed the habit of pretending to listen to them, nodding as they spoke, but keeping his mind focused on the words on the page.

Seetharama was right when he told Pushpanjali that Sreepada wasn't ready for marriage. Sreepada had told him that marriage was a luxury he couldn't afford. He needed to finish his studies, establish a practice, and help his family escape the poverty of the village. Everything else had to wait until he accomplished his goals. There were times, of course, when he felt lonely and wondered what it would be like to have a wife he could confide in, but those thoughts quickly faded. He was twenty-three. Far too old for silly daydreams, far too young for marriage.

After weeks of watching his daughter mope around the house, Seetharama promised Pushpanjali that he would ask Sreepada if he would marry her. One day he broached the subject over a light breakfast at the hotel.

"I'm sure you've noticed how sad Pushpanjali is these days," Seetharama began.

"She does seem to cry a lot," Sreepada said. "It is probably a part of the monthly women's issues. Hormones create such instability in women."

"It is much more serious than that. She has received a wedding proposal, but she has confided in me that she is in love with another man."

"Put your foot down," Sreepada said. "You simply cannot allow such foolishness."

"But I think I am partly to blame. I introduced her to the man. And her choice is a good one. It would be a perfect match."

"Well then, why the problem? Simply arrange the alliance." Sreepada paused. "Ah. But the man probably wants a large dowry. And you are worried about setting such a precedent with so many more daughters to marry."

"Nothing of the sort."

Sreepada sipped his coffee.

"I really don't know what help I can be on this issue. Marriage is a completely foreign subject to me. As are women. My guess would be that you should just mention the issue to the boy. You are well respected. The boy may end up agreeing. Or is it that he is a lazy fellow? Or is there some dark secret to him?"

"Sreepada," Seetharama said, latching onto his hands, "she has fallen in love with you."

"Me? How?" Sreepada spluttered. "I barely talk to her! Please believe me. I did nothing to encourage this."

"I know," Seetharama said, "and yet, somehow she has set her heart on you, and I feel as if her happiness, and now, even mine, depends on your decision."

"Do you want me to marry her?"

"I do not want you to do anything you do not want to do."

Sreepada sat silently eating, shaking his head.

"Do you refuse?" Seetharama asked quietly. "I will not be angry if you do."

Sreepada swallowed.

"I will marry her. But please, send word to my mother and make sure she gives her blessings as well."

Although Seetharama may have guessed why my father married my mother, he never asked. But my father told me, many a time. "I married her because I loved him. Because I couldn't bear the thought of disappointing him."

The town I landed in, less than ten miles away from the college, rumor had it, was the incest capital of the world, a seedy little working-class town best left to its own misery. The college kids said that the folks in the town were a mean and spiteful bunch who would go out of their way to fuck you over if they knew you went to the college, or if they caught even the faintest whiff of money coming off you. It made me think of Cicero, a screwed-up shithole of a neighborhood in Chicago that my dad had always warned me to avoid. He said that in Cicero, people didn't take well to outsiders, and with the mob running everything, people of color were expected to keep their mouth shut and not touch the white people or any of their things and to be out of the neighborhood by nightfall, unless, of course, they were trying to attempt suicide by Cicero. If the town folks didn't like the college kids, I was pretty sure they especially wouldn't like me. Still, it was a cheap place to lie low, and I only needed a few days away from Jonas to give him a chance to cool down. Worst case, after a few days when the students came back from Thanksgiving break, I could go to one of the deans and ask to transfer out of the room. I could slug myself in the face a couple more times before I walked in and guarantee myself a nice room, maybe even a single. As well, if I stayed in the town, there was a good chance someone might save me the hassle and layer on some fresh bruises of their own.

As the bus rolled down the main drag, I could see why the town folks had a chip on their shoulder. Crumbling stone two- and three-stories coated in a sallow skin of sickly moss squeezed against each other. Years of factory fumes mingling with oily truck exhaust smudged everything a despairing charcoal grey. A few liquor and check-cashing stores had their doors open, but most stores rotted behind boarded windows, their signs faded beyond legibility, advertising only the nothingness the town had become. It made sense that the town was the incest capital of the world. What else could anyone hope to do in such a place but propagate misery, and what better target than a family member guaranteed to remind you of your fucked-upness till the end of your days.

I found a bar called the Anchor right near the bus stop and settled into a stool to figure out my next steps. The place was tiny, a trailer put up on blocks and jammed full of tables that were, for the moment, empty. A variety of naval implements that I couldn't identify hung on the walls along with curling beer posters, a cracked picture of Ronald Reagan, and a moose head, its eyes missing, its hide patchy and stained. When I asked for a beer, a policeman sitting a few stools over hollered at the bartender that he'd better check my ID, and when I produced it, the two studied it with exaggerated care.

"I'd say it's a fake," the cop said, "except that no dumbass would put a name like that on a fake ID."

"You one of them Iranian fuckers?" the bartender asked.

"I'm Indian," I said.

"Why you here?" the cop asked.

I shrugged. "Same reason as anybody. I wanted a beer."

"His story checks out," the cop said, nodding importantly. "Go ahead and serve him."

"Your English is pretty good," the bartender said.

"I practice a lot," I said. I took a long sip from the mug and looked away, hoping they would get back to doing whatever the hell it was they'd been doing before I walked in.

"What brought you into the country?" the cop asked.

I looked into my beer for guidance. I took another sip.

"Land mines," I said. "Communist land mines. Turned my family into hamburger."

The bartender shuddered.

"That's what happened to John in Nam," he said.

"Nothing but a flag to bury," the cop said.

"That's the shit of the world," I said. "Good people go down, and we're left with the pieces."

The cop and the bartender sipped from their beers mournfully, staring into the amber liquid, watching a movie only they could see. I knew they'd let me be as long as I wanted now. We were brothers who'd survived the horrors of war.

When my sister returned from India with her new husband, my parents felt it would be best if they lived with us in my parent's house. America was a tough place to get started, and it made sense for them to join in as extended family, living in my sister's old bedroom, until they could make enough money to get a place of their own. With my sister safely married, my parents let her husband know that it would be safe for her to return to college. He, meanwhile, began working up the corporate ladder, taking the occasional night class to flesh out his credentials. I loved that my sister was back at home, but she seemed different now, broken in a way I couldn't place. She reminded me of the way my mother had been after her father died, a hollowed-out person that needed all her energy to hold herself together, leaving her little chance to reach out and be a mother to anyone. Her husband seemed like a nice enough guy—he bought me comic books all the time—so I loved him like a big brother. Each night when we went to sleep, I took comfort in knowing that though my sister was sad, at least she had a nice guy to keep her company and help her through her troubles, whatever they were.

The walls of our house were thin, which made privacy a little difficult. When my parents or my sister and her new husband went to bed at night, I often heard the squeaking of their bed, and being twelve years old, I knew that the rhythmic sounds of bedsprings compressing signaled they were making love. It made me blush, and I tried to clear my mind of the thought of my mother or my sister lying in bed underneath a man. In time I learned to cover my head with my pillow and to dream of Hanuman jumping across the stormy ocean, or the knock of stone on stone as the monkey army built a bridge to Ravana's kingdom, and turn my two mothers' nighttime pleasures into a sonic entrance into the Ramayana. In the morning when I saw them I would always lower my head. It was easier to pretend that I'd heard nothing and thought nothing than to acknowledge that I'd learned too much of the world to feign innocence any longer.

I don't know how long the honeymoon lasted, or when my pleasant dreams were replaced with the screams of war. I'd hear curt voices, the smack of flesh on flesh, the muffled screams of my sister. And in the morning my parents would join me at the breakfast table with bowed heads, party to my attempts at ignorance. One night when I heard a slap, I grabbed my baseball bat and stood by my sister's bedroom door. I held the bat with clenched fists, but I did not move.

Each morning we repeated our ritual of ignorance, and each night we heard the sounds of war. One night, when my sister and her husband had gone off to an office party he'd been invited to, I came downstairs to find my parents yelling at each other.

"It is not my place," my father said. "She is his now."

My mother flung flattened dough into the deep fryer and did not flinch at the splatter of oil.

"Then we should take her back!" my mother raged. "We did not sell her and he cannot own her."

My father shook his head and continued eating.

"It would reflect badly on her. First she nearly dated some American, and then she left her husband. It is better if they solve their problems on their own."

"There is no solving!" my mother said, scooping fluffed-up *puris* from the oil. She brought them over on a plate for my father, pouring him another cup of water. He waved her off with his hand.

"You should stop cooking and eat. You are too hungry to think properly."

"She is my own flesh, my daughter, and you want me to eat and be quiet?"

"She does not need your trouble. They will adjust, just as we did."

My mother turned away, for that is what she always did. She would yell and yell, then turn away. It was what she had been raised to do.

This time though, I saw her hands shaking. She looked at her forearms, at the dark spots left behind over the years from the shrapnel of cooking. I had touched those arms before—she had told me how she rubbed that skin and wondered at why it no longer could sense the kiss of the wind, the pleading touch of my fingers.

"Their marriage was not God's will," my mother said, turning to face my father. "Their marriage was by your will, and you will be the one to end it."

My father grunted and placed another puri in his mouth.

"It is too late. He says he wants a child. Perhaps she is already pregnant."

"Just as I was with her," my mother said quietly.

"Yes. And just like us, they will find their happiness. All marriage has its adjustment."

"He will not change."

"Don't be stupid. What can you know of this?"

And my mother rushed toward him, her hand raised high.

"I am not stupid!" she yelled, her hand thudding against his scalp. "Men like him, like you, you never change!" Her hand struck again, and then she fell to the ground in tears.

My father touched his scalp, his fingers finding blood.

"You hit me?" He looked at her as if seeing her for the first time.

My mother lifted her hand to her face, shaking her head. Even from where I stood I could see the blood on her diamond wedding ring.

They say that Parvati always enjoyed a leisurely bath in the morning, but she grew tired of Shiva's habit of walking in on her while she bathed. He would playfully grope her breasts, or stand from a distance and watch her as she washed. Shiva was the God of destruction, and he was her husband, and so Parvati said nothing, even though she was a Goddess of great power herself. One day, though, she thought of a way to show him what she felt without being disrespectful. After she had anointed herself in oils, she chanted mantras of great power and scraped the oils from her skin, creating a soft putty that she molded into the form of a young boy.

"You are my son," she told him. "You will stand outside the door and not allow anyone to enter. If anyone comes, you will say that your mother is bathing inside and she does not wish to be disturbed."

She gave him a spear and the boy eagerly took to his position.

While she was in the midst of her bath, Shiva came back from his morning meditation with his trident in hand. He tried to brush past the boy, but the boy barred his way with the spear.

"I am here to guard the door," the boy said. "My mother is inside bathing."

"Step aside," Shiva said. "You cannot stand between me and my wife."

Shiva nudged the boy with his trident, but the boy struck the weapon aside with his spear.

"I am the destroyer," Shiva said. "There is no stopping me."

He shoved the boy, but this time the boy lunged with his spear, nicking Shiva in the arm. Shiva looked down at his arm and touched his own blood. He brought it to his lips. The boy thrust with his spear, but Shiva caught it with one hand. The boy struggled in vain against the God's strength.

"You cannot pass," the boy said.

"But I can," Shiva said, and he drove his trident into the boy's neck, separating his head from his body. He carried the head with him inside and threw it to the floor in front of Parvati.

"You should not have put this fool between us," Shiva said.

"He was of my own flesh. He was my son!" Parvati said, rising from her bath. "He was doing my bidding."

Shiva laughed and kicked the head aside.

"No being can stand between me and my wife."

In that moment Parvati saw her will cast aside like the boy's head. Shiva had promised her his love and respect on their marriage day, but now she realized that such words had no meaning to the God of destruction. She whispered the mantra of the ending of the world, ripped a lock of hair from her head, and dashed it to the ground.

From the ground erupted a massive four-armed being, black as nothingness, garlanded with the skulls of her vanquished. It was Kali, the devourer of time, the ender of all things. Shiva opened his third eye, hoping to vaporize her, but his gaze could not harm Kali. She struck him down and straddled him, bellowing her war cry. Shiva called for his armies, but Kali only grew larger, devouring them as they came. Shiva called for Vishnu, the preserver, for perhaps the two powerful Gods of the trinity could stand against Kali. But Vishnu could not draw near—Kali held him at bay with a wink of her eye, devouring his army as they raced toward her.

Kali began to dance, her ponderous steps shaking all of creation, cracking time and earth. All the beings of the three worlds, the Rakshasas, the Gods, and the mortals, screamed in terror at the ending of the world. Brahma, the creator, finally heard their calls.

His voice boomed across the skies. "Kali cannot be vanquished. Once released, she can never be contained. Only Parvati can stop her, for she is the one who called her. Appease Parvati or all of existence will vanish from my dreams."

With Shiva pinned beneath her feet, only Vishnu could act. He raced off into the distance, and, finding an elephant cowering in his path, lopped off its head and returned to Kali. He placed the elephant's head on the dead boy's body and beseeched Brahma to raise the boy to life.

Parvati smiled when she saw the boy alive again, and with her smile, Kali vanished like a wisp of smoke.

As I sat there at the bar, sipping my beer, I wondered about the choices available to the women I had known. My mother, powerless in her own marriage; my sister, held hostage in hers. Sita had been chained to a tree by Ravana, Draupadi raped by the subjugators of her husbands in the Mahabharata. When Sita had returned from Lanka on Hanuman's shoulders, the people had questioned her purity, and her own husband had forced her to walk through fire to prove her innocence. My own sister, in time, tried to end her life as proof she suffered. And what of Sarah? What would happen to her? My sister, Sarah, my own mother—they wanted redressing—and who is the agent of redressing but Kali?

The cop took off about thirty minutes later, saying that he was on duty. The bartender introduced himself as "Sully" and shook my hand.

"It always this busy?" I asked. There was only one other guy in the bar, talking to an empty pitcher.

"Give it another hour and you'll be swimming."

"As long as they don't mess with me."

"You're not a nigger, or a spic. I'll let them know."

"Thanks."

He nodded and stared at me for a bit. I looked into my beer because staring back seemed like an invitation to an intimacy I wasn't willing to bear.

"You're one of the college kids, right?"

"I go to the college, but I'm not like them."

"I can see that," he said. He smacked the bar and looked away. "Fucking land mines."

"It's tough during the holidays when you've got no place to go," I said.

"I hear you," he said. "But why come out here? I mean this town, not the school. I figure any kid like you really earned a spot in that place—hell, I'd go if I could, probably. But this town's nothing much. If you were going someplace, you should check out Boston. Now that's a city."

"This town's as far as I wanted to go," I said. "I just needed to find someplace real, if you know what I mean. That school's fucked up, and filled with fucked-up assholes, and I just needed to be someplace with normal folks."

He slapped the bar approvingly.

"You found a good place," he said.

We sat in silence. I sipped my beer and he set another out for me on the house, then busied himself with polishing glasses. When he was done he leaned in close and whispered, "You don't mind if I smoke some green, do you?"

I laughed. "Hell, no. I'd roll one up if I had any."

"That's good," he said. "I always need a little something before the night gets going."

He fished around in a drawer near the cash register then came back with some rolling papers and a little bag of weed. He held the bag of weed up to the light and shook his head.

"Roll for me," he said, stretching out for a cordless phone.

All he had left was a couple baby buds dry as bread crumbs. The weed was a vaguely florescent kelly green, but it glinted with a sharp blue when turned in the light.

"Crisp, clean. Keeps you sharp but mellow. You like and I can get you some. I'm calling my guy for my refill."

"How much?"

"A dime's a dime."

I held it to my nose. The smell had an earthy peppermint base, tinged with a hint of sea salt.

Sully punched a series of numbers into the phone, then hung up.

"It smells like it came from someplace warm," I said.

"He's on his way."

"Who is he?"

Sully shook his head.

"Look, kid. Just roll the joint. If you like, you buy some more off this guy. But I'd stop with all the questions. Nobody likes questions around here."

I wasn't very good at rolling—my fingers always seemed to disagree about how to proceed—but Sully's buds crumbled to dust at just the slightest pinch of pressure. The weed spread fine and even across the rolling paper, and the joint rolled like a machine cigarette. Hanuman later told me that things only work out that perfectly when you're at the crossroads of your own destiny.

Sully and I had been talking about baseball, working out a strategy for debating the inevitable hostile outsider who would rip us for obsessing about the Cubs (me) and the Red Sox (Sully) even though the teams sucked, when a tall guy in a hoodie, sunglasses, and a sparkling silver winter coat punched through the door.

Sully set a beer out for him, but the guy waved him off.

"Got to move," he said, then, peering over the edge of his sunglasses at me, he asked Sully, "How do you know this guy?"

"Came in off the bus. Says he's from the college."

"Friend of Sebastian's, right?" he asked me. He slid his sunglasses lower and winked at me. It was Eduardo, the drug-dealing townie Sebastian had introduced me to.

I nodded. "I'd asked you about getting a lot of things."

He tugged at the collar of his coat, revealing a zippered compartment that normally would have held a thin hood for the coat. He fished his fingers in and pulled out two teardrops of green and a tinier teardrop of white, the plastic twisted tight at the top, the bags cupped in the palm of his hand. He flashed the bags at Sully, then closed his hand in a fist.

Sully pulled a couple bills from his pocket, then shook hands with Eduardo, the money and drugs switching between their hands as if by magic. Eduardo glanced at the cordless phone and nodded, and Sully silently slid it to him.

"I got my boy here," he said when the phone finally connected. "Remember what I said about college? Yeah, he was at the Anchor drinking with Sully."

He spoke too quietly into the phone for me to hear what else was said, and after a minute he slid the phone back to Sully.

"Sully, as always, a pleasure," he said.

He slapped the table twice with a laugh, and gave a final wave to Sully. He motioned for me to follow him.

"What's going on?" I asked.

"I'm going to teach you the business of addiction."

The Twelve-Step House was painted in bright lemon yellow. Walden led me past a few tired chain smokers on the porch. The first floor looked like all the walls had been knocked down to form one big warehouse that could store a good chunk of the North Side alcoholics.

Walden led me over to Tats, who was already seated at one end of a thirty-foot table. Walden then took a turn around the room, waving at people, patting others on the back. There were more men than women in the place. People chain smoked, drank coffee from Styrofoam cups, laughed. Flannels and T-shirts dominated, with a hint of leather. One person was wearing a tie.

Tats pointed a lady out to me. She was a hatchet-faced woman with chestnut crimped hair and a pouty smile she flashed at anyone looking at her. She looked to be about thirty.

"She's leading the meeting," he said. "Her name is Mary."

Some old guys got comfortable in seats near Tats, and Walden joined them, giving me a wave. One guy had to be wheeled up to the table, and once he was in place, some more old-timers took seats around him, with some younger guys pulling up chairs to be near his space. "That's Marty T.," Tats said. "He's an original member. More time sober than I have alive. If you want to find the roots of AA, go listen to him." I could barely hear his voice over the bullshit spit rapid-fire around me, but all the heads around him were craned in, nodding.

At the beginning of the meeting Mary asked if there was anyone new to AA, but nobody raised their hand. When she asked if anyone was new to the Twelve-Step House, Tats nudged me, but I still didn't raise my hand. Some other guy did, and everyone clapped when he said his name. As far as I could tell it was the same AA bullshit—a lot of clapping. Mary told her story, which was mainly her rambling about being an only child and drinking and what a tough time she had and how she decided to get sober. It wasn't anything special. I tuned out after a bit, because as far as I could tell, she wasn't saying anything new.

When it came time for the comments portion of the meeting, people raised their hands and talked about how similar they were to Mary. I looked around, trying to find someone like me, anyone. Everybody was white or black. I looked for any Hispanics, but the only one I could see never looked at me. I kept bumming cigarettes off Tats and smoking. I tried to look at his watch. I listened to a few people, then spaced out some more. For some reason I kept expecting someone to say something magical, to reveal what the trick was. Nobody said anything important.

The mantra I kept hearing was, "Don't drink; go to meetings." I wanted to ask one of the old-timers exactly how I was supposed to not drink, or in my case smoke crack or shoot heroin, but after I'd ranted for a few mintues, Tats told me to sit down. He told me to shut up and listen. But I'd done enough listening already.

Tats joined me and Walden on the walk back home. He asked me what I thought, and I said it had been a good meeting. Walden and Tats then started talking about something, the weather maybe, that was completely unrelated to alcoholism. I was feeling real edgy, my neck stiff, my palms sweaty. They just kept talking.

At home a guy gave me a piece of pizza and sat down at the dining table and talked with me. My mind was in a cloud. I don't remember much of what he said. Every time I swallowed a bite of pizza, I tasted the bitter aspirin taste of cocaine sliding down my throat. When I inhaled off a cigarette, I held my breath like I was taking a hit off the pipe. I flexed my arms and looked for good veins.

More guys came into the dining room, shook my hand, said their names: Mike and Bob and Bill and Ted and on and on. They said I was in the right place. They told me they were painters and plumbers and carpenters and electricians and on and on. There was nobody like me in the place.

As soon as I got a chance, I slipped past them and went up the stairs to my room. I crawled into bed, clothes and all, and covered myself completely in my sheets. I concentrated on breathing. I tried to make my mind blank.

In my dreams I saw Hanuman carrying a mountain of crack toward me. I climbed it, using my pipe as a piton, smoking all the way. At the top, I discovered that the snowcapped peak was actually heroin. I didn't waste time trying to cook it up. I buried my head into a drift and breathed deep.

10

Before an individual can be saved, he must first
learn that he cannot save himself.

—**M.R. DeHaan**

Eduardo and I squeezed into his black hatchback. The
rear window had been replaced with a garbage bag,
and duct tape coated the back seats, a replacement for the ripped and
torn vinyl, but Eduardo was proud of the car.

"Turn off the lights at night, and the cops can't see this baby. And
it cooks—hell of a lot faster than it looks. It even can go off-road, and
that's saved my ass a couple times."

"I'm glad I caught up to you at the Anchor. I didn't think I'd run into
anybody I know."

"What the hell were you doing there anyway?"

"Roommate trouble."

"The kind that'll be a problem if you're dealing?"

"I fucked his sister."

He laughed and smacked me on the thigh.

"It's a serious problem," I said. "He's huge and he's psycho-religious. I don't know if I'll be able to get back into my room."

He shook his head.

"Don't worry about it. I'll take care of it for you. I can be pretty persuasive."

"We going there first?" I asked.

"My place first. I got what you need there."

"Then why'd it sound like you were getting permission from some-body when you used Sully's phone?"

"Because I was getting permission. I clear everything with Teddy T."

"Who's he?"

Eduardo cocked his head and gave me a quizzical stare.

"This is business. Teddy's real smart about not getting caught. That's all this is."

I shifted in my seat and tried to calm myself into thinking I was only taking a scenic drive.

"What's he like?" I asked.

"He's alright if he likes you," Eduardo said. "I mean, he gets tweaked sometimes and does stupid shit—you probably heard that story about him killing those college kids—but it's all about the money with him."

"You work with him long?"

"Since high school. I'm not officially part of his crew, but give it a couple years. He's starting to let me build my own crew, under him. That's when the big money starts to roll in, when you're a boss and not just a hustler. My big advice as far as he goes is don't lie to him and don't try to steal from him. And if he tells you to do something, don't bitch about it. He's got folks higher up the chain he has to answer to, and they shit on him enough."

Eduardo was surprisingly open about what he knew. Teddy had gone to a rival high school and wasn't much older than Eduardo. He'd been a legendary defensive lineman—all-state his junior and senior years—infamous for having paralyzed the opposing quarter-back with a cheap shot in the state championships. Some said that

Teddy hadn't gone on to college football because they wouldn't have let him enhance himself with speed and steroids at that level, but Eduardo thought the real reason was because Teddy never had the grades. There was no point going to a school to kick ass for a team when you could stay at home, party whenever you wanted, and kick ass for family and friends. People knew and respected him and his family here, and he had a real future running things in the area. If he went anywhere else, he'd just be another dork with a helmet working his ass off for nothing.

As for his nickname, Teddy "Two Doors," Eduardo had heard a lot of rumors. Most likely it was something given to him by his family because of his size, because his shoulders were so broad he always had to turn sideways to squeeze through doorways. Teddy himself liked to say it was because of his fists—there were the door to heaven and the door to hell, and if you ran into Teddy's fists, you were going through one of them.

"So it's just a reputation thing," I said. "He had to sound like a badass because of what he does, but as long as you're his friend, he's cool."

"Where'd you get that from what I've been saying?" Eduardo asked with a laugh. "Teddy's one serious fuckup. Maybe when he was a kid he was nice or something, but all the shit he's done and keeps doing's got him in a twenty-four-seven bad mood. Maybe some psychologist could give you all kinds of sweet-sounding bullshit, but the truth is, folks like Teddy only smile when they're hurting someone."

We gunned down the road, fog whipping by as Eduardo stuffed a massive wad of chewing tobacco into his mouth.

"My cousin came up short with Teddy once," Eduardo said, rolling his window down. "Teddy wrote the amount he owed on two blocks of wood, had me and some guys hold my cousin's hand between the blocks, then Teddy screwed the two pieces together. One of the screws had a tough time getting through the bone, so Teddy took a hammer to it."

He spat out the window, flecks of brown spittle splattering the window behind him.

"Be cool, listen to me, and work smart. Everybody starts out like this. You do right by Teddy, and he'll do right by you. You're a professional now."

Eduardo lived in a decrepit studio above a Greek pizza place on the main college drag. The thin, once-beige carpet was coated in stains that had layered atop each other over the years, smears of blood and jelly and mold congealing into sticky ridges. A boom box lay next to a sleeping bag in one corner of the room, a mountain of clothes piled beside it. A rusted, greasy stove leaned against a wheezing refrigerator at the other end. Stale smoke mingled with the fetid scent of the molding carpet, the pizza-oven aromas of melting cheese and garlic thick enough to taste. Nobody could ever really live in such a place. People rested in places like that for moments in their lives, breakdown lanes for lives with blown engines, and remembered it later with the nostalgia befitting of a temporary grave.

Eduardo opened the freezer and pulled out a strongbox with a combination lock. He popped the lid, revealing dozens of bags of weed rolled tight like cigars, a thin hint of frost coating the bags. He tossed me one of the bags, locked the box back up, and put it in the fridge.

"Teddy wants you to move that ounce this week. Two hundred dollars for the ounce. I'd say sell dimes to start, ten bucks a gram—that'll clear you two hundred eighty, leaving you eighty dollars profit. Do an ounce a week, in dimes, and make people get used to you being reliable and having good shit, and in the first month you'll pull a clean three hundred, with a couple grams for yourself. If you can move more, you can buy more—and you'll get a break for half pounds and pounds. Start offering coke, acid, shrooms. Know what they want, then get them to want more. Easy money."

"How am I supposed to break this up? I don't have a scale."

Eduardo laughed.

"Steal one from one of the college labs. Until then, borrow mine."

He handed me a foot-tall blue bong.

"She's clean and ready to go. Test her out. I think you'll like our green."

I packed myself a bowl while he fished around in his pile of clothes. Finally he stood up, a sleek and shiny gun in his hand. He jammed a clip in it and stuffed it in his pants.

"Where's your problem live?" he asked.

I gave him a blank stare. My biggest enemy was the asshole that shared my own skin.

"You know, the guy whose sister you fucked?"

"You mean Jonas. My roommate." I paused, staring at the butt of the gun peeking out from Eduardo's jeans. "You're not going to go do anything to him, are you?"

"What the fuck you mention him for if you didn't want him taken care of?"

I told him about Sarah, the Smith family, and Jonas's heavy fists.

"But he's a good guy," I said. "It's just that he'll never forgive me, and there's no way I'd survive living in the same dorm with him if he didn't. But you don't need to kill him over it."

"Kill him?" Eduardo laughed. "I was just going to negotiate a truce."

"You don't need to take a gun then."

I sucked a thick tube of smoke from the bong. I coughed, trying to hold the smoke in. It felt like I'd swallowed a tube of toothpaste, but the weed had a nice warming kick that tickled me into not caring.

"You said you had a roommate problem," Eduardo said, "and Teddy doesn't like problems."

"Don't kill him," I wheezed, trying to get my breath back. "And don't hurt Sarah."

"Don't worry," Eduardo said. "Whatever happens, it won't get back to you."

I hoped Sarah had gone home—I could write her a letter to explain the situation, work out a way to meet again, and neatly sidestep any problems her family might cause. If she was still in the dorm, though, Eduardo would have a problem. If he came in with his gun drawn, Jonas would try to take him down to protect her. If he came in peacefully, Jonas might stay calm for a bit, but if he scoped Sarah out, or mentioned my name, Jonas would slam him into a wall. The scenarios all ended the same—Jonas, startled, his mouth a big red "O;" Eduardo, gun held horizontal like a gangster, pulling the trigger with a demonic smile. The cops would come searching for me, and I would inevitably buckle under questioning. Then, while being led in chains to a courthouse, a black car would pull up, the window open, and I'd be silenced by bullets.

Eduardo set out his scale, a precision instrument enclosed in glass and labeled "Property of the Geology Department," and showed me how to tare it so every subsequent measurement would be accurate to a thousandth of a gram.

"You can use my sandwich bags in the fridge to divvy your ounce up," he said, pulling his gun from his waistband and double-checking the clip. He stuffed the gun into the back of his pants at the small of his back this time, and tugged his shirt out to cover it.

"I'm going with you," I said. "I can't let you do this for me."

Eduardo cocked his head.

"You know I'm just going to talk to him, right? I might scare him a little, but I'm not going to hurt him."

"It would start out like that," I said, "but you don't understand Jonas. You need me there to translate."

"You come, and there will be trouble. If I go, and he starts acting tough, I can let him know he's just a punk without lifting a finger. Trust me. It's like I've got special military training in this. I'm Teddy's ambassador to the college, and I don't start wars unless he tells me to."

I pushed myself to my feet, the buzz of the weed making the air feel thick and soft, the floor an unsteady mattress.

"Show me how to weigh out the bags," I said, "and when we've got everything divided, I'm going with you to talk to Jonas."

"I thought you were afraid of him."

"He's got that effect on people," I said. "That's why I need to see him."

.   .   .

Eduardo drove us over to the dorm, even though it was only a couple minutes' walk from his place.

"You could be a professional chauffeur." I laughed as he whipped around the speed bumps on the dorm drive.

"You think this is all I want to be," Eduardo said, slowing smoothly in front of the door to my dorm, "but me working for Teddy is only temporary. It's training for better."

"You listing him on your résumé?"

"I'm going into the Coast Guard," he said. "In a couple years, maybe."

"Don't they drug test?"

We got out of the car and hopped up the steps to the door.

"I'll be clean. I'll kick ass there, impress people—I'm a good leader, good with a gun too."

"You could end up a diplomat, brokering peace deals at the UN."

Eduardo nodded fiercely.

"You think you're fucking with me, but it's the truth. The world needs guys like me in those kinds of positions, guys that aren't afraid to make a decision."

Eduardo slid a card through the reader and the front door clicked open.

"I thought only students got an ID card for those readers," I said.

He shrugged.

"Can't do my work on campus if I don't have one. Don't worry, though. It's not mine. I've got a bunch of different student cards, so even if the cops got the reader to tell them who was going in and out, I'd just look like another student."

It made sense that the college's feeble attempt at security would only inconvenience students who'd forgotten their own cards. Doing anything more was a waste—the added expense would never keep out people like Eduardo.

"You're invisible," I said as the door slipped closed behind us.

"That's the point," he whispered.

. . .

The dorm was eerily silent as we walked up the stairs. Eduardo slid from step to step on the balls of his feet, his hand at the small of his back, waiting to snatch his gun. I clomped up the stairs, my hand thudding the railing. Despite Eduardo's glares, I kept it up, pretending I didn't understand what the fuss was about until he finally hissed "Quiet!" He was too late. Our door up the stairs slammed open.

"You'd better find someplace else to stay," Jonas yelled.

"That's what we're here to talk about," Eduardo called back. "I was told that you assaulted this young man."

"You don't know what he did."

"I'm coming up to find out your side. I need you to guarantee that you won't give me or him any trouble. This is out of your hands now."

"He's the only one that has to worry," Jonas called out.

Jonas was sitting on the couch, his hands neatly folded in his lap, when Eduardo and I entered the room. Sarah was nowhere to be found, but since the door to Jonas's bedroom was closed, I assumed she was hiding in there, her ear pressed to the wood.

Eduardo steered a chair up in front of the couch and sat down, pulling the gun from his back and resting it on the armrest. I stood by the door, propping it open with my foot, ready for another sprint down the stairs.

"I thought you were the police," Jonas said, staring at Eduardo.

"In a way, I am," Eduardo said. "You call the police when the bad guys are fucking with you, when you need protection and you don't know how to get it. I've been called in to deal with you."

Jonas glared at me.

"You're a coward," he said. "You'd rather hide behind a man with a gun than face up to what you did."

I couldn't look at him.

"He's not the one you should be concerned about," Eduardo said.

"Fine," Jonas said, crossing his arms over his chest. "Say what you need to say. I'll listen, but it won't change anything."

Eduardo shook his head wearily.

"This isn't some movie where you're guaranteed a happy ending. Be smart and shut up and listen very carefully. My employer has some plans, and he won't be happy unless those plans work out. If anything looks like it's going to get in the way, my employer will remove the distraction."

"I'm not afraid of you," Jonas said. "The moment you walk out, I'll call the real police."

"I might come back and be less friendly, or one of my fellow employees might need to pick your sister up and continue where my associate left off."

"I don't believe you."

Eduardo rose from his chair and picked up his gun. He pointed it at Jonas and clicked the trigger, then clicked it again.

"The only difference between what just happened and what will happen is that I didn't put a clip in. My associate wanted to talk. I think it would be in your best interest that you do. He's not going to be able to move out of this room for a while, and until then my employer wants him to be able to do good work for us. I think you'll find that you and your family are much safer and happier if my associate is able to do the work my employer wants. Do we have a deal?"

Jonas scowled at him, but nodded anyway.

Eduardo stuffed the gun back into his pants and pushed past me through the door. Before he went down the stairs, he leaned his head back in and looked at Jonas.

"I know how you feel. I don't like that this is how it has to be. Do me a favor and help us out. The sooner you understand that you have no choices here, the better."

When the door slid closed, Jonas and I could only stare at each other. The door to Jonas's bedroom popped open and Sarah peeked out.

"What was he talking about?" she asked.

I made my way to the chair Eduardo had been sitting in and fell into it.

"I didn't expect this to happen," I said. "I was just following up on something, and I let slip about the fight, and they decided what they were going to do without telling me."

"What, exactly, are you doing for them?" Jonas asked, anger seeping into his voice.

"I just wanted some pot," I said, "something cheap and decent that I could maybe make a few bucks with. I'd heard these guys were the way to go."

"Drug dealers?" Sarah asked. "What made you think you knew how to handle these guys?"

Jonas held his head in his hands.

"God is always testing us, isn't he," he said.

"They're killers," I said. "Eduardo—the guy you just met—he's not so much like that, I think. He acts like it, but he's a pretty nice guy. The others, though, Eduardo was telling me stories."

"Who's this employer he keeps talking about?" Sarah asked.

I shook my head.

"Some local punk. Crazy guy. You wouldn't know him. He goes by Teddy something."

"Teddy Two Doors," Jonas whispered, looking up at me in shock. "Do you have any idea who he is?"

"Is he the one, the guy at the lake . . ." Sarah said, her eyes wide.

Jonas nodded.

"There was a friend of ours from the church who tried to lead a prayer group in a town nearby," he said. "He went missing. A year ago they found his hands. There was a rumor that there was a witness, that Teddy T was involved. The guy's parents ended up mysteriously drowning in the Chesapeake Bay, and nothing ever happened to Teddy T."

"I'm just dealing a little pot for him," I said. "I'm sure he'll ignore me. He won't hurt any of us because he won't have any reason to."

Sarah crouched on the floor, hugging herself.

"We're all going to die," she said, looking at me with tears in her eyes.

"No," Jonas said. "We can't go to the police because Teddy will know if we do. We can't go to anyone. Only God can give us strength. God will see us through."

Jonas spoke with such a fierce determination that Sarah's tears stopped, and she looked at him expectantly. He was like Hanuman, full of faith and strength and free of fear. I had to turn away. He would make it his mission to help me; he would believe it was God's plan. And I, I would help him help me, I would make him think that I believed. But in the end, if it came down to choosing sides, I would trade him like a pawn. I would sacrifice him.

"You okay with what happened between me and Sarah?" I finally asked. "You willing to put that to rest?"

Jonas got up from the couch and walked into his room, closing the door behind him.

Sarah gave me a weak smile.

"At least he didn't hit you," she said.

Jonas put Sarah on a bus back home the next morning, but he grudgingly allowed me to go with them to the bus stop. He even allowed me to hug her good-bye, though I heard him firmly tell her that she shouldn't tell anyone about what had gone on during her visit. We walked back to the dorm in silence, though I kept catching Jonas glancing over at me as if waiting for something.

"I'm sorry," I finally said. "I didn't mean for anything to happen between us. It's just that when I was with her, it felt like we'd known each other all our lives, that we were meant for each other. It was like she was my wife and always had been."

Jonas stuffed his hands deeper in his pockets.

"Would you marry her?" he asked.

"I don't think that's legal."

"But if you could, would you?"

I didn't hesitate.

"Of course. I can't stop thinking about it."

"She said the exact same thing," he said. "I've never seen her like that. She kept saying it's what God wants for her."

"I feel the same way. Like it's destiny. You know, my dad married my mom when she was sixteen. He was nearly ten years older than her. I've got relatives that were married when they were twelve. If people are meant for each other, age doesn't matter."

"This all feels wrong to me."

"Jonas," I said, pulling him to a stop and forcing him to look at me, "I promise you that I will never hurt Sarah. I will protect her and love her as much as you do."

Jonas shook his head, his body twitching with an involuntary spasm.

"There's a voice inside me that says all of this is wrong, but I'm not sure it's God's voice," he said. "I don't know what it means."

"Judge me by what you see," I said.

"You shouldn't have slept with her!" he roared. "If God is okay with that, then everything I've been taught is wrong."

"I'm not sure you are wrong. Maybe this is just an exception. Is it that hard to believe that God allows some exceptions to his rules?"

Jonas pondered the question in silence as we walked, his hands ripping branches off passing trees, littering the sidewalk behind us with snapped twigs and shards of bark.

"My father always says that man looks to bend God's rules only when he begins listening to the devil's whispers."

"No way to know what this is until it plays out," I said. "But can you be cool with this, cool with me?"

Jonas looked me dead in the eye.

"I never will, but I'll pray for guidance and do as God sees fit."

With Sarah gone and the college students returning to campus, my life became a blur of studying and dealing. Semester finals were less than a week away, and I needed to cram a semester's worth of reading. I wasn't sure if failing all my classes would get me kicked out of school, and I didn't want to look at the academic guidebook to find out the specific punishments that lay in store if I did, but it was clear that not doing anything would be as bad as an hour session of torture with Teddy T. Flunking out of college would get me disowned, which would inevitably lead to me working full-time for Teddy. At the same time, if I didn't peddle Teddy's green, I'd end up dead, or, best case, have to try to write my finals with fingerless hands.

The moment that Hamilton and the boys were back in town, I hurried over to begin taking care of my life. I played it quiet at first, kicking back during the poker game, listening in on their stories of home while I fiddled with my cards. One of the guys had brought back a joint, and the guys passed it around, greedily sucking the smoke down.

"This all we got left?" Alex asked. "I'm jonesing big time."

"You guys should have saved some of your stash," I said.

"Wouldn't matter if we did," Hamilton said. "I had an eightball of coke in my room, and the janitors fucking stole it."

"You're shitting me," Micah said. "One of them snagged my U2 collection, but an eightball?"

"Dude, Jessica took the U2 before break when she dumped your ass—remember? It was hers," Alex said.

"Bitch kicked a hole in my speaker. Yeah. She back?"

"You sure it was the janitor?" I asked.

"Yeah, she's back. She's probably banging the guy that took Hamilton's eightball."

"Who else could it be?" Hamilton said.

"She's fucking the janitor? I'm going to kick his ass," Micah said.

"We got to do something," Alex said, rising up from the table.

The other guys stood with him, ready to find the janitor.

I pulled the ounce out of my jeans and slapped it on the table.

"I've got green if you want green," I said. "I got it off a townie over break."

"Oh man. Roll me some," Micah said. "I've got a fucking crisis over here."

"You were here over break?" Hamilton asked, staring at me.

"No reason to head home," I said quickly. "Thanksgiving sucks at my house, and, besides, the Moonie was stuck here, so I had some company."

"The fucking Moonie," somebody said. "You get him to smoke green, or he just preach at you?"

Alex grabbed the bag of weed and began dumping some out to roll.

"Hold up," I said. "I can't just give it away. The townie fronted me that. Charged me $300 for it."

"It any good?" Micah asked, eyeing the bag like it was a panhandler asking for a quarter.

"Solid," I said. "Good clean high, nice taste. Cheaper than I thought it should be, but this townie seems cool. He keeps talking about spreading the weed, spreading the spirit. Nice to see that not everyone's in it to make a buck."

"Those are the people you can trust," Hamilton said.

I scooped the weed back into the bag.

"I could maybe roll us one," I said, "but I need to get him some cash soon. It wouldn't be right otherwise."

I snapped my fingers, as if suddenly remembering.

"He said he had coke too. Maybe I could ask him about buying some of that."

The guys looked from me to the bag and then at each other. I saw the slight nod, the giddy lick of the lips. Hands dug into pockets. Twenties started flipping onto the table. Hamilton took the bundle of cash, counted it in his hands, then looked me in the eye, a thin smirk playing across his lips.

He dug into his pockets and added three crisp hundreds to the wad of cash.

"You've been busy while we've been gone," he said. "We've got enough for two here. Take the cash and get us another."

I took the cash from his hand and stuffed it into my pocket, sitting back down as Alex and Micah eagerly rolled joints.

"Now," Hamilton said, gripping my forearm and pulling me to my feet. "Get the second ounce now. And ask this townie of yours how much he wants for his coke."

Within twenty-four hours I'd sold three ounces of weed and a quarter ounce of coke and had orders for a lot more. I needed help, and so I looked to the guys in the room. Nobody wanted to help, and they all seemed pissed by the frequent ringing of the phone. I bought a stereo system for our suite with some of my cash, but that didn't appease anybody, and so I had to camp out by the phone so I could answer it immediately. The incessant ringing screwed with their ability to study, they said, and they didn't like the shifty-eyed folks who came over at all hours looking to score another bag. I told my roommates they were being assholes. I had just as much right to the phone as them, and it wasn't my fault if all the calls just happened to be for me.

The week of finals went by in a blur. In order to cram in a semester's worth of reading, I needed to stay up as many hours as possible, so I started taking a few sniffs of coke whenever my energy started to lag. Sometimes the mix of coke and my own anxiety about the amount of studying I needed to do got me too speeded up to think straight, so I puffed weed until my nerves calmed down. Hamilton laughed at all the fuss.

"If you want," he said, "I could find you some papers or whatever you need to get past your classes."

"I'm not worried about the papers," I said. "I took care of that stuff pretty easy. It's studying for these chemistry and bio finals that's got me worried. There's a whole lot to cover."

"Why are you taking chemistry and bio?" he asked. "Those classes are filled with those psycho premed jerks who study all the time. Good luck trying to surf the curve."

"I promised my dad I'd do the premed stuff."

"Why the hell would you make a promise like that?"

"Being a doctor is the new family tradition. Didn't your dad tell you what classes you should take?"

Hamilton shrugged.

"Just get a guy to take the tests for you. Maybe Alex could do it. I think he's premed."

"Alex's a nitwit. How the hell is he a premed?"

"Any idiot can be premed, and he totally knows how to work the system. He's a senior. The stuff you're doing is probably easy as hell for him, and if its not, he'll know how you can scam the test."

"That's alright. I'd rather risk it on my own."

"I'll get you the tests from the past few years at least. They don't change much. Profs are lazy bastards, especially here since we've got the honor code and they don't expect anyone to ever cheat."

I didn't take him up on it, though as the nights of cramming crept past, I often wondered why I was making things tough for myself. Hamilton had an easy out, and there really was no reason I shouldn't take it. I could always study the stuff at my own pace if I really wanted to learn it. Besides, how much of what I was memorizing was really going to be valuable to me anyway? I didn't see my dad spouting off on valence shells and gene expression. If I were a doctor, all that would matter was being able to talk to people in a friendly way and being able to look up their symptoms in a medical textbook. If I needed to learn the material, I could do that when I needed to. Still, despite all the good reasons to cheat, a part of me wanted to study and earn a grade on my own. Hamilton and his crew could get their good grades whatever way they wanted to, but if I was going to flash an A to my family, I wanted to feel like I'd earned it.

When I walked in to take my exams, I was still buzzing from the nights of endless coke lines. In high school my mind would have flipped through its mental pages to find the correct answers, but for the first time I found myself struggling to recall facts and theories. It felt as if each time I approached a question, I was plunging my hand into a river of knowledge, hoping to pull out something useful, and often pulling out a useless pebble instead. As students got up and handed in their exams, all I could think of was that there once was a time when I was always the first person to finish, where I was the person who set the curve.

The last of my finals came toward the end of the exam period, and so I found myself alone in my dorm room as the test approached. Salvatore, Jonas, and Kenny had finished up their exams and headed home for the winter break, leaving me to freak out on my own. I disconnected the phone rather than deal with the constant calls from students desperate to get high—if they really needed something, they would come looking for me. My regular customers knew to drop by my dorm room or look for me in the student union study area, but word of mouth had spread my phone number across campus, and so during finals week I kept getting calls from people I'd never met who were looking for some kind of edge that could keep them studying. Not answering the phone probably cost me several hundred dollars a day, but at that point I was more concerned about passing finals than earning Teddy T extra profit.

After I took my last final, I made my way to the student union to give my mailbox a final check. My dad had set up a plane ticket home for me, but I wasn't leaving town for a few days, and so I hoped I might run into some people at the student union and find a way to waste some time. I usually didn't check my mailbox at the student union that often—my high school friends weren't the kind to write letters, and my family called when they had something to say. When I did check my mailbox I'd usually find it stuffed with campus flyers and catalogs for J. Crew or L.L.Bean—I'd never bought anything from those places, but from the way everyone else dressed on campus, those companies must have assumed their clothing was part of the school uniform. That day, though, I found a curious letter mixed in with the usual assortment of junk: a plain white envelope from the Red Cross. I dumped the other mail in the garbage and ripped the envelope open. At the top of the first sheet, in big block letters, it said, "Your blood has been rejected."

I sat on the ground beside my mailbox and slowly read the letter, then reread it again. I could remember donating blood during one of the first weeks of school. The letter noted the exact date, then went on to say that I didn't have HIV. It repeated this statement, then explained that the Red Cross thanked me for my donation, but that it could not accept my blood. Finally, at the bottom of the letter it said that my blood had tested positive for hepatitis C, that the disease was potentially fatal and could be transmitted through blood. The Red Cross suggested that I talk about the situation further with my doctor. I kept double-checking the letter, hoping that somewhere it explained what the disease was, how I might have contracted it, or what I could do, but the letter was curiously silent on all the details I really cared about.

I pulled my knees against my chest to try to quell the feeling of terror shuddering through my body. My dad probably knew what hepatitis C was, but telling him I had it would bring up all kinds of uncomfortable questions. I didn't know how I'd gotten it, but he would want to know. If he determined that I'd gotten the disease by sleeping around, that would be it. He'd cut me off. I could see myself huddled in an alley, covered in festering sores, waiting alone for a painful, inevitable death. My family would disown me and feel good for doing it. That was the Indian way of dealing with shame.

I don't know how long I sat like that, caught in a despair that made all my worries about Teddy T or passing my exams seem like the troubles of some other fortunate soul. The thin winter light crept past my shoes as the sun set, pooling across the carpet until I could no longer distinguish it in the harsh overhead glare of the student union fluorescents. Outside the student union windows, snow lay like freshly pressed sheets, and I wanted to burrow deep within it and let the chill soothe me into sleep.

A wisp of hair tickled my cheek, and when I tried to brush it away with my hand, the sensation traveled down my fingers, settling in my palm. I held my hands away from me, blinking my eyes to try to shake the feeling, but the tickling persisted, jumping from hand to hand. There was nothing around me except for other students' discarded junk mail, gently rustling when a puff of air from some open door elsewhere in the building blew in. I shook my hands out, then clenched them into fists. For a moment it felt like my hands held a furry rope. I felt a sharp tug, and the sensation was gone.

"Where are you?" I asked, searching the mail room. No one was around, and the doors to the main hallway of the student union were closed. Either someone was fucking with me good, or all the nights of coked-up studying were finally getting to me.

I kicked the garbage can over, spreading the trash with my foot and finding nothing but paper and wrappers and empty cans.

That was it. I'd lost it. I swore to myself I wouldn't keep myself up three nights in a row with cocaine again.

I felt a flick of hair across my nose and sneezed.

I slumped to the ground and pulled myself into a ball.

Dainty pink snow boots tapped my feet until I finally looked up.

"Why're you sitting in the trash? It's too early to be wasted."

Eva grinned at me, whipping me playfully with the tassel from her Grinch-style knit cap that dangled down to her knees.

"Don't tell me you flunked out," she said.

"I didn't."

"Then what are you doing sitting here? Come on and get some dinner with me before the dining hall closes."

"You come here looking for me?"

She shook her tassel and grinned.

"You'd like to think that, wouldn't you?"

"How'd you do that earlier? I didn't see you but then you touched me and I still couldn't see you . . ."

Eva laughed.

"Whatever you're on, you definitely need to share," she said.

"You weren't here? Where were you?"

She raised an eyebrow.

"I had a psych final. Brutal. And then a long walk in the snow. I think my boots leak."

She stamped her boots for effect.

I shook my head.

"Never mind," I said. "I'm just glad you're here."

I grabbed her hand and pulled myself to my feet.

"So what is it? You get some shrooms? Or did acid finally hit this shit town?"

I handed her the letter from the Red Cross. She scanned it quickly and then looked up at me with a fierce determination. She grabbed hold of my hand and pulled me along behind her.

We sat together in the dining hall, Eva goading me to eat once I told her I hadn't had anything since before my morning final.

"You'll need your strength," she kept saying, and I could only nod at that.

"I don't know what I'm supposed to do," I said.

We went over my options. The first step, clearly, was to contact the Red Cross and figure out if they had made a mistake. If they hadn't, I needed to talk to a doctor and figure out what the hell hepatitis C was, how I'd gotten it, and if it was as bad as the letter from the Red Cross made it out to be.

"They could at least have given you an eight-hundred number to call," she said.

"I could call the infirmary," I said. "Maybe the nurse there will know what to do."

Eva shook her head.

"The nurses at the infirmary are nice ladies, but the only thing they ever do there is help kids who've passed out get sober. I saw them help a friend when she was having an asthma attack, but that's about the limit of what they do. They're really sweet if you get a cold and need someone to play mommy for a while, but if there's any real medical problem, they just send folks on to the hospital."

Eva had been babysitting for one of the doctors who did a weekday shift at the college infirmary, and since she knew his home number, she insisted on having me call him right away. She had been babysitting for him as a kind of family favor—her dad had gone to college with the doctor—and she was sure he'd know what I was supposed to do and be willing to tell me discreetly.

She dialed his number from one of the phones in the student union, and after a few seconds of friendly chitchat, relayed my situation and put me on the phone.

"I'm not sure what hepatitis C is," he said. "I know they found something that they were calling non-A, non-B hepatitis, but I can't say anything more than that for certain without looking it up. I wouldn't be surprised if it's a false alarm anyway. Regardless, hepatitis isn't all that big of a deal. Come in tomorrow, I'll check to make sure you're doing fine, and everything will work out. Don't worry about it."

"But what if it's real? What's it going to do to me?"

"I'll know tomorrow. In the meantime, don't do anything silly. Hepatitis is very contagious. Put Eva back on the phone."

Eva got back on.

"Please," she said, rolling her eyes. "I'm not fucking him, so don't worry about it."

She hung up and smiled at me.

"He always wants to act like he's my daddy. It's just because he's secretly got a crush on me."

"What did he tell you?"

"Not to touch you. In so many words."

"So I went from Brahmin to untouchable just like that?"

Eva laughed.

"Come on," she said. "Let's get you drunk."

While Eva fumbled to find the keys to her dorm room, I fought a desire to run off. I heard a whisper somewhere inside me, a muffled voice growling warnings about an invisible line I shouldn't pass. I was trying to have a relationship with Sarah, after all, and Eva was Salvatore's girlfriend, and it felt wrong to be too friendly with her, but I wasn't sure if that was because of the attraction I felt to Eva, or because of years of admonitions from my mother about the dangers of women. I knew from observing others that it was theoretically possible to have a platonic friendship with a woman, so I figured that if I treated her as I did Salvatore, then there wouldn't be any problem. The more I thought about it, the sillier I felt for worrying. Regardless of any hormone-inspired fantasies that might attempt to grab the reins of my consciousness, nothing would happen because Eva wasn't going to be interested. She was with Salvi, and she was trying to be a friend when I needed one. The worst thing I could do was mistake friendly affection for passion.

It helped that as soon as we entered her room she put on a Sarah McLachlan CD, thunked some candles into the open mouths of a row of empty wine bottles perched on her window, and then shoved me onto a bean bag and began dealing out my future with a deck of worn tarot cards. She uncorked a couple bottles of wine—she had a case ready in the corner—and gave me one while she swigged hers. She had a nice, cozy single room, thanks to the influence of her father, and she'd decorated it with batiks and tacked up posters of fierce and sultry sirens—I recognized Edith Piaf, but the rest were too hip and modern to be familiar to me. She yammered on about why she was a Wiccan and how great it was to be free of the chains of Christian fascism while flipping through a book that translated the pattern of cards she had laid on the floor. Finally she paused, lowered the music a notch, and earnestly pronounced that the cards said I was facing a big choice in my life, that I would struggle with my decisions, but that everything would work out for the best in the end. Then she said something about pentacles and swords, rambled about k.d. lang and how cool she was, and wasn't that a funny quote, that thing she'd said about penises being cute but useless, and that honestly, and I should swear not to tell him, but she was going to come out to Salvatore since she was bisexual and he'd better know about it and respect that since it was her choice, really, and anybody who said anything different was only trying to control her like her dad.

By the time her monologue finished, her pale, moony skin had flushed a gentle rose, and I was done with my bottle of wine. Her words had been a soothing melody, and I wished she'd continue with her lullaby.

"You're a quiet guy," she said, as if surprised. "That's a good thing, you know. Most guys are so boring going on and on about stupid sports or trying to impress you just because they think that'll get me to take my pants off."

"I wouldn't want you to take your pants off," I said.

"Why not? You don't have to lie. Everybody always wants to fuck. You know, the reason people go nuts is because they're repressing what they want. If they just cut loose and did what came natural, there would be no suicides."

"Was that on your psych final?"

"Oh, come on. You know it's true."

"Indians are repressed. My family more than most. But we're not suicidal," I lied. "That's a purely American sport—everybody competing to find the most painless yet spectacular way to die."

"That's because everyone in America is repressed. I bet if you really looked you'd find that people are killing themselves in India all the time. You just don't know about it. Suicide is a part of being human. It's what comes natural when you realize that life is just meaningless bullshit."

"Life is *maya*. Illusion. We get caught up in the bullshit, but that doesn't mean it's all bullshit," I said, leaning back with a deep sigh.

"It's sad, isn't it?" she said. "I mean, my family, we've got all kinds of money. And still we're all slowly suiciding. My dad has enough money to make a difference in the world, but all he does is sip Glenlivet and cut people down. That's why I'm so spiritual. I know all our money, this college degree, whatever—it won't do anything. Our only hope is if we find a deeper truth that makes sense of it all."

"Wicca is spiritual?"

"Of course it is!"

"I thought it was a cult."

Eva glared at me.

"But hey," I added quickly, "people think Hinduism is a cult too, so what's it matter?"

Eva shook her head and reached for her stereo remote. Tori Amos started wailing in the background.

We sat without speaking, nodding to the music. One of the candles in the wine bottles near her window burned down to its end, and as it finished, the last layer of wax crumbled and the flame plunged into the bottle.

"Even the candles commit flaming suicide," she said. She suddenly got up and moved closer to me.

"Why aren't you hitting on me?" she asked.

I sat up at that and eyed her warily, then tried to laugh it off.

"There's nobody around," she said. "Don't you want to?"

"That's like asking why I'm not out trying to rob the bank in town."

"It's not like we'd have to start dating or anything. Aren't you curious? We can pretend together for a night, make it feel like there's nothing else but us in the world."

"I don't want an illusion."

"It's that kid—Jonas's little sister, right? Maybe you're a pedophile. Were you abused when you were a kid?"

I shook my head, but words of defense didn't come to me right away. I felt like a beetle nestled deep in the sweet meat of a mango. She held the fruit in her hand, and she craved the sticky, seeping nectar. What would happen when she bit deep and felt me scurrying on her tongue, tasted the rot of my bed? When I opened my mouth to speak, it felt as if I wasn't the one in control of my voice.

"What we both need is what we already have," I said. "If all the world is crap, if life is meaningless, I'd rather try having something true with you than conjure a temporary lie."

"This is true," she said, leaning in and kissing me deep on my lips. She pressed her body against me and I could feel my body thrumming in response. She rested her hand on the bulge in my pants. "This is as real as anything can ever be."

I pulled away.

"Then it doesn't need to be secret," I said. "It can wait till after break, till after you've told Salvatore what you want to do. It can wait till I've worked out what's going on with Sarah. Otherwise, we'll be like thieves."

"I knew you were interested," she said with a sly smile. "Jonas's sister was just a fling. And now you're ready for another."

"That's all you want this to be?"

"That's all anything ever is until it proves to be more."

"We shouldn't do anything until the doctor tells me if I really have hepatitis C," I said.

"Don't worry. I have condoms."

She took my hands and forced them to her waist.

"There's nothing wrong with this," she whispered.

A voice inside me told me I should pull away, go back to my room and curl under the covers with my conscience intact. It was firm and logical, sensibly calm, quietly insistent and confident that it was right. And for that reason it was cold. It did not care for me, really— it wanted me to be a monument to some silly morality, a hunk of polished marble in the temple of the good and the right. It preached noble solitude, the *sanyasi*'s path to the land of virgin snow where the Gods sat calmly in judgment within the crown of mountains, sad-eyed at the sight of humankind squirming like maggots in the charnel pit below. But there was another energy within me that did not speak in words. It gave a taste of the electricity of skin on skin, the melting of mind and body into mercurial passion. It was the fire starter, the quick twitch that launched fists. It shunned word and thought, for those were the tools of deception. Only the visceral could be believed, for it was the common tongue of all humanity, the one shared proof that my existence wasn't a construct of another's imagination. By staying true to personal pleasure, by combining feeling and action into an indistinguishable one, my life could be simplicity. There was no such thing as wrong. There was only what I felt, and the authenticity of what I could feel, the promised sharing and conjoining of sensation, was the only power that could dissolve the illusion that I was alone.

My hands gripped her blouse and tore the cloth from her skin. I took her breast in my mouth and bit until I could taste blood. Her fingers clenched and she pulled back for a second, her eyes wide with a sudden fear. But she did not run. She looked down at her nipple, the red welling from the mark of my teeth. And I think, in that moment, she saw me as I was. She cringed at what was before her and yet she leaned toward me, gently biting my lips to taste her own blood.

The college infirmary was in a quaint yellow sided house a few blocks from the center of the college and would have been indistinguishable from the other houses on the block if not for the paved parking lot that consumed the front lawn.

When I gave my name to the receptionist and mentioned that I'd come in for hepatitis C, it seemed like I'd broken the rules. The little old ladies scurried around, and I could overhear them asking each other what hepatitis C was and if it was safe to take my temperature, or if I should be quarantined until the doctor could look at me. They left me alone in a corner of the waiting room, peeking out from time to time to make sure I hadn't keeled over yet. I finally had to yell out that the doctor knew I was coming and that he said the hep C wasn't anything to worry about just to get them to look me in the eye. One of them finally came out with her hands safely ensconced in gloves and handed me a glass of orange juice while I waited.

When they hustled me in to see the doctor, I found him waiting for me with gloved hands and a mask over his face. I handed him the sheet from the Red Cross and he gingerly accepted it, nodding to himself and huffing slightly as he scanned the page. He motioned me to the examination table and took a seat in a chair on the other side of the room.

"Do you know what you did to get this?" he asked.

"I don't even know what it is."

"Nobody's really sure," he said. "That's the reason there's no cure."

"I thought you were going to look it up. Should I head to a hospital and find some real doctors?"

"We'll need to be very careful with you," he said. "The last thing we need on this campus is a deadly epidemic."

"Look," I said, "I seriously doubt anything's wrong. I don't feel sick. Aren't there some tests you can run that'll prove I don't have this thing?"

"That would require a blood draw," he said. "Nobody here is comfortable doing that for you right now. And even if we did, we'd need to send the blood out to be tested, and it could take weeks for results to come back."

I hopped off the exam table.

"I bet if I grabbed a needle, gave myself a stick, then plunged the motherfucker up your ass, you'd find a way to figure out real quick."

The doctor got up and stood in front of the door.

"Sit down and listen. Think of the bigger picture for a change," he said.

"For a change?"

"You want other people's deaths on your hands?"

"What the hell are you talking about?"

"Hepatitis C is deadly. It's at least as contagious as AIDS."

"I thought you said you didn't know anything about it."

"I said I didn't know anything that could be done about it."

"I'm telling you. I don't feel sick."

"Nobody ever does at the start. Now's the time to act, though. It's not too late."

"I thought there wasn't a cure."

"I'm talking about protecting the community. We need to let the college know. We need to track down all your partners. Anybody you've shared a needle with, anybody you've slept with. We'll need to test everyone in your dorm. We might need to test everyone in the school. I'm going to recommend that we shut down the campus until we're certain how many people you've infected."

"Why don't you put a fucking poster up on everybody's door with my name and face on it? Tell them to find a shotgun and blow their heads off before they infect the rest of the world."

"You need to take this seriously. Your concern should be saving lives."

"Maybe you could start by trying to save mine."

He shook his head wearily.

"That's the problem with you people. You're only ever thinking of yourselves. Maybe if you'd paused and thought about the consequences of your actions, you wouldn't be here right now."

"This isn't my fault," I said, moving toward the door.

"I can't let you leave." He held his arms out and braced himself against the door.

I leaned in close.

"I'm going to see a real doctor," I said. "My dad will know what to do."

"Any doctor is going to tell you the exact same thing," he said.

"A good doctor would try to help me," I said.

He turned his head, and for a moment, with his arms stretched out, his head lolling against his shoulder, he looked to me like the asshole Jesus of my nightmares, the symbol the British had tried to ram down my ancestors' throats in order to save them.

I spat in his face. He let out a horrified scream, his gloved hands slapping at the spittle trickling down his cheek. I shoved him aside and opened the door.

A gaggle of the old ladies stood outside the door, but as I strode out, they bolted down the hall.

I felt stronger than I ever had before, full of righteous rage and power like the Rakshasas of old. If I was already dead, as the doctor claimed I was, I had nothing to lose. I must have seemed like Ravana when he roared through the kingdom of the Gods, an unspeakable evil, an unstoppable curse upon the world. All I was, though, was a scared college kid trying to figure out why he'd been sentenced to die. All my life my skin, my religion, my parents' beliefs had made me feel like I didn't belong. Now I knew the truth. It was my blood. My very blood was poison.

11

Yes, God is motionless, because there isn't any place where
He is not. When a child is sitting in his mother's lap, he can cry
for a million things, but he cannot cry for his mother to come.
We are all in the lap of the infinite Truth. It is nearer than your own
eyelashes. There is no distance between you and It.

—Swami Tejomayananda

When I arrived in Chicago, my dad picked me up at
the airport, eager to talk with me about how my first
semester had gone. All I wanted to do was dig through my suitcase
and fish out the eightball of coke I'd hidden in my deodorant. It had
been a long plane trip, and I needed a line to keep me going, especially
after the stress of waiting for my luggage to come down the conveyor
belt. I'd waited patiently long enough, forcing myself to look calm
when cops passed by the conveyor belt. If I'd been on an international
flight, there would have been at least one cop patrolling the area with
a drug-sniffing dog, ready to cuff me as soon as I touched my suitcase.
With the danger safely in the background, my dad chattering on about

some mundane piece of family trivia, it didn't seem right that I had to wait any longer for my coke.

"Can't you get us home any faster?" I asked him.

My dad motioned to the cars thronging the highway.

"You cannot rush in rush hour," he said.

"You can if you pick the right lane."

"No, that lane is where people are coming onto the highway and leaving it. That is always the slowest lane."

"The correct lane," I said with a sigh. "You've been in this country for, what, three decades? And you still haven't figured English out?"

"What is to be figured out? The language itself is foolish. It uses the same word to mean many things. Like how they say the food is hot and they mean it is *bishe*. And then they will say, 'Oh, I very much like hot food.' And that is when they mean *carra*. No wonder they are always killing each other. And then if you go to the south, they speak with such a *swara*! How is one to understand anything when they pronounce the same words so differently?"

"You knew what I fucking meant."

My dad smashed the horn with both fists and glared at me.

"There is no reason to speak foully to me!"

"What the fuck's foul about 'fuck'? You just said English has all these useless words. 'Fuck' is another fucking one of them. Do you even know what the fuck 'fuck' means?"

"Being in college gives you no right to speak like a hooligan."

"Jesus Christ. You need to chill out. Get us home already."

"You sound like a druggie. You go to a good college, I pay so much money for you to get an education, and you speak like this?"

"There's nothing wrong with drugs. Don't start up with that propaganda."

My dad shook his head, his jaw clenched.

"You cannot get my goat. I know what you are doing. I will not stand for it."

"Like that time you got pissed off over our Rubik's Cube and threw it out the window and then smacked us for crying about it?"

My dad eyed me carefully as the car slowed to a halt in the bumper-to-bumper traffic. He squinted for a second, then reached out and gently touched my forehead with his palm, then gripped my wrist, his fingers finding my pulse with practiced ease.

"Are you on drugs?" he asked quietly.

I looked him in the eye and took a deep breath.

"I just found out I have hepatitis C. The school doc said they're going to kick me out because of it."

Unlike the quack at the college, my dad didn't freak out. He gripped my palm tightly, then gave my shoulder a reassuring rub. He asked how I'd found out, and when I explained about the Red Cross letter, he nodded and said that it was highly likely they had it right. They would have tested the blood multiple times. They were a thorough group and wouldn't send out a letter like that unless they were certain. He paused and nodded to himself some more, as if jogging useful bits of information from the recesses of his memory. Hepatitis C, he said, was an interesting virus. There was some debate on how the virus was transmitted, but it seemed like it mainly propagated through blood-to-blood contact. He theorized that I must have received it from blood transfusions I'd received in the hospital as a baby—transfusions for platelets typically used multiple donors. Since that transfusion had occurred in the early seventies before anyone knew about the virus, let alone screened for it, it was the most likely cause for my disease. I didn't look jaundiced, and I'd been in good health for most of my life, so it wasn't likely that the virus had been doing any severe damage to me. If it became active, it could rapidly damage the liver, eventually resulting in liver cancer. Still, as long as I didn't drink or do drugs or anything silly like that, nothing would really aggravate my liver, and so the virus would most likely remain dormant.

"An American," he said proudly, "would have died from it by now. All their drugging and foolishness. But we are a healthy people, and you will not drink or be drugging, so there should be no worry."

He rubbed my shoulder again.

"Don't worry. I will bring you to the hospital with me. We will do some more blood tests, investigate your liver panels, measure the viral load. If there is any problem, we will find a way to fix it. But there will be no problem. God is watching over us."

I nodded and turned my head away from him, trying hard to control my breathing. He had such faith in me, such incredible love, but I couldn't recognize it as that at the time. To me, in the moment, it felt like he was trying to take control of my life, and my lungs tightened as if my family's tentacles were squeezing the life out of me. All I could think of was how quickly I'd take my suitcase up to my bedroom when we got back home, and how I'd draw myself a nice fat line. I could already taste it in the back of my throat. But I also resolved right there to slow down on the drinking. Drinking was bad for the liver, and my dad was right—I needed to be more careful. I could cut back to drinking maybe only once or twice a week, maybe only a few beers at a time. No way was I going cold turkey just because he thought I should— that was clearly just him trying to impose his screwed-up morality on me. No, I could make things work my own way. I could substitute with weed, spice things up with coke. It wouldn't be too bad at all.

When we got home, my father took me immediately to the family room so that I could revel in our Christmas tree. The only reason we had a tree was because we had been conditioned in school to expect presents and believe in the fairy tale of Santa Claus, and my father, reassured by his colleagues that presents and Santa Claus had nothing to do with religion, decided that we too could take part in the annual ritual of consumerism. Each year the old tree inevitably toppled over when feet tangled in the extension cords, causing branches to bend and shed their plastic pine needles. We'd strangle the tree in lights, cover the bare patches with clumps of tinsel, then heap on whatever Christmas ornaments we'd made in our grade school years. Topping it off was the star I'd made in kindergarten out of tongue depressors— the glitter long lost, the wood showing the stains where glue had once been. We kept the tree near a wall so that we could hide the fact that we'd somehow lost a third of the branches in the transit from family room to storage box to basement. But this year he'd bought a new artificial tree, double the size of our old one, as if, now that the last of his children had headed off to college and returned, the lurking danger of his children being corrupted by the magic of Christmas and converted into Christians had passed. Of course, the tree still looked like it was chained down by the tinsel and our incompetent childhood attempts at ornaments, but my dad seemed proud of it.

"More space for the grandchildren's gifts," he said.

My sister had two kids and was on the verge of a third. Her college education stalled during her first pregnancy, and though she finally graduated with honors in biology, she now chased her children while her husband scrutinized management books in his attempt to crack American corporate culture. The family celebrated her motherhood, taking pride in her fertility, talking about how wonderful it was that she had brought more children into our family, giving us an excuse to continue the charade of Christmas. She didn't seem unhappy anymore, and I wondered if Hanuman had rescued her the way that Agni, the sun God, had rescued Sita, if he kept her safe in his kingdom in the heavens while my maya-sister doppelgänger suffered on earth with us. When I asked her if she was happy with her life, she smiled brightly and said that all was working out well for her, that she had no complaints. I thought that perhaps, in time, Hanuman would return my real sister to me, but I didn't know if Hanuman answered prayers, and I wondered if having a Christmas tree in order to fit in with the American holiday spirit was a blasphemy that prevented us from receiving his presents.

Over dinner, while my family filled my sister's children with the lies of Santa Claus, my dad announced we would be traveling for Christmas. A few days before the holiday we would caravan toward the green hills of West Virginia, where my father's youngest brother had become a medical god to the black-lunged coal miners. My grandmother, Varadha, would be there as well—she had been shuttled off to live with my uncle and to help with the rearing of his young kids. I remembered her as a silent woman, trapped in America, longing for the clay huts of our ancestral home. She lived in nostalgia, remembering the simple life in service of Kali that Narasinga and Kupana Bhagavatha lived, but when I was young, she had been kind to me, teaching me to tie my shoes, whispering to me that my family did not belong in America and that she would convince her sons soon to return to the land and the duties that owned them. Instead, she was shuttled from son to son, acting as a nanny for their children while her sons anchored themselves further to America. Not knowing English, her only understanding of the country came from her interpretations of the concerned faces of newscasters and the images of violence flashed on the nightly news. It was why she would never walk outside the house alone anymore. She believed that America was the world of Rakshasas described in scripture.

I looked forward to seeing Varadha again. I knew she would have found a comfortable couch somewhere in my uncle's house where she could read prayer books and keep her eyes on my uncle's children while being close enough to the kitchen to tell my aunt how to cook dinner. I imagined sitting beside her, listening as she quietly told me stories in Thulu of the way our family had been. I longed for her nostalgia, for I could imagine myself in that ancestral place where a part of me still belonged, at peace, confident of who I was and what I was supposed to do with my life. She was a reminder of the simplicity that came with dharma, with doing what one was destined to do.

Before we left for the trip, I wrote Sarah a letter. My first letter had been written out of a sense of guilt and obligation, gesturing toward sincere notions of love so she wouldn't feel that I'd used her, but the more I wrote, the more I began to believe that there had been something magical between us. I had written her a few letters after Thanksgiving, but hadn't received a response. I wondered if Jonas had told his parents what had gone on between us and if they now took it as their responsibility to ensure that she never heard from me again. I'd called once from the dorm, hoping to get her on the phone, but I'd hung up when her dad answered. I'd realized at that moment that he probably controlled the phone and was the first to the mailbox, a snarling guard dog vigilantly protecting his family from disruptions in faith. Still, I'd resolved to write her a letter every week. I'd stop if she ever wrote back and told me to stop sending her letters. But until then, I wanted her to know that I thought of her constantly, that I kept imagining ways of rescuing her from her family. I told her the story of how Sita had been captured and held against her will, and how Rama kept searching for her and finally found her with Hanuman's help. I'd carefully implied she was my Sita. If her dad looked over her letters, he'd only see me retelling some pagan story, and perhaps be less inclined to burn the letters. But Sarah would know, and in knowing that I was searching for her and that I would not give up, she would find a way to reach me. With each letter it became easier to write to her about myself, about what I imagined for us, because I cloaked my confessions of self, my proclamations of desire, in the veils of myth. My father's advice on the hepatitis C was transformed into a speech by King Dasaratha on the Rakshasas in our blood, the way my mother annoyed me was retold as a speech by the venomous Kaikeyi who had convinced Dasaratha to ban his son Rama to the forest. And I told her even of Eva, and of Teddy T, couching the situation as the problems brought on by a Rakshasa king and his beguiling seductresses. The truth became blurred in myth, the myth confused by the truth, but through it all a single thought scintillated on the page: I would find her and I would rescue her. Myth was the best way to capture what I felt for her, because what was occurring between us was not some typical love story. We would come together or be split apart, actors in a grand play teetering on the verge of tragedy.

As we drove to West Virginia along the ribbons of highway suturing America together, I stared out at the barren fields, the snow like tight plaster protecting the seeds of future grasses and corns. I wanted to lie beneath that shield of ice and whiteness, to let the cold turn my blood into a slush that would slow the churning of my mind. I was being very careful with my coke, snorting thin lines during bathroom breaks to keep my edge up and to try to preserve the meager eightball I had. But I was afraid of West Virginia. My uncle and aunt were there, with their New World Indian views of what made a person worth knowing. It never crossed my mind that what they thought of me was irrelevant.

We had set off from my parents' house before the first hint of dawn, and by the time we reached West Virginia, night once again reigned. My young cousins scampered out eagerly to greet us, their parents smiling from their position at the door. Everyone seemed happy to see each other, but I felt a sense of dread. I quietly made my way inside, dropping my bag off near the door and looking for my grandmother. She sat on the soft couch near the kitchen, just as I imagined she would, her head turned toward the noise of the door, an expectant look on her face. I walked toward her and gave her a wave.

"Sreepada?" she asked.

"No, Srinivas," I said. "Sreepada's son."

She laughed.

"I may not be able to see well anymore, but that doesn't mean I don't know whose son you are!"

As I came closer to her, I felt the lingering ache of my coke craving dissipate, and my worries about my uncle and aunt disappear. It was as if an aura surrounded Varadha that immediately transported me to someplace safe. It was like when I was younger and I ran to my grandmother after cutting up all the negatives in my mother's stack of family photos—I'd been entranced by the color of the negatives and had wanted to slice them and place the images in new orders and create a new movie for the lives of the people within them. My mother chased me, scolding me, but at that young age, the difference between being yelled at and beaten seemed very small. I'd run bawling to my grandmother, and when she held me in her arms, my mother had turned away. And my grandmother told me that whatever I'd done, it must have been God's will. If it hadn't been, I wouldn't have been able to do it.

Sitting beside her, I felt as if no time had passed. The safety she offered now was the same as that she offered then, and I felt that as long as I stayed near her, Teddy T and all his henchmen would be as powerless to harm me as my mother had been so long ago.

My grandmother took my head in her hands and squinted as she brought her thick glasses closer to my face. She shook her head and smiled.

"You grow like a giant," she said. "You have Kupana Bhagavatha's size, but your father's face. How come it has taken you so long to visit?"

"My college is far away," I said.

"Not so far as our village is from here," she said, "and there are roads from your college to here. Not so for our village. There are many seas between us, I have heard. Much water, and very deep. How many days' walk would it be for you from your school?"

I shrugged.

"Nobody walks in this country. I don't know how long it would take to walk anywhere. I'm not even sure how far away I am."

She nodded. "That is the problem. None of you know where you are or how far you are from where you need to be."

We sat smiling at each other. Suddenly she raised her forearm and shook it, marveling at the loose skin hanging like an empty sack off her arm.

"Isn't that strange? I feel like I am a young woman still hiding underneath this skin. Maybe it will peel off when I have passed away and I will emerge from it when I am near your grandfather and we will be as we once were."

"What about rebirth?" I asked. "I thought we were all to be reincarnated?"

She laughed.

"I am done with being reborn. I feel it. I am ready for more."

"I think reincarnation is just another lie to make us less afraid of dying."

She gave me a stern look.

"I hope not. That would mean we have all wasted a lot of time." She cocked her head. "Or is that your reason to disobey your parents?"

"Have you been talking to everyone else like this?"

"Oh no. They think I have nothing worthwhile to say." She laughed and rubbed my arm with her hand. Suddenly she stopped laughing and took her glasses off, leaning in close and staring at me.

"Something is wrong with your skin. Are you sick?" she asked.

"I'm not sick," I said, but then I suddenly felt like I couldn't lie. "In some ways I've been sick for a long time."

The rest of the family burst in, laughing and smiling as they walked past us toward the kitchen.

"They should treat me like Kunti, a mortal woman whose children revered her even though they were sons of the Gods," she said, "but they will only realize that when I'm gone." She nodded and whispered to me, "You at least always listened to me. Did you know that I was always telling you important things even when you were living far away? I have been trying to do for you what Kupana Bhagavatha has done for me in the years since he died. He tells me important things when I need to hear them. He started when he was dying, telling me to send Sreepada to him. He thought of me and just like that, I heard his voice in my mind."

I nodded and smiled at her.

She patted my arm.

"In this family, we know how to watch over each other, even after we have passed from this world. It is a blessing we have. All your ancestors are watching you, you know. They always know what we do, and they have been talking to you like they talked to me. I can tell."

"I'm not so sure about all that," I said, "but maybe I just don't know how to hear them."

"You hear them," she said. "They ensured you came here, didn't they? They have been watching over you. I know this for certain."

Then she raised herself slowly to her feet and creakily made her way after the throng congregating by the coffeepot. I sat on the couch, running my hand over the depression she had created in the cushions from months of sitting in the same spot without moving. It made me think of the sages who would sit in one spot doing tapas to the Gods for years in search of a boon. They would sit like that, ignoring their hunger and their thirst, ignoring the bites of insects, until trees grew around them and enveloped them in their bark.

That night, I had a number of opportunities to sit down and talk with my grandmother. There was a moment before dinner when she sat on her sofa and looked expectantly toward me. And after dinner, when she was again sitting on her sofa, I could have taken a spot beside her. Later, when the television was boring me, I could have gotten up and walked over to her. Or when she slowly dragged herself across the room to take a spot beside me, I could have waited for her and talked. But I didn't. I saw her looking at me, and I knew she knew what was wrong with me. She could sense the coke, I was sure, that little baggie in my pocket. She could sense the hepatitis C running hot in my veins. I thought her sad eyes staring longingly toward me were a sign that she would spill my secrets in front of the family. So I avoided her.

I'd locked the door so I could wash up for bed and do a line of coke in peace, but when I lifted my head after my line, there she was, smiling at me in the mirror. Other people might have freaked and dumped their coke right there, wondering how and why she'd unlocked the door without making a noise, but with the sharp edge of the buzz lifting me up, I just smiled back at her. She wasn't wearing her glasses. I calmly twisted my baggie back up and put it in my pocket. Odds were she had no idea what I was doing.

"I'm too old for you to just come walking in the bathroom," I said. "Did you lose your glasses?"

"I don't need them anymore." She tapped her nose. "There is still some on your nose."

I wiped it off.

"I shouldn't be doing snuff," I explained. "I keep it secret because my father wouldn't understand."

"Snuff is brown," she said, the smile creeping back onto her face, "but you can keep lying to me if you want to."

"It is a new kind of snuff," I said. "Just like what Grandfather used, but a better kind of tobacco." I put toothpaste on my brush and went to work on my teeth.

"When I have gone to the forest, when I am in Hanuman's hands, you will feel sad about lying to me."

I rolled my eyes.

"I swear, I'm not lying to you."

"I wanted to tell you good-bye," she said, her hand lingering on my elbow.

"We're not leaving until after Christmas."

"Still, I have been wanting to tell you good-bye." She pulled my face to her and gave me a peck on the cheek. "Remember to listen for me. I will be watching out for you with our ancestors, and we will guide you when you need our help."

I knew I shouldn't, but I decided to tease her. "But how will I know it is your voice and your advice and not some Rakshasa's?" I asked.

She stared me in the eyes and smiled.

"That is not what is difficult. We always know. The only issue is which voice we choose to follow."

And then she was gone, vanishing from the bathroom when I blinked my eyes. I thought little of her words, more worried that she was going to tell my family about the coke. As I fell asleep, I decided I would have another talk with her in the morning to gauge if she was about to tell my parents what was going on. I could discredit her pretty easily if it came to that—she was old, and I could convince them she was imagining things based on some wild TV show.

I didn't get the chance. The next morning, I was woken by the sound of frantic bustling in the house, and off in the distance, the sound of an approaching ambulance. They took my grandmother out of the house in a stretcher, a mask bathing her in oxygen, her face frozen in a peaceful smile.

We waited in a room sterilized of all emotion except grief, my cousins and my aunts quietly searching each other's faces for some hint of strength.

When a doctor passed or a nurse bustled by, our heads turned in unison, hoping for someone to come in bursting with news, to pass out cheer or misery like cigars ending the pregnant pause left in the ambulance's wake. My father and my uncle were deep within the recesses of the hospital, blurting out suggestions to the doctors caring for my grandmother that any medical student would have thought of, these twin medical gods reduced to quivering children, helpless in the hands of fate. Only my mother stood strong, quietly reading an ancient piece of paper she had safely pressed between clear vinyl sheets, her voice a low, soothing hum.

"What are you reading?" I asked quietly.

"The Hanuman Chalisa," she said.

"Is that the same prayer I catch you reading every night?"

She was always reading her prayer books at home, usually until three in the morning. I'd always liked it when she did that because then at least she wasn't complaining about her knees, joints, the hassles of menopause, and the latest villain: her diabetes.

"One of them," she said, nodding. "I always read it when someone in our family is in danger. It calls for Hanuman to help us. He is the bringer of cures."

"What happened to the rest of your prayers?" I asked.

She fished into her purse and pulled out a plastic bag. Neatly wrapped within were torn and worn pieces of paper, the words faded.

"That's not cool," I said. "One of the kids tore them up?"

"Oh no." She looked down sadly. "It's my own fault. I read them so much that now the paper is dissolving in my hands. I don't really need to hold them, though. I know the prayers by rote. But still, I like holding the prayers when I pray. It is a comfort."

I felt a sudden surge of generosity strike me.

"Give them to me," I said, "and the Hanuman Chalisa too. I could take it to a copy place while we wait and get them done up nice."

She looked up quickly, carefully placing the Hanuman Chalisa into the plastic bag.

"Good," she said. She turned to my aunt and asked her about the copy places nearby, then fished into her purse and handed me ten dollars.

"Go to Kinko's," she said. "The nurses will tell you how to get there."

My aunt dug out the car keys from her purse and handed them to my mom.

"I want you to photocopy everything. Do it very carefully." My mother paused, rubbing her hands against her sari. "If they have a computer, I want you to print borders for the pages. Something nice and colorful, with flowers. Laminate the pages. I would also like a spiral binding."

She put the keys in my hands. I looked from them back to her, then back to the bag.

"Go! Go!" she said, "Copy, decorate, laminate, and bind. If they ask for more than ten dollars, bargain them down."

I waited at the Kinko's counter for the curly-haired lady who'd taken the prayer sheets from me to return. I hadn't bothered with trying to do any additional design work—Kinko's had a computer I could have used to design the flowery edges my mom wanted, but I needed some act of rebellion to show my mom that I wouldn't be so easily conned into doing everything she wanted. I'd already wasted enough time trying to explain to the lady what I'd needed done. She'd at first told me it was impossible, that the heat of the lamination process would burn the originals beyond recognition. Only when I attempted a West Virginia twang, turning my Is into Ah's and lengthening my Us, drawling a bit for clarity's sake, did she understand that I needed her to photocopy the originals and then laminate the copies.

"These things look really old, darlin'. They antiques?" she asked.

A part of me wanted to lie and tell her that she was holding a sixteenth-century document in her hands, that the Hanuman Chalisa was an important scriptural document handed down through the generations by my family, and that I'd been sent to the Kinko's to find some way to preserve it. As ludicrous as the story was, I had an instinct she would believe me, that she would take her time with my mom's prayers and treat them the way I wished my mother treated me.

"No," I said. "They're just my mom's prayers. One of them is pretty neat though. It's called the Hanuman Chalisa and my mom was saying that it's a special prayer that—"

"Just looks like scribbles to me," she said. "And your momma tore 'em up? Not much respect for religion, if you ask me, but that's your business."

Before I could respond she'd turned and headed into the back. While I waited at the counter, I saw her toss the prayers on a photocopier then walk away. Soon I heard yelling in the background, and I saw a pudgy man in shirt and tie hustle out, waving off the woman as she came after him complaining about her hours, that it wasn't her shift, that it wasn't her fault if Jason was too drunk to come in for work, that she had kids, she had responsibilities. The manager kept shaking his head, repeating, "You do what you got to do."

Finally the woman ended up in front of the photocopier, and while she continued her tirade against Jason, calling him a "no-count sonuvabitch" before quieting into a series of mumbled epithets, she slapped my mother's prayers one by one into the photocopier, smacking the copy button with such force that the machine shook each time.

A black man in sunglasses stepped up beside me at the counter. I looked over at him and gave him a friendly smile. He shook his head.

"Why she so angry at you?"

"It's not me she's angry at."

"Maybe she is and you just don't know it."

I nodded. The woman continued her tirade, then glanced over at us at the counter. She gave a big sigh and her shoulders slumped. Her hands moved more quietly in their pummeling of the machine.

"What she copying for you?" he asked.

"The Hanuman Chalisa. It's an Indian prayer. My mom's favorite."

"I know what it is. I always wanted to go to India."

"I didn't know what it was until my mom told me."

"I been a bus driver thirteen years, a carpenter for over twenty-five."

"I sometimes think I'd like to be a writer, but I'll probably just end up a doctor."

"My mom's a writer. She's the one kept telling me to go to India with my wife. Said it would open my eyes. I never listened to her."

"I try not to listen to mine."

"I shoulda gone. You get the chance, you should go."

"There's nothing stopping you," I said. "Just get a couple tickets and fly. Figure it out when you land."

"Breast cancer. Took my wife last year."

He was holding three pieces of paper in his hands.

"I'm sorry," I said, and I meant it. Not just because I was uncomfortable, but because he looked like my dad did when I'd last seen him at the hospital.

"Sorry about the sunglasses. I should look a man in the eyes, but I can't. Never know when I'm going to cry."

I folded my arms across my chest. That much honesty is never a good sign. I kept my eyes on the papers in his hands.

"You want a mint?" he asked.

They were drugged. I'd slip a mint into my mouth, and the next moment I'd be bound and gagged.

"I'm not into mints."

"They were my wife's favorite."

He pulled off his sunglasses, dabbed at his eyes with a handkerchief, then turned away, leaning against the counter heavily.

"I always hated them. But I liked that she liked them."

That didn't mean they weren't drugged. But I also couldn't rule out that he'd been carrying the hated mints in his pockets for a year. Had he bought new ones, or were they the last ones he'd found in his wife's purse?

He held one of the mints up in the light.

"She popped these like medicine. They didn't do anything. They just dissolved in her mouth, a little at a time, until they were gone. She said she didn't need to suck on them. She bought them and put them in her mouth, and they disappeared. A little bit at a time until there was nothing left."

He pressed his handkerchief to his eyes, and his chest heaved silently. He looked up at me, his eyes red, then put on his sunglasses and looked away.

"I been meaning to quit smoking for a long time," I said.

"Smoking?" He shook his head, staring at the three pieces of paper in front of him. "How long you been a smoker?"

"Six months," I said, hurriedly adding, "but it feels like longer."

"We used to both be smokers. She quit with mints. I didn't."

I wanted to quit smoking. If for no other reason, so I wouldn't be the motivation for somebody else's mints. The mints in his hand, they seemed more important than the Hanuman Chalisa. They had become memory that never leaves.

"You mind if I have one?" I asked.

"I can't stand them. Go ahead and have one."

He pulled his hand out of his pocket and deposited a slightly melted mint in my palm. For a moment his hand lingered, and I could see his other hand fumbling with something in his pocket, the noise like the clicking of a rosary. I put the mint in my mouth. It had a sea tang, salted by his sweat.

"We should have gone to Egypt. We wanted to. It's a wonder anyone built the place, and it made us proud thinking that someone did. It's lasted so long."

"My grandmother's dying," I said. "That's really why I'm here."

He pressed the handkerchief up under his sunglasses.

"It's tough," I said. I wanted to find the right words, but all that came to mind were clichés. I told him I understood, that I sympathized, that God's blessings were with him and that he had to keep going. "At least she had you," I said. "My grandmother—I don't think she had anything but her memories."

"What I remember most are the arguments. I can't lay down my sack of stones. Dr. King said undeserved suffering is redemptive. Not for her. I told her she was my best friend, a month before she died. But all I remember are the arguments."

He took his sunglasses off and flung them in disgust at the ground.

"I'm dying too," I said. The tests we'd run in my uncle's hospital were clear. The viral load was high. The ultrasound showed abnormalities in my liver. It was only a matter of time. The only question was how long. "But we all got to stay strong."

"I got to stay strong for the grandchildren, for my kids."

"My mom says she's praying for my grandmother. She's also praying for me."

"I want a copy."

"Of what?"

"The prayer you're copying."

"The Hanuman Chalisa? It's a bunch of crap that won't mean anything to you."

"Hanuman can cure anything, even the past."

"You won't understand it. It's a Kannada translation."

"You ever pause to think that if I know what it is, maybe I know how to read Kannada too?"

I looked him over again. He was smiling, but I couldn't tell if it was because he was feeding me bullshit, or because he knew I thought he was bullshitting me.

When the woman came back with my mom's laminated prayers, and I ended up being short seven dollars, he covered the difference. I handed the money to the woman, and she stared at me, as if expecting more.

"I'm not tipping you, if that's what you're hoping for," I told her.

"You haven't even paid what you owe yet!" she said.

"I paid you," I said firmly, turning back to the man. If she couldn't count the money right, it wasn't my problem.

The man asked for my mom's beat-up originals, so I gave them to him, keeping the laminated copies.

"Hanuman can forgive the past, you know," he said.

I shrugged. "I don't know much about what he can do. Only what my mom told me."

"Ask her," he said. "Ask her if suffering has purpose."

The woman was still staring at me.

"Are you planning on paying for your copies?" she asked.

"I already did," I said, showing her my empty wallet.

"You can use a credit card, you know," she said.

"Can you believe this woman?" I said to the man. "Some people will try anything to make a buck."

The man nodded and passed his three sheets to me.

"Ask your mother about these poems. From my wife. She said her cancer was a demon, but I know she meant me."

I folded them and put them in my pocket.

He tapped his chest with the scraps of my mother's prayers.

"These mean something," he said. "Don't think they don't."

"I never said they didn't."

He smiled.

"Your mom prayed with these a long time, didn't she?"

I nodded.

"You tell her I think that's beautiful. That's true faith. And true faith, it always heals. I take these with me, I know I'll heal too. I thank the Lord for putting you here today," he said.

"I'm glad I could help," I said.

The woman shook her head and rolled her eyes, huffing off toward the back of the Kinko's.

He laughed. For the first time. A small laugh that warmed me.

"Charleston is a beautiful place," he said. "Enjoy your time here. Tell your mother God will be with you on the way back home."

He smiled, bent over and picked up his sunglasses, then walked out the door. I looked after him for a moment, then, realizing I had no reason to stay, walked out after him. I wanted to ask him a question. But he was gone. I stood outside, pulling my pack of cigarettes from my pocket and lighting one up. I reached in my pocket for the papers he had handed me. They weren't there and when I went back in and tried to search for them, the lady told me I'd better leave before she called the cops.

"What's your problem?" I asked.

"You're the one with problems, honey," she said, shaking her head. "I start talking to myself the way you just was, I'd ask somebody to shoot me and put me out of my misery. You're lucky I don't report you for trying to skip out on your bill."

"I was talking to the black guy. The guy with the mints."

"Sure you were," she said, rolling her eyes, "and I'm Santa Claus's wife."

"We were talking right in front of you."

"Honey, the only person that's been in here is me and you and my manager."

She pointed to the door.

"You and your imaginary friend aren't welcome here."

12

The price of anything is the amount of
life you exchange for it.

—Henry David Thoreau

My father didn't want to leave his mother's side. He
and his brother took turns at her bedside, investigating her chart like astrologers waiting for an auspicious shift in
the planets. When my father brought me in to visit her, I saw my
grandmother's scans with him, the geography of her mind reduced to
two-dimensional black and white. On first glance the image looked
innocent enough, the expected blob of gray ensconced in a tidy white
cage, but in the corner, near her neck, loomed an encampment of a
large, dark army, paused for a moment before the final charge. The
radiologist's report was paper-clipped to her file, and stated that the
patient, a seventy-five-year-old woman who had presented in the ER
unconscious, had a cerebral embolism.

"She will get better," my father and uncle kept saying to anyone
who asked about my grandmother. They said it to each other before
my father led our caravan back home. My father said it again to me as

247

I prepared to get on my plane back to college, as my grandmother lay tucked between sheets, her arms and legs still twitching in movement as if ready to finally follow where her mind had already journeyed.

"My grandmother's dead," I told Jonas and Salvatore when I got back to the dorm.

"That is what Eduardo is saying about you," Salvatore said.

"She's actually not completely dead yet. A coma," I said.

Jonas nodded, whispered his condolences, then repeated that Eduardo had already been by our dorm room looking for me and that he seemed agitated. Salvatore went off on a long story about his grandmother that had something to do with a festival and lights and the taste of something special.

I couldn't hear him. If Eduardo was looking for me, I was probably in trouble with Teddy T. And if I was in trouble with Teddy T, then my grandmother and I were closer now than we'd ever been, caught somewhere between the dying and the dead.

Kenny banged through the door and paused upon seeing me. He gave Jonas and Salvatore a cursory nod, then looked uncomfortably at me.

"You need to see the deans," he said. "Right away."

I gave the room a suspicious once-over. Salvatore and Jonas shifted on their feet, hands in pockets.

"You guys trying to get me kicked out?" I asked.

"Don't blame them," Kenny said. "You're the one with the problem."

"We saw your grades," Jonas said. "You left all your work strewn around the room."

"Are you failing?" Salvatore asked.

"You guys went snooping through my stuff?" I shoved a chair against the wall.

"That's not the problem," Kenny said, his arms crossed over his chest. "I just got a note in my mailbox. From the infirmary. There anything you were planning on telling us?"

"That's none of your business either!" I yelled.

"It sure as hell is." He looked toward Jonas and Salvatore. "He's got some disease. They say we need to get tested."

"What disease?" Jonas asked, his voice cold.

"It's nothing," I said. "Hepatitis C. I just found out. And it's not contagious."

"How, then, did you get this hepaceces?" Salvatore asked.

"Blood transfusions. When I was a kid."

"And you just found out?" Kenny raised his eyebrows and gave Jonas a knowing look.

"It is contagious how?" Salvatore asked.

"I'm not sure," I said. "Don't worry. It's not a big deal," I lied.

"It kills people," Kenny said.

I felt Jonas's hand on my shoulder, heavy and strong. His grip tightened and I could feel my vision blur.

He leaned into my ear and whispered. "How long have you known?" he asked.

"End of semester," I squeaked.

He shoved me against the wall.

"And you wrote her letters!" he roared. "And you knew all the time and you didn't say anything. You called yourself Rama. Told her she was Sita. And now she'll die because of you."

He raised his fist, and I wanted him to hammer me into oblivion.

"You make me sick," he said, charging out the door.

"What was he talking about?" Kenny asked.

"His sister."

Salvatore and Kenny shook their heads and walked out after him.

I'd snagged my grades out of my parents' mailbox before I left, and my parents had been too oblivious to notice. When my dad asked, I told him that my official grades weren't in yet, that there had been some issue in one of the classes, and so grades would be delayed for a bit. I wasn't about to tell him that my best grade had been in poetry, and that I'd gotten Cs in my philosophy and chemistry classes, with a solid F for biology. The philosophy class grade I could understand—I hadn't cared for "dead old white man philosophy," and so the professor had taken a disliking to me. But the grades in my science classes had to be mistakes—I'd gotten perfect fives on the AP tests for biology and chemistry in high school, and we hadn't come close to covering the same material yet in the first semester. My professors must have made a mistake adding up my scores, and I wasn't going to have anyone lecture me about my grades when the only reason I'd done so poorly was professorial incompetence. When I'd applied to colleges, I'd received a notice from Northwestern claiming that all my materials hadn't reached them yet. When I'd investigated the issue, it had turned out they had created two files for me and split my admission materials between one that listed my first name as my last name, and the file that had my name listed correctly. My professors had probably made the same mistake and hadn't had a chance to correct it yet.

I would make an appointment with the dean and settle the grade mix-up and the hepatitis C nuisance. Both could be taken care of easily. Jonas might be a bit more difficult, but I was sure that if we talked things through everything would work itself out. Salvatore and Kenny would fall in line right after. There was no reason to worry.

But first, I wanted to call Eduardo to get some more coke and see if Teddy T was after me. Pissing Teddy T off was a death sentence. I knew what my priority had to be.

Eduardo and I flew over the icy roads, Eduardo accelerating so the car took air over bumps. He'd lay off the gas on the turns, spinning the wheel furiously, the car fishtailing before he wrested control from the forces of momentum. I had no idea where we were headed, and he hadn't volunteered any explanations.

"You could slow down, y'know," I said, my hands braced against the dashboard.

"You should take off your seat belt," he said. "If the car flips, the seat belt will kill you. We'll land on the roof, and that seat belt will hold you up. The weight of the car will drive you through the ground like a nail."

He grinned at me.

"I'm getting good at this. Next year, I'm going to get in a rally. You know, like *Cannonball Run*. Just tear across country. Flipped out of my mind, tripping. Win the whole motherfucking thing, get the cash, start something big . . ."

The right side of the car sliced into a snowdrift on the shoulder and Eduardo yanked the wheel left. Somehow we kept on down the road.

"Why you trying to kill me?" I asked.

Eduardo shook his head and laughed.

"Jesus Christ, you're uptight!"

He leaned across me, one hand on the wheel, one hand digging in the glove compartment.

"Quit fucking around!" I yelled.

He tossed a large freezer bag from the glove compartment in my lap, then looked up at the road just in time to skid us back on track.

"Quarter ounce of white, half pound of green. Two varieties on the green, good and better, so make sure you don't sell it cheap. But here's the magic—an ounce of shrooms, and twenty-five hits of acid. Teddy's being real cool about it—just twenty-five hundred dollars, and you can get it to him next week. Anytime you call me, I can deliver the same package. Thing is, he said you owed him some bills—I forget how much. But he wants to see you catching up, and I told him what you're getting on campus for this, so he's getting impatient."

"I already owe him about five hundred dollars. I took an eightball home for Christmas instead of selling it," I said. "I'm not sure I want to be responsible for moving this much."

"That's not your decision to make. And he said you owed him about fifteen."

"That's bullshit!"

"Maybe it is, maybe it isn't. I'd suggest taking him at his word."

"Then I'll get him his fifteen hundred dollars, but that's it for me. He can't jack me around like this."

Eduardo laughed and punched me in the thigh.

"That's funny. But, seriously, keep moving this stuff for him, and he'll lay off after a while. You've got to prove you're a reliable worker.

You're good at this, and once he's sure you won't flake out on him, you'll start seeing some big benefits. Trust me, okay?"

"What kind of benefits?"

"A lot of good things happen when you're a friend of Teddy T. He's got connections. The folks he answers to love guys that do good business. Teddy said you got a future."

I shook my head.

"I already had a future. I don't need him giving me one. With him, all he can offer me is two choices—either he kills me or fucks me over."

Eduardo shrugged.

"Yeah. That sounds right. But it's too late to whine about it."

My chest felt tight. I tried to take deep breaths, but it hurt to breathe. I leaned my head against the cold glass of the window, the jouncing of the car causing my head to smack against the glass. The pain felt right, but I felt like I was going to throw up.

"Don't freak out, man," Eduardo said, reaching a hand over to give me a reassuring rub on the shoulder. "Take five hits and down an eighth of the shrooms. You'll feel better."

"I can't move this much crap that fast! People just got back from break."

"Wake up, bro. You think I don't feel the pressure too? Trust me. Take a few hits of acid, some shrooms. You'll see things clearer. You won't worry about moving the stuff. It's the selling season. Time for you to sell, sell, sell! Winter study, man. Don't you know the way your own school works?"

Eduardo knew more about my college than I did. I'd assumed that classes would start up right away, but Eduardo explained that I had another month of holidays ahead of me. His voice became a soothing lullaby that I let convince me that things would work out alright. There were people like us and Teddy T, and the weak people of the world. We were always the ones in control so long as we never let ourselves forget that the weak people would do what we said because we were the ones who controlled what they most desired, who brokered the line between happiness and sadness, between the darkness and the light. I took a few hits of acid, chewing the paper to pulp and packing it in a corner of my mouth, following it with the shrooms, the stems and caps dissolving into a bitter powder that felt like tiny worms wriggling their way into the back of my throat. Eduardo did the same, banging the horn with a smile while he kept his car careening down the road.

When he'd finished swallowing, he took a swig from a bottle of soda and passed it to me. He tapped the freezer bag that lay in my lap and told me that being the one who delivered that on campus would transform my life for the better. People would want to be with me. People would care about me in a way I'd never experienced before. I would have a power over them, and with that power would come a loyalty and an openness. Winter study was my time to convert the entire campus. That month break between semesters was when students got the chance to take an experimental course for a pass/fail grade. It was a time to try something new, and it also was a time for students to kick back and party endlessly through the winter. Eduardo theorized that it was the college's way of keeping people sane during the harshest months of the year.

"This is the time of the year when it's best," he said. "Pretty soon we'll get the Den of Iniquity going, and—*Que chingon!* Did you see that—" He turned his head to follow something fading into the background, then snapped his head back to the road.

"Snow in this light, it just . . ." He shook his head and gripped the wheel tighter. "Okay, we need to get back before I forget what the road looks like." He gunned the accelerator, then slammed the brakes and put us in a spin, leaning into the wheel. Then he snapped the wheel back, his feet pumping the pedals, and suddenly we were rocketing back the way we came.

"Are you feeling it yet?" he asked.

I wanted to lean out the window and throw up. I looked at him, holding my hand to my mouth, motioning with the other hand for him to lower the window.

"Yeah, you might need to let it go out the window, but that window's frozen shut."

He pulled the car to a skidding halt, and I tumbled out the door, heaving into the snow on my hands and knees.

"Now is when it really begins," he said, patting me on the back, lifting me up.

I felt like we were still driving, my body rising and falling as we rocketed along. I couldn't feel the cold though I knew I should be freezing. I took deep breaths, the cold air crackling in my throat, but felt like I could never breathe deep enough. And through it all, my body thrummed, as if it had been humming a note all my life, and only now, in this moment, could I sense it, feel it doubling on itself, magnifying. My body shook from the soundless sound, a plucked string on an instrument wielded by chemical hands. I staggered with Eduardo toward the car, the gray and white of the landscape bursting with a hint of color at the edge of my vision, as if the world were a kaleidoscope everywhere except where I was staring in the moment. Off in the distance, atop a drift, I saw a massive creature. I squinted at it, tried to get a sense of its shape and form, but all I could make out was that it was large, that it was far away, that it was dark, and that it was looking at me.

"What's that?" I whispered, pointing.

Eduardo looked up and laughed.

"Ain't nothing but what your mind wants to see. Take another tab and whatever it is will get closer."

I'd never tripped before, and so as we drove back, I was unprepared for the rush of thoughts, the sensations that come with tripping. I'd heard rumors that people who tripped sometimes went insane, but I'd always thought it was just typical say-no-to-drugs scare tactics. In the moment, all I could feel was the rush, the chaotic jumble of my own thoughts, the insistence of my own senses asserting that colors surrounded me, that dust motes were dancing up my skin and trying to crawl underneath my fingernails. For most of us, our brains filter out much of what we see and hear—our brains protect us from the entirety of the world. It's not as if we don't sense or feel the world, just that our brain limits what we have to deal with so we can process and interpret the essentials. When you're tripping, anything the mind or body senses, you feel. All of it comes to the fore, and unless you are in control of your own mind, unless you know what to expect, the sensations will batter you to the ground. Hallucinogens are a poison, their beauty the result of the mind's struggle to reconcile its own impending death with the overwhelming vitality of the world.

I crouched in my seat, holding myself tight, trying to find a way to bring my mind under my control. The feel of the vinyl of the seat through my jeans, the chill of the air tickling my skin, the fog of my breath—all battled on equal ground for attention. My mind, meanwhile, surged with voices. There was not one voice of conscience and another of reason. There was a babble of voices, each one insistent on being heard. I was going to die, one of them said. I wanted to die, another said. I was going to flunk out of school, another whispered. Eduardo was going to kill me, they all agreed.

I felt Eduardo's hand on my back, rubbing.

"It's okay, man. Let it flow through you. I'm here for you," he said.

I could feel his nails. Why was he touching me? What did he really want?

"I'm gonna get you home," he said, "and we're going to take some bong hits, and that'll kick you off right."

"I want it to stop," I said, my hands shaking.

"Oh man, there's no stopping now. You'll be going until lunchtime tomorrow, at least."

"At least?"

"This your first time?"

I nodded, trying to take a deep breath but finding my lungs shivered too much for me to do more than gasp.

"Well, I guess we'll find out what you're made of. You're in for a ride, man. Just remember, go with it. Follow where it leads you. But remember, it's not supposed to be permanent. If it gets bad, I'll lock you in a room, okay?"

My throat constricted, and I had to remind myself to swallow and to breathe.

Eduardo patted my hand.

"Don't worry, man. I'm looking out for you."

Though the wind blew cold on my skin, when I closed my eyes, the heat of Madras summers filled me. My cousins and I, we were all fans of romances, trapped as we were in a house walled with Harlequins. Before the elders we kept our eyes averted, chaste and upright like the saints we aspired to be. But at night, as the flicker of torchlight took up the curve of the beach, we clambered up the latticework to lean against each other on the terrace.

My cousins' parents went off to a disco to dance. Four of us took care of the house, all of us only eighteen years old, yet ancient with the trickeries of lust. I taught them poker, licked rum off their breasts.

Afterward, they whispered about desire, eyes askance with respectable shame.

We were children at war, I said, and our bodies capitulated willingly. We strode through the lands the ancestors claimed were filled with fire, and we emerged unsinged. We made the journey together, because only in family is loyalty unconditional. Our bodies prospered, our hearts unfettered by expectation.

I taught them how to move their lips, the subtle pleasures of the shift of hips, the lovely lasciviousness of fingertips.

When Eduardo got me back to the dorm, Jonas told me I had an appointment with a dean. I stood dumbly, the doorknob in my hand, until Jonas came over and closed the door for me. I thought I was just starting to rise up out of the trip, but my mind felt raw and fatigued, hard on the edge of a headache, the thoughts and sensations dimmed by a static that overwhelmed all else like a sun flare. Jonas had to remind me to change out of my dirty clothes, and I slowly pulled out a set of clothes and showed it to him for his approval.

"I didn't know you had green jeans," he said.

I looked at what I'd set out and nodded my approval. Grass-stained jeans that I rarely wore, a green turtleneck that felt soft and alive, and a thick cable-knit green sweater that fit me snugly.

My mind buzzed with a spectrum of responses. I was afraid of what might happen with the dean, yet excited by the danger. I ticked off a list of acceptable answers, from a strident thumping of my chest to curling on the floor and weeping. I tried to focus my eyes on Jonas but found my gaze drawn to the movement of my hands, the way they still created faint trailers as they swished in the bright morning light.

"I need green," I said. "It's so cold out there."

"You're late for the meeting," he said, "but she said she would wait."

Salvatore walked in, saw the two of us, and walked back out saying that he was going to lunch.

"I'm taking you to the dean personally," Jonas said. "I need to get dressed properly and I want to show them the letters you've been sending my sister. Wait here for me."

He went into his room.

I nodded, grabbed my backpack, and headed out the door.

I kept pausing on the walk to the administration building that housed the deans. I thought I saw the shadow of a bird flitting across the snow, but when I looked up, it was only the wisp of clouds that would suddenly fade away, leaving me staring at the bright, hypnotic sun. I stumbled along the sidewalk, tripping over chunks of ice that suddenly materialized, pausing to touch the ground beside me where snowdrifts seemed to rise and then melt, rippling away from me as if carried by the wind. I was seeing beyond the illusion of the world into a canvas that I could transfigure with a thought. Time did not seem a one-way road. It froze, like my breath in the air, and moved if I brushed at it with my hands. Meeting the dean did not worry me. The dean was of the mortal world, but I was no longer chained by the same rules.

Jonas caught up to me at the door and steered me to the secretary, who steered me in to my meeting with the dean. The dean mentioned her name but I promptly forgot it, squinting my eyes so I could look out at the glare of the white fields melting and reappearing in the large picture windows behind her.

"Wouldn't it be better to be outside?" I asked.

The dean shuffled some papers on her desk and looked up.

"We need to talk about how to deal with your hepatitis C." She leaned forward expectantly.

I waved my hand at her, trying to loop her hair around my fingers but finding that she was five feet farther away from me than I thought.

"I love your hair," I explained. "What color is it?"

"Brown." She tapped the papers in front of her with a pen. "Your roommates are concerned about the health risks."

"It's not contagious," I said, shaking my head.

"You should tell your roommates that. You should talk to them about this. Have you told your family? During tough times, it's friends and family that get you through."

I nodded. I couldn't see her face clearly in the shimmering light, but my gut told me she was lying.

"You're very pretty for a dean," I said. "But I don't believe you."

She leaned back in her chair and steepled her hands in front of her face.

"Let me guess. The reason you're on academic probation has nothing to do with drugs."

I waved her off and smiled.

"I'm doing fine. I'm not on academic probation."

"Yes, you are. Your grades weren't up to standard last semester. We'll expel you if you have a repeat this semester."

"The grades I got weren't the grades I have."

"What?"

"I got good grades."

"I have your transcript right here."

I nodded.

"I'm getting As. They made a mistake."

Her pen tapping her desk made me think of woodpeckers. I got up, walked over, and took the pen from her hand, tossing it into her garbage can.

"You don't need it. It'll give you a headache," I said.

The dean stood up, her hands planted firmly on her desk, and glared at me.

"You can play games all you want, but we know what's going on. You're dealing drugs and you're failing your classes. To top it off, you may have infected half the campus with hepatitis C."

"It's not contagious."

"It can be transmitted to another person. And it can kill. We're not going to quibble over semantics when public health is concerned."

I took a deep breath and unsteadily rose to my feet.

"It's not contagious. It's a curse. And it's meant only for me."

She rolled her eyes.

"Don't count on us pretending with you. You're a danger to the community. We'll act if you don't. I want to see you making steps in the right direction, and I'm going to be checking up on you."

I shrugged.

She pointed toward the door.

"You should go and sleep off whatever you're on. Stop with the drugs, and start with the studying."

"Sleep," I said, and I smiled at her. "Perchance to dream."

I walked out and Jonas walked in, his eyes firmly fixed on the envelopes in his hand.

I did need sleep, but it wasn't the magical solution. Jonas hammered on my door close to dinnertime, and we joined Salvatore and Kenny and headed off to the cafeteria.

As soon as we'd set our loaded trays down, Jonas opened a notebook and began to tap his pen on an ominous list of discussion points.

"I think I made a bad impression on the dean," I said. "You shouldn't have let me go."

"You would have gone even if I told you not to," Jonas said.

"You're the one that made me go," I said.

Jonas shook his head and looked to Salvatore for support, but Salvatore was staring at something on Jonas's notebook.

"Many people have been calling," Salvatore said, "while you sleep."

"If they call again, tell them we have shrooms and acid now too."

"Hamilton called several times."

"I'll drop by his place sometime after dinner."

"He said he had moved. He is out of the dorms. A new place."

"I didn't think anyone could do that before the beginning of fall semester," Jonas said.

"He give you directions?"

Salvatore nodded.

"What about the rest of his crew. Those guys call?"

"Here's a perfect example of what I was talking about," Kenny said. "If he gave a damn about classes, he would spend more time in them instead of being a dope peddler. And you guys encourage him."

"I'm not peddling dope," I said.

"You know what I mean. And if somebody handed you dope, you'd be peddling it, no questions asked."

"What is this dope?" Salvatore asked.

"I'm just working for Teddy T for now. It's not permanent."

"When you flunk out, it will be," Jonas said.

"Is this dope, is it injected?"

"Sometimes," I said to Salvatore. "And I'm not flunking out," I said to Jonas.

"So the dean didn't say anything about your academic probation?"

"Maybe you should focus on your own life, your own shit, instead of worrying about me," I said.

"We all want to focus on our own lives," Kenny said. "Problem is that your life won't let us."

"You should not have touched his sister." Salvatore nodded.

"All of you can stay out of that one," I said. "That's between me and Sarah. It's none of your business."

"When she's fifteen, it's everybody's business," Kenny said.

"You've exposed her to hepatitis C. Did you bother to think to let her know that? You started up your drug operation in our room, and put us all in danger, but you didn't bother to ask us about that either," Jonas said.

"We talked. You knew the situation. There wasn't any other way."

Kenny got up.

"This is absolute bullshit," he said. "You guys can deal with this crap if you want, but I'm done. I'm going to ask for a new room."

"Go for it, asshole," I said.

"You coming, Jonas?" Kenny asked.

Jonas snapped his notebook shut and pointed it at me.

"You and I will talk later," he said. He patted me on the arm as he got up. "You need to start doing the right thing."

I waved Jonas off and motioned to Salvatore.

"Come on, Salvatore," I said. "We should head where we're welcome."

"I thought we were all having a dinner together?" Salvatore said.

"Not tonight. Not with them. I've got better shit to do than be lectured."

"You know what's right," Jonas said. "You don't have to be this kind of person."

I walked off, Salvatore hurrying after me. "He means no harm," Salvatore said.

"Maybe, but him and his judgment, his God bullshit—that's a hassle we don't need."

Salvatore looked at me, then looked down at his feet, but he followed me when I kept on walking.

Hamilton's new place was on the northern edge of town, wedged between the local highway and a road that branched off it; a solitary sign between the tip of the triangular house and the fork in the highway warned drivers. Candlelight glimmered in the bay windows, but it was the hint of techno-pop seeping through the aluminum siding that drew us.

We knocked at the door, and Hamilton yelled us in. The house had only one room. A sparkling new stove and oven, bracketed by a knife-scarred countertop and rusted sink, consumed the right-hand wall. A halogen lamp warmly lit one tip of the room, Hamilton's plush bed squeezed as close to it as physically possible. His sofa and TV filled the space between the bed and the front door, a couple chests of drawers bridged the gap between the two bay windows on the left wall, and though nothing cluttered but the candles by the window, the house felt cramped.

Hamilton lay sprawled on his bed in his boxers, a blond girl wearing only bikini bottoms hugging his leg, her head resting on his thigh. A nude brunette filled the space next to them, her hands folded neatly across her breasts, her legs spread wide with the disregard of the unconscious, Hamilton's fingers absentmindedly threading her pubic hair. At the sight of us, Hamilton carefully disentangled himself, the girls giving low sleepy groans, and sat up with a grin.

"You should cover them," Salvatore said, staring at Hamilton's sofa, "for their honor."

"Honor." Hamilton laughed. He shook his head. "They're from that boarding school outside town. The one for all the fuckups."

I'd heard of it—a private prep school for troubled upper-class kids gifted in hedonism. Some probably were there only because of overprotective parents, but most were genuinely screwed up. The school promised the parents salvation, offering a curriculum steered by good religious values. Since it was a boarding school, they also believed they could protect their students from temptation. Like most such arrangements, the only people who believed the lie were the administrators of the school and the parents who'd locked their kids in its temporary prison.

"We should come back when they're gone," Salvatore said.

I nodded. It was one thing to hand off drugs to Hamilton, another thing entirely to have underage naked girls witnessing it.

"They won't even know you're here," Hamilton said. "They're too wasted to know what's going on."

"Don't they have a curfew or something? How're they going to get back?" I asked.

Hamilton shrugged.

I said, "If they don't get back by curfew, you know they're going to be asked a lot of questions. It's one thing screwing around on campus, but I guarantee the police will come visiting if high school kids get involved. I can't deal to you with them as witnesses."

"Relax already," Hamilton said, getting up from the bed. He grabbed hold of one of the girl's feet and pinched it hard. The girl sleepily pawed at her face, but didn't move. "They won't remember anything, so there's no problem."

Salvatore eyed me uncertainly.

"They going to be okay?" I asked. "The shit will come back to me if you end up killing one of them."

"With what I gave them, no way they remember a damn thing," Hamilton said, striding over. "Now why don't you hand over what you brought me and get out?"

Salvatore shook his head and turned away. I looked at Salvatore and suddenly felt like I knew what the right thing to do was.

"Prices went up," I said, "and the way things work now, you've got to pay up front. And pay for what you owe."

Salvatore muttered something and walked out. Hamilton furrowed his eyebrows.

"Since when did you turn into an asshole?" he asked.

"That's just the way those guys are treating me," I said. "If I don't pay up, they cut me off."

"You people are all alike," Hamilton said. He walked over to one of the dressers and opened the top drawer. He fished out a wad of cash, stripped off a finger-thick bundle of twenties, and tossed the wad back into his drawer.

"My dad always said people show their true colors when there's money involved," he said, stuffing the cash into my front pocket.

"Business is business," I said weakly, handing him a rolled-up brown paper bag filled with his allotment of coke and shrooms and weed.

He flipped the bag onto his sofa and walked toward his bed.

"You can leave," he said coldly, dismissing me with a wave of his hand.

Salvatore wouldn't look at me as we walked back toward campus, and I wasn't going to try to coax him into being friendly. If he wanted to be pissed off, then I had no problem letting him sulk. It wasn't like he was my girlfriend. The longer we walked, though, with his muttering steaming out into the cold night air, interrupted only by the dull thunk when he kicked a chunk of ice ahead of him, the more frustrated I became.

"You've got to grow up," I finally said. "All that matters is keeping Teddy T off our back. You can't get caught up in the little shit."

"Hamilton is not some little shits. Do you see those girls? You think that is right what he is doing?"

"I can't say I know for sure what he's doing," I said. "It's not my place to judge."

Salvatore stopped in his tracks and spat off to the side, then glared back at me.

"You would do what he does?"

"What the fuck, Salvatore! It doesn't matter! Can't you get that? I've got to sell to him because Teddy T wants his money."

"Hamilton is an asshole," Salvatore said, enunciating the word with relish, "and you become like him. You become his friend."

I grabbed Salvatore by the shoulder.

"I don't have the luxury of being able to give a fuck," I said. "What you want me to do? Call the cops? Have them go over there and bust him and then bust us when he talks? He'll walk, we'll be locked up, and then Teddy T's guys will find a way to keep us quiet."

"There is always choice," Salvatore said quietly, "but you do not want the choosing."

I threw my hands in the air and walked ahead of him. I had enough to worry about without his bullshit. I walked fast to ward off the cold, and now I was mumbling to myself too. The dean was giving me shit,

Teddy T was riding me, and now I had to worry about people I thought I didn't need to worry about. Nobody seemed to appreciate that no matter what I did, there would always be shit to deal with. I'd thought my friends at least understood that, but friends were supposed to be friends. They were supposed to stick with me.

"You make no fucking sense, you know that? You want to be pissed, fine, but you know I'm right," I said, turning around.

But Salvatore wasn't there.

Alex cleared off the desk in his room, sending books and a bong clattering to the ground. While he freaked out about the spilled bong water, searching for something to wipe it up with and then finally stripping off his own shirt, Micah pointed at him and laughed. I wearily sidestepped them and began laying out my wares on the table. Eduardo had given me two different cuts of coke, so I ripped a piece off the brown paper bag I'd bundled everything into and set it on the table to provide contrast. I loosened up the bags of coke and let a bit of each cascade onto the brown paper bag. One had a touch of French vanilla in its color, a graininess in its texture that made it seem as if it had been chipped off a block of marble, ground up halfheartedly, and then left forgotten beneath the sun on a muggy summer day. The other bag was ivory white, smooth and consistent, as if it had been gently scooped from the shores of a pristine beach and untouched until I'd opened the bag. In a circle around the bags I laid out the other goodies Eduardo had made available—a chunky ounce of Mexican domestic brick weed, a few tightly rolled eighths of weed he claimed had been shipped by air and which seemed to fluoresce with a purple glow when held up to the light, and a couple ounces of his standard mint-twisted reefer. The tabs of acid lay neatly wrapped in plastic beside the weed, the dull matte of the paper concealing the power of what they contained. Right beside them I piled the earthy shrooms— the serpentine stems seeming to writhe amidst the cerebriform caps as if they were already alive with their own hallucinations.

When Alex and Micah got up from rolling around on the floor making fun of each other for intensifying the mess, they took one look at the table and nearly fell down again. Alex plopped into a chair, but Micah teetered on his feet, his mouth working soundlessly.

"As you can see, I've got two kinds of white," I said, "and there's no price break. They're both good candy, but the china white—I mean, I call it china white, but . . ."

"All of it," Micah said, nodding. Alex coughed and abruptly got to his feet with a big smile.

Micah enveloped me in a bear hug. "This is the most beautiful thing I've ever seen."

"I don't know if I can sell all of it to you guys," I lied. "I have to keep some for other folks, and I did promise some people . . ."

"We need it all," Alex said.

"But you know those assholes dealing to me—good variety, but they're jacking me on price. I don't want you guys thinking I'm ripping you off. This shit costs more than what it used to."

"It's worth it," Alex said.

I could charge them just about any price. Addicts like them could never walk away from that much candy on the table, and rich addicts like them might whine about price for a moment, but would hand over cash in an instant because it was as easy to obtain as a glass of water. But as I stood there with them, trying to slow my breathing, I realized I wasn't any different. The sight of so much candy on the table filled them with a desire that required instant gratification. And though a real dealer would have taken their money and moved quickly out the door, the thought that came to mind was that I would rather stay with them and dice lines all day.

"I can get this whenever you want," I said. "It's the new way of things. But as I said, it's got a cost. I peeled off some for Hamilton . . ."

"That fucking asshole. Moved into the death-trap house rather than stick with us. Called us fucking mooches. Can you believe that?" Micah said.

"I get the feeling he thinks everyone's a mooch," I said.

"Hope a truck plows into that place when he's sleeping. You know they've rebuilt that place three times?" Alex asked. "Every few years, a cranked-up trucker misses the turn."

"Yeah," I said, but I couldn't keep my eyes off the coke. "Cut me a line, will you? I'm feeling a little low."

"Yeah, no problem." The two started dicing the china white and quickly laid out a field of pin-thin lines. They each took a line and settled back, smiles spreading across their faces. Alex shook his head like a wet dog climbing out of a river, and Micah lifted up one of his hands and high-fived him. I grabbed the card from them and swept a few lines together so I had a nice one pinky thick and ripped it down with one of their rolled-up bills. I unrolled the bill as the coke kissed me hard, feeling a flush washing over me like a warm ocean tide. It was a hundred-dollar bill, and the sight of it made me smile. "For this, and I'm being a friend on this because I split off some for Hamilton, I need thirty of these," I said, snapping the hundred tight between my hands.

Alex and Micah exchanged a glance, and Micah grabbed my hand hard.

"We've got your money," he said.

Alex went to the bookshelf and yanked a row of books down, grabbing them one by one off the floor, thumbing through the pages, pulling out crisp bills that he'd hidden between them.

"Great hiding spot," I said.

"Nobody reads books," he said, counting out his cash and handing it to me.

"I don't got to run just yet," I said. "A couple more lines for the road."

The two nodded in unison and we settled down with the coke, carefully moving the rest of the weed, shrooms, and acid back into the brown paper bag.

"The deans said they were onto me," I said.

"They always know something about what's going on, but they're just fishing." Alex laughed. "They won't do shit. Too much hassle, and it makes them look bad that they let drugs on campus."

"But maybe the cops are pressuring them. Cops put undercover narcs on campus all the time."

"You're letting the coke get you paranoid, man," Micah said. "That only happens in the movies."

The two started thumbing through the shrooms and Micah pulled out his four-foot bong and packed a fat bowl with the good weed. They were giddy and laughing like children who had just discovered their Christmas presents under the tree.

I couldn't sit with them. I could feel danger lurking. Did the deans have cameras in their room already? Were the police listening in? I stuffed their cash into my front pocket and pushed myself away from the table.

"What the fuck?" Micah said. "Enjoy the buzz, man!"

"I've got things to take care of," I snapped, and I rushed out the door.

When Kunti was a young princess, her father sent her off to serve Durvasa, the greatest of the tantric sages. She served him dutifully, so Durvasa taught her a powerful mantra. She could use it anytime, and as many times as she wanted, but he asked her to be careful with it and use it only after she was married. When she said the mantra, whatever God she concentrated upon would be compelled to come to earth and give her a son. Kunti did not believe Durvasa would reveal a mantra of such power to her, so the next day she said the mantra while looking at the sun. Sunbeams pierced her womb, and she spontaneously gave birth to a son. She made a basket for the baby out of grass, and floated him down the river.

Later, she married the powerful King Pandu, a king cursed by a sage to die if he ever made love to a woman. Pandu kept the curse a secret, so everybody blamed Kunti for the lack of heirs. He was compelled to take a second wife, and when he took his wives to the forest with him for a spiritual retreat, he finally revealed his secret, and Kunti told him about her secret mantra. She called on Yama, the God of

Death; Vayu, the God of the Wind and Hanuman's father; and Indra, the God of lightning and the king of the *Devas*. She told the secret to the second wife, and that wife decided to call on the twin Gods, the Asvins. Unfortunately, Pandu could not restrain himself with the second wife, and died upon making love to her. In grief over having allowed his death, the second wife killed herself. Pandu's brother took over the kingdom, and Kunti was left alone in the woods to mother the children.

Her children were the sons of Gods, children of destiny. They listened to their mother. One of her sons, Arjuna, returned with his new bride, the princess Draupadi, whom he had won in an archery competition her father had hosted.

"Come outside, Mother, and see what I have won," he said.

"Whatever it is," Kunti said, "share it equally with your brothers."

So he did, alternating visits in a rigid schedule with his siblings.

And later, after his eldest brother, Yudisthera, had lost all their fortunes and gambled away their wife, Draupadi, in a game of dice, he watched as his enemies raped her before his eyes.

It was the path of dharma. He could not object. The path his elders set before him was to be followed without objection.

He would get his revenge in war, the great Mahabharata of Hindu legend. Kunti's children would shed their own cousin's blood and regain their father's throne. And when the throne was finally theirs, as Draupadi faded into the anonymity of their new harems, they watched Kunti walk off into the forest and throw herself on a funeral pyre. They did not join her. The kingdom needed ruling. The sons of the Gods had legends to attend to.

I took the stairs down, past the ballroom, through a wide archway that led to a long, ornate hall. Cheap gray carpet cloaked the wood floor, but the delicate alcoves along the walls hinted at a nobler past. A bay window at one end of the hall overlooked the last slope of the hills the college crowned, and at sunset, the shadows of the college buildings curved out into the valley below like a protective hand. The thick tide of years of paint couldn't wash away the scent of importance that clung to the walls.

Only one door opened off the hall, and it led to the best room in the building, a top pick in the annual housing lottery. Wisps of smoke curled from under the thick wooden door, the acrid scent of cigarettes entwined with the tangy smell of skunk weed in a seductive embrace.

Sebastian opened the door when I knocked, smiled at me, then swung the saxophone hanging from his neck to his lips and trilled a brief composition of somber notes that made me think of a languid sunset in the dead of winter.

"I like it," I said, clasping him in a bear hug, "but I've never been a big fan of music. Where's that from?"

Sebastian opened his mouth in mock horror, then patted me paternally on my back.

"College civilizes and educates most people, you know," he said. "Give it time and you will learn."

"Beethoven?" I guessed.

"My own composition," he said proudly. "An original, created on the spot. Your own private theme song."

He steered me into the room, waving his hands over his head to draw everyone's attention. About a dozen people lounged about the spacious room, most perched with drinks in hand on the burgundy-sheeted bed at the far end, chatting quietly or nodding their heads to the jazz whispering from the stereo. Indirect lighting gave the room a seductive sense of warmth. A series of tiny abstract oil paintings dotted the walls, vivid swirls of red and black warring with faint pastel lines that wove between stenciled words—"love" and "lust" in one, "war" and "Jesus" in another. Eva and Salvatore looked up from a corner of the bed, Salvatore's face frozen in an expressionless mask. Eduardo crouched in the middle of the room atop a threadbare Persian rug the size of my dorm room, nodding vigorously at the words of a big-breasted brunette who stretched beside him. He tilted his head in my direction with a wry grin.

"Everybody know my Indian friend?" Sebastian asked.

"As well as anybody should," Eva said with a smile. Salvatore stared pointedly at his hands.

Sebastian handed me a glass of white wine, sipping it first with a wink. Banging at the door called him away, and I sidled near Eduardo, who shooed me away without turning from the big-breasted brunette. I had a moment to glance at Salvatore whispering fiercely in Eva's ear, his hand a vise around her thigh, and she stared straight at me, cheeks flushed, before a wave of the sweat-drenched stumbled their way in, exhorting everyone to start dancing. Sebastian nodded approvingly until one of the hyper-drunk made a rush for the stereo. He blocked the path, scowling, but another in the throng offered up a CD. Sebastian looked the CD over and rolled his eyes, but when he turned to play it, the mob cheered. Nine Inch Nails thudded from the speakers. Eduardo and the brunette hopped up when feet started clomping around them, Eduardo throwing a good-natured elbow in the spirit of the mosh. Somebody clicked on a few green-bulbed table lamps in the center of the room, and candles sparked to life in the corners. The music, overly familiar and expected, an annoying ritual at every party, drew everyone into the middle of the room all the same, and I closed my eyes and let the rhythmic ebb and tide of the bodies carry me. The boundaries of cloth and self faded before the sweating insistence of flesh pressing against me, and I could smell in the heat of the bodies around me a simmering charnel passion that would subsume us all.

Something tugged the back of my shirt, and before I could brace myself, I lay sprawled on the floor outside the crush of dancers. I opened my eyes to the candlelit flicker of a jaw working furiously, spittle flying. I shook my head, tried to pull myself up, but a boot crashed into my chest and the world swam away. Rough hands yanked me up, spun me around, and a heavy punch dug into my gut, followed by another that caught me sharp in the teeth, sending a dull tingle down the length of my back. The taste of iron suffused my tongue, and my fingers, when pressed to my lip, revealed a wetness that glimmered darkly in the candlelight.

It bellied up to me, its sharp teeth frozen in a grimace, and I shoved the heel of my hand into its jaw. I kicked hard at its leg, and when it stumbled, I jumped atop it, hammering my fists, closing my eyes, my arms drumming. A strange new light came to the room, and the music faded. The wood floor was drizzled with red, a puffed and swollen face, its cheek pressed to the wood, staring wild-eyed at my fist. A keening, broken howl slipped past its misshapen mouth.

Eduardo pulled me away.

"Serves him right," he said, loudly. "Attacking a guy, no reason, from behind."

"Salvatore?" I said, crouching beside him. He lay weeping on the floor, one hand fluttering near his face like a butterfly with a broken wing. A pair of elfin green boots, a black ribbon lacing them up the side, delicately stepped outside the pool of blood.

"Is he okay?" Eva asked, crouching down.

"Salvatore! What the fuck happened?" I asked.

He blinked his eyes, stared at me, then shut his eyes tight. He gave a deep-bellied groan. His eyes snapped open and he reached a hand out to grip my collar. He pulled me close and spat in my face.

He growled something in Italian, then slumped back to the ground.

"Get him to the infirmary," Sebastian ordered, pointing to a few of the dancers.

A couple guys slowly lifted Salvatore up and carried him out of the room, followed by a handful of others. Eva stayed.

"What did he say?" I asked her.

She, like everyone else in the room, could barely look at me.

"I didn't know it was him," I said.

"It was dark. He surprised you," Eduardo said.

Everyone nodded and a few sat down and started talking quietly to each other. Sebastian flipped on some jazz to change the mood. Eva looked at me and nodded. She grabbed hold of my hand and squeezed. We moved over to the bed and sat beside it, pressing our backs into the softness of the mattress.

Sebastian mixed up a series of stiff drinks, passing them out to soften the tension of the moment. We sipped our drinks, murmuring quietly to each other, and I grabbed for more when the image of Salvatore's broken face flitted before me. Sebastian passed around a couple finger-thick joints, and while we passed and puffed, he and Eduardo set up a card table, placed a gilt-edged mirror atop it, then poured out at least an eightball of coke. Eduardo ripped through a few quick lines, then motioned for everyone to come to the table. We formed a line, kneeling before the buffet when it was our turn, rising to receive a communion wafer of acid when we rose. One by one we sprawled on the bed.

"That's the last time he's invited," Sebastian said, squeezing himself into an open spot beside Eva and me.

"I told you he was one inch from psycho," Eduardo said, "but my man was here to deal with it." He leaned over and reached his hand to give me a high five.

I left him hanging and shook my head.

"Salvatore's a good guy," I said.

"Good for an ass-whupping!" somebody said, and I heard the slap of a high five somewhere behind me on the bed.

"I hope he's okay," Eva said quietly.

"He'll be fine," I said though I knew better.

"I told him about us."

"I figured as much."

"You think I shouldn't have told him."

"That's the least of my worries."

"You should have heard the things he was saying about you."

I looked at her, then looked away.

"Any details about dealing?" I asked coldly.

"No," she said.

"What did he say?"

"Nothing you don't already know," she said.

Eduardo and I discussed the situation briefly when we went up to refill our drinks. Salvatore, we agreed, would be a problem. The only power he had left lay in what he knew, and he'd soon figure out that the best way to hurt me was to start talking to the right people.

"He's got to go back to the dorm to sleep," Eduardo said. "We catch up to him there."

"He'll understand if we play this right."

"This ain't the time to play," Eduardo said. "We need to make sure about this."

"I can smooth this out. Just don't involve that paranoid fucker Teddy T."

"Teddy T's already involved," he said. "He was the second Salvatore decided to be trouble."

Before I could respond, the lights in the room dimmed.

"Is everybody drunk enough?" Sebastian asked.

A murmur of agreement filled the room.

"Acid kicking in?"

"It's more than kicking," someone said to a chorus of laughter.

Sebastian went to the front door, turned back to us with a wink, and went outside. He came back a moment later leading a young woman and young man by the hand. Both were blindfolded, a thick black cloth wrapped tight around their eyes. A thin slip of iridescent green gauze covered their nude bodies, and where their skin shone through, red glitter twinkled.

Eduardo turned to me with a grin.

"Teddy T can wait," he said.

Sebastian led the couple to the bed and arms gently pulled them into an embrace. Eva slid the slip off the woman and kissed her belly. Sebastian's belt clanged to the floor with his pants. Eduardo strode over from beside me, flinging his collared shirt to one side, yanking his T-shirt off while walking. The lights clicked off, only a few candles lighting the bed. I lingered in the shadows.

Bodies plunged in, grips tight, lips hungry. The wet smack of lips, of flesh suddenly pressing into flesh replaced the buzz of zippers and the clink of buttons. I saw Eva sit up, silhouetted in the light, and then a large shadow blocked her from view.

A body rose from the shadows and came over to me. A hand tugged at my belt. A hand brushed my face, tracing my lips with wet fingers heavy with the scent of damp clay and vinegar.

"You're not allowed to watch," Sebastian whispered in my ear. He pressed his erection into my hand.

I swallowed the shock and shame that surged like bile, and discovered that underneath lay a current of desire. My people believed in an ascetic rejection of the pleasures of the Den. In Sebastian's room, their rules had no meaning. Navigating pleasure with wordless bodies, we were safe from the consequences of morality.

A good Indian would be satisfied with the pleasures of a good meal, or a day of work completed, the mantras chanted on time, the ritual performed precisely as it should be. But I was tired of being a body chained under mantras, my acceptable pleasures ritualized and diminished, the full potential of my human experience restricted and feared. The others in the Den would clamp down after college when they were measured by their billable hours. They would have their jealous spouses and nosy neighbors to hide from. A few, the artists and writers full of plans of catalyzing canonical change and revolutionizing human expression, might continue the exploration of the Den longer in life, unless they wandered aimlessly into the enforced dilettantism of trust funds and self-doubt and lost all sense of pleasure. In Sebastian's room, our desires made us one.

Our bodies drew together, our breaths indistinguishable. In the bed, Eva's lips found mine, and then the woman in the blindfold rubbed her thigh across my ribs. Lips traced from my knees up along my thighs, and I reached up to pull another body closer. Hints of lavender and patchouli pinpricked an electric musk. The scratch of a beard at the shin, an earring pressed against the navel, a warm and wet breast flush in the eye. We were desire.

The morning light revealed bodies strewn throughout the room. Some lay spent in bed beside me, others curled against each other on the Persian rug. Eduardo sat in a chair, rubbing his eyes and stretching loudly. The blindfolded woman straddled him, snoring quietly, one of her hands tied to an arm of the chair with the blindfold. Streaks of chocolate marred the sheets and the walls, evidence of the chocolate fondue Sebastian painted in the middle of the night on those who were still unsated. Eduardo gently lowered the woman from his lap. She curled on the floor, one hand still attached to the armrest by the blindfold, chocolate ringing her lips.

"We better go deal with Salvatore," Eduardo said, grabbing a towel and wiping himself off. He threw the towel to me and hunted for his clothes.

"Salvatore won't be back," I said. "They'll keep him for a while at the infirmary." The towel was coated in chocolate and damp from other people's fluids. I kicked it away and used a clean corner of the bedsheets.

"Good," Eduardo said. "We can get to your place and wait for him. It'll be easier that way."

"Forget about him. He's not going to be a problem."

"This your shirt?" Eduardo asked, lifting mine up. I nodded and he threw it to me. Eva opened her eyes and adjusted her head on my thigh.

"I think somebody stole mine." Eduardo said, hands on hips, staring around the room. Finally he said, "Fuck it," and yanked the belt on his pants a notch tighter.

I nudged Eva aside and slid my shirt on. Eduardo tossed me my pants. He ticked points off his fingers.

"First, I need a smoke. Then we get Salvatore. Then we take him to Teddy T."

"Come on, Eduardo," I said. "We owe Salvatore better than that."

"That's not important," Eduardo said, rooting through the clothes on the floor in search of his shirt. He stood up and shrugged. "The bastard that took my shirt got my pack of smokes. I got an extra in the car. Let's go."

I sat frozen on the bed.

"It's him or us," Eduardo said softly, "and he's the one that fucked up."

"Give me a second," I said, nodding toward Eva.

Eduardo grinned.

"Five minutes," he said. "And grab my shirt if you find it."

He hitched his pants up again and strode out the door.

I shook Eva awake. She brushed her brown curls out of her eyes, and kissed my thigh.

"You need to wake up," I said. "Find Salvatore before Eduardo and I do."

"Salvatore? After last night, I'm not talking to him. Ever again."

"You need to get him to leave town. Tell him I think he's in danger, and that I'm not the reason why. He'll understand."

"You're overreacting," she said. She lay her head back down and closed her eyes. I grabbed Sebastian's phone and called our room, hoping to catch Salvatore, but no one answered. I laid out a line on the mirror and huffed it down, then ran out the door after Eduardo.

13

If thou wouldst rule well, thou must rule for God, and
to do that, thou must be ruled by him. Those who will not
be governed by God will be ruled by tyrants.

—**William Penn**

My dad eyed me intently on the walk to the outpatient
treatment wing of the hospital, as if expecting I'd
bolt at any second. The thought did cross my mind, but I quickly
discarded it as a waste of energy. I didn't have any money, and I didn't
have any place to stay other than my parent's house. My folks had
done a good job of trapping me. Sure, I could probably sneak out of
the treatment wing and do some shit on my own for a while, but inevitably I'd have to return to my parents to refuel on cash and sleep.

My dad signed me in at the desk, lingering uneasily until one of the
counselors led me off down the hall.

"Be good. Do right," he called after me. "I will be here for you at
the end of the day."

"He's a sweet man," the counselor said to me as we walked on down
the hall past a series of small cubicles. "You have no idea how much
he's done for this community."

"Yeah. He's always had my best interests in mind," I said evenly. "I'm just glad he brought me here. I really needed a wake-up call."

"I'm surprised to hear you say that," she said, pulling up with a start. "That really shows me something."

"I mean it," I said. "Enough is enough, you know?"

She gave my arm a friendly rub and steered me on down the hall toward a meeting room that was empty except for chairs arranged in a circle in the middle.

"You sit quiet in here," she said. "The rest of the group will join you soon." She nodded and gave me a warm smile. "I'm glad to see you came here ready to make a change."

She looked at me expectantly. I gave her a little shiver, as if I suddenly felt cold creeping into me.

"I'm just scared," I said, looking down, taking a deep breath.

"You should be," she said. "Rest easy now. We're all here to help you."

As she closed the door behind her, I couldn't keep the smirk off my face. I quickly pinched myself and forced myself to breathe easy again. If they caught me laughing at them, I had no doubt they'd bring out the chains. In time the room filled up. Some came in quietly, their hands stuffed in pockets, eyes on the floor. Most of them looked like middle-aged housewives or working stiffs—casual in jeans and plain T-shirts or blouses, a hint of a frown on their faces, suspiciously eyeing those around them. A couple men came in looking sharp in business suits, taking their seats quickly, their hands snapping out in a wristwatch salute as they checked the time. They popped open their briefcases and made themselves busy with paperwork. A handful of folks, seemingly no different from the stiffs, came in chattering, giving each other big smiles and waves, sitting down and quickly flooding the room with eager talk about meetings they'd checked out, good things they'd heard speakers say, talking loud on purpose like desperate guys in bars who hoped bullhorning the news to everyone that they'd just bought a new boat or come back from a luxurious trip to Europe would draw the pretty girls in. At last the counselor came back in, a skinny black man about my age clinging to her arm, his left side jerking along in semi-paralysis as if it knew that it didn't want to be there.

"Everybody," she said, "we have two new people today. This here is Tavorian, and over there, the young man in the glasses, that's Sire-sarin." She paused, pulled a sheet from a pocket, looked it over, then said, "That's Ray-O."

I shook my head. She might as well have said the crippled nigger and the sand-nigger for the way most of the people stared at us.

"Good to meet you brothers," one of the loud guys said. "Welcome to the group."

"I ain't your brother, motherfucker," Tavorian said, his words slurring out from the paralyzed side of his mouth.

The room gasped in shock.

"What you all looking at? You expect a grateful nigger saying 'thank you, massa'? What you looking at?"

Everybody looked away, but I couldn't help smiling. Tavorian caught me grinning and a tiny smirk came to his lips as well.

"Nice to meet all of you," I said, quietly. "I'm just grateful to be here."

Tavorian gave me a nod as if he knew I was his brother in arms. The counselor explained to the group that we would spend the first half of the day going over some things to think about regarding recovery, the basic danger areas, the common triggers, then take a break for lunch. We would return for an afternoon session where we would share details of our stories and help each other see how our addictions had damaged our lives and led to our need for being in that room, then try to help each other find ways past our individual triggers. At the end of the session, a couple of the members would be asked to present their fourth step, a "searching and fearless moral inventory of themselves." From the way most of the people in the room stared off into space, or at the breasts of the women in the room, it seemed like the counselor was repeating her daily plan for Tavorian and me alone. Everybody else knew what was going to happen. The loudmouthed brownnosers peppered her with questions, asking if she was going to give a talk on a story in the Big Book, or explain some semantic confusion about one of the steps. They waved a blue tome around, opening it from time to time and lovingly tracing passages with their fingers. The book was prominently labeled in gold lettering *The Twelve Steps of AA*, and I could tell they cherished literal, idiotic interpretations of it like a pack of militant Christian fundamentalists at a Bible reading. When one of them asked her if the passage that said that addiction was like a physical allergy meant that they should avoid skin contact with other alcoholics still in the throes of addiction, I heard a collective groan. The fundamentalists, however, seemed to be the ones whom the counselor praised the most, and so I figured that the best thing I could do was try to find a way to fit into their con.

I tried to keep focused and pick up on their lingo. One of them proudly proclaimed that he'd overcome his aversion to the third step, which said it was important for us to have "made a decision to turn our will and our lives over to the care of God as we understood him." I perked up. He talked for a bit about how tough it was for him to even think about the step because he didn't believe in God at all, that he'd always considered religion a crock of shit. That made sense to me. Then he said that what he'd done is realize that the key was that we just needed to define God as we understood him, and so he'd turned his will and life over to the lightbulb above his bed.

"Because, you know, that lightbulb, it's a miracle and it's got more power than me. I mean, all that electricity, and somehow it becomes light. It's this amazing, unexplainable thing, and yet I take it for granted. But there's a power there and it's greater than me and I know that it will watch over me because it's lit my room for a long time, even when I didn't think about it. And isn't that what God is? A power we don't understand that looks over us even if we don't realize it's there?"

"That's good," the counselor said. "It's important to find a definition that works for you. You find something that works, and then you can move on to the next step."

I nearly fell off my chair. Tavorian and I exchanged a look while most of the others groaned audibly again.

The guy who said the crap about the lightbulb looked hurt, though, at the reaction.

"Don't criticize my recovery," he said. "I'm keeping sober."

"Look, guy," one of the suits said, "being sober is all fine and good, but if it turns you into a moron, then I'd rather stay drunk."

"You don't like what I've got to say? You can always leave!"

"Trust me, guy, I would if I could. I should tape your wisdom for my judge. He said I was disturbing the peace. I'd say you're disturbing my peace a hell of a lot more than what those whiners at the office complained about me for."

"Fucking DUI judges," one of the stiffs grumbled.

"Am I in the right place?" one of the housewives asked the counselor. "I only accidentally put someone else's pills in my purse."

The counselor finally began cooing to settle the throng. Nobody listened to her. I bit my lip and stared at the carpet, carefully adjusting my wrist so I could keep my eye on my watch. One of the stiffs and the lightbulb brownnoser were chest to chest, spittle flying as they yelled. The counselor tried to pull them apart, enlisting another brownnoser to help her out. The only escape from the madness was lunch break. I busied my mind by calculating how many minutes had passed, what percentage of the time we were required to stay in that room still remained, and how that percentage changed with each passing second. Then I calculated the numbers relative to the three weeks of outpatient sessions I had to attend. It was too much to bear.

Tavorian stuck a cigarette in his palsied hand and then tried to light it up. If he was lighting up, I was going to as well. I pulled out my pack and lit one up.

"Smoke 'em if you got 'em," one of the stiffs said, and a wave of lighters came aflame.

"No smoking!" the counselor shrieked. "No smoking!"

She snapped the cigarette out of Tavorian's fingers and flung it across the room.

"What the fuck," he said.

"No smoking!" she said.

The brownnosers and a few of the stiffs joined her in the chant. I stubbed my cigarette out on the carpet. The rest of the smokers in the room guiltily did the same while some of the nonsmokers chose that particular moment to begin hacking as if their lungs had been damaged beyond recovery.

The counselor flapped her arms in the air.

"Please, everybody, please settle down. Do you want me to have to report this on your record?"

Immediately the room quieted down.

"Goddamn DUI judges," a suit said.

"Just tell me this, lady," Tavorian said. "Why you take my square first?"

"You all can smoke at lunch," she said.

Tavorian shook his head and slumped back in his seat while the counselor motioned to a brownnoser to begin reading from the blue book.

"Where should I start?" he asked.

"There's something to learn on every page," she said, slumping in a chair.

I looked down at my watch. We were 2.7 percent closer to lunch, less than a hundredth of a percent closer to the end of my outpatient treatment. I knew I'd never make it.

We marched down to the hospital cafeteria for lunch, the counselor quickly disappearing once we'd all passed through the doors. I nudged Tavorian in the cafeteria line.

"How much you want to bet she's back in her office downing a drink?"

"Yeah," he said, sliding his tray along with his good hand, then dragging his paralyzed half after.

"You need help with that?" I asked.

He glared at me.

"Did I ask for help?"

"Chill, Tavorian," I said with a smile. "I didn't know you were a magician."

He grabbed a wrapped ham sandwich and slammed it on his tray.

"How you going to fill that tray and then carry it to a table?"

He stared at me for a second, then turned his head away and shoved his body forward, muttering, "Alright. You can carry it. But I didn't ask."

I loaded up my tray with fries and threw in an apple. Tavorian shook his head, a hint of a smile cracking his face. With a pointed look, he filled his tray with a colorful meal of peas and mashed potatoes with gravy, a slice of cherry pie, a ham sandwich, and a bowl of tomato soup.

"You can't eat like that if you tryin' to keep from getting brain-washed," he said. "You need energy, otherwise these fuckers start sounding sane."

I took our trays to a nearby table and Tavorian slowly followed. The rest of the group had splintered off to sit alone at tables and sullenly fork their food.

"Thanks," he said quietly, lowering himself into a seat.

We ate in silence for a bit, Tavorian leaning over his tray and shoveling food in.

"What you in for?" he asked when he finally paused for breath.

"Get my parents off my back," I said.

"What's your DOC?"

I paused, thinking it through.

"My dad," I said. "He's a doc. He's got some kind of pull in this hospital and made sure I got in. He said this was the best outpatient treatment in the city."

Tavorian laughed.

"D-O-C. Drug of choice," he said. "I didn't know you were a first-timer."

"Oh. Sorry. I don't know why they've got so much lingo for this treatment shit. Maybe they think if they've got a secret language, it'll make us want to get cured faster so we can be a part of the cool club talking in code and shit."

"I never thought of that," he said, nodding. "You probably right. Been here three times now, and the shit they say sounds dumber every time."

"I'm in for coke and pot, Tavorian," I said. "At least, that's all my folks know about."

"These fuckers'll get a blood and piss test on you 'fore today's over. Tell your folks now what you done, otherwise these fuckers'll make it sound like you a junkie and a liar."

"I didn't know they could do that."

"Soon as you sign on, they got the right to test you. You got no rights anymore. Nothing's private."

"Thanks for the tip."

"I know how it goes. My dad's a preacher. Big-time Baptist. South Side. He pulled strings to get me in here, too. When you got folks like that, you know nobody gonna have your back. Folks want you to look bad, and they'll flip on you first chance."

"I'm not in the business of talking. That's why I'm here. Coulda smoothed things out if I'd turned for the cops, gotten some protection. But I didn't. Now it's like everybody's against me, Tavorian."

Tavorian nodded.

"Call me Tav," he said. "You dealing? Where?"

"East Coast," I said. "I had to run."

Tav laughed.

"We always running. I was with a crew South Side. We flipped a lot of H. Cops got me because I can't run, but I didn't turn. Crew thought I did, though."

"Heroin? I never done that."

"Me neither, really. I ain't no addict. I like a bump time to time, helps with the CP. But rolling He-ru-on, that the big money. I was making my cash cuz nobody want to look at me. I'm invisible."

"That's so beautiful," I said. "It's just so perfect."

A wistful smile crossed his face.

"Yeah. It was, wasn't it? It was."

We smiled at each other like the best of friends.

. . .

He-ru-on. The way he said it, his tongue lingering over the vowels, spreading them out so they washed upon the ear with waves of warmth, conjured a sense of a mythic kingdom of the ultimate high. When people said "heroin" it sounded so cut and dry, the syllables clipped. That did nothing but make me think of overdoses and needles, junkies too wired to do anything but chase the next fix. Heroin was what newscasters lamented in the nightly broadcast. Another dead of a heroin overdose, another gunned down peddling heroin. But He-ru-on, three lilting syllables that his tongue savored, was a word of love. I could see throngs nodding blissfully, smiling in each other's arms, chanting the name of the God of drugs.

I made my way through the afternoon session by meditating on the word "He-ru-on," by imagining the world that Tav had described. My parents had always painted the South Side of Chicago as a seedy, dangerous place best avoided, full of killers roaming wild in a valley of evil. But Tavorian described a different land. Sure, there were dangers, but there were dangers everywhere. A brown man like me could walk without fear so long as he had someone in the neighborhood backing him. And if he did, the South Side opened up in all its wonders. Working-class families filled the streets, and they were for the most part honest and decent. You could find drugs if you wanted to, quite easily in fact, but the people were about more than that. The drug spots were fierce fiefdoms dotting a peaceful land, and as long as one didn't encroach on the other, nobody got hurt. Uniting all the people was a fierce antipathy for the North Side. The North Side was where the rich lived. The North Side had all the money, and so it drew all the benefits that came with money—fancy restaurants, vibrant theater, a varied and energetic music scene. But everyone knew the South Side was a thinly disguised internment camp for the black and poor. Cops strutted through communities like prison guards, hauling people off for the slightest offense to courts where the judges threw them into prison for life if they tried to deal. On the North Side, justice was more kind, offering community service to the poor citizens unfortunately snared by addiction. Two different worlds stood side by side, and Tavorian knew which one he belonged in. The more he talked about it, the more I believed it was where I belonged too.

We hadn't found Salvatore back at the dorm, but since Kenny and Jonas weren't around either, Eduardo relaxed on our couch while I went to take a shower. When I got back, one of Jonas's shirts hung loosely on Eduardo, who sat hunched on the couch, the phone pressed to his ear. After a series of yeses, he hung up the phone and rubbed his forehead. I threw on the cleanest clothes I could find, which meant I dug through Kenny's stuff until I found a shirt that fit, then put the pants I'd been wearing the night before back on. I couldn't remember the last time I'd done laundry.

"Teddy's arranged a meet," he said when I sat down. "We have to bring him Salvatore."

"Don't even think of selling me out just to save your own ass," I said.

"You're freaking, man. We get Salvatore and we'll be fine. If Teddy thinks we've got all the angles covered, he'll lay off."

"Until next week when he's flipped out again. He hassle you about how much I owe him?"

Eduardo nodded.

"Third thing he asked about. Business is business."

I fished in my pocket and pulled out my money. I tried to count it, but I kept losing track and having to start over again. Finally, I gave up and stuffed the wad back in my pocket.

"If it's enough, it's enough. And if it's not, fuck it. I can't think straight," I said.

"Do a couple lines and get your head straight!" he yelled, closing his eyes and rubbing his temples. "You get fucked, I get fucked. If you could shut up for a second and start thinking shit through, maybe we could figure a way out of this."

"You already got your way out," I said. "You'll tell Teddy the shit's all my fault, then trade me in. Just go ahead and try that shit with me!"

"I've screwed folks over before," Eduardo said quietly, "but this is different. We've got legitimate payback with Salvatore."

"I've got nothing against Salvatore." I rubbed my eyes and tried to get my thoughts to walk in single file. Instead, rude children that they were, they ruckused in the back of my mind, screaming at the top of their lungs.

"He knows who you are and he knows who I am. If he turns, you go down. If you go down, you take me and Teddy with you. And now he's got a reason to turn. He's a mess we've got to clean."

"Teddy's being a moron. Going after Salvatore is a stupid bullshit plan and you're encouraging him."

Eduardo rolled his eyes.

"You're the one who made the plan. Last night."

"I did?"

"You're a complete fucking waste of space when you're crashing, you know that?"

Eduardo pulled a thin case from the front pocket of his jeans, popped it open, and pulled out a small bag of coke. He ripped the first line, but as I knelt over the table, I realized that my nose was congested beyond hope.

"Fuck," I said, tapping my nose. I tried to blow my nose, but only blood came into the tissue.

"You're such a rookie," Eduardo said, laughing. "Lean your head back and I'll pour some down your nose for you."

"That's never as good."

"Well, either that or a pinch under your eyelid. One way or the other, I'm getting some coke in you."

"You're shitting me."

"Way you are now, I figure you'd fuck everything up. A little white in you, though, and you'll be cool and tight. I could do you up real good if you weren't a pussy."

"Whatever, man. Just quit fucking around."

Eduardo popped his case back open and pulled out a spoon and a thin syringe.

"This freak you out?" he asked.

Freebasing was a line I'd never thought I'd cross. It was one thing to snort a bit of coke. Everybody from lawyers to used car salesmen did that. Syringes, though, marked the line between the casual user and the drug fiend.

"Best way to get high," Eduardo said. "Snorting's like taking a walk. Freebasing is stomping the pedal in a convertible. You know that feeling in a roller coaster when you just get over the top of the big climb and you know you're about to rocket?" He tapped a bit of coke onto the spoon. "Once you start, you'll never want to go back."

My body felt tight and sore, on the edge of an ache that made sunlight and movement seem a dream other people had. If I didn't get something, my body would curl up on itself, a bug trying to protect itself from the jab of a stick. Anyway, it was just a onetime thing. Once my nose cleared up, I wouldn't need to do it again.

"Just don't put it in my arms," I said. "People notice that kind of thing."

"You don't see needle tracks on me, do you?" Eduardo said. "I'll do you between the toes. It stings a little, but you'll get over it quick."

I turned my head toward the window, my foot on his lap. I would have watched him, how he held my foot, but instead I was closed eyes on a first kiss, my heart trilling at the thought of steel penetrating skin, the needle mark branding me as one who crossed into the forbidden. My ancestors chanted in the mountains, cloaked in furs, starving until fervor brought a glimpse of the divine. The needle was my conduit, full bodied, to the Gods. Foot first, I could soar through the mist of maya, one step bridging the universe, and nap in the gardens of the Devas.

The needle pricks with the bite of an ant. At first, it is as if I am ankle-deep in eddies of foam, my toes scalding on south Indian sand, a thick sun languorous overhead. But quick rushes the summer tide, ocean firing fast past knees, melting flesh into water, bone into salt, my body effervescing, for I am the water, stretching out, embracing the ocean, becoming ocean. I reach wide waved toward the horizon, sun tickling my back, feeling the scrape of ocean floor in the chill of my depths. Frantic lives of fish and humans churn above and within me, only the steady blink of sunrise beyond my reach.

On the horizon a speck appears, growing larger, becoming a mountain racing the sky. Underneath strains a monkey, his tail trailing in my water. I whisper that he should leave his burden, come swim within my warmth. He will not listen. He draws me in with his tail, drinking me from the ocean, and together we jump past the sun.

When the Rakshasa demon king Ravana first prayed for power, the Devas thought they could trick him. He'd spent years chanting, but the Devas would sneak by and throw trees at him, mocking his dark skin, his large nose, his ill-fitting clothes. He ignored them, layering mantra upon mantra, until the weight of his words threatened to tear the fabric of the universe. But when Brahma came to appease him and to grant him a wish, the Devas cast a spell upon Ravana that temporarily twisted his speech. He wanted divine awareness, to sense the soul of all living beings, but instead his words knotted in the blinding presence of Brahma, and he asked only that he be able to *see* the living no matter from what direction they approached him. And so Brahma gave him ten heads so he could see in all directions, and the Devas laughed at Ravana's foolishness.

But Ravana was not ashamed. He had lost hold of language due to a trick, but he discovered that the words held power, and that he could become power through wielding the words. So he took the words of the Gods and began again with his mantras, weaving them into a new fabric to rival the universe. And when Brahma tried to ignore him, Ravana cut off one of his ten heads, the head still humming with the mantras of creation, and sacrificed it to Shiva. When a thousand years passed without Shiva acknowledging him, he sacrificed another head. Every thousand years, he sacrificed a head, until finally he had only one head left. His words had become like the ticking of time, a harmony to the ever-present *om* of creation, and Shiva could not bear the thought of the loss of Ravana's life. He came to Ravana and offered his blessings. Ravana asked for immortality, but that was not possible for Shiva, the destroyer, to give. Ravana, remembering the laughter of the Gods, asked instead for power over the divine, and invulnerability from the Gods. No longer would he let them bully him. No longer would he be afraid of their words. He would be the king of the universe, and nobody would mock him ever again.

Shiva pitied Ravana, for Shiva was a God of power, the destroyer of injustice, and his ears perpetually rang with the lamentations of the powerless. Ravana had beseeched him beautifully and proven his faith, and for him, Shiva would bend the universe and cloak Ravana with divine might. When Shiva departed, the other Gods fleeing in his wake rather than face the wrath of the now invincible Ravana, Ravana finally loosed his hair from its sanyasi's *jada*, and laughed. The mantras he had chanted were mantras of praise to the divine, the starry-eyed babbling of humble devotees. But Ravana was not a humble man, and he was not a devotee. He was the Rakshasa king playing a con, lying through faith and ritual so he could kill the Gods, so he could become a Rakshasa Shiva. He had used their mantras against them, and now he had become an ender of worlds.

We roared down the highway, Salvatore and Kenny's laptops stacked neatly in the backseat. We'd considered grabbing Jonas's computer too, but he had a desktop. Both laptops fit neatly in my backpack, though, so that meant I could get them out of the dorm without anybody noticing. Teddy would appreciate the gift.

Eduardo hadn't shot up because he said he needed to keep his edge if he was going to talk our way out. Teddy had a sixth sense for bullshit, he said. If I was smart, I'd let Eduardo do the talking for me.

With the flush of coke still humming in my veins, it made sense to let Eduardo handle Teddy. If I tried to talk, there was no telling what I'd say, or if I'd have the sense to shut up at the right time. I didn't want to think about it or worry about it, so as Eduardo talked I nodded and ignored him.

. . .

A van with tinted windows pulled up beside Eduardo and me at the rest stop. Two Jeeps took up spots next to it. Before we had a chance to open our doors, two toughs pulled us out and steered us to the back of the van. They patted us down then tossed us in. The doors slammed shut behind us and a dim overhead light came on.

"You two are pissing me off," Teddy T said, running a thick paw through his tight blond crew cut. His red and blue tracksuit heaved with his breathing.

"We can track him down, and even if we can't, he's no problem anyway," Eduardo said, rubbing his hands on his pants. With the long sleeves of Jonas's shirt draping over his hands, the collar stretching wide over his scrawny chest, Eduardo looked like a kid trying to play daddy.

I jumped in to help out. "Salvatore's pissed because his girlfriend has a thing for me. It might feel like it's a big deal, but it's really not. I've got it under control."

"Shut the fuck up," Teddy T said.

I saw a twitch in his arm, the heel of his hand approaching, and then a dull buzz became dim light and the sound of Eduardo talking in a tunnel. I rubbed my jaw, pushed myself up off the floor of the van, felt the taste of blood from new cuts in my mouth. Strangely, I didn't feel any fear, only the reassuring warmth, the seemingly indefatigable confidence of a coke high. The coke gave me faith, and so I believed that everything would work out for the best in the end.

"I got your money," I said doggedly. "And we brought you a present."

Teddy looked to Eduardo.

"I thought you said you didn't have him yet?"

"He's talking about the laptops," Eduardo said.

Teddy jabbed me in the chest with a finger.

"Shut the fuck up."

I pulled the wad from my pocket, fanned it out, then tried to hand it to him. Teddy glared at me. The soft blond fuzz on his cheeks glistened with sweat, his face flushed. In that moment, he seemed like a petulant child wearing his anger like a mask. I couldn't fear him, not with that baby down struggling on his cheeks.

"You trying to set me up?" Teddy yelled.

Eduardo grabbed the money from my hands.

"You're short," Eduardo said, then, leaning into me, he whispered, "*Never* try to hand him money."

I said, "The laptops—"

Teddy banged on the side of the van and the back doors opened.

"Get this fuck out of my sight. Marco—straighten this shithead out."

A guy about my height, but a hundred pounds heavier, nodded and yanked me out. He slammed the door shut, dusted off his black track-suit, and ran a leather-gloved hand over his gleaming scalp. I'd noticed a number tattooed in black on the back of his scalp when he'd closed the van doors, but now my gaze was fixed on his dark sunglasses. I couldn't see his eyes, couldn't gauge where he was. His breathing was calm and steady. A trickle of fear dripped into my consciousness, and a voice within me said to pay attention to it, to follow it, but the coke brought confidence in waves and I couldn't find where the fear had gone.

"So you're Marco," I said.

He nodded, then shoved me toward one of the Jeeps and gruffly told me to get in.

"You going to kill me? Mind giving me a gun first so I have a chance?" I asked.

Marco paused, tilting his head to look over his sunglasses at me, his brown eyes steady, a whisper of a smile on his face.

"That's funny," he said. He motioned to the passenger seat. "Get in."

I gripped the door. The rest stop was deserted. There was a little building with vending machines outside and signs for restrooms, but they'd corner me if I ran there. There were some trees off behind it, though.

"Get the fuck in," Marco said. "You thinking of running? You wouldn't make it to the shade."

"Might as well take my chances," I said. "I'm pretty fast."

Marco laughed. "Eduardo said you were a bullshitter. Seriously, get the fuck in. We're just gonna do some business and talk about some new things. I ain't got no problems with you."

I couldn't read him, but I couldn't run from him either. At least not yet.

"Didn't seem like Teddy was feeling friendly," I said.

Marco shrugged. "He don't like you. You're a fuckup. But I'm here to change that."

"Everything's under control," I said. "Teddy's just flying off the handle for no reason."

"Yeah? What if I told you your buddy Salvatore's working with the cops?"

"You guys have proof?"

"Got proof he ain't?"

I knew what came next. He'd drive us to some deserted area, make me walk out of the Jeep ahead of him, then pop two bullets into the back of my head. The only surprise would be in how he chose to dispose of my corpse.

"Before you do this," I said. "Let me get back to my dorm so I can write my family a letter to explain things. A farewell. I owe them that."

Marcos shook his head, flashing me a sharp-toothed grin.

"Trust me," he said. "You're gonna help me, I'm gonna help you, and by the time we're done, everything'll be cool."

Marco took me to a diner, pulling a Red Sox hat on when we got out of the Jeep. Inside, we hung out over a basket of cheese fries. Aside from never taking off his sunglasses or gloves, he acted like a normal guy. He said please and thank you when we ordered, and he looked at the waitresses' asses whenever one passed. He pulled a notepad from his fanny pack and wet the tip of his pencil as he took notes. He asked me how I'd been running the business, what I'd been charging, what I'd been paying. He nibbled on the tip of his pencil, then tapped the notepad and made some quick marks.

"Why don't you ever take off your gloves?" I asked.

He grabbed my water glass and lifted it in the air. With his eraser he drew circles around smudges on the glass.

"Your fingerprints are on everything," he said.

"So it's about leaving evidence? Is that why you're bald? So you don't leave hair behind?"

"I'm bald because I'm bald, dumbass," he said.

"So you didn't shave off all your body hairs?"

"No, you fuck."

"Just asking."

"You should be asking me what's next, what you got to do."

"So you're saying it's smarter to worry about what my friends are doing than worry about the cleaner Teddy's got sharing cheese fries with me? Give me a gun and I'll chill out."

He grinned.

"So you got a point," he said. "That makes you a smart-ass instead of a dumbass. Now shut up so I can think."

"Can't you think and talk at the same time?"

He smacked his pencil on the table. "You gave me a bunch of numbers, and I've got to figure them out."

"Let me look," I said.

He turned the notepad to me. On one side he'd listed the price I said I was buying at. In a column next to it was the price I was selling at. Next to that was another column with much smaller numbers.

"So what are all these numbers?"

"What you buy for, what you sell for, and what Eduardo gets it for."

I could feel a familiar heat rising within me.

"You been doing good," he said. "You set your prices right, and it looks like you collect on it all."

"Eduardo sells to me, and he collects from me," I said. I made a rough estimate, double-checked it, then checked it again. I didn't owe Teddy anything. I should have had nearly five grand in profit. "I'm getting fucked," I said.

Marco laughed. "Yeah, Eduardo's fucking you," he said, "but that's the way things go. At least I know you're still earning right."

I slapped the table. "So collect from Eduardo. That's your problem. You don't have to worry about me or Salvatore."

Marco scowled at me.

"Nothing's changed. Your Eduardo's boy, so he's got a right to a cut of your earnings. And if he says you're light, then you're light. Your word against his. Eduardo's been loyal."

"Can't you see the angle?" I said, leaning back into the booth in disbelief. "How many college guys has he fucked like this? He skims the cash, Teddy gets pissed, but Teddy thinks it's our fault, so he comes after us. If we don't do anything, Teddy puts us in the dirt. And if we do try to get the cops to protect us, Teddy cuts us up, then puts us in the dirt."

Marco took a sip from my glass of water. "Maybe I'll tell Teddy the story you're telling." He tapped the glass with his finger, then cocked his head.

Tapping the glass, cocking his head—those were nervous gestures, poker tells. He was hiding something. I tried to navigate the possibilities, but my mind was beginning to slide into the fog of a headache. I lit a cigarette, the nicotine giving a hint of clarity for a moment. It faded before I could form a complete thought.

I blew the smoke in a cloud above me. "Once Teddy knows, he'll get rid of Eduardo. That's just good business," I said.

Marco drummed his fingers on the table, a smile flickering across his face.

"Teddy's about the money," I said. "Once you tell him what's going on, he'll ease up."

"You don't know Teddy," he said, flipping a twenty on the table for the waitress. "Uppity fuck like you, I figure he'd rather skin you just to wipe that shit-eating grin off your face."

"You're just screwing with me," I said, forcing a smile. "You and me wouldn't be talking like this if Teddy wanted me dead."

"And why's that?"

"No surprise. You don't tell your target you're about to shoot it. You let it nibble grass and think it's any other day."

"You make it feel comfortable," he said. "You let it relax."

He grinned.

"Don't worry, though," he added. "I ain't a malicious fuck. I hate motherfuckers bawling and sniveling. If it's your time, and I'm the one he calls, I'll end you quick and kind."

We ran, Tav and I, during the afternoon smoke break. The counselor scribbled notes, everybody smoked and milled, but we snagged a wheelchair and Tav suffered the indignity of sitting in it, and I pumped my monkey legs and got us rolling fast, hot into an elevator, bam out the doors through the emergency room, and then sweet rolling in a summer drizzle down some Chicago road—I didn't care which, I didn't need to know right then. Tav yanked a smoke out and lit it on the first try. I popped him into a wheelie and let out a whoop.

"What the fuck, man," he said. "I got a square going."

"Just celebrating, man," I said, taking in a deep breath. The air was cool with the memory of rain, the fog of exhaust pressed down for a moment by the wetness, so it felt like I could smell beneath the city itself, to the ancient earth slumbering underneath years of solid concrete.

"Slow down. I'm walking from here," he said, banging the armrest with his good hand, cigarette dangling from his lips.

"I do something wrong?"

"No, man. Just I don't needs to be going so fast. It's outpatient. Nobody gives a fuck what we do."

"That why nobody stopped us?"

He laughed.

"Grab yourself a square and settle," he said.

I lit up, gazed at the street signs. We were way west on Belmont, near Central Avenue. I had no idea where we were. Aside from school field trips into the city, I'd never been. Once my parents moved to the suburbs, we stayed there, except for occasional trips to Devon Avenue to investigate the Indian stores. Sometimes we drove by Michigan Avenue to see the Christmas lights. There was no point in visiting the city. The suburbs had all we needed. The mere mention of the city was enough to get us to lock our doors.

"So where do we go from here?" I asked.

"We're West Side, smack in the middle between North Side and South Side. There's a spot a little south of here," Tav said.

"I mean after that. What's the plan? You have a place I can stay?"

"I never agreed to nothing. You on your own."

He had a point. During smoke break I'd asked if he wanted to leave, and he'd said yes. That was it. I'd daydreamed about roaming the South Side with him, but we hadn't discussed that possibility. He had implied the possibility during lunch, though. I was pretty certain about that.

"I've got no place to go," I said, "but you know the city. We'll do better together. I can help you. Because, you know, you've got that—" I motioned to his paralyzed side.

"Why you always bringing up my disability?"

"Well, you're disabled, right?"

Tav wagged a finger at me.

"It's the way you bring it up. You got to think about that. I have CP, but I'm still a man."

"I never said you weren't."

"That's right. You keep it that way." He puffed a bit more on his cigarette. "I can't go on the South Side," he said. "I got people looking for me."

"What about the suburbs?"

"Fuck the suburbs. I know some good spots North Side," he said. He paused and looked me over. "You gonna run if we get into some trouble?"

"Where would I run?"

He nodded.

"I don't need you," he said, "but I'm going to do you a favor. As long as you keep cool, do what I say, we'll be fine."

He limped down the street and I followed.

14

He who has a why to live can bear almost any how.

—Friedrich Nietzsche

Tats woke me up at four in the morning. He handed me a pack of cigarettes, a book of matches, and two bus tokens. He saw me to the door. He took the coffee can that he kept for cigarette butts from the shoe rack, brought it out with him, and sat down on the porch, lighting up a smoke.

I'd worn what he told me to—old blue jeans, a long-sleeved T-shirt—though I knew the weather report for the day said that it'd be in the high eighties.

"Trust me," he'd said. "You need the protection."

When I got to the place on Western, it was still dark. There was a line of other guys standing in the parking lot, lit up by the streetlights, all in jeans and long-sleeved shirts. A group of five Mexicans spoke rapid-fire among themselves: one short and fat, one tall and fat, one with an arm in a cast, one lying on the ground with his arms making pillows for his head, and another taking swigs from a forty of Colt, offering it to the others, them refusing. A mix of black and white guys formed a ragged line behind, not saying much of anything at all, examining the calluses on their hands, looking at the ground, staring at the Mexicans, or examining the calluses on other people's hands. Light was pouring out of what looked like a little backyard shed. The door was open, and the sign above it said "Day Labor." I walked inside.

A bald guy with a thick black handlebar mustache and Corona T-shirt was sitting on a lawn chair behind a card table, just inside the door. He had a cell phone on the table, a beeper beside it, a stack of papers in the middle, and a rusted file cabinet behind him. He looked me over.

"*No hay trabajo ahora. Necesita venir mañana.*"

"I'm an American," I said, and I pulled my real papers from my wallet.

He examined my ID, scanned my Social Security card, held my ID to the light, and looked me over again.

"Tats sent me," I said.

"You're awful thin."

"I'm a hard worker. Tats said I could handle it."

"You work with Tats before?"

I nodded.

"You good with concrete?"

"Depends on what you need."

"We need someone who can handle a wheelbarrow."

"No problem."

"Somebody who won't quit."

"How long you need me?"

"At least for today."

"I'm your man. You're paying cash today, right?" I asked.

"Don't worry."

He handed me my Social Security card, ID.

"Stand outside."

Thirty minutes later a rusted-out school bus with "Day Labor" painted on the side pulled up. The guy came out from the shed and walked down the line, pushing guys out of the way, pulling others by the collar over to the bus. He chose the tall, fat Mexican, shoved the others out of the way, picked a tall black guy, a short white guy, pushed ten more out of the way, no rhyme or reason as far as I could tell, until he came by me, grabbed me by the collar, and threw me in. He walked back to the shed, closed the door, put a padlock on it, and walked back to the bus. A couple of the guys that he had pushed away started yelling at him, the Mexican with the cast grabbed hold of his hand and started pleading and crying, but he stiff-armed them all away.

"Maybe tomorrow," he yelled out the bus window, and we were off.

The seats were filled, and guys gave me a stare when I came near them to let me know that there wasn't enough space. The Mexican guy who had been chosen was sitting in the back of the bus, and he smiled at me as I made my way back. He slid over to the window and gave me a place.

He started talking in Spanish. I smiled and nodded. At the appropriate spaces I told him my name, where I was living. When he'd quieted down a bit, I started with some simple questions about the pay.

"*¿Cuanto paga por trabajo?*"

He stared at me for a bit, shrugged, then said, "*Veinte o treinta dolares. Depende.*"

"*Por cuantas horas?*"

"*Depende.*"

After that he didn't talk much.

We were dropped off at a grammar school. They were going to be pouring new concrete, but they needed to get the old cracked concrete out. They had some professional guys working with jackhammers to break the stuff up, and it was up to us to clear the pieces out. A rusted Bobcat stood nearby, but the scoop on it was missing, which left all the hard work up to us. A couple guys would shovel the pieces into a wheelbarrow and then the pieces would be carted to a truck, and then the pieces would have to get into the truck, and when the truck got filled, it cleared out. I was one of the wheelbarrow guys. It felt like I was hauling dead bodies, and I had to grit my teeth to raise the wheelbarrow. Over time the wheelbarrow handles blistered the skin on my palms. It burned at first, but I kept working. At least I didn't have to bend down and lift the concrete into the truck, or hammer away at the cement chunks the professionals hadn't gotten small enough. The guys who had to hammer had the worst of it. You need the right tools. One of the guys who were hammering had a piece fly up and hit him in the face. He went down hard, bleeding, holding a hand to his eye. He was moved over to a shady area under the overhang of the school where he spent the next half hour using his shirt as a compress. When he came back to his work, I could barely see his right eye under the swelling. I got used to it, though. It was work, and they gave us water and a break for food. Nobody talked to me. Nobody looked at me, not even the Mexican. And at the end they loaded us on the bus and took us back.

The guy called us into the shed one by one. I tore the sleeves off my shirt while I was waiting in the bus and wrapped them tight around my palms, so when he called me in, it would look like I was just taking care of my hands.

"You didn't slack off. A good ten hours I got out of you."

"I'm a hard worker," I said.

He turned around, opened the file cabinet, then turned back to me.

"Put out your hand," he said.

I blinked. The gig was up. He was going to check.

"Don't you want to get paid?"

I stuck out my hand. He laid two twenties in it. And then, with a smile, added another ten.

"That's a bonus," he said.

I ran out the door. Four dime bags! My mind buzzed. A nice pipe, a good lighter, and four bags, all to myself. I felt a familiar itch in the back of my throat.

After going south a couple blocks, I realized that the itch in the back of my throat had turned to a burning. And my hands! The feeling in my hands was like when I had tried to help a cokehead who had caught on fire while freebasing. The idiot had kept running, and

I'd had to trip him or see the whole crack house go up in flames. I'd tripped him and rolled him with my bare hands, the hairs on my fingers and forearm singeing to the skin. I looked at my hands and saw that the cloth was soaked in red. I tried to swallow. My tongue wouldn't move.

I stopped at a gas station on the corner and bought myself a pack of Camels and twenty ounces of Coke, laughing at the irony of it all when I put the bottle on the counter. "Twenty ounces for a dollar," I told the lady behind the counter. "That's a great deal." She had a confused smile.

I had her open the bottle for me, and using both hands, I lifted the Coke to my lips and drank. I asked her to open my pack of cigarettes. She lit one for me. I looked at her. She had long wavy blond hair and a moon face, bulging gray eyes, buckteeth, but a nice solid figure. I smiled at her. She smiled back. She didn't run away.

I walked outside and took a deep breath. People nodded at me as they passed.

On the bus ride back, I looked everyone in the eye. And I'm sure, if they looked at me, they could see it in me too. First money I'd ever earned doing honest work.

When I got back to the Oasis, the front door was open and the coffee can was in place, nestled between the wall and somebody's cowboy boots. I took off my gym shoes, placed them in their spot, and turned just in time to avoid an elbow and a mop handle.

"Could you watch it with the mop?" I said.

"So you're the new guy?"

I nodded. The guy in front of me had a mess of dirt-brown hair that he gelled straight back. Short, chubby nose, monobrow across his forehead, but a genuine smile, good except for a missing incisor. I shook his hand and winced.

"What happened to your hand there, guy?"

The T-shirt strips had turned dark brown.

"There a first-aid kit in the place?"

He leaned on the mop head, looked up at the ceiling.

"Maybe Tats has one," he said. "Yeah, Tats has one. And if he doesn't, I'll buy you one. I got a problem hand too, see?"

He showed me his right hand. His pinkie was missing.

"When I was on the streets, this situation came up, and some street punk cut off my finger." He flexed his remaining fingers. "Still stings and whatnot from time to time. Let me see your hand again."

I gave him my hands to inspect. He prodded the cloth with his thumb. I grimaced.

"That's very serious there. You'll need antibiotics and maybe some stitches and stuff. Definitely see Tats. Could be infected. And don't let any flies near it." He shook a finger in front of my face. "You'll get maggots. That's what Zhivago says. How's it feel? The hands?"

My hands felt like they were holding hot napalm.

"My name's Bob," he said. "We met yesterday, but I forgot your name. You know how it is."

"Eddie," I said.

I shook hands again, like an idiot. Through the cloth, I could still feel his missing pinkie, but more than that I felt excruciating pain.

"Where's Tats?"

"Dining room. I gotta finish detail though. You know what time it is?"

"Don't have a watch."

"Oh yeah," he nodded, looked down at his wrist, noticed a watch, and looked at the time. "It's 4:30."

I pushed past him as quick as I could. There were a couple guys in the TV room, a couple more in the kitchen. I'd reintroduce myself later. Tats was in the dining room with T.T. and another guy I didn't know, drinking a cup of coffee, one hand pressed to his head. He had a Monopoly board in front of him.

He looked up when I came in.

"You get paid?"

"Yeah."

"Good."

He returned to looking at the board.

"I'm sorry, Tats," T.T. said. "I think you need to throw in Illinois, Indiana, and Kentucky."

Tats nodded.

"Don't you got to be at work, T.T.?" I asked.

"I got fired."

"Boardwalk, Park Place, and railroads for yellows and oranges, and now he's saying reds too," Tats said, taking a sip from his coffee.

"You're going to lose," I said.

T.T. shook his head. Tats took a long swig from his coffee, then turned and stared at my hands.

"Show me your hands," Tats said.

I gave them to him. He carefully undid the cloth to reveal a mess of blood and blisters and shards of skin. It looked like something you'd buy at a butcher's.

I sat down beside him. He gave me a cigarette. He sent T.T. to get the kit.

It ended up being a job too big for Tats, so he called in Zhivago. Zhivago was six and half feet tall and full of muscle, and had thick black hair that seemed to cover every inch of him. He had hair coming out of his ears, hair from his shoulders, thick, black and curly. He also could bench over three hundred pounds, according to Tats, and liked to show it—he had detail for two weeks because he'd taken to wrestling with Bob the past weekend, after Bob had claimed to have been an all-state wrestler in high school, and he'd ended up breaking the coffee table in the basement in two when he'd tripped on a takedown. He was also reckoned by everyone in the house to be the medical expert, as he'd been an animal vet out near Peoria until a run-in with the DEA cost him his license.

Zhivago decided to call the house spaghetti pot into action, boiling water in it and sterilizing a few tools he had: scalpel, tweezers, some good needle-nose pliers of Tats', as well as his toothbrush, which he'd accidentally knocked into the toilet during detail. He set aside a big roll of gauze, Band-Aids, three different antibiotic ointments, as well as T.T.'s foot fungus spray, which both he and T.T. thought might come in handy.

After he cleared out the rest of the guys from the house, most of whom had collected in the dining room either because they were fascinated by the sight of blood, or because they felt it was their duty to help out since they'd said they'd been in Nam and had been around battlefield wounds, he sat down to work. Tats kept me company, in case it got bad, and to keep an eye on Zhivago in case he tried to do more than he should.

Zhivago rinsed his hands in the spaghetti pot water, dried them off, and holding both my hands palms up in his, asked, "So how long has this been hurting?"

"Since today."

"How long have you had it?"

"I cut 'em up at work."

"Will you quit with the doctor bullshit and just fix him up?" Tats yelled.

"I'm just trying to make sure there are no complications. You ever seen gangrene? You want this kid to lose his hands?"

Tats lit up a smoke and leaned back.

"If he loses them, then it'll be that much harder for him to grab a crack pipe," Tats said.

Zhivago looked over my hands a bit more, then laid them face up on a towel on the table.

"Here's what I'm going to do. I'm going to clean your hands, real gentle. It might hurt, so just bite down on something. We got a towel, Tats?"

Tats nodded. He pointed to a clean towel that was folded on a corner of the table.

"Right. You bite down on that. So I clean up your hands. Then what I do is cut off some of the dead skin—germs hide in that stuff. I'll cut the blisters too. If you're gonna work tomorrow, you're going to need them drained. Then I wash it again, put on some antibiotic ointment, and wrap your hands good with gauze. I'll change the gauze in the morning and when you get back from work. We do this process each night, and it'll hurt, but that's how it goes."

"Are you sure everything has been sterilized?" I asked. I'd been premed.

"You want to do it yourself?"

I shut up.

"What about showering? He stinks," Tats said. I hadn't had a shower yet.

"Can't get soap on it," Zhivago said. "Gangrene and soap are like a nuclear bomb."

"We could put gloves on him," Tats said, "rubber band 'em up for when he takes showers so the soap and water don't get in there."

"That's right," Zhivago said. "And if they do, we use the fungus spray."

He waved the can in front of my face.

"Got it?"

I nodded, swallowed hard, and closed my eyes. This was a shitty excuse for medicine. Tats stuffed the towel in my mouth, then held my hands down, standing up to lean the full weight of his body on my wrists.

"To think," he said, "a couple months ago we coulda filled you with Jim Beam and there'd be no problem."

"Welcome to sobriety," Zhivago said.

Rama needed the cure, or better heroin. He twitched on the ground, his skin turning blue, eyes rolled back in his head, blood trickling from his nose. Black lines inched up his arms, throbbing, sending off finer black lines that spread across him like he was caught in a fishing net. His men were in a tight circle around him, battling with long, curved swords that had mantras emblazoned on them, their armor glistening with blood underneath the wine-red sun. The Rakshasas pounded against them, wave after wave, their army stretching all the way back to Ravana's castle. The Rakshasas threw tree trunks, they fought with talons, they bent down and tore huge, dripping mouthfuls from the dead. Indrajit, Ravana's son, played grand-wizard over the battlefield, floating in a black chariot. A monsoon of arrows rained down upon the screaming men from his open mouth.

In the heart of India, Hanuman snorted a little coke to get himself ready for the next jump. The Hill of Herbs was damn heavy. He was thirsty. He needed to take a piss. His hands were sweaty. He had no idea how much longer he could hold on to the hill. His arms hurt. He wished he had shot up before he'd begun looking for the damn hill. He wished he could shoot up now just to take the edge off. He grit his teeth.

He jumped.

Zhivago later told me that I passed out when he got to the removing-the-skin part. They called in T.T. to prop me up, and with Tats' weight on me, they were able to finish the job. When I woke up I was wearing gauze and my hands were so big I felt like a boxer.

Tats handed me some extra-large sky-blue latex gloves that the guys used for cleaning the toilets, and after I got them tight on my hands and sealed at the wrists, I felt safe to take a shower. I walked slowly up the stairs, anticipating the feel of the water, the smell of the soap. I would turn the water on as hot as my skin could handle and just stand there, feeling the steady drumming on the back of my neck. I could close my eyes.

When I got in the shower, I felt like I was finally at home. I've never felt so safe in my life as I did at that time, in a steaming hot shower, with a big bar of soap, and a dozen guys roaming the house who cared about whether or not I stayed sober, and who wanted me to be able to work the next day, to have use of my hands, not because I owed them and they needed my cash, but because, one way or another, they'd been in the same place. So what if I was conning them? I sank to my knees in the shower. I opened my mouth and drank the water coming from above. It was hot and clean.

When I got out of the shower and got dressed, Zhivago inspected my hands to make sure I hadn't gotten them wet, and the rest of the guys stopped by to talk and introduce themselves, pat me on the back, and say welcome. They led me to my room and sat on my bed. I told them that I needed to sleep if I was going to get to work the next day. I liked the way they kept laughing, how one guy asked me if I'd jerked off in the shower with my new gloves. One of them, a guy named Bill, said he'd take me out for ice cream the next night.

Zhivago ended up coming into the hell room at four in the morning to wake me up. He did a good job changing the dressings on my hand. My palms looked worse, if that was even possible, but he said that it was all part of the healing process. "You gotta get worse before you can get better, just like in recovery." He threw me a bottle of Advil and told me to take ten right there, and ten every four hours. With that, I left the house.

I took the bus out to Day Labor, found the same line of guys, stood in the exact same place, and got pushed aside. The guy took one look at my hands, and even though I told him the gloves were just so I could grip the wheelbarrow better, he knew better. I stood with the crowd watching the bus rumble off, and I started to panic. I walked back home rather than waste the bus fare.

Tats was on the porch smoking when I finally got back home.

"No work, Eddie?"

I swallowed.

"No."

I took a deep breath and looked at my hands.

"Tats," I said.

"Yeah, Eddie?"

"Tats," I said, "my name's not Eddie."

He nodded.

"My name's Cheeni," I said.

"It's actually Srinivas," he said, pronouncing it correctly. He smiled.

"It's good to finally meet you," he said. "I was waiting for ya."

I felt a strange feeling well up inside me. I looked up at Tats.

"You don't happen to know Hanuman or anything, do you?"

"What kinda name's that?"

"It's an Indian name," I said.

"What kinda Indian? Indian like with bows and arrows, or Indian from India?"

"I'm from India."

"Couldn't hardly tell, Srinivas. You look like a plain old alcoholic and drug addict to me."

I nodded.

"So what do I do now?"

"Find a job. I need that deposit soon."

"That's all you got to say?"

"That's common sense."

My mother always said I didn't have any common sense. People were book smart or street-smart, but she said I was too lazy to make anything happen with my book smarts, and too oblivious and insensitive to get by on street smarts. Tav saw it different. Maybe I didn't have his street experience, but I had potential. I was long and lean and strong. I could wedge my fingers in mortar gaps between bricks and clamber up the sheer face of a brownstone to the open third-floor window. I could crack a deadbolt, boot a door off its hinges. I could rip a purse, stiff-arm a Samaritan, and outrun a cop.

We'd made the neighborhoods around Wrigley Field our stomping ground. Suburbanites thronged to the Cubs games, wallets fat with cash, and the drunk stumbled the streets, tanked with beer and ready to talk about the Cubs. Tav could limp up, raise his hand for a high five, and talk Cubs, and, caught between fear of the black stranger and pity for the poor cripple, they'd quickly slip into the safe camaraderie of statistics babble. I'd rush in, knock Tav down, knock them down if I could, and make the quick grab. They'd try to help him, and by the time they discovered they were light, I was already in an alley investigating the loot. Tav claimed that as long as we didn't hurt anybody, the cops wouldn't care too much what we did. The area immediately around Wrigley Field was off-limits due to hidden cameras and hypersensitive cops, but enough fat cash staggered around the surrounding blocks to gorge us for weeks.

"It don't last," Tav said. "Keep that up front. Moment cops get wise, you better be moving elsewheres."

Sure enough, even though we were careful, flyers with vague descriptions of us began popping up on store doors or stapled to telephone poles. I was listed as six and a half feet of beefy violence, while Tav was depicted as a quick but short knife man, if he was noticed at all and not just considered another victim of my thuggery. I was sometimes white, sometimes Hispanic, sometimes black, and none of the flyers made any mention of Tav's CP. Either people thought Tav's CP was a good act, or they were too embarrassed to consider the alternative.

One time the cops shone a bright light on us as we came out of an alley, but Tav's limp seemed to put them at ease. I figured it was because, like most folks, they thought cripples can't be crooks, that they're just victims of life's cruelty begging for some good, old-fashioned Christian compassion. Instead of barking at us to spread-eagle or empty our pockets, the ritual of any veteran North Side cop when encountering nonwhites in an alley at night, these cops talked soft.

"Are you hurt?" they asked Tav.

"I'm always hurtin'. What the fuck you care?" Tav asked.

"There's a vicious fuck mugging people out here," one answered. "Best way you can get back at him is to make a statement if you've seen him."

"Do I look like I been mugged?" Tav asked, glaring at them.

Tav was a natural of the street. I could feel my nerves, and I wanted to play kiss ass with the cops until they rolled off, but Tav knew that being nice would be a dead giveaway. The cops were used to guys like us. Anything sweeter than hate was a sign of a con.

I slipped into a thick Indian accent. "He is being my patient," I said. "He has the CP."

The cops exchanged a look and planted their light on me.

"You don't look like a doctor," one of them said.

"I am not being a doctor," I said. "I am massaging therapist and I am teaching him mantras. His chakras are—how is it you are saying?" I mashed my hands together and nodded, then tapped Tav's back along the spine and nodded.

"And you're giving him therapy here?"

"Motherfucker promised me a beer," Tav said.

"We were watching Cubs game, and now I am looking for a bars. Where is this Clarks Street?"

The cops shook their heads and laughed.

"Goddamn tourists," one said. He pointed at the streetlight ahead. "Around the corner."

A pickup blaring salsa music ran a red light, plowing into a blue-striped Cadillac with a Cubs flag on the antenna. When the salsa pickup's driver popped out with a beer bottle in hand and shoved the Sandberg-jerseyed Cadillac passenger, who held a wailing redhead slung over her shoulder, a crowd erupted around the cars. Tav and I slipped off as the cops tunneled in.

We took a bus down to Division, dipping into our stash of mugged tokens, and hustled to Cabrini Green. I could feel a despairing anger around us, as if it leaked slowly from the cracked and weary concrete of the projects, poisoning anyone who lived there. R&B love ballads whispered at each other in the night air, but warring jacked-up speakers on the street drowned out the sounds with machine-gun raps. At least I could fantasize about a magical transformation for myself, some fairy-tale life in the suburbs with a fenced-in yard and friends and respectability. I could compare my life against those of everyone in my family and all the kids I'd run into in school and know that my current situation had to be an anomaly, that people like me were destined, at least, for nine-to-five middle-class ennui. But the folks of Cabrini Green were in a prison, and everybody knew it. They had the world to be pissed off at, the pattern of their lives, the migration of good luck from their ancestral line. There was no one battle to overcome so they could feel the satisfaction of vengeance. There was the concrete of their worlds, the rigidity of the prisons their lives had become, and the unhappy brotherhood with everyone else in Cabrini Green. So they fought with music and words, the occasional bullet, and they searched for whatever salvation could make the night pass easily. Time loses meaning when you're homeless, or in the projects, or in jail. The near future, the near past, the distant future, the distant past—it all fades to inconsequentiality in the face of the vindictive, sadistic now. All you want to do is live with the current moment, forgetting the regrets of the past. When the smoke of the pipe, the sting of the needle, touches deep, you get what you want. You slip time. You live an eternity of ecstasy in that moment, freed from body and mind, freed from yourself. Nothing else matters anymore. Nothing needs to.

I glared at the darkness around me, thinking I could ward off the hoods who wanted to roll me by keeping my hand in my jacket pocket, clenched around a chunk of concrete. I hoped that from a distance it might look like I had a cop-killer cannon in my jacket. The paranoia nauseated me, but I couldn't escape it—the air was so thick with fear that anyone walking through soon fevered with the infection. They did not want to leave us alone, but they would have to let us go about our business in peace. We were devotees of the man with the bags of rock, and nobody would ever trouble those willing to pay his tithe. Our latest wallet lift had netted fifty-four bucks, so we pocketed seven bucks apiece and flashed four fingers at a bald guy in a dingy wife-beater puffing a blunt beside an immaculate white van. I slapped him our forty bucks. He spit four rocks skinned in red plastic into the palm of his hand and transferred it to me with a handshake. He gave Tav a nod, then opened a door in the van and disappeared inside. For a moment, as smoke billowed out from the van, I thought I saw the smack of cards and the flash of cash.

"They play poker?" I asked Tav.

"Shut the fuck up," he said.

"You gotta get me into that game," I whispered to Tav. "I guarantee I win us slabs."

Tav spat on the sidewalk and shook his head.

"I don't care how good you say you were. That game ain't meant for you."

Tav led the way to a warehouse and pointed out the fire escape. I knelt down and he wrapped his good arm around my neck, and I pulled his good leg around my waist. I climbed up the ladder slowly, Tav's arm a noose, and heaved us onto the roof, sprawling on my back. The tar top was still warm from the summer sun, the night sky above reflecting a faint orange from the city lights below, a few murky stars nestled in the glow. A stiff breeze blew in off the lake, heavy with heat, but I couldn't smell the city, couldn't feel it. The city felt like a stage backdrop, a stale irrelevancy drowned out by the promise of the pipe.

I flipped Tav a rock—he always needed to go first, that was our deal. It worked better for me that way too since I'd sometimes get so twitchy from wanting a hit that I'd fuck up the pipe and huff the rock into the chore. I'd have to dig bits out of the copper wire or brillo we used as a filter and try it again, but I'd get so pissed, feeling like I'd been cheated, that the hits I got were never enough. Tav was cool about it, after the first time he cussed me out. There was always a bit of jealousy going on with him, the way he'd look at my legs or I'd catch him rubbing his arm—he was trapped in a rusted-out hooptie of a body, and I was the jackass revving next to him at the light in my natural-born-monkey turbocharged Mustang. When it came to crack, though, he was the master of the pipe, lord of my senses.

Tav settled in with the pipe and I waited, fidgeting with the rocks we had left. He took his sweet time blasting the pipe hot, the rim of the glass a glowing orange halo, and inhaled. I picked out the rock I wanted for my hit and unwrapped it, holding it up against the stars. Light framed the edge of the rock, dull and dirty, but as I traced an orbit with the rock against the night sky, the bright spark of Venus caught the rock's milky heart for a moment, and it blazed like my own personal moon.

. . .

In second grade, the day after my teacher had told my class I was retarded and made me wear a plaque proclaiming my inferiority, a kid brought in his dad's rock collection for show-and-tell: golden, silver, polished, rough, red, sparkling. In the center of the table he placed a biconical pink diamond the size of my fist. The other kids gaggled over the petal of turquoise or the conchate hunk of fool's gold, but I grabbed the pink diamond. Past its polished surface of diaphanous carnation, at its center I saw a milky diamond, a perfect replica in miniature. The boy had no idea what he had, saying his dad thought it was quartz, that it was worthless, but I knew the pink diamond was precious. Such things could not possibly occur naturally. The only reasonable explanation was that the diamond was the prison of some Goddess, and fate had brought her finally to me. I waited until everyone sat down in their seats, and during a moment of busywork I asked to go to the bathroom. I walked past the table with the show-and-tell stones and grabbed my pink diamond. When I brought it home at the end of the day, my parents asked where I'd found it. In the sandbox, I lied. I took the diamond with me into the garage and smashed at it with my dad's hammer. For the next months I spent a few hours every day hammering at it, using anything I could find in the garage. I needed to free the Goddess and hold her close. I felt that if I had her in my hand, the troubles of my family, the sadness that leaked into my life, would fade and disappear. She would help me if I freed her.

One day my grandmother came into the garage, pleading with me to stop my hammering. I told her I couldn't, that much depended on my work.

"You will never find answers searching through rocks," she said. "God does not live in the unliving. Only Rakshasas are imprisoned that way."

Still, that summer when my family went to India, I smuggled the diamond with me. Every night I would take it up to the terrace and bang on it. A crack widened in the pink exterior, so I stole an old chisel from a worksite at the temple and wedged it in the crack, raining blows on it with a brick until the brick crumbled. Nobody minded me—I was just a kid screwing around in the summer. At least I wasn't off buying fireworks with my brothers and waging bottle-rocket wars with the beggar boys. At least I wasn't spitting from the terrace on the devotees as they passed on their way to the temple. Only Varadha would come up to look on me, shaking her head.

"That you are wasting so much time with this, in this heat—you must feel like you are in a teakettle! Come inside! See how much you are sweating? This is not natural. It is not good."

But I was a boy and she was just an old woman, so I didn't think I needed to listen to her. Nobody in my family listened to her anymore. She had aged into irrelevance.

Later that day, I brought the diamond back up to the terrace. The terrace concrete scorched my feet, but the cool breeze off the ocean soon brought sharp rain. As I hammered at the diamond, the clouds doubled on each other, rising high into the sky, a dark black wall flickering with its own lightning. Slivers of hail shot toward me, but still I worked the stone. My oldest brother came up to look for me. He saw me with my diamond and asked what I wanted to do. He traced his hand over the finger-thick groove I had chipped out of the rock's skin, then motioned me to a corner of the terrace shielded from the wind. He went downstairs and came back up with a plastic bag of fireworks. He wedged the groove with squat and fearsome charges, then nestled my diamond between two fist-sized bombs. He gave me the match, and I lit the fuse.

My brother kept his head down, warning me about shrapnel, but I needed to see. The explosion blazed light with a belly-reverbrating whomp, thunking me into submission with its hail. Sunlight shaped as woman rose from where the stone had been, twice as tall as my father. She strode toward me, her skin sloughing off in opalescent streamers until all that remained was shadow shaped as body. Her mouth opened wide—large red fangs caged a dying universe, pinprick stars fading into nothing. She reached out and shyly caressed my hand.

I woke up in a bed with a damp cloth over my eyes, Varadha rubbing my hand. I tried to remove the cloth, but she said my eyes were burned, that we would need to see a doctor. In another room, she promised, my mother was beating my brother soundly. My grandmother asked what happened, and I told her that we had freed the Goddess from the stone. That we used fireworks. That the Goddess had walked toward me and held my hand.

"What did she look like?" my grandmother asked, squeezing my forearm.

"She was bright. She had long white hair," I said. "But she saw me and she changed. Then she was so dark."

She patted my arm.

"You looked at her and it was like staring at the sun. I saw Sita once, before I was married. She came in white and with her were five maidens in white saris. They blessed me, but they were too bright for me to look at long."

I shook my head.

"There was only one," I said. "She was naked. She looked like ice. And then she turned dark and she had fangs."

"Kali," she whispered. I heard rapid footsteps, the bang of doors. I removed the cloth from my eyes and tried to open them, but they were sealed shut. I heard yelling in another room in the house, but no one came back in for me, not until hours later, not until the doctor had come, not until Seetharama was hours into chanting mantras and tossing ladles of rice into an open flame beseeching the Gods for protection.

A few days later, Seetharama, while climbing the steps to his restaurant, coughed once, closed his eyes, and slumped to the ground. When I went onto the terrace that night to escape the throngs that had come to visit his body, I found Grandmother crying amidst the plants. I always liked going on the terrace at night because I could walk between the potted plants kept there and smell the scents of coriander and mint, gardenia and rose, and feel the soft kisses of the leaves on my cheeks as I walked. I could take some of the flowers and rub them in my palms, and when I slept I could smell the flowers all night long. I could look over the edge of the terrace wall and see all of Madras: the bright yellow lights of the streets, the squat concrete buildings, and the tall thickets of trees everywhere, dropping coconuts, mangoes, bananas, and leaves the size of small children, so many trees that it looked like a forest had set up camp and was waiting for the right day to eat all the buildings. And I could look to the east and see the Marinas Beach, the bobbing lights of the lanterns of the fishermen in their long wooden boats on the sea, the waving flashlights of the families sitting on blankets in the sand. I could imagine the vendors chasing the children around with balloons and kites and squeaking toys trying to make the children beg their parents to buy something, anything, and other vendors rolling wooden stands along, enticing families with peanuts or corn daubed in chili powder and lime, which they would roast over a pile of coals right in front of them. And at the edge of sight, when the lighthouse beacon flashed, I could imagine seeing the last stone temple that some ancient kingdom had carved out of the hills, home now only to seagulls and the bones of fish, and sometimes I could even see the waves of the ocean as they slammed against it, trying to destroy it. It is the ocean that I always found myself looking at last, stretching to the east, full of waves and anger. The Rakshasas slept in that ocean.

My grandmother stood staring at the ocean from the edge of the terrace, her tear-streaked face glistening in the moonlight. In her hands she held long strands of a flowering saffron-colored vine, and each time her lips moved with the unmistakable repetition of a mantra, she twined the vine around her fingers. She did not notice me, and so for a long time I watched as the vine slowly bound her hands together, pollen and ocher flowers flurrying to the ground, staining her skin with phosphorescent lines.

"Grandmother," I said.

She turned slowly and stared through me.

"Don't worry," she said, slowly unlooping the vine from her fingers.

"It is loud downstairs. So many people coming to see Grandfather, and all of them are crying," I said, looking over the edge of the terrace.

A long line of people extended from the front door off into the shadows down the street.

She nodded and the tears began again. A thick haze hung in the night, veiling the fat and orange moon with the smell of burning.

"Grandfather died because of you," she said. "Nobody else will say so. But you know. You are willing to believe what my children are embarrassed to know. He sacrificed himself to Kali to save you."

I felt the memory of guilt for a moment, a sharp rock stuck in my throat, but when I took a breath, it disappeared. I knew I should cry, but I couldn't remember the feeling of sadness. I tried to think of happy moments with my grandfather, but all I could sense was a vast grey landscape of memory, cold and irrelevant, meaningless. I was a body without emotion.

She began twining the vine around her fingers again, whispering to herself.

"I'm sorry," I said, feeling the need to break the silence. I leaned close to her, pressing my cheek against her hip, the soft touch of her familiar cotton sari providing reassurance. She rested her vine twined hands on my head and we stared toward the turbulent ocean, breathing in time with the waves.

In between the alpha and omega rock, when the highest trill of a smooth-torched crack hit backslid from God's aria of creation to the keen of a half-drowned demon dragging itself onto the beach, was when Tav and I had our best ideas. We could think about more than where we were getting our next rock. We could make plans for our future.

"We need to hit something big." I said. "Something where we get enough cash to keep us in enough rocks so we can lay low for a while. The cops ain't stupid."

Tav nodded. "We got to move. I figure South Side, near the college."

"I'm talking hitting something for big money. That's how you get ahead."

"What the fuck you know about getting ahead? You go big, you go down big. There ain't nothing big we could get in on anyway."

"Poker," I said.

"I'm telling you," Tav said, shaking his head, "you just gonna get fucked."

"But what else we got? You said something about South Side, the college. That's nickel and dime shit, right?"

"Nothing wrong with what works."

I smacked the tar top with my hand. "It's boring. First time, yeah, it's kinda a rush. But then? Same small shit all the time, and for what?"

"You want to go into rehab again?"

I waved him off. "I'm not saying that and you know it. I'm saying we should have a little ambition. What if we scraped together a big stack of cash, started buying, maybe even being the guys making the rocks. Then we're in control and we're comfortable and we got rocks all the time and money all the time."

Tav shook his head. "Give me the pipe," he said.

I held it from him and stepped back.

"I dealt in college," I said coldly. "And I'm a good poker player. You been running things for us, and I appreciate it, but now you listen to me. I got an idea, and we're going to go with it."

"Fuck you. Give me the fucking pipe."

I took a few more steps away and torched it.

"Give me a fucking hit," Tav said.

I walked to the edge of the roof and held the pipe over the alley.

"I can get another pipe easy," Tav said.

"Yeah," I said. "But how you gonna climb down?"

Tav shook his head. "I knew you'd try to fuck me. Everybody always does."

"We're a team," I said quietly. "Long as you respect me, we play it all equal. That's all I'm saying. I ain't your servant."

"I never said you was. I was just showing you how things was, what you got to watch for."

"Fine," I said. "But now we're going to do something my way. We're getting me in a poker game. We find some dealers, set it up."

"Better to just head South Side."

"You said you'd get fucked South Side."

"Yeah, but maybe not. Better than this poker bullshit. That's guaranteed to get fucked."

I nodded. "Then this is how it works. We're doing poker. A couple times. I guarantee I'll make it big for us. And then we go South Side with the cash. Do whatever, but we use the cash to keep it low. See what I'm saying? Poker means cash, and cash makes South Side safe since you won't need to stomp on any toes. It's the best chance we got."

"Just give me the fucking pipe," Tav said.

"We cool then?" I asked, handing him the pipe.

Tav didn't answer. He stuffed the last rock and jacked the lighter so long the pipe glowed like a new sun. He sucked on his singed fingers, then stared into the pipe, looking for more.

15

Spirituality is about acting out of your inner humanity, if you go deeper, you'll be acting out of inner divinity. This has nothing to do with morality . . . the maximum damage to this world has been done with good intentions.

—Jaggi Vasudev

Marco's beeper went off just before we left the parking lot of the restaurant. He took one look at the number, rushed over to a pay phone, and screamed at whoever was on the other end of the line for a full two minutes. When he got back to the car, I kept my eyes on the road and breathed quietly.

"I got something come up," he finally said, stomping the accelerator. "I'm dropping you on campus. You sit tight in your place till I call."

He didn't speak for the next fifteen minutes of the drive. When he left me at the steps of the dorm he finally said, "Don't fuck around. Sit tight," then squealed his tires and roared off. I wondered if he was rushing off to meet up with Teddy T and a bound and gagged Salvatore or Eduardo, outlining for himself how he would go about torturing them before their broken bodies were discarded near the landfill, or if he was going to pick up some tools so he could carve me into an example. I didn't have to waste much time thinking about what to do. I had to escape, and the longer he was gone, the better chance I had of doing so. As for Salvatore or Eduardo, it was probably already too late.

I ran up the stairs of the dorm two at a time. The other students moved out of my way, glaring as I passed. Whatever reasons they had for disliking me, I was sure their feelings would only intensify as more news came out and the hint of the rumors solidified with the facts. The door to our dorm room stood open, and I went in hesitantly, expecting campus security at least. Instead, only shadow and silence greeted me. I grabbed my pipe from my bedroom, sat down on the couch, and blazed a super-kind mint julip bud the size of my thumb.

A wall of shadow moved from a corner, and for a moment I saw the glint of a golden crown and earrings, a tail whipping to slide out the chair across from me. It sat heavily before me, cloaked in darkness. I knew his name from the stories my family had told me, the same God I could always sense lurking in the corner of my fantasies and nightmares, watching. My grandmother had said that the ancestors of our family line watched out for us, but not until that moment did I realize that they could do so through a God. I dropped to the floor and prostrated myself before him.

"I'm sorry, Hanuman," I said, sobs rising up unbidden. My muscles quivered, as if with their own emotion, and would not support me. Alone in the dark, with a God prepared to judge me, I had no will left for excuses. Everything I reached for I destroyed, and so a part of me passionately strove for my own destruction. My grandmother had warned me. Now a God had come to claim me, and I had no regret, only an expectation for the relief promised from the burden of being.

"Should I thank you for not taking my computer? Or is it just that you forgot to get it on your way out and came back for it now?"

I blinked, and slowly the form in front of me took on the shape of Jonas. A part of me wondered if I was going through some kind of hallucination, or if my brain chemistry had jumped the rails of its own volition, but deep inside, beyond sense reaction and intellectual interpretation, I knew who stood before me. Still, if a God presented himself as another person, it was wise to continue the charade until the God fully revealed himself.

"I needed the money, but I don't know why. It's not really about getting high anymore, or trying to stay alive. I used to know myself, but now . . ." I buried my head in my hands.

"Then ask for help," he said quietly. "And ask for it from the right people."

"It's too late," I said. "I'm either dead or in prison. One or the other. That's the future."

"Salvatore's safe," Jonas said. "He's started talking with the police."

"Then it's prison at least," I sighed, more out of a sense of relief than regret. "How many years you think I'll get?"

Jonas smiled, leaning back in his chair.

"You've never understood Salvatore, have you? He would do anything for you. He's on your side. He would never tell the police anything that could hurt you."

"Either you know what he's said, or that's bullshit masquerading as faith. You ever notice that the ones that get fucked worst are the ones with the most faith?"

Jonas's face tightened into a grimace, but then he looked away.

"You can end all of this right now," he said. "You can go to the police, admit everything, and then work from there."

"I'll get kicked out of school for sure," I said, "and you can bet Teddy T's got guys that can get to me even if the cops protect me. They'll get Salvatore. Just watch."

"Then those are the consequences. If you don't do anything, this will definitely get worse. You've surrounded yourself with the worst kinds of people—they will never do anything to help you. If you accept your mistakes, at least then you have a chance to begin doing the right thing, and then God can begin working through you."

I shook my head.

"Jonas, that's bullshit. If my folks find out I had a run-in with the cops and got kicked out of school, they'll never talk to me. And then what? I've got nothing. My family wouldn't have anything to do with me. And the world—the world fucks people if they ask for a second chance. You seriously think anybody would let me back into college after this? You think anybody would hire me if I had a felony? Only way to play this is to work shit out with Teddy T. Settle things without the cops. Otherwise I might as well be dead."

"You want to do good," Jonas said quietly. "Your family would stand by you. So would any good person. My church would help you because I would tell them that you want to do good, that you genuinely regret what you've done."

I laughed.

"Jonas, that's sweet and all, but let's face it. Best thing you can do is stay as far from me as possible."

"That wouldn't be right," Jonas said solemnly.

"It doesn't matter," I said. "I've got to settle this. And I've got to do it on my own."

"You can't do this alone."

I grabbed Jonas's hand and squeezed it tight.

"I appreciate it, Jonas, really. But get the fuck out of this. You've got nothing to gain here, and so why do it? All I've been is shit in your life—I won't blame you for bailing out. In fact, I want you to."

Jonas squeezed my hand back.

"That's why you can count on me."

When the phone finally rang it was Eduardo.

"I cleared things up," he said, "so we got some time to set things right. Can't find Salvatore, but Teddy's got folks on it."

"Marco rolled off in a hurry," I said, "and he looked pissed. You figure you know why?"

After a sigh and a pause, Eduardo responded.

"Nothing you need to worry about right now. We need to meet and talk. Ten minutes? On the corner by that shitty coffee place? Can you do that?"

"I'm there," I said. "There's stuff Marco said that I need to ask you about."

Silence greeted me again, followed by a "Really?"

"Yeah, really."

"Well, he's full of shit, so I wouldn't pay him much attention. He's probably just trying to fuck with you."

"Ten minutes," I said and hung up.

Jonas, who had been sitting quietly by my side, nodded as I filled him in on Eduardo's side of the conversation. He'd listened patiently as I told him all that had happened over the past few days, even taking notes and drawing a diagram for himself as I explained where I thought Teddy T was based, where I thought the dump was, what I thought was going on.

"You go to the coffeehouse," he said quietly. He flexed his knuckles and nodded at his hands. "You should show up alone."

"Don't bring the cops," I warned him.

He shook his head.

"Bringing the police would be the smart approach. Just us two showing up is a very dangerous proposition."

"Eduardo's not going to pull anything stupid in a public place," I said.

Jonas shook his head, rubbing his fists.

"It's not him I'm worried about."

"There's no way I will either. Shit hits the fan, I'll run."

Jonas smiled.

"A good choice. Now you only have to worry about what I'll do."

I sat in the coffeehouse facing the door, Jonas lurking outside amidst the trees. Our plan was for Eduardo to wander in unsuspecting and grab a seat opposite me in the booth. Then, while he was in the midst of wooing me with bullshit, Jonas would sneak in unnoticed through the door and squeeze into Eduardo's side of the booth. If Eduardo tried to pull a gun, Jonas would slam him through the plate-glass window. Most likely, though, Eduardo would play quiet and do what we asked, answering any questions. He'd always been a bit afraid of Jonas. Most people were. Being a giant tended to have that effect.

Eduardo pulled up outside the coffeehouse. He saw me inside and waved me out to join him in his car. I waved for him to join me inside. He honked. I waved for him again. He honked. I stood up and motioned him inside. He honked.

"We're trying to eat in here," somebody yelled. "Can't you Mexicans communicate like normal people? Quit with the honking!"

I should have stayed in my seat, but the people in the coffeehouse were all staring at me, the stupid foreigner, the silly brown man, ruining their meal. If it were one guy, I would have called him an asshole and waded in with sharp fists. But this was an entire coffeehouse staring at me. Eduardo had never looked at me that way, had always treated me like a brother. He might be trouble, but I knew him in a way other people couldn't. I could manage him much more easily than the glare of the coffeehouse patrons, against whom I had no defense but my sudden and overpowering sense of shame for the color of my skin, the disruption I'd brought into their idyllic lives. I ran outside rather than face their eyes. I slid into Eduardo's car, my head bowed in embarrassment.

"Now's not the time to be fucking around," Eduardo said, slamming the car into drive. One of his silver guns lay on his lap, the barrel pointed at me. Outside the coffeehouse, amidst the trees, Jonas stood guard. I stared after him as Eduardo screeched into traffic.

The wind whipped past, the land a gray and brown streak of melt and mud and skeletal trees. The air promised spring just around the corner, but the pale sun warned differently. Months of cold lay ahead, the bitter, bone-chilling cold of the real New England winter.

"You're lucky I'm looking out for you," Eduardo said. "This is the shitty time of year."

"Nothing a sweater can't handle," I said.

"Ain't that. When it melts like this, it's a lot easier getting rid of people. The ground's softer. Lakes and stuff aren't frozen all the way through. And then it refreezes and you've got guaranteed time when nature's your secret keeper."

"Tell me straight," I said as calmly as I could. "Is there a way out of this for me?"

"Teddy T told Marco to take care of you. He was going to take you to a place he likes, drop you with a Taser, carve into you a bit, wake you up, kick the crap out of you, and then . . . I forget the rest of it. He has this ritual. Sick fucking bastard. I've seen him go in with a guy and come out with garbage bags, and it's the only time you'll ever catch him really smiling. But I got them off you, at least for now. I bought you back."

"What do you mean you 'bought me back'?"

"I bought your rights. As an earner. You're all my responsibility now. But we owe a shitload to Teddy T, and we better get it fast or else Marco'll be working us both over."

"You're the one who owes him," I said. "Marco showed me. I was making good money. You're the one that fucked up."

Eduardo gave me a sidelong glance.

"Yeah." He drummed on the steering wheel. "Yeah, it's pretty much my fuckup." He shrugged. "Can't waste time with blame, though. We come up with enough cash to keep Teddy T happy, pay him so you're free and clear, and that's it. That's how you get free."

"How much?"

"Ten G. I mean, there's other shit too, but if we get him ten G by next week, we're off the hook."

"Forever?"

Eduardo banged the horn.

"Off the hook! Who gives a fuck for how long?"

I shook my head.

"And what if it's all bullshit, and he's just trying to get as much cash out of us before he fucks us? You seriously think there's enough cash in the world to keep his paranoid ass from flipping out about us?"

"I'm in charge here," Eduardo said coldly. "Maybe it's not the best, but it's all we got. We don't get him the money, we're dead. No escape, I guarantee. At least if we get the money we got a chance. So you gonna help me get this shit cleared, or do I need to start worrying about where I'm going to bury you?"

My hands faltered into cowardice and shook from their secret fear. I pressed them together in prayer to steady them.

Outside, as the hills darkened into dusk, a shadow bounded alongside us, the reflected light from its golden crown like a star chasing us across the night.

"I can get us the money," I said.

Hamilton wasn't in his shack, and one of his windows was open a crack, but we kicked his door down anyway. I had gloves, but Eduardo couldn't find his, so we improvised. Hamilton had rigged a lock and latch to his dresser, but once we whaled on the wood with our feet, and threw the dresser into walls, it surrendered into splinters and clothes and a roll of close to three thousand dollars. His kitchen cabinets didn't have anything other than pots and pans. Ripping open sofa cushions scattered only foam. Under his mattress, though, we found more money. Another five hundred dollars and a manila envelope filled with pictures of women and rope, bruises and blood, each face branded with a trickle of Hamilton's semen. Eduardo let out a slow whistle as he flipped the pictures one by one. I recognized the high school girls we'd seen with Hamilton before. I recognized a girl from my dorm. There was a young woman who looked like Sarah, her lips pressed tight, her eyes staring up and to the right, unfocused.

Eduardo didn't say anything when I asked him for his lighter, but he started yelling when I flicked the photos on fire, and I had to kick him off me to set the bedsheets aflame. He was already out the door when I turned on the gas stove. Outside, when I fell while running away, my breathing collapsing into sobs, he grabbed my arm and dragged me to his car.

"Nice play, asshole," he said as we rolled away from the blaze. "My prints are everywhere."

I was beyond caring about what he said. I could feel my monkey fur, dank and foul from the overripe mangoes and rotten eggs the Rakshasas throw at me. They invited me into their kingdom, they paraded me around and showed me every inch of their defense, and now they wrap me in oiled cloths, light me on fire, and laugh at the thought of the torch I must become. They know my name, but not my history. I am son of the wind, friend of fire. They do not know the next step in our story.

We drove to Eduardo's place to hide out for the night. The "play," as far as I could gather, was that I'd pinned the arson of Hamilton's place on Eduardo. Since only his prints were there, he'd be the prime suspect. I was the only one who knew he didn't do it. If I ended up dead, he'd have no protection, and if he fucked me in other ways, I could clue the cops in to him if they hadn't picked up the trail yet. Eduardo said this meant I had power and that meant we were legally partners now and that we should take the time to really get to know each other for once. I figured he was only saying that because he hadn't figured a way out yet and was hoping to sight a new angle from whatever he could figure out about me.

We kept Eduardo's bong lit the entire night, a dim lantern in the dark of his room that we passed between us whenever our throats seized up at the unfamiliar honesty of our words. We laid highways of coke to keep our voices rolling. I told him about Sarah, Eva, my sister, trying to explain the rage that had come over me when I saw Hamilton's photos. I told him about my parents, their expectations, how I knew I would never live up to them. It was safe territory—honest information, so it looked like I had no idea what he was up to and was spilling my guts, but limited. He told me about his mother, carving a nine-to-five in a nearby buffet that catered college parties, bringing home leftovers she'd rework by her magic into a sumptuous feast. She'd put Eduardo and his siblings to bed with stories about the stupid college kids, whispering that they too had a chance, that America really was the land of opportunity, that she'd leave their dad soon, she promised. His jail-guard dad deserved leaving, but she never did get away in time. He was a former punch press operator who'd gotten the job through a friend at the plant, and though the jail-guard swagger came naturally with his personality, he had trouble keeping the punch press mentality restrained. People were just big blanks of sheet metal. The only way to get what you wanted was to pound them into the shape they should become.

Eduardo grabbed the bong and pulled a thick hit. He nodded with a slight smile and pointed at me, blowing a column of smoke in my face.

"I rip people off," he said. "Most kids call on Daddy and get the money. That's the way it's supposed to work. Teddy's his own deal. Teddy's just a mean-ass motherfucker."

I yanked a hit, letting the smoke curl slowly from my nose as I exhaled.

"You ever kill anyone?" I asked.

"You're an arsonist, man. You know how shit just happens some-times."

"I've never killed anyone."

He shrugged.

"Guys like us, it's only a matter of time."

"The only person I'll probably ever kill is myself," I said.

"Spoken like a true pussy."

I grabbed the bong and took a thin hit.

Eduardo reached for his case and waved a syringe in the air.

"You up?" he asked.

"Not tonight," I said. I resolved I'd never shoot up with him again. I did a few lines instead.

He put the case away and did a few lines as well. He rubbed his temples and leaned back.

"I was serious about Teddy wanting ten grand," he said, staring up at the ceiling. "We get him that, you promise to get the fuck out of town and never come back, and I guarantee you never have trouble with us again."

"What about Salvatore?"

"Fuck him. Seriously. He's not worth the hassle."

"So he's free too?"

Eduardo rolled on his side and laughed.

"Look, man. You got enough on your plate. If you're dead, you can't do shit for anyone. Take care of your problems and worry about the rest later."

"And all my problems are settled for ten thousand dollars."

"Only about six thousand to go," he said, a friend's smile frozen on his face.

Hamilton's place burning down was big news on campus, but nobody had mentioned arson. For the time being, officials pinned the blame on a toppled candle. From the way Hamilton reveled in the genuine concern of the other students, lamenting the tragic loss while strutting about his daily routine of bong hits and plagiarism with an air of stoicism, I doubted that his family was covering up the details. If Hamilton had heard anything, he would have been the first to announce that he was a victim of a crime. The cops knew nothing, and that bought me time. I told Eduardo I'd written a letter detailing how he was the one who set the place on fire, that I'd witnessed him doing it and that he threatened to kill me, and that I'd left copies of it with a bunch of friends. They'd mail it to the cops if anything happened to me. Eduardo had seen enough movies to understand the threat, and so he took me seriously. Naturally, I kept meaning to get around to writing the letters, but stayed too stoned to do anything. Instead, I told Eduardo it would take some time to get the cash together, two weeks. That gave me a nice honeymoon to keep dealing, where Eduardo and I could pretend we were best of friends.

I went to a few of my classes during some sober moments only to discover that I was way behind. Winter study had ended at some point and the new semester charged toward midterms. My teachers were, in general, sympathetic with my situation. I told them about the hepatitis C, that it made schoolwork difficult, and that I was going through an emotionally difficult period. I would catch up when I had the chance, I promised. My creative writing teacher was the only one who pieced the puzzle together. He realized that the sheaf of pencil- and beer-stained paper that I'd handed in as an attempt to make up for a semester's worth of missed assignments, which I claimed to be a short story in progress, was actually the drunken ramblings of a semiautobiographical journal where I called cocaine "candy," weed "green eyed jane," and described the intricacies of my drug dealing in terms of a lemonade stand. He told me to get off the drugs and get into class, that my writing was incomprehensible crap, and that, no, there was no fucking way in hell he was going to pass me. I told him that "Mr. Fuckhead" was a real character and a good friend of mine and that shit would go down if things didn't break my way. The next day I had to visit with the deans, and I was genuinely confused when they asked about the threats of violence and attacks that I had apparently orchestrated. Soon it came out that they were primarily worked up about the Salvatore issue, which I explained was just a love triangle gone wrong because Salvatore had an alcohol problem. A few days later they yanked me into a panel discussion of my academic and behavioral issues at the college. To my surprise, Alex was on the panel as a student representative. He was called on to announce that I'd also been caught cheating on a genetics homework assignment—I vaguely recalled ripping off somebody's work from the professor's "return" basket and resubmitting it as my own. Aside from Alex, nobody seemed to buy the hepatitis C story, even though it was true—true at least that I had the disease, even if I couldn't really see any effects of it—and it took me a few minutes of bullshitting to recover my stride. I finally hit on a fake breakdown concerning my "drug problem," how I'd become agitated and violent and felt like I was losing myself. I dabbed at my eyes and honked my nose a few times. As was mentioned to me repeatedly, admitting I had a problem was a very big step. Everyone patted me on the back and agreed that I should seek treatment and counseling and that all would work out, that I had to keep a positive attitude, that they were all pulling for me. The college cared. Alex sidled up as I left to let me know there was a monster madhouse planned for the weekend, and that they desperately needed someone to deliver the cool.

"And, hey, man," he said, toeing the ground uncertainly, "sorry to hear about your grandmother."

"That was a while back," I said. "The stroke. She's actually just in a coma, but thanks."

He looked up at me, then looked away.

"I thought you heard," he said. "I mean, we heard. Your family called looking for you. She kicked it . . . I mean . . ." He snapped his fingers and furrowed his brow. "She passed on."

"She has prostrated herself at the feet of Hanuman," I said quietly.

I turned away quickly and ran back toward the dorms.

A bombastic bass line greeted me at the door of the dorm, a crowd of shivering smokers puffing on the steps, bopping to the music like joggers waiting at a stoplight to keep warm. A thick punk I didn't recognize tried to bar my way, saying fuckwads weren't allowed, but I was in no mood to negotiate verbally, so I kicked him in the groin. Just as I was about to knee him in the face, the world flipped and I found myself staring at the sky, my head ringing, my chest feeling like I'd been T-boned by a semi. I touched my hand to the back of my skull and felt the warm stick of blood. I braced my hands on the concrete and pushed myself up. The smokers snickered on the steps. Jonas loomed over me.

"Nice tackle, big man!" one of them hollered, hopping down a few steps to give Jonas a high five. Jonas looked at him in disgust.

"Get up," Jonas said to me, clasping my hand and lifting me up before I had a chance to consider the possibility. "What are you doing here?"

"I live here."

"You're not coming in tonight. Not while Salvatore's here. Not on his birthday."

"Salvatore's here? Get him out of town! It's not safe."

"You'd be better served looking out for yourself."

The door to the dorm opened and a throng tumbled out. In the center of the group, in an oversized purple Hawaiian shirt unbuttoned to his navel, stood Salvatore, flushed and beaming. Eva hung on his shoulder, giggling as she tried to wrap her coat around the both of them.

Jonas slung me over his shoulder and began to stride away, but it was too late.

"What is that crawling back?" Salvatore yelled. "You think you are scaring me, yes? With these guns and these fools. You come stand here and I will show you what is being a man!"

"Let me talk to him," I said to Jonas, trying to squirm from his grip.

"There's nothing to talk about," Jonas said.

"Asshole!" Eva yelled. "You motherfucking asshole!"

"I didn't do anything!" I yelled.

"Fucking you, motherfuckers!" Salvatore yelled, yammering on in Italian, his face beet red, spittle flying from his lips. He threw his beer can at us and missed by twenty feet, but his throw inspired others, and soon cans clanked dangerously close.

Jonas loped off with me as the folks on the step erupted in cheers.

"You should have let me in," I said. "I need to call my family. I wouldn't have done anything. I just need to ask about my grandmother."

"Not after what you did."

"What the hell are you talking about?"

"Don't pretend you don't know. Taking our computers, your threats to Salvatore. That was stupid. What do you think you are? Some kind of gangster? You're an idiot!"

"What the fuck, Jonas! I talked to you about that. I'll get them the money back for their computers—I was just doing it because I needed the money or else Teddy would have killed Salvatore. I was buying time. You know that! I told you!"

Jonas dumped me off of his shoulder and when I stood up, he shoved me away.

"You need help," he said. "You don't even know when you're lying anymore."

"You were there! You remember, don't you?"

Jonas shook his head and stuffed his hands in his pockets.

"Whoever you think you were with, it wasn't me." He sighed and reached forward gingerly and patted me on the shoulder. "Get help," he said. "I've tried to be there for you, but this is too much. You need God in your life, and I don't know anymore how to guide you to him."

"So what am I supposed to do now? Where am I going to sleep? You guys have to let me into the dorm for that at least."

"I have your things packed. Call us and let us know where you want them delivered. But don't come back. You're not welcome around us anymore. You're on your own."

Jonas turned. He looked back at me, his mouth opening as if to say something, his eyes watering up. Then he turned and vanished into the night.

Alone in the dark, I wanted to curl up on the cold ground and sleep until the world faded away. I couldn't call my family—their first instinct would be to judge me, to scold and reprimand me, to bemoan the shame I had brought upon the family. The school had already made their position clear—I would need to set up counseling and drug treatment, navigate my troubles on my own with only their silent approval to keep me motivated to stay on course. I had nothing. No friends, no future, no hope for happiness except what the needle could provide.

So I went to the last safe place I had left. I climbed the steps to Eduardo's apartment and when he didn't answer the door, slipped his lock and entered. His strongbox of weed lay unlocked on the floor, his case of cocaine and syringes next to his bed. I loaded a bowl and sucked the smoke down until my throat burned. I loaded bowls until my lungs were singed and my fingertips black with resin and ash. I opened Eduardo's case and laid out a sidewalk of cocaine and snorted until I could feel my blood trickling down the back of my throat along with the bitter aspirin paste of coke and mucus. In Eduardo's fridge I found two bottles of pills, one filled with ruby gelcaps, the other with unmarked white tablets. I ate ten of each, prepped a syringe, and plunged it between my toes.

I lay in Eduardo's bed and closed my eyes. Through the filter of my eyelids, I saw a universe of light tinged the color of my own blood, suffused with constellations of black motes. My breath heaved in and out, an invisible tide shuddering the motes into new orbits. This was my body, my life, and what I saw was nothing more than the light passing through my eyelids and playing tricks with the flotsam behind my retina. I knew this, and yet I also knew that I was witnessing the universe, that I was the fabric of creation, that my breath was God's own voice of creation. I could feel cool sweat and clammy skin, but in my center a flame grew stronger, my heart charring in the cage of my ribs, my lungs flashing into smoke.

"Open your eyes," a deep voice said.

The universe blinked away. The shadow with the golden crown knelt beside me. He brought a pale white flower to my nose.

"Breathe," he said.

Eduardo was finally allowed to visit once the nurses had me hooked up in the critical care unit. I didn't mention meeting Salvatore, Jonas, Hanuman, or the doctor who pumped me full of charcoal, nor being sacrificed by an ancestor who had caused my entire family line to be cursed. Instead I showed him my hands, the hair singed off, the criss-crossing burns, and said, "God is real."

"Damn right," Eduardo said. "What the fuck made you think you could break into my place and take my stash? You owe me. Big. And, by the way, I also saved your ass."

"No, you didn't."

"Like hell I didn't. I'm the one that called the paramedics. Good thing I'd only stepped out on a drop-off—any longer and you'd have been toast. Had to haul your fucked-up ass out of my place first too. No fucking way was I letting you die and pin the arson rap on me. Stupid time to overdose, man. What the hell were you thinking?"

"I was looking for something," I said.

Eduardo laughed.

"You stupid shit. But catch this—the hospital dorks actually think you were trying to commit suicide."

"I wasn't."

"Yeah, well you'd better not try to fake your way into a psych ward."

"So what happens now?"

Eduardo looked at me incredulously.

"You get the hell out of here as soon as you can, and you get me my money. Teddy T ain't the kind of guy that's going to let you slide because you overdosed."

I closed my eyes and wished for him to go away.

He tapped the bed rail.

"Alright then," he said. "I'll let you pass out. Just call me when you get out and I'll pick you up."

The door banged behind him as he left.

I ended up staying in the hospital for only a couple days. I admitted to the nurses that I'd been trying to get high, and that I felt stupid about it, and they took kindly to me and kept the secret. One of the nurses brought in her seventeen-year-old son during visiting hours so I could give him a quick lecture on the evils of drugs, and stepped off to deal with other patients so that he could feel comfortable asking any question. I told him the truth. Drugs were damn good in excess, but it cost a hell of a lot, and unless you were born rich, you were better off just becoming an alcoholic. Drugs also tended to kill you quicker. What about pot, he asked. Pot, I assured him, was totally cool. He thanked me, wrote down his phone number, and asked if I knew where he could get a decent eighth of weed. I promised I'd help him if he could find a way to get me out of the hospital and deliver a ride back to campus. He told me that it wasn't a big deal, that he knew how to unhook my IVs, and that he had a car. He found my clothes, ran off hollering for his mom as a half-assed way of distracting the nurses, and twenty minutes later, we were rolling out of the parking lot.

My clothes were coated in puke, so our first stop was to the mall for burritos and a sweater. He decided to buy a pair of *Terminator* sunglasses, and suddenly began insisting that I call him "Snap" for the "cool factor." I told him that Snap really didn't have any cool factor at all, but in the end I let it be and navigated him toward the Poker House. The guys at the house were unsure of what to do about me— rumors spread quickly on campus—but Snap hopped right into the path of a five-foot bong and ripped a massive hit without coughing. The guys told him to stick around for the monster party going on that night, and while they were hollering love at him, marveling at his Teflon lungs, I snagged his car keys and took off.

I could have kept going. Before that overdose, I was the kind of person who would have. But I knew that Teddy T and Marco and Eduardo weren't going to just disappear, and I knew Salvatore was Salvatore. They would find him, or I could stop them and do good for someone for a change. I should have called the police. I could have asked for help. Instead I drove to Eduardo's place.

The Poker House was just starting to flow when Eduardo and I arrived. Alex greeted us gleefully when we waved our brown paper bag in the air, and led us down to his room. We closed the door behind us, and Eduardo pointed one of his guns in Alex's face. I picked through his wallet, skimmed cash nestled in the books on the shelves, fished through drawers, then stuffed the brown paper bag with what we'd caught. Eduardo bound him with his bedsheets and stuffed a T-shirt in his mouth, and then I led the way up to the poker room. Snap waved when he saw me, but soon he looked as surly as the rest. They handed over their wallets and money clips silently, their eyes locked on Eduardo's guns.

"You assholes are going to get what's coming to you," Hamilton yelled.

"Is that right?" Eduardo asked. He nodded toward me. "My associate was just telling me I should shoot one of you, that you'd be the perfect one."

He aimed his gun at Hamilton's chest.

"We should go," I said.

Eduardo nodded.

He touched his gun to the tip of Hamilton's nose.

"This is just a tax," he said, "just protection money. No complaining, okay? You guys don't want your parents knowing how much coke you're doing, do you?"

"Let's go," I said.

Eduardo caressed Hamilton's quivering jaw with the barrel of his gun.

"I'm coming back for you," he said, and then we both ran out the door.

Eduardo drove until we hit a gas station. When we stopped, he counted out the money in the brown paper bag, then rolled up the bag and stuffed it down the front of his pants. He hopped out of the car and plunked quarters in the pay phone, and minutes later he was back in the car, grinning.

"You did great. Teddy T's real happy. We're going to meet right now and settle this," he said.

"Why now? Where?"

"Out by the dumps, and it's gotta be now. You think he's going to let us sit on this and think about it and maybe run off with his money? He wants it now."

"How much did we grab?"

"More than we needed," Eduardo said, thumping me on the thigh. "And now all this shit is finally going to be over."

"I'm taking off after this," I said, "and I'm never coming back."

"Good," Eduardo said. "You'll never be welcome here again."

The drive to the dumps was long and silent. Eduardo rolled the windows down a crack so our cigarette smoke could escape, and the chill night air lent my thoughts a touch of clarity.

"I need to borrow a gun," I said.

Eduardo gave me a sidelong glance.

"I know you don't trust me, but come on, man. If I was going to take you out, I'd have done it already."

"Then there's no problem loaning me one now."

"I thought you hated guns."

"I do."

Eduardo nodded to himself.

"It won't make any difference, you know. Even if they don't pat you down, they know how to use a gun, and you don't. Marco was Special Forces or some shit for crying out loud. You'll just end up putting a cap in your own ass."

"Either shoot me now or give me a gun. Quit fucking around."

Eduardo laughed.

"Alright," he said. "When we get there."

One set of headlights beamed from the dump. We pulled close, rolling slowly, our high-beams on. When we got near, Marco flagged us to a stop.

"We got some guys out there, so don't be stupid," he said, reaching in and pulling the keys out of the ignition. "Eduardo, let's take a walk. College boy, kick back and have yourself a smoke."

Marco opened the car door and took a firm grip on Eduardo's arm.

"Hold up a second," Eduardo said, reaching under his seat.

"Don't move," Marco said. He twisted Eduardo's arm behind his back and pulled him out of the car. Just before I lost sight of him,

Eduardo looked me in the eyes, looked down at the driver's seat, then looked me in the eyes.

"I'm sorry," he said.

"Yeah, you dumb shit." Marco laughed. "Yeah, you're sorry now. This has been a long time coming."

He steered Eduardo off and I was left for a moment in the darkness. I reached under Eduardo's seat and felt the familiar steel of his gun.

"Run," a deep voice whispered in my ear.

In the distance, I heard a crack. My hand clenched around the gun, then let go.

"Run!" the voice yelled in my ear. Sharp teeth nipped my neck, and my door popped open.

"Motherfucker's trying to bolt!" somebody yelled.

A bang rang in the near distance and something pinged off the car.

My body dove out of the car, its hands scrabbling dirt, and then the legs began pumping. It dove left, and I heard a bang and whoosh and soft thud nearby. My body was worn and battered, still raw from the ravages of the critical care unit. It should not have moved one more step.

But I was not my body. We were tight cords of muscles with skin like stone and steel-wire hair. Our tail gave us balance. The wind lifted our steps. And the night, our friend, cloaked us in her mystery. We kept running.

16

Are you not haughty and arrogant
Whenever a messenger comes to you
With what your selves do not desire?
Some you have branded liars,
Others you have killed.

—The Qu'ran

After our disagreement on the rooftop, Tav and I needed a few rocks apiece in order to get over the emotional trauma. Since we didn't have much cash on hand, and were pretty sure it was a Sunday, we decided to scope the brunch crowds for a target. Tav, playing lookout from the rooftop, spotted a crotchety grandmother with a purse the size of an elephant ear and an old man in a walker with a backpack strapped on. I went down to street level, tagged them from behind, and by the time they had recovered from the shock, I was already halfway up to the rooftop. We sifted thirty bucks from a mess of outdated coupons, expired prescriptions, hotel soaps, bus tokens, condiment packs, a Bible, and a fistful of school mug shots of grinning grandchildren. Thirty bucks wasn't nearly enough, and we'd burn the coupons and grandchildren, but the other stuff had uses. The prescriptions had the potential to get us high, and the soap, tokens, and condiments covered hygiene, transport, and sustenance. I popped down by the church and tried to trade the Bible in for cash— I stood outside as the church crowd tumbled out, held a lighter near the Bible, and yelled that I'd torch it right there unless somebody got me twenty bucks. Nobody seemed to give a shit, though, and I was about to give up hope when the pastor popped out, handed me a ten, and told me to put the lighter away and read the Good Book instead. It wasn't that bad of an idea, I decided. I didn't have anything but left-over newspapers to read, and if the Bible was boring, I could at least use it as a pillow.

I figured I needed at least a hundred bucks to get into any real poker game, but with how fast Tav and I smoked rock, it was tough to build a stake. For weeks Tav pestered me, saying the South Side was easy pickings, that the trouble he'd had down there could be easily avoided, that things were getting too hot for us North Side. When he got annoying about it, all I had to do was open the Bible and begin reading aloud. I'd use my Shakespearean voice and insert bits of my own bullshit. That would get him yelling. His dad was a Bible-thumper, and as a result Tav had issues with religion in general, but only assholes disrespected the Bible. I told him I wasn't disrespecting it, just reinterpreting to fit the moment, but he believed there wasn't a distinction.

I finally relented and Tav guided us to Hyde Park. After a couple days there, I apologized to Tav for being a jackass. I still gave him Bible readings to keep him on his toes, but none of the other North Side interpersonal shit traveled with us. The college kids in Hyde Park were sweet groves primed for picking. The University of Chicago filled its ranks with intellectuals immersed in minutia, and the strain of keeping their moorings while buffeted by theory and abstraction led to a collective tunnel vision. They knew the surrounding neighbor-hoods were filled with crime, and they knew the surrounding neigh-borhoods were filled with blacks, and so although they shouldn't have been victim to the same tired racial equations, in the dark of the night, with their minds fumbling through the day's research, they froze at the sight of Tav and eyed him, not me, until it was too late. I'm sure a few got a good look at my face, but if they told the police anything, it must have been some vision of the night filtered through the same racial arithmetic. We soon saw warnings posted about two dangerous black men. The cops searched relentlessly for them, finding villains who fit the description twice a week, on average.

Tav also hooked me up on another sweet con that ran well on campus. If I saw a suit late at night, the guy's eyes flitting, not with fear, but hunger, all I had to do was smile and ask if he needed a friend. Whether or not you fucked the guy didn't matter—he'd want to be someplace discreet. A knife at the throat, and he'd hand over cash, never a whisper, and you'd know that he'd never talk about it to anyone. Some nights we scored hundreds.

Tav finally popped the question one night when we were getting some slabs to celebrate a big haul I'd gotten off a horny chemistry prof. The guy in the van was in a good mood, puffing a blunt of skunk, and when Tav said he'd heard they played cards, that he had a player who wanted in and pointed at me, the guy laughed. I flashed a thick wad of twenties.

"Hell, yeah, we'll take your money," the guy said, sliding open the van door. "Crackhead coming in!"

I went in, but he slid the door shut before Tav could join me. I wasn't worried—Tav had his slab, and I knew exactly what he'd be doing with it.

The inside of the van was hot and thick with pot smoke. Three muscles and a skeleton crouched on the van floor, slamming cards. The inside was completely stripped of seats and carpet, but the side molding had been left in place. I couldn't tell where they kept the drugs, but it had to either be on their bodies, or hidden in the side panels.

"What you playing?" I asked.

"Cards," the skeleton said.

Twenties smacked the floor, the skeleton dealt cards, twenties smacked the floor, muscles bellowed and grunted and flung cards in the center, and then one of the muscles grabbed the money and roared.

"You guys play poker?" I asked.

"Fuck poker," a muscle said.

"I play poker," I said, fanning my money out in front of me.

The skeleton looked at the muscles and they nodded.

"Seven card stud."

There are as many ways to cheat at cards as there are variations of games. You can mark the cards so you always know what the sucker is holding. You can be a mechanic and work the shuffle and deal so you always get the right cards. You can have guys playing together, re-raising each other when they know one of them has a killer hand, just to drain the sucker dry.

They let me huff a rock, and then I puffed a spliff laced in something—one of the muscles said it was PCP and juice—formaldehyde. Counting cards is a huge advantage in seven card stud, but I soon had trouble counting my own fingers. It didn't help that the guys played as a team, signaling by card taps and hand position, or that the skeleton was clearly a mechanic—I could tell from the tight curl of his index finger along the edge of the deck. If they'd marked the cards or done anything else, I was too far gone to notice, and so high that I was dangerously close to not caring.

Some hands, I thought I had them beat, only to discover one of them holding a hidden straight. Other times, I thought I had a monster, only to realize that my blurring vision had mistranslated the cards. I won a few hands by fluke, and I'm sure they scooped some pots that I'd actually won. By blind luck, probably because the mechanic had made a mistake, I finally found myself sitting on rolled-up trips that became four of a kind by the turn. I bet and raised, and the muscles bet and raised, and though the pot didn't make up for all I'd lost, it at least brought me within sight of even.

"That's it for me, boys," I said. "That's all the lesson I can handle today."

"Boys?" one of the muscles said.

"You ain't done yet, motherfucker," another said.

I tried to get up, but a wave of nausea forced me to pause. I bent down to pick up my cash.

"You hear what I said?" a muscle said.

"I'm done," I said.

"He's done," the skeleton said sympathetically. "Let's let the boy go home."

The muscles laughed as I tottered to the van door. The skeleton banged the door and I stumbled out into the light, then yanked the door shut behind me.

Tav got up from his perch on the curb and limped over to me.

"What took so fucking long? My slab's gone, smoked, man, and I've been waiting."

"They have some good shit in there," I said with a wistful smile, holding on to his shoulder to help with my balance.

His fingers twittered on my forearm.

"I need me a slab, man. You got the cash?"

I nodded. I fished in my pockets. I patted myself down. I looked toward the van, then toward the man standing by the door.

"Let me back in," I said.

The man laughed.

"Go home," he said.

Tav looked at me wildly.

"Come on, man! Shit, man, I'm—you owe me a fucking slab!"

My hands kept searching my clothes even though they knew nothing was there.

"They took it all?" Tav asked.

I looked toward the van, my hands fumbling.

Tav bumped chests with the man. He grabbed hold of him with his good arm.

"You got to let us back in, man!"

The man stiff-armed him.

"You'd best get walking," he said, his voice suddenly low and tight.

Tav bumped him again, his hand tracing over the man's jacket.

"Just a rock, then, man. You got us good, it's all cool, but just a rock, man."

"Get the fuck off!" the man growled, jacking Tav in the nose.

Tav fell and bounced back up, a trickle of blood coming from his nose. We could have walked away, grabbed a bus, headed South Side, built up cash, gotten some rocks. It would hurt for a while, but we'd get us our rocks and when we did, we'd forget. We'd be okay.

"Let's go, Tav," I meant to say, but the PCP and juice had knotted my tongue, and I could only sway on my feet, senselessly grinning.

"You got a rock," Tav said, pressing against the man, his good hand digging into a coat pocket.

The man leaned back, grabbed Tav's hair with his left hand, then hooked his right arm into Tav's gut. His right arm drew back, then plunged in again. He shoved Tav to the ground, and looked at me. I swayed on my feet, my face trapped in a smile. He banged on the van door, yelled "Go," hopped in, and off the van roared.

Tav lay on the ground, his good arm clutching his chest, his fingers red with his blood. His eyes found mine, his lips blew pink bubbles. He opened his mouth wide, gasping.

When I first started gambling, no stake was too low. I was a novice, a beginner at taking risks, and each loss stung, even if only a penny. As time passed and the fall of cards became familiar probability, as pots won and lost blurred into each other, the numbness of acceptance replaced the pain of loss. For most gamblers, when winning and losing has no charge, they raise the stakes, they take themselves to the edge of their own destruction. They gamble with their lives. I had gambled with my life, and I had gambled with others' lives at college. And though, when I look back now, I am filled with a guilt that chokes my breath and I have nightmares that I know will never leave me, in that moment as I stood over Tav, I felt nothing.

"What's going on over there?" somebody yelled.

Tav shuddered on the ground, his eyes locked on mine. He could not speak, but he mouthed one last word to me.

"Run," he wanted to say.

Footsteps thundered toward us and the sound sent a current down my spine. I jerked a foot free from the ground and lurched west, chasing a van I knew I'd never catch. I looked back at the crowd. They stayed with Tav. They looked toward me. They knew better than to follow.

Alone again, with nothing but my pipe for company, I lived as Tav had taught me. My cravings were simple masters and excused anything as long as I kept the glass torching. For a moment, rock granted a temporary passport to the heavens. For the privilege of that moment, I was willing to surrender myself fully to the cravings, to the innocence of pure gluttony and the violence it inevitably required.

I called my family collect, but often hung up before someone answered. When I didn't, I would say that I was fine, that I was getting better, that I might come home, but I needed a bit of money, just a little bit. They begged me to come home, kept begging me, until finally it became too difficult to talk on the phone with me, and I would only hear my mother and sister crying, or the sound of my father breathing, or the comforting noise of my brothers yelling about the evil I'd become. A part of me wondered at the possibilities of rehab, but the cravings shouted that idea down. A life without drugs was a coffin—no sunlight, no moon, nothing but the damp and the dark every day, the dissolution of decomposition the only possibility of change. I sought the company of addicts, thinking that I might feel less alone amongst my people. When they didn't try to steal from me they eulogized their lives, recalling each cruelty visited upon them, bemoaning the unfairness of life. If they had been willing to share their drugs, I might have tolerated them, but their self-obsession, their inability to see their own role in the misery they now lived, infuriated me. I was the victim of a curse, trapped by forces beyond my control. They had choices, but insisted in believing they were powerless. We could not relate.

With no one else for company, the voices in my mind grew louder and began to engage me in conversation. At first they kept our conversations private, but it soon became clear that secrecy wasn't essential, and so we began taking turns speaking with my voice. Passersby took little interest, giving us wide berth, occasionally flipping coins in our direction. A few invited me to church groups. One handed me a translation of the Koran, and told me I would find my answers within its pages. The voices and I devoured the book and revisited the Bible. We argued long into the night.

One voice took control, her soft voice insistent. Why was I searching out other paths when I knew the path already, she asked. The world did not care for me, so why did I care for the world? At each moment of my life I had witnessed the strong tormenting the weak, and though I had strength of my own, I had stood silent. But I was the descendant of Kupana Bhagavatha. I served Kali. How is it that I had forgotten my birthright? I needed only look to my nature, Kali whispered. I was the caretaker of vengeance. I needed to walk amidst the evils of the world and destroy them.

I walked out into the world with a new sense of purpose. The drugs, the violence, the desires that made others simper and lament, these were my gifts from Kali. I need only sever my ties to the world, my attachment to my body, and eliminate the compassion that could only weaken my resolve. Drugs gave me Kali's power, scoured my body clean of its weakness, and filled me with a fury that overwhelmed any pain.

Between crack binges and mugging, I did my duty against the evils of the world. I heard a woman screaming in Humboldt Park and punished her attacker, holding his head in the water of the pond until he bucked me off and fled down California. I found a crack house near 43rd, where a child had been raped the week before, and burned it to the ground. I saw a little boy toddling across Lincoln, and saved him from the wrath of a blue car. I saw a couple arguing outside a restaurant, and beat the man until he fled. I found a car parked in front of a fire hydrant, and bashed its windows in. I took from the rich and I took from the poor. I gave to myself to punish them.

Every few weeks, or when trouble hung thick around the corner, I took a new form. I became Eduardo, with his long and lean swagger, unleashing Spanish when the mood struck me. I became Tav, limping down the street, a skullcap pulled tight, my body hunching in on itself. I was a Christian when I was asked if I had accepted Jesus as my Lord and personal savior, and I was a Muslim when greeted by the brotherhood. One day I was Nasir, the next I was Chaz. I sacrificed myself and lived in other forms, replacing the ashes of self with a multiplicity of identity. The voice praised me for my devotion and told me that nothing in the mortal world could harm me as long as I lay in the embrace of Kali.

But there were powers at work beyond my understanding, long prayers in the night by my family, jolts in the consciousness of the world as my old friends wondered to themselves where I was and what had happened to me. My ancestors called to me, but their voices could not match Kali's, and so they turned their voices to the heavens, to the Gods who were so often too busy to listen. And so it was that Hanuman searched for me and tracked me down behind a tacqueria on Division as I stood over the sacrifice of myself, a junkie priest of Kali caught between worlds.

After my family disowned me over the phone, tears and pleading replaced by the tough-love click, it was Hanuman who held me in the alley and told me I wasn't alone.

"If they really did love me, they wouldn't cut me off," I wept. "I haven't done anything to them!"

Hanuman raised his bushy eyebrows.

"They love their son. They don't love you."

"I've never abandoned anyone," I said fiercely. "What good is love if you can ditch a person like that? That's not love. I stood by Tav; I even stood by Eduardo. That's what being a man is all about."

"You have stood next to many people, but how often have you really stood with them?"

"I'll show them," I hissed, flicking my lighter in my hand, the flame dancing seductively. I could see our house burning, my parents trapped at their bedside window, screaming to me. I would stand there on the lawn and laugh. Then they would know.

Hanuman tilted his head and hopped close, sniffing my hair. He plucked a few hairs from my scalp and sucked on them, his eyes clouding, then glowing with a keen yellow light. He stepped back from me and smacked the brick wall of the alley with the palm of his hand. A thunderclap snapped overhead, and rain poured down in sheets.

"Strange," Hanuman said, a smile flickering across his lips. "So much rain so suddenly." He stretched his arms as if to encompass the world, his fur slicking so I could see the golden skin underneath.

"I'm getting soaked, you asshole," I said.

Hanuman laughed.

"Of course you are! Why don't I take you someplace warm where you can change your clothes and we can sit quietly and talk about your family."

"Fuck that," I said. "All you've got for me is bullshit. I'm getting some rock."

Hanuman nodded.

"I'll show you where to go."

As the weeks trickled past, Hanuman persisted in fucking with me. I'd start figuring plans for scores and scams, and he'd distract me. I see the police, he'd say, just as I was about to jack a purse, and I'd hide in a corner. Looks like rain, he'd say, and the skies would open up. Just around the corner, he'd say, and I'd run smack into a church freak hustling pamphlets and salvation.

"I don't need you here," I said.

"Of course you do."

"I don't want you near me," I said.

"That's Kali talking," he said with a shake of his head.

"So what if Kali talks to me? She at least makes sense. She doesn't fuck around with me."

"She doesn't care for you. She's never cared for anyone. Ask her to leave. See what she says."

I searched within myself, and Kali whispered back.

"She would leave if I needed her to. But what about you? You're nothing but lies and tricks. I didn't ask for your help."

Hanuman smiled.

"Oh Kali," he said to me, "we are too old for this game." He tapped my forehead. "You're a silly little boy. Why do you think Kali is here? Why do you think I have been called to you?"

I shrugged.

"I know there's a curse on our family, but Kali has always been good to us."

"Good?" Hanuman furrowed his brow. "Kali is not good or evil, just as a sword is neither good nor evil. Your family has guarded the world from her for centuries, and I have guarded your family from Kali."

"If that was true," I said, "I'd have heard it from my family. Or there would be a story about it somewhere. The only story out there about you has to do with you helping Rama. You can bullshit me all you want, but I know what's real and what's not."

"A very human answer," Hanuman mused. "A very human answer."

I rolled my eyes.

Hanuman grinned. "What proof do you think faith needs?"

"Something real," I said. "Something I can see."

"Like you can see me?"

"That's a start."

Hanuman held up a paw.

"How many fingers am I holding up?"

"Four."

"Wrong. Twenty-seven."

I squinted my eyes. He had only four fingers up.

"The human eye can only see so much," Hanuman said. "You see light so long as it is within certain wavelengths. With your technology, you see more, and with your technology you have proved to yourself that this is all there is to see. An interesting god you have made of this technology. You deify the child you have created and expect it to teach you all mysteries."

"Typical religious crap."

"Then how do you explain me?"

"Maybe I'm crazy."

"That's the problem with humans. If one sees something different from everybody else, you call it insanity."

"So you're saying you're real?"

"That's a very difficult question. Humans live in a world where they can only perceive and comprehend a fraction of what is around them, and yet you have created rigid boundaries between the real and unreal, even though the truth of the world remains a mystery. Yes, I exist, but not as you see me. Others will not see me and they will not hear me, and so they will say I do not exist. Humankind believes that all thought, understanding, and action come from the brain, yet you have only guesses as to how your brain operates. You have uncovered your own DNA, but persist in believing that large segments of it are junk and do nothing for the soul or body. In the face of such arrogance, how could I ever prove my existence? Weren't your hands burned when you visited your ancestor during your overdose? And yet you still doubt."

"So I'm not crazy?"

"Nobody ever is. Sometimes people gain the ability to see and feel more than the rest. That's why the sages and rishis loved to go into seclusion in the forest—if they stayed in a city, they knew their true sight could overwhelm their fragile mind. It is a hard thing to step between worlds and return. Most that do never come back. Look at all the addicts you know. How many see the divine and never return? Through drugs you launch your body into the divine and transcend the human form, but your mind is not prepared. Each time, you leave a part of yourself in the other world until nothing is left on this mortal plane but the shell of your soul, an undead corpse. Kali would take great pleasure in seeing that happen to you."

I heard her insistent whisper in the back of my mind.

"Kali only wants to help me. She's always helped my family."

Hanuman shook his head.

"You look at us and call us Gods, and so you think we speak in absolute truth or absolute falsity. We are living beings, my son. Some of us lie for our own agenda, and some of us lie without knowing. Of course Kali thinks she wants to help you. Of course she believes she has always helped your family. But Kali is vengeance personified. She is the scimitar of the heavens, our greatest regret. She was unleashed during a time of great need during the wars of old, a weapon beyond our control, a being of pure emotion, of pure anger, so ancient that she had only been a myth when our people came into being, and only through our combined efforts, an agreement between the Devas and Rakshasas to set aside our difference, was she restrained for a moment. Our universe and yours exist side by side, and if Kali is unleashed again, we will all be destroyed. For she is the ender of all things, my son. In order to hold her, the Devas, the Rakshasas, and the humans each had to volunteer one of their own to be the seal against her entrance. From the Rakshasas, Ravana was chosen, the most powerful being of his race, one who could walk between the universes, the only one strong enough to touch Kali without being consumed. From the line of the Devas, Rama was chosen, wise and steadfast, incorruptible. And from the humans, they chose my son, part Deva, part human. But Ravana grew too proud, and sought to end Kali on his own, and she ensnared him. She worked through him to spirit Sita away, and so Rama destroyed Ravana, and now, though Kali could not fully enter the world, she could begin to influence it, her powers seeping through the shattered seal. And so it was that the people in Rama's kingdom began to doubt Sita, Kali's whispers in their minds too persistent to ignore, and so she drove a wedge between Rama and Sita. Rama forced Sita to walk the test of flame to prove her purity, and when she left, filled with the rage of Kali that had leaked into her during her time with Ravana, Rama had no will to continue living. He passed the seal and the responsibility to his daughter, and he dissipated rather than face an eternity alone. My son married his daughter, and the two seals against Kali became your birthright. Now, Kali works through you. She will destroy your family

359

through you, and then she will consume you. From your ashes she will rise, her mouth devouring all creation."

"If that's what's going on, doesn't sound like there's much I can do," I said. "You should check in with my brothers or my sister. Maybe one of my cousins."

Hanuman squeezed my shoulder firmly with his paw.

"Kali chose you," he said, "because you are the one most like your father. Because your father loves you most of all. She chose you the moment you were born, slipped in with the blood the doctors pumped into you, and began to twist you to her way. I have fought her all your life."

He shook his head, and could not look at me. I could hear Kali whispering to me, a tickle behind my eyes.

"You're too late," I told Hanuman.

Tats had told me to find work, suggesting the want ads as a place to start. Since T.T. was freshly unemployed, Tats ordered the two of us to work together.

"I don't need to be looking at want ads," T.T. told him. "I'll get an unemployment check. No problem."

"So, you think you're going to sit on your lazy ass in my house?"

"I'll go to meetings three times a day."

"Like hell you will! That's not enough. You need to be working."

"It's none of your fucking business, you Nazi," T.T. said.

Tats thumped the table.

"You just got yourself a week of detail," he said.

"A week?" T.T. said.

"Alright then," Tats said, a gleam in his eyes, "two weeks."

"What the fuck, Tats," I said. "He didn't do anything wrong."

"You get a week too, then. And you better scrub good. I want to be able to eat off those toilets."

T.T. kicked me to keep me from yelling at Tats, but since I'd been about to mutter "fuckingassholecontrolfreakNazi," the kick made it come out more like "fuckingassholecont—Jesus Christ!"

"What'd you call me?" Tats growled. "How about a month then?"

T.T. and I sat down at the table and grabbed the want ads.

"You better be lined up with a job by tomorrow," Tats said, walking into the kitchen.

T.T. flipped the want ads back in the middle of the table and sat back with a sigh.

"There's nothing in there for me," he said, shaking his head. "I always got jobs by referral or when they got a sign-up. This want ad shit never works."

"What kind of jobs can you do?" I asked.

"I'll do anything but a desk job," he said.

I flipped through the pages.

"Can you drive?"

T.T. laughed.

"Sure I can. Just don't have a license no more."

Finally, I found it.

"How about telemarketing? Says here no experience necessary. And they pay by the hour. And they've got commission."

"Sure they don't have anything for a punch press guy in there?"

"You said you didn't see anything."

"Yeah," T.T. said, his eyes darting away from mine. He looked back at me. "Telemarketing? How's that work?"

"You talk to people on the phone. Sell them shit."

"You ever done that?"

"Well, I've talked to people on the phone. And I've sold shit, weed and coke mostly."

"What are these guys selling?"

I looked over the ad again.

"No idea."

"I don't know," T.T. said.

"You got anything better going on?"

He shrugged.

"The unemployment check ain't bad."

"You want a month of detail too?"

He stood up and grabbed the ad. I followed him into the kitchen, where we found Tats foaming up some milk. Tats grabbed the paper from us, looked over what we'd circled, and laughed.

"Which one of you nitwits thought this was a good idea?"

"What's wrong with it?" I said.

Tats rolled his eyes.

"You could get a respectable job, you know," he said. "Especially you, T.T. You've got real job skills. You okay with how much this pays?"

"How much does it pay?" T.T. asked.

Tats sighed. He gripped me by the shoulder and pulled me close to whisper in my ear.

"T.T. can't read."

"So how's that my problem?" I said.

Tats nodded slowly.

"I want you to teach him."

"Teach me what?" T.T. asked.

"How much you going to pay me?" I asked.

"I'm making you two roommates," Tats said. "You get the second floor front room."

"With the window facing the street, and the Butera, and that sexy little . . ."

"That's right."

T.T. clapped me on the back, giving me a knowing nod.

"What's your angle in this?" I asked.

Tats smiled.

"Alls I ask is this: T.T., until you get a job of your own, you got to make sure Srinivas goes to his and comes right back. Take him to meetings, introduce him to the guys. Talk to him."

"No problem," T.T. said, solemnly nodding.

"And you, Srinivas, all I'm asking you to do is help T.T. get himself a good punch press job again. And maybe you could help him with that other thing we talked about."

"What other thing?" T.T. asked.

"Knock two weeks off my detail and you got a deal," I said.

"How about I kick your ass out of my house?" Tats said.

We shook hands.

"I'm using deodorant! I showered!" T.T. said.

"No, T.T., we weren't talking about the hygiene thing again," Tats said. "You done good with that."

"I got cologne samples from a magazine," T.T. said to me.

I nodded, grabbed the ad sheet, and headed back into the dining room.

Hanuman and I headed for Hyde Park because it was too good of a feast to pass up on for long. At least, that's why I headed there. Hanuman said there was a *vasana* emanating from there, a scent trail of an old soul that he couldn't quite place. He'd hopped South Side one night to check out my old stomping grounds and had come rushing back to tell me the news. He said I needed to head there, the vasana so pungent and familiar that even I would smell it. He kept yammering on and on about it, getting me so pissed off that I took a swing at him like an idiot when I had my pipe in my hand. I missed him completely and my rock tumbled out of the pipe down to the ground below. I spent the next thirty minutes in the alley torching every white pebble I could find, Hanuman blathering on about vasana this and Sita that, until finally I gave up and decided to roll with him since I knew where I could get some rocks real quick by the Hyde Park Metra station.

As soon as we got there, Hanuman led the way, sniffing gently, the tip of his tail darting about in tiny jabs and flourishes of excitement.

"It is an old scent," Hanuman said, licking his lips. "Do you remember it?"

I sniffed the air and got a good whiff of bus exhaust.

"Tuberose, a touch of vetiver," he nodded, "She always loved vetiver."

He curled his tail around my forehead, and for a moment I felt a tingle in my nose, a scent like cheap incense mixed with turpentine. A girlish voice giggled in the corner of my ear.

Hanuman leaned in and pressed his forehead against mine.

"Kali, you bitch, you can at least let him smell her vasana."

"Maybe there's nothing to smell," I said.

"You would remember it," he said.

"How the hell would I remember something I never smelled?"

"Because it is in your blood."

"Even if it was in my blood, which is bullshit by the way, it would be from way back whenever."

Hanuman counted on his fingers, perhaps using some I couldn't see.

"Maybe it is three thousand five hundred years old? Or is it four thousand?" He blinked slowly, then looked at me. "It is now in the end of your twentieth century?"

"Mine? Or humankind's?"

"Yes. Anyway, that is all irrelevant."

"Why'd you bring me down here then? You kept yelling about this vasana and now it's suddenly no big deal."

"No, no," Hanuman said, waving his hands. "I was thinking how useless it is to try to tell you what time you last smelled this scent. I am no good at measuring time."

"You should get a watch."

He jabbed his finger at me triumphantly.

"A wonderful idea! They are so beautiful, so naïve. It would remind me of your limitations. When my people first discovered the irrelevancy of time, a war broke out. Nobody likes hearing that the passage of time is only a construct of our imaginations."

"Time doesn't exist?"

"Of course it exists. But all time is the same. No point is different from the next. It is a nondimensional closed loop crowding the same point as the other loops of the other universes."

I rubbed my temples and looked back down the street.

"I need to get me a rock," I said.

"Yes," Hanuman said, with a knowing nod, "Rama would get the same way too. I wouldn't be surprised if a part of him was goading you toward rock. After all, Kali was with him too."

I looked at him blankly.

"Come, come," he said, sniffing the air again. "Just around the corner."

The Gothic architecture of the University of Chicago, oxidized gargoyles guarding fortresses of concrete, came into view.

"A good school, you know," Hanuman said. "You should go there."

I wasn't so sure.

The guys in the house gave me and T.T. high fives when they found out Tats had hammered us with weeks of detail. As long as we had to do it, they didn't, and though everybody liked the idea of a clean house, it was always better when somebody else had to dust mop the floor after a long day of work. We all went out to the Twelve-Step House for a meeting and then loaded up on ice cream at Zephyr's—we had a loyalty to the place, in part due to its proximity to the Twelve-Step House, and in part due to the semi-confirmed gossip that Zephyr's had been run by a recovery guy and had been about to go national when he got on the wrong side of a .45. We understood about failed dreams. Plus, the place tended to have the prettiest waitresses in the area, and though most of the guys were at least twenty years older than them, masturbation fantasies require fodder.

It was only when we got back that we realized Zhivago hadn't come back from work. Tats told us that if we saw him, we were supposed to keep him out of the house. Zhivago had been out on an overnight, but he was supposed to catch up with us at the Twelve-Step House. When he didn't, Tats had looked through his stuff and found an empty bottle of vodka. Zhivago eventually showed up close to midnight. T.T. and I had gone to bed early, trying to get ready for work. Zhivago had tried the door, but since Tats changed the combo anytime someone broke bad, Zhivago started kicking it. Since our room was directly above the front door, we got an earful. At first he swore and banged and swore some more. Tats stepped out and I heard him talking to Zhivago. He told him to get the hell away and check into detox, that all his yelling was only going to get the neighbors phoning the police, and that would make the house look bad, and that could threaten the house, threaten the sobriety of all the guys in it. Nobody wanted a house of recovering addicts on their street, and the first chance they got, they'd stick it to us. Zhivago started weeping and saying he was sorry. Tats told him he was going to take him to detox. Tats rumbled his chopper, and they were gone.

"That's his second time," T.T. said.

"You think Tats'll let him back in?" I asked.

T.T. sighed.

"Normally, first time you break, that's it. Tat's had a soft spot for Zhivago, though. Maybe it's because they're both big guys. Maybe because Zhivago's a cool guy—no questions—always has your back. Whatever happens, I can't get worked up about it. Neither should you. We got to focus on our own recovery. There but by the grace of God go I and all that. It's tough enough dealing with our own shit. Worrying about other people's just gets you drunk."

The next day, T.T. and I were up early. I'd set up an interview for myself for the telemarketing job over the pay phone and it wasn't until ten in the morning. I could have woken up late, but the Zhivago situation had set off a flood of familiar nightmares. So, I sat in the dining room with T.T. and Walden, nursing a cup of coffee, brainstorming about what to do about T.T.'s job issue.

"You should prepare a résumé," Walden said. "If it is well done, you will stand out. We could help you. We could write it longhand here, and then I could find a typewriter. I think we have one at work."

"What about doing it on a computer?" I asked. "We could create a draft and fine-tune it as necessary, keep track of where you've sent it with a spreadsheet."

Walden and T.T. laughed.

"Now what would make you think we have a computer in this house?" Walden asked.

"You could use a computer at a copy place. I've seen them starting to have that available. Or the library. Or you could sneak into a college computer lab. It wouldn't be hard."

"If they don't mind letting drunks in," T.T. said. "They can always tell I don't belong."

"The more pressing issue is that none of us knows how to use a computer."

"I do," I said. "Hell, I could make you one."

Both looked at me slack-jawed.

"Tats didn't mention that you had gone to college for electronics as well," Walden said.

"Nothing like that. Me and my brothers used to tear things apart all the time—broken-down TVs, VCRs, stereos—and then when our dad got us a computer, we took it apart real careful to see how it looked inside. My brother custom-built himself a computer when I was just getting ready to go to college. I helped him out. It's not hard."

"You're so full of shit," T.T. said with a laugh.

Walden, though, looked at me keenly.

"You should mention this to Tats," he said.

"I will."

"Well, whiles you both are still tripping, maybe I can get you to do my résumé for me."

I promised Walden I'd look into the computer situation, and then we pulled out a sheet and peppered T.T. with questions about his job history. He had an impressive résumé, usually rising quickly within whatever machine shop he worked in. There were a couple major problems, though. He had never left a job on good terms, and he had a five-year gap in his work history.

"So how have you explained your frequent firings in the past?" Walden asked.

"I just tell 'em my bosses were assholes or that the place went belly-up. Nobody checks too hard. Plus, I'm good at what I do. When they see that, no problem."

"Perhaps you should try honesty. Tell them that you are in recovery."

"Yeah," T.T. said, nodding. "That's a nice move. I'll try that one out if they don't look like they're buying the bullshit."

Walden shook his head but didn't press the point.

"What about this gap—1983 to 1988?" I asked. "You need an explanation for it."

"I was in the state lockup."

"What for?" I asked.

"That's for me and my sponsor to know."

Walden tapped his notepad pensively.

"How have you explained it in the past?" Walden asked.

"That I took a vacation. Stayed in Mexico for a while."

Suddenly it struck me.

"You learn anything while you were there? Take classes, or learn a trade, or anything?"

T.T. nodded. "They had me making license plates."

"Then that's what you say. You did coursework in industrial manufacturing. At Illinois State. Didn't finish your degree."

Walden shook his head.

"We should be helping him to create an honest résumé," he said. "Recovery is about honesty."

T.T. waved him off. "I'm trying to get a job here," he said.

"Don't worry about it," I said to Walden. "Everybody lies on their résumé. We're just doing what normal people do, and isn't that what this house is about? Learning how to fit in with normal people?"

As Hanuman led me through Hyde Park, sniffing the air, Kali sulked in the back of my mind.

"Maybe you both got it wrong," I told them. "Maybe I'm not who you think I am. Kali only came to me after I broke open that diamond in India. She must have been trapped in there. So maybe all that stuff you were talking about, the Gods and wars and seals and all that, maybe that doesn't apply to me."

Hanuman laughed.

"It will still be true whether you believe it or not," he said.

"It was not a diamond," Kali whispered. "And I was not trapped within it. I was trapped within you, voiceless, shielded from your mind. But you so wanted to see me and to save me. I could hear you calling."

Hanuman nodded.

"Now it makes sense," he said. "In the moment when the rock shattered, when the debris struck you, you passed into a state between consciousness and unconsciousness. That is how Kali gained control. She was alert, waiting, and then in that moment, when your mind was unprotected, in that gap between dreaming and living, she joined you completely."

"I never meant to hurt you," Kali whispered.

"Once again, the lie . . ." Hanuman began, but he froze. He pointed across the street.

Mahogany ringlets and a lime green jacket. She was smiling, a backpack slung over her shoulder, a cup of coffee in her hand. A couple guys in button-downs chattered at her.

"Eva!" I yelled, running across the street, Hanuman bounding along beside me.

She looked toward me, squinting her eyes. The two guys stepped in front of her and glared at me. When I got close, one of them pinched his nose and looked toward Eva with a pained expression. He kept his arms extended to ward me off.

"We don't have any spare change," he said.

"If I need your change, I'll take it, you fuck," I said.

"Cheeni?" Eva asked. She took a step back, her hand over her mouth.

"You know this guy?"

"What you doin' here?" I asked.

"I'm transferring." She took another step back. "Are you okay?"

"Hanuman's been taking care of me," I said.

"Hanuman?"

I nodded.

"Everything cool with you?" I asked.

"You need to get moving, mister."

"Me and Eva got no problems," I said, "except maybe you, if you don't mind your own fucking business."

"Stupid fucking bum," the guy said, shoving me.

"Stop," Eva said, yanking on the back of his shirt. "Stop. This is Cheeni. The one I mentioned."

The guy looked at me again, wide-eyed. He backed up a bit and his friend looked at him uncertainly.

"I'm not here to cause any trouble," I said as softly as I could manage. "I just saw you, and . . ."

"I've missed you too," Eva said softly. "I've wondered what happened to you. Do you need help?"

"I'm fine," I said. "You good?"

She looked away, her eyes wet with tears, then looked back at me.

"How's Jonas? How's Salvatore?"

"Salvatore went back to Italy," she said. "And Jonas . . . He's taking time off."

"Missionary stuff?"

"I thought you heard," she said. "His sister committed suicide."

I felt my legs crumpling under me, but Hanuman grabbed me by the arm and held me up.

"So the police didn't get you?" she asked.

"No, I just came out here. Been living."

"They came looking for you. Looking for Cheeni. But that's not your real name, is it?"

"Srinivas," I said. "Cheeni's a nickname."

She opened her mouth to say something, but her lips began to quiver, and she buried her head in the chest of one of her friends. She clutched his shirt, whispered.

"We've got to go," the guy said, staring at me coldly. He began to walk away, Eva draped over him, the other guy guarding their rear.

"Hold up, Eva," I said. "Where are you staying at?"

She didn't answer. I wanted to run after her, but Hanuman held me back.

"How did you know she was here?" I asked him.

He gazed at me with sad eyes.

"I know where all my children are," he said. "Even the ones who have forgotten my name."

17

When you demand nothing of the world, nor of God, when you want nothing, seek nothing, expect nothing, then the Supreme State will come to you uninvited and unexpected.

—**Shri Nisargadatt Maharaj**

The telemarketing gig was in a cramped dive near Melrose and Western. Boxes of pinchy plastic sandals and blistering faux-leather loafers jammed one front corner, propped against vinyl carry-ons and duffel bags. Cubicles extended to the back, about ten in all, but only three folks staffed the phones. A guy in blue jeans, a white dress shirt, and a fat red tie enveloped me in a bear hug moments after I walked through the door, then pumped my hand like I was a slot machine.

"You ready to get to work?" he asked.

"What do you do here? Don't you need to interview me?"

He put both arms on my shoulders.

"Can you read?"

"Yes."

"Can you talk on the phone?"

"Yes."

"Ever committed a felony?"

I paused and looked down, Walden's words about the need for honesty ringing in my mind.

"I've never been convicted."

The guy laughed.

"I like the way you put that. Same here," he said with a wink. "You're hired."

"So what do you do here? Telemarketing?"

"What we do here is make people's days better. We're doing exciting work here. Let me show you the script."

The deal was pretty simple. People would head out to their mailboxes and discover a postcard that said they'd won a prize, that all they needed to do was call our 800-number to answer a few questions and claim it. The prizes ran the gamut—they could win a Ford Mustang, ten thousand dollars, a cruise package to the Carribean, boutique luggage, or designer shoes. When they called, we read through a script crafted to entice them—deliberate pauses as we checked to see what they had won, careful verification of their number, and then, genuine excitement in our voices as we told them they'd won the cruise package. Once they'd gotten over their excitement, we'd take them through the minor processing details: their preferred mailing address and phone number, good times to call, if they'd ever been on a cruise before and did they know how much fun it was, and, finally, how they wanted to cover the processing fee, which ran about $500. Our catch phrase when they got annoyed at the processing fee was elegance itself: "I'm sorry if you expected something for free, but don't blame us. I wish we didn't have to charge you tax on the amount you've won, but that's what the government requires, and we like to ensure that everything we do is ethical and legal." If they still had issues, but hadn't hung up yet, it was a pretty simple thing to switch them over to the designer shoes and boutique luggage, which only had a processing fee of $65. Regardless of what they chose, we'd pump them up for the brilliant decision they had made and congratulate them on their good luck.

Of course, nobody ever won the car or the ten thousand dollars, and the cruise was nothing more than a crap jaunt on a shitty ship—they had to cover their own airfare and pay for hotel rooms for the three nights the ship docked in tourist traps. Every once in a while we had to deal with complaint calls about the luggage or the shoes, but most people, I assumed, simply gave up out of embarrassment over being hooked by such a simple con. Given the shitty location we worked out of, I figured our boss kept himself just one step ahead of the law.

Still, the job paid $6 an hour, and I got a $75 commission on every cruise and $5 on every shoe or luggage con. To top it off, there were additional cash rewards if we sold more than three cruises in a day or if we were the big money-earner for the week. Though I was trying to wean myself off my addiction to lying, Tats had told me to get a job, and so I rationalized that since the telemarketers had advertised in the paper, they qualified as legit, or, at least, a hell of a lot more legit than pushing dope. Compared to what I had been doing, it was honest work.

The three other folks working the phones were a desperate bunch. Two looked like high school dropouts—pimple faced and terrified. They read their scripts in monotone and rarely sold anything. Most of the time the person on the other end of the line would start yelling at them, and instead of hanging up, they'd sit there and listen, as if they thought they deserved the punishment. One, heavily pregnant and with a serious Diet Coke addiction, broke down in tears and couldn't be cajoled into handling the phone for a half hour. The other person in the group was a Hispanic guy who gave me a quick smile and a nod when I came in. In talking to him, I often had to switch to Spanglish in order to be understood, but when it came to the phone and the script, you'd never know he had any issues with English. He didn't even need to look at the script or the comebacks and rebuttals. He'd memorized them and practiced the pronunciation, and if a sucker sprang a surprise question on him that he wasn't prepared for, he asked questions of anyone around him until he'd devised a proper response and knew how to pronounce it like a good American. "Well, I'll be," he'd say. "Looks like you're a big winner!" During a break he let me know that if he ever got a Spanish speaker on the phone, he hung up right away. He had principles.

Three hours into working, I'd broken his single-day record for sales. As our boss kept tallying my hits on the board, he cajoled the others to work harder. "This guy can sell ice to an Eskimo," he said. "Figure out his magic, and you'll all get rich too!"

As our last hour of work ticked off, the boss herded the others around my cubicle.

"I want you all to listen in on this next call. Notice how he works the target. Notice how he turns them into his friend."

The others nodded, except for the Hispanic guy, who clearly had no idea what our boss just said. I translated for him. He grabbed a pen and paper and looked intently at me.

When the next call came in, our boss turned on the speaker phone. I heard a tired grandmother, a Southern twang in her voice, and took a pause from the script.

"You sound a little run-down," I said, feeding a touch of the South into my voice. "How are you feeling today?"

My co-workers looked at me in confusion, but my boss grinned broadly and gave me a thumbs-up.

"Oh, my, I guess I am a little run-down," she said. "I didn't know anybody could tell."

"Don't you worry about it," I said. "We all get a little run-down from time to time. I'm only thirty-seven, and I'll tell you what—some days I feel like I'm twice as old!"

"I'm sixty-eight myself," she said. "Some days I wish I was thirty-seven again, but then I remember all the tough times, and I guess I don't mind being as old as I am because things are good these days."

"I know what you mean about tough times," I said. "If it weren't for the Lord, sometimes, I tell you, I don't know."

"I looked to the Lord a lot. He surely is a strength. I just got back from the hospital, you know. I had to have surgery and now radiation. Breast cancer, and they say I'll lose my hair, can you believe that? I've always had long hair."

"I'm just happy to hear you're doing better," I said. "Maybe you'll have a little less hair, but that'll grow back. I hope you had good insurance and they took care of everything for you."

"Oh, insurance. You know how those people are. I took a look at my first bill. Came in the mail. Maybe that's why I sounded a little down. But then I saw your card and I wondered, maybe this is the Lord acting to help out."

I felt my voice catch for a moment, but I bulled on. I asked for the code number on her card, gave her the pause, then delivered the good news.

"I'm just so pleased to be able to tell you this," I said. "You're one of our big winners. You won the five-day cruise! Have you ever been in the Caribbean, those soft blue waters, that luscious sand? I wish this was a ticket for two, because I'd be pestering you right now to let me come with you!"

"Praise heaven!" she said. "Oh my. Oh my. I need to take a breath here."

"Now don't get too excited," I said. "I want you in good condition for this cruise. After all you've been through, you deserve this."

"I sure feel like I do. Me and my husband, we've always wanted to go to Egypt. It's a wonder anyone built that place, and it makes us proud thinking someone did, maybe even one of our ancestors. But the Caribbean! For free? When do I get to go?"

"As soon as we get you processed, you can go at any time."

I got her name, her phone number, the times she liked to be called, and she volunteered the name of her daughter and let me know she liked piña coladas.

"Now the final little detail we need to take care of is the tax and processing charge. You know how the government is, taxing everything. I wish it weren't the case, but what can folks like us do?"

"How much is it?"

"It's only five hundred and seventy-five dollars, not too bad considering the cruise is worth over six thousand.. How would you like to take care of that? We can process a check or a credit card over the phone right now."

A pause followed by a sigh greeted me. My boss leaned in, the Hispanic guy jotted notes, the dropouts shook their head because they knew she wasn't going to go for it.

"That's so much money," she said. "With all these medical bills, I just don't know."

"That's okay, ma'am," I said. "I would never want this to be a burden on you."

"I'm sorry," she said. "I was hoping so much . . ."

"I really want you to have this!" I said. "If ever there was a person who deserved this, it's you. You know what I'm going to do? I'm going to check with my boss. I want to see if I can't pay your processing fee for you."

"You would do that?"

"It's the Christian thing to do."

"God bless you," she said, and I put her on hold.

I looked to my boss and nodded. I counted to ten, then got her back on the line.

"He won't let me," I said, sighing heavily. "He said there are legal issues since I'm an employee of the company. I couldn't understand it all. I'm so sorry."

"Oh, honey, I appreciate you trying."

"After all you've been through, you definitely deserve this. Are you sure you can't find a way to put this on a credit card? You've been through so much; you owe yourself a vacation. I'm surprised your husband didn't think of that. So, you know what? Think of this as a vacation coming from a good friend. This one is coming from me."

Her breath quickened on the other end of the line.

"Is Visa okay?"

As I took her info and closed the call, the others nodded at me. My co-workers slowly walked back to their seats, but my boss hung back. He put both hands on my shoulders and gave me a momentary massage.

"You've got a future in this. A very big future," he said. "I'm going to get you a bump in pay, and I want you to start training people." He pointed to the empty cubicles. "I'll fill them, you train them, and we'll get this business flying."

I nodded. I looked around me, my co-workers hunched over their phones, the dingy cubicles, the crap piled in the corner. I sniffed the air, and I could smell a scent of sweat, a scent of desperation. I didn't need Hanuman to tell me what to do.

"You pay in cash?" I asked.

"I can. Check is easier."

"I'd like today's pay in cash," I said.

"Going out to celebrate?" he asked, winking at me.

I shrugged. "Got that cash for me?"

He went to a desk in the corner and fiddled with some keys. He looked up at the board and tallied the figures, then pulled together an envelope with nearly five hundred bucks in it. It was a lot more money than I'd seen in a long time, and I'd earned it clean and sober, and I could keep earning it. I could make a living of this. I stuffed the envelope in my pocket and shook his hand.

"I quit," I said.

On the bus ride back to the Oasis, Hanuman plopped into the seat beside me. He didn't say a word. He kissed me on the cheek and spent the rest of the ride smiling out the window.

I wanted to punch Hanuman in the gut for showing me Eva. I wanted to make him feel what he'd done to me. There was no point, no purpose to bringing me to her. What use was the guilt? I'd just begun to get to a point where I didn't think so much about what had happened at college, what could have been, and he threw it all in my face again.

"That's what Hanuman does," Kali whispered. "He is a trickster. What else could you expect from a monkey? You are just a plaything for him."

"She describes herself," Hanuman said. "You know, deep within your instinct, why I did this. I have always worked to protect you."

But I wasn't going to let Hanuman fool me with his words again.

"You love this Eva, don't you?" Kali whispered. "I could see that she loves you too. If Hanuman truly cared for you, wouldn't he have helped you?"

"You do not love Eva. Before a being can love any other, it must first learn to love itself," Hanuman said.

"If you are really as powerful as you say," I hissed at him, "you would have fixed this. You would have done something for me. All you've done is kick back and laugh as I fuck up my life."

"Well said," Kali whispered.

"So you think others should do for you what you need to do for yourself? You are like the fools who plead to the heavens thinking that some God will hear them and come down and remedy their grief. Don't you see? We are of another dimension in your time, another incarnation of your universe. We can send a portion of our forms here, but it is not enough to directly physically affect your reality. Instead, we work through you, through all people. What you see as the power of God is the power of our good intentions, our influence slowly pushing each one of you along the better path. And at the same time, there are those like Kali who leak into your world and spread their violence. Each one of you must fight your own battle, must choose for yourself which voice you will listen to. And when you are weak, when you are afraid, you must trust in the good of others. For no one of you is a god. All of you, the sum of human consciousness, compose the divine. And so is divinity ever purely good or evil? It is neither and it is both. You are neither, and yet you are both. Why do you insist on looking to the heavens when all the heavens exist within you and around you?"

"See how he twists his words," Kali whispered.

"Close her from your mind," Hanuman pleaded. "She is a poison in this world."

"Let us find Eva," Kali said. "Let us love again with her. She ran because of Hanuman, but I will help you."

I could see Hanuman's lips moving, but no words came forth. Slowly, he faded into mist.

"I will shield you from his lies," Kali said.

With Kali's aid I found Eva again outside a bar. She smoked a cigarette in the night, smiling with some guy. Another girl came out and the three started laughing at some joke.

"That feeling you feel," Kali whispered, "is love. You two were always meant for each other. It is a destiny Hanuman should not have hindered."

I nodded. First there had been Sarah, but I was pretty sure Hanuman had been working through Jonas to ensure that I would never meet her again. Though they called it suicide, I knew it for what it was: calculated murder. And then with Eva, spinning her off with Salvatore, that sudden and inexplicable rage she had shown on the steps of our dorm when I saw her last. She and I had felt a real connection, a true passion. And then? For that to dissolve so quickly, to turn so completely into hate, that had to be the influence of Hanuman.

Eva and the guy started walking west on 53rd, so I followed, Kali tucked safely between my ears. They walked up to an apartment building and Eva paused at the steps to give the guy a quick peck before she stepped inside.

"Hanuman sent that Rakshasa to try to lure her," Kali said.

I snapped a tree branch, as thick as my forearm, and ran for him. At the last second he heard my steps and turned. I could feel Kali dancing within me, and with each stamp of her feet, I struck. I hit him in the knees and he fell to the ground, clutching a fence railing. I smashed his hand off the fence, then crunched him in the back. He gave a groan and tried to turn toward me. I caught him flush in the nose, and he curled on the ground.

He turned his face to me, raised a hand to ward my blows. His lips parted and I could see them trying to form words. A river of red flowed down his face. A pink bubble of snot ballooned from a nostril.

I remembered a man in a van, a knife. A friend? Something flitted at the edge of sight.

"You must kill him," Kali said.

"I can't," I whispered, my hands shaking. I dropped the branch, held my hands to my ears.

"Then you must kill yourself."

"I don't want to die."

"Do you think Eva could ever love a coward? What kind of man are you? Wronged and you do nothing? Have you no honor, no shame?"

"I have honor," I whispered. "I am ashamed."

"There is a better way," a different voice whispered.

I looked up. Standing guard over the boy was Hanuman.

"She would have you become like Ravana, twisted by desire. She would have you find the way to destroy yourself."

"He opens his mouth and only lies come forth."

"No, Kali," Hanuman said, "that is you. From you comes the negation and destruction, the un-being, the un-truth."

Hanuman opened his mouth, and I saw myself inside him, a tiny flickering star nestled amongst many, swirling around other stars. My light, by myself, was nothing. A shadow loomed across it. But around me were brighter lights. I stretched toward them.

"You must reject Kali," Hanuman said.

"It is an honorable and necessary path," Kali said, "fit for a god. You can join me in the heavens. All you need to do is kill the boy."

He lay unconscious beneath Hanuman's feet. I grabbed the branch and raised it. I looked Hanuman in the eyes. He did not flinch.

"You must choose," he whispered.

I brought the branch down with all my might, and broke it across my knee.

Hanuman smiled, he reached for me and I could feel his soft touch on my shoulder. As though a switch had flipped, Kali's whispers became the soft rustle of grass. In the distance I heard sirens.

"It's time to run again," I said.

"Not much longer," Hanuman said.

"I don't want to run anymore."

Hanuman smiled.

"Can you guide me where I need to go?" I asked.

He nodded.

I knelt down beside the boy. I took off my jacket and propped his head up, then wiped the blood from his nose with my T-shirt.

"I'm sorry," I said.

His eyes were closed, but his breathing came calm and steady.

I nodded to Hanuman and we set off west.

"Where you leading me?" I asked him.

"Detox," he said.

I nodded.

"It's the best way to stay free of Kali," he said. "Without drugs, you slip less easily between worlds, you make yourself less vulnerable to her."

"That sounds like exactly what I'm looking for."

"There's one small catch," he said.

I groaned. There was always a catch.

"Oh, you'll be okay with this one," he said. "Without drugs, she won't bother you as much. But, then again, neither will I. Not because I don't want to."

"So if I'm drug free, I'll never see you again?"

"You've been speaking English all your life, and you still don't understand what I said? I said we won't bother you 'as much,' not 'never.' We'll still see you from time to time, moment to moment. It will all depend."

"But I won't be able to see you anytime I want?"

"Oh, if you want to do that, there's a good method. You'll be able to control things better. Ever hear of meditation?"

"Well, sure, my dad has all kinds of books, and then there's the stuff in scripture . . ."

Hanuman waved me off.

"Those things are no better than tabloids. The original message has been changed so much by mistranslation and politics and social agendas. I'll show you the right way."

We walked, hand in hand, down the street as he began to teach me his lessons.

Tats was on the porch, tapping his stogie in the ash can, when I walked up.

"How's that telemarketing thing working out?" he asked.

"I quit."

"It's a shit job, people hanging up on you, cussing you out. I got an air horn I like to use, but I kinda feel bad about it after. Poor guys trying to get donations, or sell papers, and now I go and blow that air horn and they're deaf probably. Better to be face to face if you're selling something. That's the way I do it."

"I was pretty good at it," I said, "but it was a con."

"Best not to be doin' that no more."

"I got about five hundred bucks from it, though. I figured I might pay up rent for a bit and save a little for food. I also had this idea about a computer."

I filled him in on the plan I'd discussed with T.T. and Walden. Tats nodded, then ticked off his objections.

"First off, you bring in a computer, it's just going to get stolen. Next time a guy breaks bad, that thing's at a pawn shop. So that makes it a waste of money, money you should be spending on rent and food and getting yourself the next job. Then there's the porn. Guys in the house won't know jack shit about computers, so the only thing they'll figure out is how to get porn on it. I like it traditional. Strip clubs. Magazines if you're desperate. But keep it real, you understand? None of this fantasy bullshit."

I told him I could lock the computer down, anchored to the metal table next to the washing machine in the basement. Money wasn't going to be too big an issue either—I only needed a hundred or two hundred to get parts and discards. Computers that other people junked, I could salvage for parts. And as for the porn, as long as I didn't put a modem in the thing, there was no problem. Guys could bring in porn on a floppy, maybe, but if they were half as techno-illiterate as he thought they were, they'd be more likely to torture the orifices of the floppy with their sweet love than load any images from one.

After a few more pensive puffs off his stogie, Tats gave me the green light on a budget of $150. Then he took me in and introduced me to a young pasty-faced gangbanger named Lonny who was a first-timer in the Oasis, and who was replacing Zhivago. Lonny hitched up his jeans, wiped his hands on his legs, then hitched his jeans again.

"So Zhivago's okay?" I asked.

"He's fucked up," Tats said. "But then again, we all are. At least we're fucked up but sober. That gives us a chance."

Lonny nodded uncertainly at this and hitched his jeans.

"New to recovery?" I asked.

"I ain't seen much of it. Don't know how it's supposed to work. Not much school in me neither, so it better be simple like they say, otherwise . . ." He shook his head, looked up at me and then away, fixing his stare on the window, then wiped his hands on his legs. "I seen some things."

"You're never too dumb to get the program," Tats said, "but sometimes you can be too smart. Like with religion."

"You need faith," I said.

"In each other and yourself," Tats said.

"Exactly," I said.

Lonny nodded and bit his lip and hitched his jeans.

"Take him to the Twelve-Step," Tats said.

"We going out? Ain't this a lockdown?"

"It's okay," I said, patting him on the back.

"Can I borrow a belt?" he asked.

Tats put his arm over Lonny's shoulder.

"You can borrow one of mine. With the silver buckle. I was thinking your saggy drawers was some kind of fashion bullshit. Good to hear it wasn't. I'd have had to get you detail on that."

"Damn it!" I said, remembering. "I've got to take care of detail!"

"That's right," Tats said. "And then the Twelve-Step."

I took Lonny that night to the Twelve-Step, hung out with him and the guys at Zephyr's, shot the shit and felt the camaraderie and felt like this Lonny kid wasn't half bad, a little rough on the edges, but a good heart. I resolved to go out of my way to help him. Most of the guys in the house were upper 30s at least. Lonny and I were about the same age. We could relate. I talked about it with him and he agreed, and we decided right then and there that we would be recovery buddies, looking out for each other, ensuring we'd both make it through. Sometime in the middle of the night he changed his mind, grabbed his shit and Tats's belt, and bolted.

I interviewed at a psych facility down the road for a secretarial job a few days later, and an Indian doctor on senior staff took pity on me and hired me. He decided I was too qualified to be just a secretary and started having me go around and organize activities for the psych lockdown patients. That usually involved handing out cups of apple juice and cigarettes in the smoke room, then dancing around to make sure I didn't get cornered and burned. It wasn't much of a challenge, but since the facility had already failed inspection and didn't look like it was in a rush to remedy its issues (such as the chains sealing most of the exits), nobody minded much if I was technically unqualified. During my secretarial hours, I worked on résumés for guys in the house, and during my group sessions, I hung out and chitchatted with the patients, who seemed to understand that there was very little distinction between us. One time I talked a bit with the Indian doctor about that friend of mine who had been heavy into drugs and had developed this fixation on Hanuman. He laughed and shook his head. Get him here, he said. Your friend needs medication.

I didn't take him up on it, though on some of my bad days I was tempted. Pulling the computer together was a lot harder than I'd thought it would be, and I made mistakes with my limited budget. When all was said and done, I spent close to $700 on that first computer. It became a nightly spectacle for the guys, coming down into the basement, alternating between watching the foosball game or the TV or me, swearing in a corner as I tried to figure out how the hell I'd blown yet another motherboard. When I finally did it and got the computer up and running after weeks of nothing to the point where they thought I was just bullshit, the guys busted out in a holler that got the cops called on us. I got them some porn from one of my geek connections, because I thought they deserved it, and showed them how it worked. Tats popped on down and scowled at me when he saw it, but I pointed out the anchor on the computer, the steel canister next to it for donations for future refurbishments that the guys had already begun donating into (also anchored), and he allowed me to teach him how to use the mouse.

Word spread through the Twelve-Step that I was a computer genius, and though I told everyone who asked that I really didn't know what the hell I was doing, I started getting orders for custom-built computers and tech service. Soon it was like I had two full-time jobs. Between the work and meetings, I had very little time to screw around. I'd kick it with the guys and watch baseball on TV, unless the Red Wings were on, in which case we all had to watch hockey with Tats. I'd play some foosball, board games, card games—but not for money—whatever fit the schedule. And then I started playing Scrabble with Tats, T.T., and Walden. Tats was solid, though he tended to plunk the same swears in the squares and giggle as if he'd done something naughty. Walden was sharp and wielded two-letter words like a knife. T.T., we all agreed, could use my help. We agreed on a system—he could use the dictionary to form his words, so long as he then used the word in a sentence of his own creation. It took a lot of time, and our games dragged on as T.T. would take his turn with me at his side, but he became better. I got him to start reading comics, and we kept pushing from there.

One day Walden pulled me aside.

"You could do more," he said.

"What else is there? I mean, I don't mean to be lazy or anything, but between the two jobs and . . ."

"Tats and I agreed. We want you to finish your college education."

I laughed.

"They don't let guys like me into college," I said. "I had my chance. I blew it. I'm okay with it. Don't worry."

Walden grabbed my arm.

"They do let guys like you into college. You need to try. You're still young. You could do this. You could get a degree."

"I don't know if I need it. I'm not sure if I want it. Sure, it would lead to more money, but college is where this all started. Maybe college and me just don't mix."

"You're a different person now."

"I'll think about it," I said.

I put it out of my mind. College was for other people. I didn't have any money, and there was no way a school would give me a scholarship. And whoever heard of anyone loaning money to a crackhead? And then there was the whole issue of whether or not I had it in me, if I was smart enough, if I had the right work ethic. All I knew for certain was that I was an addict. Addicts don't graduate.

During the Sunday meeting, during the personal venting session, Walden hit me with it again.

"All of us have agreed on this. We want you to apply for college."

"You'd be a good teacher," T.T. said.

"A computer guy," Tats said.

"The point is, we believe you should take the chance."

"I just don't see what difference it makes," I said.

"It makes a big difference," T.T. said.

"You have no idea," Tats said.

A few of the other guys looked up at me and held my gaze.

"That time, with that legal trouble," Freddie, a six-week veteran of the Oasis said, "you was the one that read the papers for me. You helped me figure that out. Nows I get to see my kid," he thumped his chest. "For that, I owe you."

"You've been helping us," Walden said. "You can help the world more if you go to college."

"Ain't none of us ever going to do it," Tats said. "Alls of us, we're just the working stiffs. Drunks. Nobody thinks much of us. Nobody gives a damn fuck. But you could walk in their world, you know? You could talk for us."

"This is about more than you," Walden said.

The guys banded together to help me out. I told them about how scared I was of going into college again, and Tats decided that as long as I was in school, he'd reduce rent for me. I'd tutor the guys as necessary, and that would even things up. That way I could keep staying in the Oasis, in a sober environment, until I was sure I could handle things. They helped me get the college admissions forms and then critiqued my personal statement and essay questions, weeding out bullshit. The final result was an honest picture of who I was—scared, unsure, a wounded veteran of the drug wars. I explained my poor transcripts and pointed to my high school ones to show I had potential. And when it came time for interviews, I said it as it was. No bullshit. Straight and simple. I'm a recovering crackhead, I said. I live in a halfway house, I said. College is about more than me.

And then I forgot about it. The days passed and work kept me busy. I played Scrabble and actually lost a game to T.T., which only made him start telling everyone that he should be the guy going to college. I got better at foosball, figuring out how to bank a shot. I started writing a journal to record my memories of my time on the street. I went to meetings. I stayed sober. And late at night, as I drifted into sleep, I would sometimes dream of Hanuman, and I knew that he was nearby.

I was coming back from the psych job, my head down. It had been a shitty, shitty day and I could hear Kali whispering as she always did on crappy days, and I was pinching my palm to get her to shut up. One of the psych patients was getting me down—a poor little guy, physically twisted up, barely able to eat or talk. His file said he had an unknown psychosis, but his file also said that he had an IQ of thirty-five. It didn't seem to me he needed to be in a psych facility where other patients took offense at his outbursts and burned him with cigarettes. I'd just gotten another circle of char on my forearm for trying to help him.

I looked up, and saw Tats on the porch, puffing his stogie. The moment he saw me, he hollered into the house, "He's here." The guys poured out, shit-eating grins on their faces.

"Tats, don't tell me I just got landed with detail again. I cleaned the toilet. I swear. This morning. If somebody pissed in it since then . . ."

"Yeah, I saw your cleaning this morning. You did a shitty job as usual. But that ain't nothing compared to this."

Walden stepped out from the throng, T.T. by his side carrying a cake spotted with cigarettes acting as candles.

Walden broke the news. "We got a letter in the mail, from the University of Chicago."

The guys rushed forward before he could finish.

"How's that feel, college boy?" T.T. said, hoisting me in the air.

The guys clamored underneath. I could feel their arms all around me. They dropped me down and we jumped and hugged and then shied away, men unsure of the meaning of such close proximity, and then we bumped again, merging, together.

"Shakes are on me!" Tats yelled. He pointed toward Zephyr's.

Walden grabbed the cake. I passed out the smokes. T.T. unleashed his Bic. We ran down the street, a family.

.   .   .

That night I saw Hanuman in my dreams. He was standing outside the Oasis, and he had a hill on one shoulder. The moonlight made his brown hair glow, and the crown on his head blazed like a ring of fire. He reached up and grabbed something green from the hill and placed it on the porch. He placed the Sanjeevani root in Tats' ash can.

Then he left, jumping high into the air, pausing momentarily to flick out his tail, sending it harmlessly through the wall of the Oasis, so it could reach inside and kiss me gently on my forehead.

EPILOGUE

The Oasis is still helping people reclaim their lives. There are two houses now, and though the names and faces change, they are all still like family for me. Tats continues to run one of the houses and I visit him as often as I can. Of the men I knew in the house, some have transformed their lives for the better, but others have fallen by the wayside, ending up in prison or surrendering to death. Too many do not survive the battle with addiction, but if not for places like the Oasis, none of us would.

My friends from college are still my friends and I stay in touch as best I can. Some of the thugs I knew are behind bars or dead, but enough remain to make returning to my old college an unsafe proposition. Some of the people evoked in the pages of this book became very nervous when they heard that this book was going to be published. It is for this reason, as well as to protect the privacy of others, that I have changed names, adjusted situations, and disguised people's characteristics. One of the casualties of this narrative brought on by our increasingly litigious society is that, though the core of the book is true and the stories reported about the individuals are true in their key respects, I sometimes had to fictionalize details in order to be allowed to share my story with you.

My family and I are on much better terms. Life since the Oasis has not been easy, but my family and friends have helped me through the tough times. I have had two failed treatments for hepatitis C, been married and divorced, and continued to battle my addictions. Kali has not left me alone, but Hanuman hasn't either. For that, I am grateful.

SHRI HANUMAN CHALISA

The Hanuman Chalisa is a sixteenth-century devotional poem written in Hindi by Tulsidas that has tremendous protective power and can enable the devout to overcome any obstacle. The poem translated here is my own version of the prayer that I used during my darkest times.

The dust of my Guru's lotus feet
Is the pollen that polishes the mirror of my heart
So pure that now I can sing the truth of the glory of Rama,
Bestower of the four-fold fruits of life:
Dharma, artha, kama, and moksha.
I know so little, but I remember you,
Hanuman, Son of the Wind,
And I ask you:
Grant me strength, intelligence, and true sight.
Relieve me of the imperfections that bring me sorrow.
Hail Hanuman, the ocean of wisdom.
Hail the monkey lord, the fountain of power,
Bringer of light to the three worlds.
You are the divine messenger of Rama,
A vessel of pure strength.
Son of Anjani
Son of the Wind.
Valiant hero, mighty as the thunderbolt,
From you is born good sense and wisdom,
For you are the dispeller of the darkness of evil thoughts.

You are golden perfection
Cloaked in the essence of beauty.
We will know you by your earrings and your curly locks.
In your hands is your lightning mace and victory banner;
But the sacred thread too drapes your shoulder.
An incarnation of Shiva and Kesari's son,
the glory of your omnipresence
brings honor in all time and space.
Wisest of the wise, virtuous and clever,
You are the eternal servant of Rama.
You are an ardent listener,
always keen to hear Rama's stories,
for in your heart live Rama, Lakshmana, and Sita.
You appeared before Sita in diminutive form,
spoke to her in humility.
But in Lanka you revealed your terrifying form,
And cleansed the earth with fire.
Bane of all demons, you destroyed the Rakshasas
And so Lord Rama completed his task on this world.
You brought the Sanjivani,
Magic herb of life,
Reviving Lakshmana and Rama,
And so Rama encompassed you with his joy.
He praised you to the heavens:
"You are as dear to me as my own brother."
"Thousands will chant hymns of your glories!"
He embraced you in his heart.
Prophets, even the all knowing Lord Brahma,
the great story teller Narada himself,
Goddess Saraswati and Ahisha, King of Serpents
Even Yama, the God of Death, Kubera, the God of Wealth,
and the Digpals, the guards of the four corners of the universe,
have vied to express your glory.
How then can a mere poet's efforts compare?

You rendered a great service to Sugriva,
Uniting him with Rama,
Elevating him to the Royal Throne.
By heeding your advice,
Vibhishana became Lord of Lanka.
This truth is known to the universe.
Though it is thousands of thousands of miles away,
You swallowed the sun,
thinking it to be a luscious fruit.
With Rama's signet ring in your mouth,
There is no surprise that you could leap across the ocean.
All the difficult tasks of the world
Become easy by your grace.
You are the sentry at the door of Rama's divine kingdom.
No one enters without your permission.
Those who take refuge in you find happiness;
Those who you protect know no fear.
You alone can contain your power;
The three worlds tremble at your roar.
All the ghosts, demons and evil forces
Are kept at bay
By the mention of your name, O Hanuman!
Those that remember you in thought, word, and deed,
Are released from all diseases, pain, and suffering.
Rama is the supreme lord and the king of penance,
But you carry out all his work.
One who comes to you for fulfillment of any desire
with faith and sincerity
is granted the imperishable fruit of life.
Your glory fills the four ages;
Your name is known in all the universe.
Guardian of saints and sages,
destroyer of demons,
You are the darling of Rama.

You can grant the eight powers and nine treasures
By the boon given you by Mother Janaki.
Rama's name is an elixir when you say it,
For in all rebirths you are his most dedicated servant.
Through hymns sung in devotion to you, one can find Rama
and become free from the sufferings of rebirth.
At death one enters the divine kingdom of Rama,
And is forever reborn as the Lord's devotee.
Why worship another?
Devotion to you, Hanuman, gives all happiness.
One is freed from all the suffering
if they remember their mighty hero, Hanuman.
Hail, Hail, Hail, Hanuman, lord of the senses.
Let your victory over evil be firm and final.
Bless me and be my guru.
Whosoever recites this one hundred times
Is freed from bondage and welcomed into bliss.
One who reads this gains success,
For Shiva will witness your devotion.
Says Tulsidas, servant of the divine,
I will prostrate myself at your feet, O Hanuman!
Make your temple in my heart!
Son of the wind, destroyer of sorrows,
Embodiment of blessings,
with Rama, Lakshmana, and Sita, live in my heart!

WORDS OF INSPIRATION

Writing this book was nearly as difficult as the experiences it depicts, and so I searched out the wisdom of others to guide me. The following quotes deeply influenced my depiction of the mythology of my life.

I say, ye human beings, among all the species on the earth, you are the greatest. You are the greatest for you can change your destiny, you can build your destiny, you can enlighten yourself.

—Swami Rama

It is better to conquer yourself than to win a thousand battles. Then the victory is yours. It cannot be taken from you, not by angels or by demons, heaven or hell.

—Buddha

When we blindly adopt a religion, a political system, a literary dogma, we become automatons. We cease to grow.

—Anais Nin

Faith certainly tells us what the senses do not, but not the contrary of what they see; it is above, not against them.

—Blaise Pascal

This is what I believe:
That I am I.
That my soul is a dark forest.
That my known self will never be more than a little clearing in the forest.
That gods, strange gods, come forth from the forest into the clearing of
    my known self, and then go back.
That I must have the courage to let them come and go.
That I will never let mankind put anything over me, but that I will try
    always to recognize and submit to the gods in me and the gods in
    other men and women.
There is my creed.

—**D.H. Lawrence**

When men destroy their old gods they will find
new ones to take their place.

—**Pearl S. Buck**

This is my simple religion. There is no need for temples;
no need for complicated philosophy. Our own brain, our
own heart is our temple; the philosophy is kindness.

—**The Dalai Lama**

Our deepest fear is not that we are inadequate. Our deepest fear
is that we are powerful beyond measure. It is our light, not our
darkness, that frightens us most. We ask ourselves, 'Who am I to be
brilliant, gorgeous, talented, and famous?' Actually, who are you not
to be? You are a child of God. Your playing small does not serve the
world. There is nothing enlightened about shrinking so that people
won't feel insecure around you. We were born to make manifest the
glory of God that is within us. It's not just in some of us; it's in all of
us. And when we let our own light shine, we unconsciously give other

people permission to do the same. As we are liberated from our own fear, our presence automatically liberates others.

—Nelson Mandela

I love you when you bow in your mosque, kneel in your temple, pray in your church. For you and I are sons of one religion, and it is the spirit.

—Kahlil Gibran

Out of Compassion for them, I, dwelling in their hearts, destroy with the shining lamp of knowledge the darkness born of ignorance.

—Bhagavad Gita 10.11

The Blessed Lord said: You are grieving over those who are not fit to be grieved for, yet you speak words like a great man of wisdom. But the wise do not grieve neither over the living nor over the dead. Never did I not exist, nor did you nor these kings. Nor shall we ever cease to exist in the future.

—Bhagavad Gita 2.11 and 2.12

He who sees me in all things, and all things in me, is never far from me, and I am never far from him.

—Lord Krishna from Chapter 6